The Shifting Definitions
of Genre

The Shifting Definitions of Genre

Essays on Labeling Films, Television Shows and Media

Edited by LINCOLN GERAGHTY and MARK JANCOVICH

McFarland & Company, Inc., Publishers
Jefferson, North Carolina, and London

ALSO EDITED BY LINCOLN GERAGHTY

The Influence of Star Trek *on Television, Film and Culture* (McFarland, 2008)

LIBRARY OF CONGRESS CATALOGUING-IN-PUBLICATION DATA

The shifting definitions of genre : essays on labeling films, television shows and media / edited by Lincoln Geraghty and Mark Jancovich.
    p.   cm.
Includes bibliographical references and index.

ISBN 978-0-7864-3430-5
softcover : 50# alkaline paper

1. Film genres.   2. Television program genres.   I. Geraghty, Lincoln, 1977– .   II. Jancovich, Mark.
PN1995.S487   2008
791.43'6 — dc22   2008001074

British Library cataloguing data are available

©2008 Lincoln Geraghty and Mark Jancovich. All rights reserved

No part of this book may be reproduced or transmitted in any form or by any means, electronic or mechanical, including photocopying or recording, or by any information storage and retrieval system, without permission in writing from the publisher.

Cover image: Photospin ©2007

Manufactured in the United States of America

McFarland & Company, Inc., Publishers
  Box 611, Jefferson, North Carolina 28640
  www.mcfarlandpub.com

To Mum and Dad,
with all my love
— Lincoln Geraghty

Acknowledgments

Thanks go to Rebecca for her support and encouragement. I want to thank my parents, Malcolm and Diane, for bowing to child pressure and getting me Optimus Prime for Christmas — not forgetting all the rest of them. Those childhood memories inspired me to develop this collection. This one's dedicated to you! — LG

I would like to thank Joanne; I couldn't have done it without your support. Our thanks go to Derek Johnston for his keen eye in compiling the index. — MJ

Contents

Acknowledgments   vi
Introduction: Generic Canons
    Lincoln Geraghty and Mark Jancovich   1

PART ONE: INSTITUTIONS OF GENRE

1. Pale Shadows: Narrative Hierarchies in
the Historiography of 1940s Horror
Mark Jancovich   15

2. The Independent Film Channel: Creating a Genre
and Brand Across Small Screens, Big Screens,
and the Virtual World
Liza Treviño   33

3. "Off-Beat" as a Generic Designation in *Variety* Reviews
Jason Scott   52

PART TWO: TEXTUAL NEGOTIATIONS

4. Film Noir as Male Melodrama: The Politics
of Film Genre Labeling
Janet Staiger   71

5. Beyond the Valley of the Classical Hollywood Cinema:
Rethinking the "Loathsome Film" of 1970
Harry M. Benshoff   92

6. Rethinking the History of European Horror:
Television, *La porta sul buio* and *Historias para no dormir*
Andrew Willis   110

7. Can Rock Movies Be Musicals? The Case of
    This Is Spinal Tap
    Andrew Caine 124

8. "A Most Historic Period of Change": The Western,
    the Epic and *Dances with Wolves*
    James Russell 142

9. "A Term Rather Too General to Be Helpful":
    Struggling with Genre in Reality TV
    Su Holmes 159

PART THREE: HERITAGE, HISTORY AND MEMORY

10. Repackaging Generation One: Genre, Fandom,
    and *The Transformers* as Adult/Children's Television
    Lincoln Geraghty 181

11. Subcultural Tastes, Genre Boundaries and Fan Canons
    Brigid Cherry 201

12. Monster Legacies: Memory, Technology
    and Horror History
    Peter Hutchings 216

13. "Just Men in Tights": Rewriting Silver Age Comics
    in an Era of Multiplicity
    Henry Jenkins 229

Notes on Contributors 245
Index 249

Introduction

Generic Canons

LINCOLN GERAGHTY and MARK JANCOVICH

While many critics have criticized the notion of a canon in literature, film and other cultural forms, most studies of genre still seem to operate around canonical texts. In other words, while the canon was often supposed to be a group of great works of art that represented "the best that has been thought and known in the world,"[1] popular genres are usually discussed in terms of key works that are either claimed to be the artistic high points, the markers of key shifts within historical development, or are taken to represent key features, periods or tendencies within the genre. Such claims to artistic status or representativeness can obviously be contested in individual cases, but there are also other problems with this continuing focus on generic canons.

For example, although Méliès's silent classic, *Trip to the Moon* (*Le voyage dans la lune*), is often cited as a canonical science fiction film that represents one of the earliest examples of the genre, the term "science fiction" had not been invented in 1902, when the film was made. Furthermore, when Hugo Gernsback coined the phrase, it was to promote the particular type of fiction that he published in *Amazing Stories*, fiction that was specifically opposed to the kinds of fantasy represented by Méliès's film. Similarly, although the Lon Chaney classics such as *The Hunchback of Notre Dame* (1923) and *The Phantom of the Opera* (1925) are now commonly cited as canonical texts in the history of the horror genre, these films predate the term "horror film," which did not enter into common usage until almost a decade later — at some point in the cycle of films that followed the success of *Dracula* (1931) and *Frankenstein* (1931).

In other words, generic terms are often imposed retrospectively onto books, films and other cultural forms that predate the invention of these terms. At one level, this might seem a fairly innocent activity, but it can do violence to our sense of history. It can, for example, abstract texts from the contexts within which they were originally understood and impose alternative understandings upon them, or it can simply emphasize some details and ignore others.

Such a criticism does not claim that the original meaning is in any sense more true or authentic than later meanings, but it does require one to be careful about how one uses generic terms. If one wants to know how *Trip to the Moon* and *The Phantom of the Opera* were understood within the periods of their original release, one needs to be clear about the precise way in which they were generically identified at the time, rather than presuming that one can simply draw upon one's own understanding of generic categories. However, one might equally want to know how the meanings of these films have changed, as they become associated with different genres, or as the genres with which these films are associated have changed meaning themselves.

In addition, while different periods might use the same genre terms, these terms may not mean the same in each period. For example, in his study of film noir, James Naremore examines the different ways in which film noir has been defined since its original usage in the late 1940s. In the process, he not only demonstrates that the term had very different meanings in the late 1940s from those that it acquired by the late 1950s but that, in these distinct historical periods, different films or groups of films were privileged as canonical texts within the genre, or were excluded from the category all together. At one time, the films of Humphrey Bogart had a canonical status and represented the epitome of the genre and, at another point, their status was partially displaced by the films of Nicholas Ray. Even more significantly, while *The Lost Weekend* (1945) was seen as a central text early on, it was virtually excluded from later definitions.[2]

However, these changes in meaning are not necessarily a matter of subtle or trivial distinctions. Steve Neale has shown that the meaning of the term "melodrama" has almost come to mean the virtual opposite of what it once meant. While the term is often used today to refer to woman's pictures, and particularly "weepies," Neale has analyzed the films that were identified as "melodrama" in the Hollywood trade press, during the period of Classical Hollywood, and claims that

> the mark of these films is not pathos, romance, and domesticity, but action, adventure, and thrills; not "feminine" genres and woman's films but war films, adventure films, horror films, and thrillers, genres traditionally thought of as, if anything, "male."[3]

One therefore needs to be careful not to transfer one's own understandings of genre terms and their meanings back onto previous periods in which the terms and their meanings might have been very different.

Indeed, during the classical period of Hollywood cinema, the industry didn't even talk of genres but "story types," and while some of those story types may seem similar to the genres that are commonly identified today, the industry's systems of categorization start to look very different when these terms are placed in context. For example, in his discussion of Hollywood's attempts to make sense of its audiences, Leo Handel provides a classification of story types that the industry commonly used in audience surveys:

Comedies:	Western pictures
Sophisticated comedies	Gangster and G-man pictures
Slapstick comedies	Serious dramas
Family life comedies	Love stories, romantic pictures
Musical comedies	Socially significant pictures
War Pictures	Adventure, action pictures
Mystery, horror pictures	Musicals (serious)
Historicals, biographies	Child star pictures
Fantasies	(Wild) animal pictures[4]

Furthermore, these terms seem to have much looser meanings than academic notions of genre. While academic definitions of genre have either stated or suggested that genres are self-contained and mutually exclusive bodies of films, the categories above refer to types of material that could easily be mixed and combined. Indeed, the musical is not even given as a category in itself but one finds the "musical comedy" listed under comedy, while the "musical" is qualified by the term "serious" in parentheses.

As a result, many critics have challenged the grand claims associated with many contemporary understandings of genre, and argued for more precise and specific ways of thinking about genre. For example, Rick Altman has suggested that genre critics need to stop thinking of genres as though they follow a linear process of development, as this way of thinking creates a sense of homogeneity and continuity across periods. Instead, he suggests that generic histories are made up of a series of smaller historical cycles, each with its own identity, although these identities might end up contributing to the range of options and choices within a genre as a whole. In other words, the Universal horror cycle is very different from the 1950s alien invasion cycle or the post–*Scream* cycle. While these are all commonly cited as examples of the horror film, each cycle has its own distinct character and dynamic, and there is no simple "evolution" from one stage to the next as many histories imply.⁵

This approach offers some very useful ways of thinking about genre, but it also prompts the question why these different cycles need to still be linked together by some overarching notion of genre at all. Indeed, Barbara Klinger's work on the films of Douglas Sirk has demonstrated that it is useful to acknowledge the existence of "local genres": historically specific cycles that may actually cut across traditional distinctions between genres such as the western, the horror film, or the woman's picture. She therefore provides a fascinating account of the "Adult Film" in the post-war period, a term that linked a series of films that would commonly be associated with different genres, and this association was through their handling of supposedly serious and challenging materials.⁶

As we can see, it is not simply the case that genres are historically produced phenomena that can change meaning in different historical periods. Particular texts, or groups of texts, can also change meaning as they are classified or reclassified in relation to these definitions of genre at different historical moments. While French critics in the late 1940s defined *The Lost Weekend* as a classic example of film noir, this is not how it was understood at the time of its release in the United States, nor how it was understood in later periods. However, it is not just that a text may be identified with different genres at different points in time, but that this text may even be classified differently in different institutional contexts. For example, a text may be defined in one way within the process of production, in which a particular cultural industry has its own generic understandings of texts, and yet be marketed or exhibited in relation to a different genre. It is not always the case that the contexts of production, marketing or exhibition fix how audiences will generically identify a text.

In some cases, these differences have even been deliberately exploited. For example, in the 1940s, the Production Code Administration (PCA) viewed horror as a problematic genre, and many films were specifically developed so that they could be presented to the PCA as one kind of genre, and presented to audiences as another. One particularly interesting example is MGM's *Dr. Jekyll and Mr. Hyde* (1941). In this case, the studio was able to minimize problems with the PCA by presenting the film as the adaptation of a literary classic, while also producing a film that could be marketed as a horror film to those audiences that might be attracted to such a film. Indeed, the pressbook even presents exhibitors with a deliberately schizophrenic campaign:

> From where we sit, we have no way of knowing whether horror, melodrama or romance draws best at your box-office. But whatever that entertainment quality

might be, we DO know that the picture can be sold in any manner you select and that few productions equal it in showmanship opportunities.[7]

The film was therefore specifically designed not to fit a generic formula but, on the contrary, to be highly flexible so that it could be distinguished from specific genres, where an association might prove problematic, and associated with a wide range of genres, so that it could be marketed to a wide variety of markets.

As a result, specific films may not only be identified with different genres in different periods, or in different contexts, but they can also be identified with different genres within a specific period and even within a specific context. As we have seen, exhibitors were encouraged by MGM to market *Dr. Jekyll and Mr. Hyde* in relation to a wide range of genres, and there are often intense arguments between different sectors of the audience over the generic identities of specific films. For example, it is not simply that science fiction and horror fans dispute whether a film such as *Alien* (1979) is "really" science fiction or horror, but even within horror fandom distinctive groups will define the genre differently, including some films and excluding others in the process, and providing very different senses of what is canonical or not. While Freddy Kruger, from the *Nightmare on Elm Street* series, is a hero to some horror fans, he is an affront to others who dismiss the series as either poor horror or even "inauthentic" horror, something that isn't "really" horror but is only masquerading as such.[8]

If most of the examples given so far have been about film genres, it is also important to remember that genres are not specific to film, even if many of the key developments within genre studies over the past decade have been developed in relation to it. However, even in the case of film, many of these developments have tended to ignore the increasing inter-relationship between film and other media. For example, science fiction is obviously not simply a film genre, and was originally developed in popular literature, but many science fiction films are now produced as part of franchises that cut across a wide variety of media forms. *Star Trek*, for example, may have started as a television series, but it is now a phenomenon that incorporates television, film, computer games, comic books, and novels in an ever-expanding universe of texts and intertexts.[9]

In order to understand contemporary film genres, it is therefore important to recognize that they are often intimately connected with developments in other media. Part of the problem is that while genre terms might cut across different media, it is not the case that they necessarily mean the same thing in each medium. On the contrary, different media have very different genre definitions, and even when they appear to share the same term, the meaning of that term may differ considerably. For example, in *The Television Genres Book* (2001), horror does not even get a listing and shows such as *Buffy the Vampire Slayer* are classified as teen television drama.[10] This reflects a wider tension within both television studies and horror studies summed up by Gregory Waller's comment that "made-for-television horror would seem to be by definition impossible."[11] Of course, despite its impossibility, horror television does exist and, as Jason Jacobs has shown, the British Broadcasting Corporation produced a number of what it called "horror plays" in the immediate post-war period due to its belief that horror was well suited to the medium of television.[12] Furthermore, it could be argued that horror has remained a vital and even strategic element of television production ever since.[13]

However, the presence of horror television does not mean that horror on television has always been defined in the same ways as horror in film. On the contrary, during the late 1950s, 1960s and even the 1970s, there were a number of anthology shows that were often explicitly identified as, or associated with, horror; shows such as *Alfred Hitchcock Presents*, Boris Karloff's *Thriller*, Rod Serling's *The Twilight Zone*, and Brian Clemens's *Thriller*. Indeed, the association with horror is made even clearer by their European imitators, which also featured hosts and, like Karloff's *Thriller*, chose hosts who were known primarily for their work in horror. For example, Dario Argento hosted *La porta sul buio* in Italy, while Narciso Ibañez Serrador hosted *Historias para no dormir* in Spain (see Andrew Willis's essay in this collection).

Furthermore, the materials that were used by many of these series would rarely have been defined as horror in relation to film during the period. The reason for this was that these shows often explicitly harked back to the horror films of the 1940s, when Hitchcock himself had been strongly associated with the genre, horror films that have, in many cases, been generically reclassified since the 1940s as examples of the paranoid woman's film (*Rebecca* [1940], *Jane Eyre* [1944] and *Gaslight* [1944]), film noir (*Phantom Lady* [1944], *Laura* [1944], and *Woman in the Window* [1944]) or simply as thrillers (*Spellbound* [1945])—(see Mark Jancovich's essay in this collection). If these individual films and groups of films were no longer related to the horror film by the 1950s, a very different sense of generic memory was in operation in television, so much so that programs featuring these materials continued to be defined as horror.

Consequently, both generic definitions and generic canons are also crucially bound up with issues of memory, or rather the processes of both remembering and forgetting. This becomes particularly clear in an age of multi-channel television and DVD, where old films and television programs are recycled more and more. However, it is important to remember that this recycling is not simply an innocent process. The recycling of materials does not just re-present materials from the past, it also re-contextualizes them. Some old shows are presented as high camp to be laughed at as the products of a naïve and unsophisticated past, while others are presented with reverence, as memorials to a golden age. Nor are these options mutually exclusive.

Such issues of memory and recontextualization are not simply a matter of what "the media" do with these shows; they are also a process in which the academy is involved. Many studies of genre describe generic history as either a process of glorious progress and enlightenment, or as depressing tales of deterioration or degeneration. For example, in his book, *Hollywood Genres* (1981), Thomas Schatz presents a model of generic development that moves from a period of experimentation, before a genre has taken shape, through a classical period in which its elements have become standardized and conventional, and ending in a baroque period, in which its mechanisms have become recognized as conventions and become the subject of criticism, revision or even inversion.[14] Not only are there many problems with such a model, but it also reproduces a sense of the past as a state of unselfconsciousness against which the present is defined as a moment of enlightenment and self-awareness.

In contrast, Kim Newman presents his study, *Nightmare Movies* (1988), as a corrective to previous histories of horror, which, he suggests, presented the genre's development as a process of deterioration in which the films of the late 1960s and 1970s were simply presented as crude and unsubtle descendents of a once imaginative and inventive genre. Moreover, he suggests that many histories of the horror film are partly based on a sense of nostalgic memory. If Newman had set out to defend the horror films of his youth, such as *Night of the Living Dead* (1968), and demonstrate their cultural worth, as a response to previous generations of critics who had celebrated earlier periods in the horror film, he also became aware that his own tastes were shaped by the past, so that he came to see the horror films of the mid- to late 1980s as sadly inferior to the period that he himself had championed. As he put it:

> Recently I've started wondering if I'm turning into Denis Gifford. I'll stick by the opinions expressed here, but I keep coming across enthusiasts acclaiming the *Nightmare on Elm Street* series, *Fright Night* or *Re-Animator* as classics. There are even people out there writing respectfully about the *Friday the 13th* films and *House*. Some of these are pretty good, but I don't think they quite stack up against the best of Romero and Cronenberg, or even *Halloween* and *The Texas Chainsaw Massacre*. This sounds a lot like where we came in, only now I've got the Donald Pleasence role rather than the Jamie Lee Curtis one. When Freddy Krueger says "you are all my children now," he doesn't mean me. Some kid out there has grown up with Freddy and Jason rather than Dracula and Frankenstein, and is graduating to the books and films of Stephen King and Clive Barker. He or she knows Empire and Troma better than Hammer and Corman; reads *Shock*

Xpress for the text and *Fangoria* for the pictures but has only dimly heard of Forrest J. Ackerman and *Famous Monsters of Film Land*; probably prefers *Return of the Living Dead* to *Day of the Dead*, and is too young to remember when you could legally rent a Lucio Fulci film on video in Britain. Some day, I hope that kid will write a book sub-titled "A Critical History of the Horror Film, 1988–2008" that contradicts everything you're about to read.[15]

Like many revisions to our understandings of genre, Newman draws upon his own personal memories of films such as *Night of the Living Dead* to challenge the values and claims of earlier generations, but he also finds his tastes at odds with the films of later generations.

Newman is not unique in this process. Generic studies are continually being updated by new generations who draw on their own personal attachments to the films of their childhood or adolescence to revise the canons and values of earlier generations. If Newman championed the films of the late 1960s and early to mid–1970s in the mid–1980s, the early 1990s saw a series of studies that revised early critical dismissals of the slasher movies of the late 1970s and early 1980s. Similarly, if critics of the 1950s and 1960s championed the films of John Ford, critics of the 1960s and 1970s praised the revisionist westerns of Sam Peckinpah and others. Memory therefore plays a vital part in our understanding of genre. It can help us to remember that which has been excluded or repressed by historical processes, or to change the values and agendas of previous commentaries. However, it can also perform the opposite, encouraging exclusions and repressions. The essays in the following book therefore deal with a number of these issues and explore different aspects of the relationship between genre, history and memory.

In Part One, the essays are largely concerned with the meaning of genre within various institutional contexts such as criticism, the trade press and television programming, but these essays also demonstrate the ways in which these institutions are involved in the production and dissemination of generic definitions. For example, in the first essay, Mark Jancovich explores accounts of the 1940s in histories of horror, and explores the ways in which the period has been understood in relation to the 1930s. He therefore argues this period is never seen as one with an identity of its own, but only as a copy or imitation that is dependent upon, and inferior to, the supposedly original 1930s. In the process, the essay examines the ways in which certain traditions are privileged within these accounts and others excluded, before moving on to suggest alternative ways in which we might think about the 1940s as a distinct cycle of horror production.

The second essay is by Liza Treviño, who provides an account of the ways in which television programming can produce notions of generic identity through which films are affiliated with one another. In particular, she examines two cable channels devoted to film and the ways they work to produce specific definitions of the independent film as part of their branding as channels. In the process, she examines the extremely fluid nature of these definitions of independent film, which are an inevitable result of their operations as channels, while also exploring the ways in which these channels used a range of different media forms to anchor and secure a sense of the unique experience that they were supposed to offer.

In the third chapter, Jason Scott examines *Variety*'s reviewing practices during the 1960s, and its production and dissemination of the term "off-beat" as a generic designation. In the process, he also tracks the development and transformation of this term between 1964 and 1968, as it changed meaning and focus. In the process, Scott not only demonstrates the importance of the trade press in the generation of generic terminology, but also provides a fascinating account of precisely the kind of "local genre" that we discussed earlier in relation to Barbara Klinger.

Part Two moves on to consider specific films or groups of films, and their relationships to various ideas of genre. For example, Janet Staiger's essay explores the ways in which film noir and melodrama have been conceptualized as male and female dramas respectively, and she claims that while the former has been highly valued in cultural hierarchies, the latter tends to be correspondingly denigrated. However, she also draws attention to the ways in which film noir can be seen to operate according to a "fallen man" formula in much the same way as many melodramas have been read as operating in relation to a "fallen woman" formula. In other words, she argues, the failure to acknowledge the relationship between the melodrama and film noir raises a number of questions about the politics of these generic classifications.

In the next essay, Harry Benshoff also examines the politics of generic labels, but in this case he focuses on a group of films that were often referred to as the "Loathsome film" during the late 1960s and early 1970s. As a result, he examines the critical reception of these films, and argues that their highly judgmental classification was an attempt to police cultural boundaries. For Benshoff, these films were, in part, the product of a blurring of distinctions between mainstream Hollywood, the exploitation cinema and pornography, but he also argues that, as such, they also challenged many of the formal and ideological features of classical Hollywood films. He therefore demonstrates that the classification of these films was an attack on the ways in which these films interrogated the sexual and gender politics of classical Hollywood.

As we have seen, Andrew Willis's essay explores the supposedly impossible genre of television horror, and particularly the ways in which the format of the hosted anthology series was indigenized within different national contexts. He concentrates on the case of Spain and Italy, and presents a fascinating account of the ways in which these shows were defined in relation to a series of different generic systems. As a result, while these shows inevitably developed as a response to the success of similar television production overseas, they were also at least in part a response to the success of horror film production within their own national film industries.

In the next essay, Andrew Caine examines the ways in which *This Is Spinal Tap* (1984) has been positioned generically. For Caine, the point of interest is that while it has been identified in a number of different ways such as comedy, drama and "rockumentary," it has tended to be excluded from the musical as a genre. As Caine points out, such exclusion is peculiar, given that the film is centrally organized around music and musical performances. As a result, he uses the film, and its common generic designations, to open up a series of questions about the processes and problems of generic definition.

Alternatively, James Russell explores the ways in which generic definitions can be crucial in the shaping of film history, and he examines Kevin Costner's *Dances with Wolves* (1990), whose production company, Orion, decided to promote it as an "epic" in order to avoid any association with the western, a genre seen as box-office poison at the time. Moreover, although the success of the film did spark a minor revival of western filmmaking, with a number of films being made over the next few years including *Unforgiven* (1992), *Tombstone* (1993), and the disastrous Costner vehicle *Wyatt Earp* (1994), *Dances with Wolves* also inaugurated a far more successful and enduring cycle of "historical epics" that included films such as *Braveheart* (1995), *Titanic* (1997) and even *Troy* (2004).

The last essay in this part moves on to examine the television genre of "Reality TV." In this essay, Su Holmes argues that despite the enormous currency of the term today, and the panics over its supposed domination of television programming, the term is actually a very problematic one. She explores how the term has developed and changed over time, and the ways in which it is used differently within different discursive contexts. She investigates the struggles over terminologies, which were related to broader debates over popular programming. In the process, she not only examines the arguments over "Reality TV" but also about the question of "television genre" itself.

The focus of Part Three is more directly on the questions of history and memory, starting with Lincoln Geraghty's essay on the fan cultures surrounding the television cartoon show, *The Transformers*. Initially condemned as poorly made and little more than exploitative advertising for a line of children's toys, *The Transformers*, as Geraghty demonstrates, actually raised a number of issues about children's relationship to these toys, which in turn have become the focus of an adult collecting culture. Many of the children who once watched the show have grown up to be adults with profound and complex investments in both the show and in the toys with which the show was originally associated. In this way, Geraghty's essay is both an example of, and an examination of, the processes by which childhood memories are used to challenge and revise established generic histories, and the valuations upon which they are based.

Similar concerns can also be found in Brigid Cherry's essay on horror fans, in which she explores fans' conceptions of generic boundaries, and the subcultural tastes on which they are based. She explores the ways in which horror fans conceptualize the genre, but rather than seeing the horror fan as a homogeneous entity, she also investigates the debates and negotiations between fans. In the process, she is able to outline the operation of fan canons, and the ways in which these issues of taste are related to broader questions of identity in fandom.

If Cherry's account is based on in-depth audience research with a large number of horror fans, Hutchings's essay is a far more intimate mediation on his own relationship to horror, and the ways in which memory operates in relation to unofficial and private versions of horror history. He considers a series of issues about the repackaging of the past in the form of DVD box sets, such as the Universal Legacy Editions, and his own personal relationships to these objects and artifacts. In the process, he demonstrates how intimately his own tastes and preferences as a horror scholar are related to historical processes such as the emergence of video and institutional attempts to regulate its consumption, and the more recent development and organization of DVD technology.

Finally, Henry Jenkins' essay sets out to consider genre in the comic book and graphic novel. In particular, he examines the use of the Silver Age of the superhero comics in the late 1950s and 1960s by contemporary comic books and graphic novels, an age in which the comic book itself was being transformed by multiple factors both inside and outside the industry. Comic books were being forced to conform to the new codes of regulation that followed the moral panics surrounding the medium in the early 1950s, but were also developing new forms of creativity as the Golden Age superheroes were being reinvented to address new audience expectations. In the process, he explores how this period is approached with both nostalgia and revisionism in contemporary work, as it attempts to reimagine and reinvent this period for today's audiences. As a result, Jenkins demonstrates that these comic books not only involve a highly complex play with memories of the genre, but also that the form's handling of genre is quite different from that in film and television.

In conclusion, the essays collected in this book all seek to examine various different constructions of genre, and the ways in which these constructions are not only produced within historical circumstances, but also work to produce a sense of the generic past. Furthermore, the definitions of genre almost inevitably imply historical models, either by proposing a sense of generic identity that unites films and makes historical time irrelevant, or by providing a sense of narrative development, which privileges certain features and marginalizes or excludes others. As a result, generic definitions are bound up with memory in a variety of ways. On one hand, generic definitions are related to the processes of remembering and forgetting and, on the other hand, they also operate to produce a sense of the past. If different generations continually revise the films and television shows that are included or excluded from specific genres, it is also the case that the very notion of genre works to establish relationships above and between different forms of visual media, and so creates senses of lineage and development. Whether we can escape from the desire to provide authoritative definitions of genre, or whether we can turn our attention to the cultural processes through which such definitions are constructed and the political effects that these definitions can produce, are questions that lie at the heart of the essays collected in this book.

Notes

1. Matthew Arnold, *Poetry and Prose*. Ed. John Bryson (London: Rupert Hart-Davis, 1967), 439.
2. James Naremore, *More Than Night: Film Noir in Its Contexts* (Berkeley, CA: University of California Press, 1998).
3. Steve Neale, "Melo Talk: On the Meaning of the Use of the Term 'Melodrama' in the American Trade Press." *The Velvet Light Trap* 32 Fall (1993): 69.
4. Leo Handel, *Hollywood Looks at Its Audience: A Report on Film Audience Research* (Urbana, IL: University of Illinois Press, 1950), 119–120.
5. Rick Altman, *Film/Genre* (London: British Film Institute, 1999).
6. Barbara Klinger, *Melodrama & Meaning: History, Culture, and the Films of Douglas Sirk* (Bloomington, IN: Indiana University Press, 1994).
7. *Dr. Jekyll and Mr. Hyde* Pressbook, 1941, Margaret Herrick Library.
8. Mark Jancovich, "A Real Shocker: Authenticity, Genre and the Struggles for Cultural Distinctions." *Continuum* 14.1 (2000): 23–35.
9. See Lincoln Geraghty, "'Realities ... Blending as One!': Film Texts and Intertexts in the *Star Trek/X-Men* Crossover Comics." *Extrapolation* 48.1 (2007): 106–117.
10. See Glenn Creeber, ed. *The Television Genre Book* (London: British Film Institute, 2001).
11. Gregory A. Waller, "Made-for-Television Horror Films." In *American Horrors: Essays on the Modern American Horror Film*. Ed. Gregory A. Waller (Urbana, IL: University of Illinois Press, 1987), 159.
12. Jason Jacobs, *The Intimate Screen: Early British Television Drama* (Oxford: Clarendon, 2000).
13. Mark Jancovich, "An Unidentified Species: Horror, the Body and Early Television Drama." In *Intensities: The Journal of Cult Media*. 4 (December 2007). Available at URL: <http://intensities.org/essays/Jancovich_Species.pdf>
14. Thomas Schatz, *Hollywood Genres: Formulas, Filmmaking, and the Studio System* (Boston, MA: McGraw Hill, 1981).
15. Kim Newman, *Nightmare Movies: A Critical History of the Horror Film, 1968–1988* (London: Bloomsbury, 1988), xii–xiii.

PART ONE

Institutions of Genre

1

Pale Shadows

Narrative Hierarchies in the Historiography of 1940s Horror

MARK JANCOVICH

As Rick Worland points out, "Standard historical accounts of the horror film consider the 1940s a dismal decade for the genre. Apart from the stylish films produced by Val Lewton at RKO from 1942 until 1946, films not so highly regarded in their day despite their current stature, forties horror cinema is commonly remembered for tired sequels to respected originals ... numbing poverty row quickies ... or mocking genre send ups."[1] Indeed, for this reason, the 1940s is still a crucially under-researched period within the genre (the other being the 1960s), in which not only has the period as a whole been misunderstood but also the different horror traditions within it.

One of the problems is the way in which the period's identity continues to be defined in relation to the 1930s, which operates as a canonized period in the history of the genre in relation to which the 1940s is simply defined as a reflection or shadowy double, something which has no life of its own but is only ever subordinate, dependent and inferior. As will become clear, most histories present the horror films of the 1940s as a mere continuation of the models from the 1930s, although most accounts also acknowledge that it was actually a quite different cycle. While the cycle that began with *Dracula* in 1931 came to an end in 1936, the cycle of the forties started after the 1938 release of a double bill featuring the 1931 versions of *Dracula* and *Frankenstein*, the successes of which demonstrated the presence of a market for horror in the period. As a result, caught between presenting the 1940s as both a continuation of the 1930s and a new cycle of film production, critics have been unable to identify the actual character of the period and, as will be demonstrated, have claimed that the films of the 1940s were simply imitations of the 1930s models *and* that they represented a corruption of those models: they resurrected their form but not their spirit!

The following chapter will therefore examine the critical histories of the period (both academic and non-academic) and the ways in which they construct the period in terms of imitation and corruption. It is important to note, following Barbara Klinger and others, that even academic criticism must be seen as a form of social discourse that is implicated within processes of reception along with marketing, reviewing, distribution and exhibition.[2] For example, as Peter Hutchings argues, the "negative perception of sequel-heavy 1940s Universal horror is often intertwined with a prejudice against the sequel itself as a particular cinematic format, with the sequelization process seeming to mark the moment where innovation ends and exploitation begins."[3] However, accounts of the 1940s also raise another issue, given the negative evaluation of imitation and repetition; there is a very real issue about the value of generic filmmaking itself, given that the generic element of genre filmmaking inevitably concerns the relation between films rather than that which distinguishes them from one another. The condemnation of the 1940s therefore reveals a position on genre in which identity is valued over conformity. In other words, it tends to value exceptional cases that mark themselves off as innovations or breaks, rather than those cases that are representative of more general patterns. Furthermore, not only is this position taken for granted as an incontestable value, but it also presents very real problems for our understanding of genre history. If that history is told through a concentration on, and analysis of, the exceptional case, the more common trends and patterns are either ignored or simply guessed at: they are not the object of analysis itself and hence the critic has no basis for establishing their character. Moreover, not only are there very real problems with the gendered nature of the privileging of identity over conformity,[4] but one can also dispute the viability of an opposition between distinction and identity, on the one hand, and imitation and repetition, on the other. All texts are intertextual utterances that ventriloquize other texts, but all texts also involve a process of negotiation in which these other texts are processed. Even the deliberate attempt to copy always produces a new text that cannot have the same identity or meaning as its model.[5]

The first section therefore concentrates on the ways in which critical accounts have constructed the 1940s in terms of the 1930s, ways that can only present it as both an imitation and a corruption of the 1930s models and, in so doing, presents it as a period that has no identity of its own but is simply defined by its dependence on, and hence inferiority to, a privileged original. The second section then moves on to think about alternative ways in which 1940s horror films can be related to those of the 1930s. If most accounts privilege the 1930s so that the character of the 1940s can only be a matter of inferiority rather than difference, corruption rather than transformation, the second section demonstrates the ways in which these histories work to canonize specific tendencies and marginalize or delegitimate others. Furthermore, this process is largely conducted in relation to the hierarchy of horror monsters in which a clear preference is established for Dracula and Frankenstein, Universal's leading monsters of the 1930s, over the Mummy and the Wolf Man, Universal's leading monsters of the 1940s. In other words, these later monsters represent different interests and concerns rather than inferior copies and, as a result, the constant critical complaints about the ways in which Frankenstein's monster changed during the 1940s can also be seen not as a process of entropy, depletion or loss but of conversion and retooling as a response to changed conditions.

Finally, the third section then demonstrates that if the problem is that histories not only privilege the 1930s but also specific features of that period, then in order to understand generic history one must not only examine the processes of development over time but also the complex processes of product differentiation within a period. In other words, not only are histories dominated by the canon of 1930s horror, but this canon also privileges Universal Studios over other tendencies. Furthermore, by the 1940s, the Universal horror films were far from being the only game in town, but had settled for being a niche within a broader horror market. As a result, the critical focus on Universal not only obscures the range of horror production that characterizes the period, but also marginalizes trends that were central to understandings of horror within the period. The fact that many of these trends have been reclassified over the intervening years, so that they are no longer seen as examples of horror today, is itself a fascinating story but one that needs to be told elsewhere.[6]

Imitation and Corruption

As we have seen, most accounts of generic history are organized around a distinction between formulaic repetition and innovative transformation, or between imitation and difference, and the 1940s is firmly consigned to the negative pole of repetitions and imitation. For example, Alan Frank claims that, during the period, the "horror film continued to explore variations of established themes,"⁷ while Denis Gifford not only draws attention to a number of remakes in the period but even implies that these repetitions became repetitive: "There were more remakes to come."⁸ This problem is claimed to particularly afflict Universal's output during the period, and the studio is even seen as displaying an almost religious fanaticism in its enthusiasm for remakes and sequels. Gifford, for example, refers to the studio's "revivalist mission,"⁹ in which the word "revival" associates the studio's remakes and sequels with the missionary zeal of religious fundamentalism.

He also claims that "history was repeating itself" in other ways.¹⁰ Lon Chaney Jr. was forced to become "the New Karloff, the New Chaney"¹¹ and so stood in for earlier horror stars including his own father, Lon Chaney. Rather than a star with his own unique features, he is seen as inferior and dependent, only ever able to play sons rather than fathers, and inappropriately trying to fill other people's shoes: by the time of *Frankenstein Meets the Wolf Man* (1943), it is argued, he had played so many of the monsters that he had only "one to go for full house,"¹² a supposedly dubious accomplishment that he achieved with his next film, *Son of Dracula* (1943). Chaney's problem is therefore tied to a more general complaint about the films, which were frequently attacked for having a "rehashed plot" or for being "still the same mixture as before."¹³ In a discussion of *The Ghost of Frankenstein* (1942), Gifford claims that "Karloff's monster remained unchanged" and, in his discussion of *The Mummy's Tomb* (1942), the process of repetition is taken even further: the makeup artist, Jack Pierce, "fashioned a mask that saved a deal of make up time" and "helped stuntman Edwin Parker look like Chaney look like Tyler look like Karloff, for once again the Waters of Khar unfold with their flashbacks."¹⁴ The sheer sense of tired irritation at these repetitions is clear here, and hence the sense that repetition involves nothing more than a law of ever diminishing returns.

Others also take issue with the Mummy series and attack the first of the 1940s' Mummy films, *The Mummy's Hand* (1940), with claims that it "is not so much a sequel as an imitation."¹⁵ It is also claimed that *The Climax* (1944) "virtually duplicates" *The Phantom of the Opera* (1925), although it is "distinguished by Karloff's carefully understated portrayal of a man obsessed."¹⁶ The assumption here is that imitations and duplicates are essentially worthless and, as James B. Twitchell claims of *Son of Frankenstein* (1939), they are simply "so predictable."¹⁷

Of course, the most common term associated with generic repetition is that of the "formula," in which it is suggested that, having once hit on a particular combination of elements, studios continue to endlessly reuse it. *The Mummy's Curse* (1944) is therefore said to be "very much to the formula established in *The Mummy's Tomb* (1942) and *The Mummy's Ghost* (1944)," although it is noted that the film does feature some "pleasantly photogenic Louisiana bayou settings" that are largely dismissed as mere window dressing that cannot hide the essential lack of identity.[18] Even Andrew Tudor falls back on the term "formula" in his description of the period. The 1940s film horror therefore "drifts towards formula repetition" and *Ghost of Frankenstein* is claimed to "retain many of the standard ingredients — elaborate laboratory sets, threatened innocents, a crippled servant."[19]

Furthermore, the term *formula* identifies repetition as an uncreative process of rationalized industrial mass production. It even evokes the transgressions of horror's mad scientists who believe that life can be created simply through the reassembling of dead materials, but have no understanding of the soul. However, even those descriptions that do suggest a more creative process behind the making of these films are not necessarily positive. They also fall back on horror imagery, which directly associates the films with the monstrousness of their creatures. For example, Frank's description of *The Mummy's Hand* notes the absence of Karloff, who had appeared in *The Mummy* (1932), and claims that this "time Tom Tyler rose from the dead, chosen by Universal because of his resemblance to the younger Karloff."[20] This association between the process of sequelization and the reanimated corpses of many horror films is made even more overt by Gifford, who refers to *The Invisible Man Returns* (1940) as "Universal's second exhumation of the second wave of horror."[21] The implication here is clear: that which has lived once should not be brought to life for a second time!

Even those films that were not sequels or remakes were not immune to criticism. For example, *Man Made Monster* (1941) is seen as a product that was similarly disinterred, although in this case Universal was claimed to have resurrected an unused script from the first wave of horror that had been held back for being "too much like *The Invisible Ray*": "Down from the shelf came a script written for Karloff and Lugosi."[22] In much the same way, Carlos Clarens claims that both *The Invisible Man Returns* and *The Mummy's Hand* involved a "pirating [of] the best efforts of their originals."[23] Interestingly, critics are more generally generous to *Phantom of the Opera* (1943), and this may be because, as many note, it was a "remake, rather than a sequel."[24] It is still seen as inferior to its predecessor but, in this case, it is seen more as a homage to the original rather than the illegitimate plundering of its materials implied by the term "pirated," a term that the industry uses to describe copyright infringement.

Consequently, critics do not necessarily ignore the work involved in the making of sequels or remakes but rather that this work is seen as a meaningless addition that adds nothing but rather subtracts from the original. For Tudor, the war period "simply extends the patterns already established in the 1930s," an extension that, it is implied, has no significance or value. On the contrary, he claims that in "some cases" the process of extension was taken to "desperate limits."[25] Similarly, Gifford claims that the makers of *The Mummy's Hand* "elaborate [a] single sequence into a whole new mythos," but still sees the series as a series of derivative sequels.[26]

However, if 1940s horror has no identity of its own, these accounts do not suggest that it is the same as 1930s horror. Nor is imitation the highest form of flattery here but rather corruption, abuse and exploitation. *Frankenstein Meets the Wolf Man* is referred to as Universal's first attempt "to ginger up fading box-office receipts by multiplying its monsters,"[27] while other accounts similarly presented imitation as necessarily involving dependence, loss and degeneration. As we have already seen, Chaney came to signify many of these problems. Like the films, Chaney could never be his father but neither could he achieve separation from him: he could never become his own man. Many critics, for example, recount his failed attempts to keep his own name, Creighton Chaney, and his complaint that he was eventually forced to take his father's name: "I am *not* proud of Lon Chaney Jnr, because they had to starve me to make me take this name."[28] This is even seen as central to his star image, so that Twitchell claims he "simply could not play the title role" in *Son of Dracula*: his "father could have" but the "son couldn't." Lon Chaney Jr. was "the perpetual son, and he could act like one in his wolf man roles, but Dracula is anything but a child — he is only a parent, more specifically, only the father."[29] Chaney, it was claimed, was doomed to play those who exist in the shadow of their parents, who are unable to escape comparison with their more powerful progenitor, or are themselves mere shadows: insubstantial shapes that have no substance of their own and are entirely dependent on the presence of another, a double or reflection.

Similarly, John Brosnan claims that the films of the 1940s "were but pale shadows of the original versions produced a decade earlier."[30] However, it is also important to remember that, in horror, while the shadow may lack substance, it is also the Other, the doppelganger, that threatens the identity of the original. For example, the horror films produced by Val Lewton in the 1940s are not only singled out for praise as the main exception to the rule of 1940s horror, but the praise is specifically reserved for their concern with shadows. In these films, "the use of shadows excels"[31] and their "distinctive use of light and shade"[32] is not simply a stylistic feature but linked to their very identity as films so that *I Walked with a Zombie* (1943) becomes a "small masterpiece" because the "beauty of the film is that, hovering visually in precarious balance between darkness and light, nothing in it is any more clear cut than the good or evil of [its character's] motives and actions."³³ Critics not only associate the shadows within these films with restraint, suggestion and imagination but also claim these shadows are related to more complex philosophical and moral themes that question the claims to identity, light and reason within them. However, while many of these critics celebrate these films, and horror more generally, for its use of the shadow, the sense that the 1940s films are shadows of the 1930s threatens the notions of patrimony on which their canonization of the 1930s depends. The shadow can productively call the identity of the original into doubt in the horror films themselves, but not in generic histories and their canons.

As a result, the imitation is not the same as the original but inferior, and this inferiority is identified with absence. The sequel to *The Mummy* is therefore distinguished by the fact that "Karloff was missing under the Universal bandages and fullers earth,"³⁴ while, in *Son of Dracula*, "Chaney is no Lugosi."³⁵ However, it is not just the stars that are absent but also, with them, the soul of their creations. It is therefore claimed that *Son of Frankenstein* "reduces [the monster] to a superhuman destructive force" so that he "becomes a sort of zombie and only reveals a little of the impulse towards humanity that flickered through *Frankenstein* (1931) and flared up in *Bride of Frankenstein* (1935) in two brief moments."³⁶ Similarly, in *Ghost of Frankenstein*, the monster is even said to be "lacking Karloff's humanizing traits,"³⁷ and it is said of Chaney, who replaced him, that his "performance has robotic power, but lacks soul, even a man-made one."³⁸

However, the problem is not just a matter of substitutions, or even poor writing but is directly related to the process of sequelization itself, which is claimed to obey a law of diminishing returns in which "Each sequel was worse than the one before."³⁹ For Frank, Universal was "running out of the original inspiration that had led them to create their classic fantasy monsters," while others claimed a "lack of inspiration" within the period as a whole,⁴⁰ in which the endless sequels were exhausting the materials plundered from the 1930s films and were therefore part of an inevitable process of decline. For Frank, Universal's "mockery of the once-serious monsters" in their encounters with Abbott and Costello only had the effect of "confirming the decline in the serious side of the genre," while Hardy claims that "the forties, with few exceptions, continued the decline initiated in the second half of the 1930s."⁴¹ Similarly, for Clarens, by the time of *Abbott and Costello Meet Frankenstein* in 1948, Universal had effectively killed off whatever life there was left in their creations, and "was flogging a dead horse."⁴²

Indeed, Abbott and Costello are frequently seen as representative of this process. As Ivan Butler claims, after *Son of Frankenstein*, "James Whale's great original joined Dracula on the sad path to the Abbott and Costello travesty."[43] Similarly, while Tudor complains that most films of the war period were "simplifications of the classical model,"[44] Twitchell claims that the Abbott and Costello films represent the end result of "the process of vulgarization" that distinguishes the period.[45] For some, the problem was that these films mark the point at which "unconscious parody finally gave way to deliberate spoof"[46] and, for others, it marks the final stage in a move away from a serious literary culture through adaptation and sequelization until the films "were made by hacks to be shown *only* to kids." As Twitchell puts it: "No further innovations followed"; "there was no other more immature audience eager to 'have a look.'"[47]

Repetition and Identity

However, while most agree on the general features of the period, there is more disagreement over the quality of specific films, and quite where the break between the 1930s and the 1940s is to be marked. For example, Gifford refers to *Son of Frankenstein* as the "first of the new horror films, the last of the great ones,"[48] and it is interesting to note that Mel Brooks' homage to Universal horror, *Young Frankenstein* (1974), is a virtual remake of *Son of Frankenstein*, rather than the previous two films in the series. Of course, one could argue that he makes this choice because this film marks the moment when the series began to become formularized, but it also demonstrates that this is also the image of Universal that has passed into popular consciousness. However, others simply deal with the Universal films of the 1940s in their chapters on the 1930s, and privilege the Lewton productions by giving these films their own chapter. For example, Ivan Butler's *The Horror Film* (1967) has a chapter on Dracula and Frankenstein, which presents the Universal films of the 1930s as central, and the reprint has a chapter on "Val Lewton and the Forties Cycle," which focuses exclusively on Lewton's productions.[49] Similarly, Carlos Clarens dedicates a chapter entitled "Children of the Night: Hollywood, 1928–1947" to a discussion in which the Universal horrors of the 1930s are predominant, and then devotes an entire chapter to the RKO films of the 1940s, "More with Less: Psychological Horror, Val Lewton and Jacques Tourneur."[50] Finally, Reynold Humphries spends two chapters, in which the 1930s are privileged over the 1940s, and covers figures such as Dracula, Frankenstein, Dr. Jekyll and Mr. Hyde, the Wolf Man and King Kong, but devotes a third chapter to Lewton alone.[51]

However, the key Universal monsters of the 1940s were not Frankenstein and Dracula, the key Universal monsters of the 1930s, but rather the Mummy and the Wolf Man, and neither the 1940s films that featured the Mummy nor those that featured the Wolf Man were sequels to films from the previous decade. The four Mummy films made in the 1940s were made eight years after the first and last Mummy film of the previous decade, Karl Freund's *The Mummy*. Furthermore, while Freund's *The Mummy* is often revered for "its sobriety and refusal to shock,"[52] others have, ironically, noted that this 1932 "original" itself was "a chance to 'remake' *Dracula*."[53] In contrast, *The Mummy's Hand*, and the Mummy films that came after it, bear little resemblance to the 1932 film, which has only one brief scene that features anything like the bandaged Mummy that has entered popular memory, a figure that is the creation of the later films. *The Mummy's Hand* does not even try to present itself as a continuation of the Freund film, but clearly sets out to start the series over from scratch. A new Mummy is unearthed, with a new backstory, new set of characteristics and a new name: Karloff's mummy was called Imhotep while the mummy of the 1940s is Kharis.

Nor is Kharis the self-motivating seducer of the 1932 film, but rather a conflicted character who is caught between an eternal transgressive desire for his lost princess, and a stern religious law that binds him to its will through the figure of a high priest. In the first film, he is the instrument of holy vengeance directed against the archaeologists who have defiled the tomb of his Princess Ananka, but eventually the high priest transgresses religious law himself and so provides the opportunity for Kharis to revolt against his master. The second film, *The Mummy's Tomb*, follows much the same story although it transposes the action to New England where Kharis tries to finish off the mission of vengeance from the previous film. In the third film, however, the story shifts and while Kharis and a high priest are still trying to repair the violation to the princess's tomb by returning her body to its rightful resting place, the narrative also focuses on a young woman of Egyptian heritage who is a reincarnation of the princess and suffers a crisis of identity in which she is caught between her two selves: a modern, independent woman and the reincarnation of Kharis' lost object of desire. Furthermore, rather than a mere formula retread, Bruce Kawin has seen this film as a "self-deconstructing masterpiece" that "exploits every formula it can, turning them against themselves, right up to the climax where the monster, for once, gets the girl."[54]

For Kawin, the Mummy itself is "a walking repetition compulsion,"[55] a figure condemned by "neurotic possessiveness" to "the deathless persistence of compulsive fixation."[56] In other words, rather than simply a series based on a repetitive narrative formula, it is one in which repetition is central to the very being of its central monster. The fulfillment of his desire therefore results in death for both himself and the object of his desire. Able to finally possess her, his embrace turns her into a mummified corpse and the two sink into a boggy grave united together for eternity, or at least until the next sequel where they are disinterred and separated by what seems to be a Works Progress Administration project that is trying to modernize a backward Louisiana: it's never quite clear how they have got from New England to Louisiana. Like the earlier film, *The Mummy's Curse* follows a dual narrative in which Kharis strives to be reunited with his lost Ananka and she suffers a crisis of identity: suffering from amnesia, she is unable to know whether she is a modern independent young woman or doomed to return to Kharis's mummifying embrace. In this way, the films can be seen to raise a series of concerns about women's wartime situation, which seemed to offer social, economic and cultural independence but over which hovered a possible return to prewar domesticity when the men returned home at the end of the war.

Similarly, *The Wolf Man* (1941) has no narrative connection to Universal's one previous werewolf film of six years earlier, *Werewolf of London* (1935), and it also starts from scratch with a new character, Lawrence Talbot, and a new set of traits for its monster. Thus, while it has been claimed that *The Wolf Man* "strengthens the rather weak myth of *The Werewolf of London*,"[57] Frank claims that "the new werewolf lore dreamed up by writer, Curt Siodmak, including the now 'traditional' belief that a werewolf should be killed with silver [and] was a considerable improvement on [Universal's] previous efforts in the genre."[58] Twitchell goes one better and claims that "what Bram Stoker did for the vampire, Curt Siodmak did for the werewolf":

> In this sense, what the folklore nosferatu is to the modern vampire, the ancient werewolf is to the modern Wolfman. Both mythic archetypes had to be domesticated, personalized, elevated from lore to art, and then returned in a new form to lore. They have changed their manners, been humanized.[59]

In other words, "Universal's Wolfmen had almost nothing to do with werewolf folklore, but instead came from the genius of Curt Siodmak."[60] *The Wolf Man* is no sequel or imitator but rather the original from which our current sense of the werewolf as a figure derives.

If some critics assert Siodmak's status as the author of the Wolf Man as we currently understand it, Lon Chaney Jr. also asserted a proprietary claim that emphasized its originality. Despite the discomfort during the lengthy ordeal of filming the transformation process, Gifford claims that "Chaney loved his Wolf Man: 'he was my baby.'"[61] Elsewhere he claimed: "Of course

I believe that *The Wolf Man* is the best of my horror films — because he is *mine*!"⁶² Unlike the other monsters that he played, Chaney believed the Wolf Man to be his own creation, an original rather than a monster that was already identified with an earlier performance or incarnation. As Brosnan is keen to clarify, "Henry Hull had played a wolf man in the 1935 film *Werewolf of London* ... but Chaney's *was* the definitive version."⁶³

As a result, not only is this version usually seen as "the definitive Wolf Man,"⁶⁴ but it also is often seen as one of "Universal Pictures' three great horror films."⁶⁵ While some accounts grudgingly accept it as one of the better examples of Universal's 1940s horror films, others imply that it was one of the 1930s films exactly because it was a classic. William K. Everson claims that it was "one of the best of the new brand of Universal thrillers,"⁶⁶ that was not only "stylish"⁶⁷ but placed a greater stress "on characterization than on plot."⁶⁸ Similarly, Frank claims that *The Wolf Man* was a case of "Universal finally getting it right,"⁶⁹ and Leonard Wolf claims that the film has "a special power."⁷⁰

Indeed, the Universal horror films of the 1940s are dominated by these two horror monsters in relation to which the Universal monsters of the 1930s were clearly subordinate. There was no *Dracula* series, and although there are a number of poverty row vampire films, Dracula is largely absent from the Universal films of the 1940s. He does not reappear until *Son of Dracula*, which was made after the established success of the Mummy and Wolf Man series, and after the success of *The Ghost of Frankenstein*. Furthermore, as critics note, the film is not really interested in Dracula but rather in the daughter of a Southern plantation dynasty who comes under his influence. As Dillard notes, in the film, "Kay's morbid psychology which predisposes her to vampirism is more truly the heart of the film than Count Alucard — Dracula himself."⁷¹ In this film, Dracula does not invade America but is actively drawn there by Kay, and he remains a largely world-weary and passive presence throughout the story and is only ever moved to action to protect Kay and her desires. Indeed, in the most celebrated scene within the film, Kay seems to virtually summon Dracula up as she stands by the water's edge waiting for his coffin to rise from its depths, for him to rise from it, and be drawn across the surface towards her. It is hardly surprising, then, that there are numerous critical complaints about Chaney's interpretation of the Count and that there was no follow-up until Dracula joined the Wolf Man and Frankenstein's monster for *House of Frankenstein* (1944) and *House of Dracula* (1945).

Similarly, while Frankenstein's monster did reappear in *Son of Frankenstein*, Universal's first attempt to cash in on the success of the *Dracula* and

Frankenstein double bill, the next Frankenstein film was not until *The Ghost of Frankenstein* in 1942, which was, once again after the success of the first two Mummy films and the first of the Wolf Man series. Furthermore, while it was a major success, the monster's next appearance was in *Frankenstein Meets the Wolf Man*, a film that is clearly focused on the continuation of Lawrence Talbot's narrative and relegates Frankenstein's monster to the position of second fiddle. Indeed, these priorities become clear in the casting. The film stars Chaney as the Wolf Man rather than the monster, which he had played in *The Ghost of Frankenstein*: Chaney was insistent that "no one else [would] play his baby."[72] Indeed, this positioning of the monster is a cause of concern for many critics, which clearly demonstrates their investment in the 1930s films rather than the priorities of the 1940s.

One of the few critics to actually present the difference between the 1930s and the 1940s as being more than a simple issue of inferiority is R.H. W. Dillard. He clearly has a preference for the 1930s rather than the 1940s, but his preference is based on a choice between their ways of seeing the world: he does not see them as attempting to do the same thing but with different levels of success. Also, he does not present these differences as simply the result of a radical break but rather relates the dominant tendencies of the 1940s to tendencies that were already present, if marginal, within the 1930s:

> The films of the 1940s, which were mainly American, reduced the range of their parabolic quest from the spirit to the flesh, from the metaphysical to the psychological. Finding their roots in the sexual and psychological concerns of earlier films like Florey's *Murders in the Rue Morgue*, Lambert Hillyer's *Dracula's Daughter*, and Mamoulian's *Dr. Jekyll and Mr. Hyde*, the films of the 1940s defined the human being primarily as a physical (as opposed to spiritual) being. The human psyche was no longer capable of the metaphysical yearning and force of Henry Frankenstein, but rather became the victim of mental aberration which should be cured.[73]

As Dillard notes, *The Wolf Man* is "cast in the terms of Freudian psychological understanding," while films such as *Son of Dracula* also focused on psychological pathology rather than spiritual corruption.[74]

Furthermore, the Wolf Man and the Mummy, like so many monsters of the period, are figures driven by compulsions over which they cannot exercise their will. They are doomed by their desires and their inability to control them. It is hardly surprising then, that their films lack Christian frameworks. Both are the products of pagan and pre–Christian religions, and their monstrousness is not related to their defiance of, or opposition to, the Christian God as is the case with both Frankenstein and Dracula. Unsurprisingly, then, Christian symbols are no defense against them.

Landscapes of Fear: Mapping 1940s Horror

Again, however, there is a need for caution. If the 1940s were not a mere continuation of the 1930s, neither were the 1940s a radical break from the previous period. Decades are never neatly divided off from one another, nor is any decade homogeneous and undifferentiated. Rather, generic development is a complex process in which each period is made up of a series of different tendencies that are not only defined in relation to one another but also draw on, and rearticulate, elements from earlier periods. In other words, most histories not only privilege the 1930s over the 1940s but also Universal over other areas of production. However, the Universal horror films were not only a diverse group, of which the Mummy and the Werewolf cannot be seen as fully representative,[75] but horror-related materials were being produced by all the other major studios and by the poverty row studios such as Monogram and the Producers Releasing Corporation. Furthermore, while other studios certainly tried to learn from Universal, any attempt to simply replicate its strategy would have been to play a losing game. Any attempt to simply imitate Universal would always suffer by comparison and, as a result, product differentiation was an important element of horror production as various studios sought to enter the horror market, but also to capitalize on their own assets and distinctive characteristics.

As a result, one of the problems with most histories is that they concentrate on narrative history rather than intertextual mapping. These narrative histories tend to search for the clear line of cause and effect, in which dominant trend gives way to dominant trend as a central logic unfolds. However, historical periods can only be adequately understood if one maps the range of intertextual options available, and the ways in which the meaning of each option is defined in relation to the other available options. As we have seen, each new text cannot be a simple reproduction of an existing model but is always engaged in a process of negotiation and transformation, and this process works both within and between periods. In other words, genre history is a complex process of assemblage, in which each new text is only ever constructed through the articulation of existing elements, a process that necessarily reworks the meanings of these elements. As a result, no text or period can ever have a pure and autonomous identity that is defined outside social structures and processes, but neither can it be a simple reproduction, replica or copy.

This concern with intertextual mapping also raises another issue about genre. As Rick Altman demonstrates, many accounts of genre history impose terms retrospectively, so that later understandings of a genre can work to exclude earlier ones. Neither *Dracula* nor *Frankenstein* were seen as horror on their initial release but rather as film versions of theatrical hits.[76] It was only later, after they had given rise to a cycle of films, that the notion of the horror film even came into existence and was then retrospectively projected back onto these two films. However, it is not just that the meaning of individual films can change over time, but also that, even once they have been created, generic terms themselves change meaning. As James Naremore illustrates, the term "film noir" had a different meaning in the late 1940s to that which it had in the late 1950s and, as a result, many films that were seen as central to "film noir" in the late 1940s were seen as marginal a decade later. Indeed, some films, such as *The Lost Weekend* (1945), which were seen as central in the 1940s, were completely excluded from the category of "film noir" by the late 1950s.[77]

Similarly, a large number of 1940s films are now distinguished from horror by terms such as "film noir" and the "paranoid woman's film," although both these terms were products of later periods. However, as I have argued elsewhere, the films that are currently associated with these later terms were usually identified with horror in the period.[78] As a result, while generic terms can help us to understand how individual films have been understood in relation to one another, they can also work to obscure the ways in which they have been related to one another in specific periods. Furthermore, they may even create the sense of distinctive categories, in which no such sense had existed previously. For example, the films identified as horror, film noir and the paranoid woman's film today were not seen as distinct categories in the 1940s, but were all identified as horror films. Part of the reason for this was that horror itself had a significantly different meaning to that which it has today, and was seen as virtually synonymous with "mystery,"[79] a generic term that was not limited to a concern with detection but was more concerned with the strange, eerie and uncanny. The films associated with horror, film noir and the paranoid woman's film today were therefore seen to share a common identity through their associations with mystery and often featured narratives of psychological disorientation, in which their protagonists find themselves trapped within worlds that are fundamentally illegible and unpredictable.

It is therefore significant that the period covered by this cycle starts in 1938 and ends in the late 1940s. In other words, the cycle starts in a period of uncertainty, during which America was moving towards involvement in World War II, and it ends after the period of readjustment that followed the war, a period in which it was feared that post-war depression would replace wartime affluence and one that was also witnessing a complex renegotiation of gender relations. Not only was a generation of men returning from the war to expectations and responsibilities that they had never known, or from which they had long been separate, but many women had enjoyed social, economic and cultural independence that was no longer seen as viable as the men returned. In other words, the immediate post-war period was a period of anxiety and uncertainty for both men and women, as the terms of their relationships had to be fundamentally renegotiated.

As a result, while Dana Polan has argued that the war demanded narratives that were immediately legible and predictable, in which the resolution is known and assured from the outset,[80] there was a strong tradition of filmmaking that followed a completely different course. Nor are these films simply the deconstructive "other" of this affirmative narrative. On the contrary, the affirmative narrative itself was a response to very real uncertainties about the outcome of the war, uncertainties that were made explicit in the mystery films of the period. In other words, the period from the late 1930s to the late 1940s was one in which the social world could not be easily read and outcomes could not be easily predicted. In this context, illegibility became a central concern, and fog became a central image. Nowhere is this clearer than in the Universal Sherlock Holmes series of the 1940s, a series that, as I have argued elsewhere, were clearly marketed as horror films during the period.[81] Certainly, Holmes could always be relied upon to solve the mystery at the heart of each film but, none-the-less, most films within the series started with a credit sequence that emphasized illegibility and uncertainty, rather than comprehension and resolution. In this credit sequence, Holmes and Watson are confronted by an impenetrable fog into which they peer with fear and determination as they walk forward purposefully, a gun aimed ahead of them as they attempt to protect themselves from threats that may lie in the obscure distance.

Conclusion

It is only when one starts to move beyond a canonization of the 1930s that the character of 1940s horror begins to become clearer. Rather than simply a degenerating continuation, a shoddy imitation or a pirating of 1930s models, the 1940s was a new cycle with different priorities to those of the 1930s. Not only were the key monsters of the 1940s Universal horror films the Mummy and the Wolf Man, rather than Frankenstein and Dracula, but also the very concentration on Universal studios obscures the range of films that were understood as horror in the period or associated with the genre. For example, in 1944, the *New York Times* explicitly discussed "a new horror cycle" that was far more ambitious than "the forerunning vampire, werewolf and Frankenstein chillers,"[82] and it identified a range of films that were representative of this new cycle: *Gaslight* (1944), *Dark Waters* (1944), *Hangover Square* (1945), *Phantom Lady* (1944), *Laura* (1944), *Woman in the Window* (1944) and *Spellbound* (1945). Few of these films are classified today as horror films, and it is only when we start to reconstruct the intertextual associations by which they were understood as horror films in the 1940s that we can begin to understand what the term "horror" meant within the social discourses of that period, rather than simply accept, or simply revise, the canon of horror that was constructed by histories of horror written in the late 1960s and early 1970s in relation to the prevailing definitions of genre of that later moment.[83]

Notes

1. Rick Worland, "OWI Meets the Monsters: Hollywood Horror Films and War Propaganda, 1942–1945." *Cinema Journal* 37:1 (1997): 47.
2. Barbara Klinger, *Melodrama and Meaning: History, Culture, and the Films of Douglas Sirk* (Bloomington: Indiana University Press, 1994).
3. Peter Hutchings, *The Horror Film* (London: Longman, 2004), 20.
4. See Joanne Hollows, *Feminism, Femininity and Popular Culture* (Manchester: Manchester University Press, 2000); and Mark Jancovich, "Naked Ambitions: Pornography, Taste and the Problem of the Middlebrow." *Scope: An Online Journal of Film Studies* (June 2001).
5. See V.N. Volosinov, *Marxism and the Philosophy of Language* (New York: Seminar Press, 1973); and Pierre Bourdieu, *The Field of Cultural Production: Essays on Art and Literature* (New York: Columbia University Press, 1993).
6. For a more detailed discussion of the cultural politics of these particular definitions, and particularly their exclusion of the female-centered, "quality" horror films of the 1940s, see Mark Jancovich, "'Rebecca's Ghost': Horror, the Gothic and the du Maurier Film Adaptations." In *The Daphne du Maurier Companion*. Ed. Helen Taylor, (London: Virago, 2007). See also Mark Jancovich, "'Two Ways of Looking': Affection and Aversion in the Critical Reception of 'Lowbrow Horror' in the 1940s" (forthcoming).
7. Alan Frank, *Horror Films* (London: Hamlyn, 1977), 42.
8. Denis Gifford, *A Pictorial History of Horror Movies* (London: Hamlyn, 1973), 26.
9. Ibid., 133.
10. Ibid., 126.
11. Ibid., 131.
12. Ibid., 141.
13. Ibid., 131.
14. Ibid., 139.
15. Phil Hardy, *The Aurum Film Encyclopedia: Horror* (London: Aurum, 1985), 75.
16. Ibid., 84.
17. James B. Twitchell, *Dreadful Pleasures: An Anatomy of Modern Horror* (New York: Oxford University Press, 1985), 185.
18. Hardy, *The Aurum Film Encyclopedia: Horror*, 86.
19. Andrew Tudor, *Monsters and Mad Scientists: A Cultural History of the Horror Movie* (Oxford: Blackwell, 1989), 35.
20. Frank, *Horror Films*, 44.
21. Gifford, *A Pictorial History of Horror Movies*, 129–131.
22. Ibid., 135.
23. Carlos Clarens, *An Illustrated History of the Horror Film* (New York: G.P. Putnam, 1967), 150.
24. Frank, *Horror Films*, 47.

25. Tudor, *Monsters and Mad Scientists*, 34.
26. Gifford, *A Pictorial History of Horror Movies*, 133.
27. Hardy, *The Aurum Film Encyclopedia: Horror*, 81.
28. John Brosnan, *The Horror People* (London: Macdonald and Jane, 1976), 20.
29. Twitchell, *Dreadful Pleasures*, 144–5.
30. Brosnan, *The Horror People*, 73.
31. Ivan Butler, *Horror in the Cinema* (London: Zwemmer, 1970), 72.
32. Tudor, *Monsters and Mad Scientists*, 34.
33. Hardy, *The Aurum Film Encyclopedia: Horror*, 82.
34. Frank, *Horror Films*, 44.
35. Ibid., 47.
36. Hardy, *The Aurum Film Encyclopedia: Horror*, 71.
37. Frank, *Horror Films*, 46.
38. Gifford, *A Pictorial History of Horror Movies*, 139.
39. Butler, *Horror in the Cinema*, 46.
40. Tudor, *Monsters and Mad Scientists*, 34.
41. Hardy, *The Aurum Film Encyclopedia: Horror*, 74.
42. Clarens, *An Illustrated History of the Horror Film*, 153.
43. Butler, *Horror in the Cinema*, 52.
44. Tudor, *Monsters and Mad Scientists*, 35.
45. Twitchell, *Dreadful Pleasures*, 55.
46. Clarens, *An Illustrated History of the Horror Film*, 151.
47. Twitchell, *Dreadful Pleasures*, 55.
48. Gifford, *A Pictorial History of Horror Movies*, 124.
49. Ivan Butler, *The Horror Film* (1967) reprinted as Butler, *Horror in the Cinema*.
50. Clarens, *An Illustrated History of the Horror Film*.
51. Reynold Humphries, *The American Horror Film: An Introduction* (Edinburgh: Edinburgh University Press, 2002).
52. Clarens, *An Illustrated History of the Horror Film*, 111.
53. David J. Skal, *The Monster Show: A Cultural History* (London: Plexus), 168.
54. Bruce Kawin, "The Mummy's Pool." In *Planks of Reason: Essays on the Horror Film*. Ed. Barry K. Grant (Metuchen, NJ: Scarecrow, 1984), 16.
55. Kawin, "The Mummy's Pool," 13.
56. Kawin, "The Mummy's Pool," 15.
57. Hardy, *The Aurum Film Encyclopedia: Horror*, 78.
58. Frank, *Horror Films*, 46.
59. Twitchell, *Dreadful Pleasures*, 220.
60. Ibid., 83.
61. Gifford, *A Pictorial History of Horror Movies*, 136.
62. Brosnan, *The Horror People*, 22.
63. Ibid.
64. Frank, *Horror Films*, 46.
65. Leonard Wolf, *Horror: A Connoisseur's Guide to Literature and Film* (New York: Facts on File, 1989), 235.
66. William K. Everson, *Classics of the Horror Film: From the Days of Silent Film to the Exorcist* (Secaucus, NJ: Citadel, 1974), 214.
67. Ibid., 5.
68. Ibid., 214.
69. Frank, *Horror Films*, 42.
70. Wolf, *Horror*, 3.
71. R. H. W. Dillard, *Horror Films* (New York: Monarch, 1976), 4.
72. Gifford, *A Pictorial History of Horror Movies*, 141.
73. Dillard, *Horror Films*, 3–4.
74. Ibid., 4.
75. During the 1940s, Universal initiated a number of horror series that included the Inner Sanctum, Invisible Man, Captive Wild Woman and Sherlock Holmes films.
76. Rick Altman, *Film/Genre* (London: BFI, 1999).
77. James Naremore, *More Than Night: Film Noir in Its Contexts* (Berkeley: University of California Press, 1998).
78. See Mark Jancovich, "Bluebeard's Wives: Women, Quality and the Horror Film of the 1940s" (forthcoming).

79. Mark Jancovich, "The Meaning of Mystery: Genre, Marketing and the Universal Sherlock Holmes Series of the 1940s." *Film International* 17 (2005): 34–45. See also Leo Handel, *Hollywood Looks at Its Audience* (Urbana: University of Illinois Press, 1950).

80. Dana Polan, *Power and Paranoia: History, Narrative and the American Cinema, 1940–50* (New York: Columbia University Press, 1986).

81. Jancovich, "The Meaning of Mystery."

82. Fred Stanley, "Hollywood Shivers," *New York Times*, May 28 (1944): X3.

83. See Jancovich, "'Rebecca's Ghost'"; and "'Two Ways of Looking.'"

2

The Independent Film Channel

Creating a Genre and Brand Across Small Screens, Big Screens, and the Virtual World

LIZA TREVIÑO

During downtime at a 2000 Seattle independent film conference, I wandered into the Seven Gables Theatre to catch a movie. Climbing up creaky and worn carpeted stairs to the lobby, I was pleased to see film culture flourishing in this alternative space — so refreshing from the banal multiplexes that had been steadily overtaking the small single or double screen neighborhood theaters I enjoyed. It was in this defiantly other space to suburban moviegoing that I came across the debut issue of *IFC Rant* magazine, a bimonthly publication by the Independent Film Channel (IFC). The attitude conveyed in the cover photo and the magazine's title meshed with the alternative space in which I discovered the magazine. In this universe, independent film was not merely a film genre or a way of describing a text's mode of production or ideology, but rather a complete three-dimensional experience. By stepping into the Seven Gables, paying for my ticket, thumbing through *IFC Rant,* and later going online to register with ifctv.com to get information about receiving the IFC digital cable channel, I was participating in a specifically chosen, all encompassing, independent film practice.

Of course, one potential reading of this phenomenon is that one person's "independent practice" is another's complete submission into "capitalist commodification." Independent Film Channel's digital cable launch in 1994 offers strong evidence for the cultural pessimist that the last arena of authentic creativity of film as an oppositional practice has been breached by marketing's commercial imperatives. What had been abstract and tenuous connections circulating between independent film and an alternative sensibility in the text, the viewer, or the producer was, with the new IFC cable channel, brought into clear relief as a tangible product and identifiable genre with a shared symbolic meaning for its audience — a meaning that was to be bought and sold and inserted into the cultural forum of TV, the virtual spaces of the Internet, and the physical spaces of movie.

Film scholar Steve Neale, in *Genre and Hollywood*, suggests that a key element to understanding genre is in the "intertextual relay," a mixture of systems and forms of marketing and reception available to each media institution, that generates audience expectations and also provides labels for films and genres that create groupings for films, TV programs, and niche network offerings.[1] To that point, critic Graeme Turner makes the case for how genre groupings and intertextual relay work within a television context. Turner argues,

> Through its inscriptions in publicity, in the listings in the TV guide, in the repertoires of cultural knowledge around individual personalities and other intertextual experiences, genre helps to frame audience expectations. For the television viewer, genre plays a major role in how television texts are classified, selected and understood.[2]

By launching a multi-platform definition of independent film, IFC actively and aggressively asserted a new understanding for independent film as a genre. In this essay, specific attention will be given to television's role in establishing a center from which popular discourse surrounding the idea of independent film could be anchored and given stable genre identification.

Since IFC began solely as a TV venture, certain negative views were entrenched about the channel's alternative potential and limits. However, IFC's overall multi-platform approach at branding complicates any cut-and-dry desire to view IFC solely as a total commodification of independent film. While IFC's website, programs, and theater renovation project are, to be sure, created to sell IFC as a product, these sites also represent dynamic interactions between its product and its audience since they elicit participation, choice, and action. The interplay of popular media regarding independent film brings up two contradictory results. On the one hand, independent film is marketed and brought squarely into the realm of commerce. However, the way that independent film has been developed as a recognizable genre by IFC provides an opportunity for participation by various levels of viewer/audience participation and meaning. An analysis of IFC promotion campaigns, signature shows, and the use of geographically specific exhibition sites, demonstrates how each distribution platform promotes different experiences to construct a complete "world" of independent film that draws upon different levels of audience participation. Therefore, while charges of commodification are not taken lightly, particularly in the wake of independent film being understood as its own commercially viable and marketable genre and as the subject of two different cable television ventures, nevertheless, such a closed reading of how IFC "works" as an independent idea remains incomplete.

Independent Film, What Is It?

Trying to pin down the independent film phenomenon is difficult at best. Avant-garde, experimental, underground, trash, and counter-cinema are all euphemisms deployed over time to specify non–Hollywood films. Definitions and theories for these specific categories also proliferate in dizzying numbers. How to define these films and, what do they all have in common, if anything at all? The confusion surrounding the term *independent film* becomes clear by sifting through the myriad definitions ventured by critics attempting to make sense of the independent cinema "boom" of the 1980s and 1990s.

Economics and financial standing have played an important role in pinning down the fundamental elements used by critics to define independent film. One of the prominent markers of this alternative film practice is its lack of proper financing. This point is a crucial distinction for many fans, filmmakers, and critics alike that see this economic component as the driving force behind what makes independent film vibrant and infused with a creativity and/or adventurousness not associated with Hollywood-financed films. Writer Greg Merritt develops this economic determinant argument in his account of independent cinema, *Celluloid Mavericks*, by delineating between independents and semi-independents. For Merritt, an independent film is devoid of any studio funding or involvement. Defining independent cinema as abashedly other to Hollywood, Merritt concludes, "the off–Hollywood arena is American cinema's laboratory, proving ground, and launching pad."[3] In *The Encyclopedia of American Independent Filmmaking,* the first page jumps into a literal interpretation of independent film, stating that it "is created, financed, produced, and distributed outside the commercial, corporate conglomerate structure."[4]

Clearly, problems abound with this restrictive interpretation of independent film. Citing the earliest work of John Cassavetes and Frederick Wiseman as the rare exceptions of truly independent filmmakers, LoBrutto ultimately puts forth the idea that the release of *sex, lies & videotape* (1989) represented the "public reference point for the modern era of independent filmmaking" and resulted in the independent film becoming "a genre as much as a mode of production."[5] With this in mind, the complete subordination of independent film into a marketing label and fixed genre presents an acknowledgement at the loss of valence for the political efficacy previously attached to independent filmmakers and filmmaking. This idea surfaces in multiple accounts:

> The true independents throughout film history have been the nontraditional avant-garde/experimental and non-fiction filmmakers, many who operate as self-governing artists.[6]
>
> The original sin of the American independent cinema, when it shifted away from the avant-garde, was the introduction of narrative.... Once you do that, you're inserting yourself into a commodity system. At that point, whether or not you have seized the means of production, ala Karl Marx, doesn't matter, because what you haven't done is seize the means of exhibition, marketing, and distribution, and so you end up having to play by the rules of the big boys.[7]
>
> At present, critics are disenchanted with the flattening out of the political implications of independent cinema, its reduction to a marketing tool. The discovery of *sex, lies & videotape* at Sundance in 1989 was the event that turned the concept of independence into a tool.... Given the decline in radical film practice, the question of what should be celebrated in independent cinema remains a potent one.... At the very least, one can suggest what American independent cinema is not: It's not avant-garde, it's not experimental, and it's not underground. With few exceptions, there is not much edge, formal experimentation, or serious challenge to dominant culture. A shift has taken place since the underground and avant-garde work of Cassavetes, Andy Warhol and Paul Morrissey.[8]

The almost wistful and certainly nostalgic tone about the corrupted current independent cinema — especially in comparison to its earlier progenitors — is plain. The loss of independence among independents as one monolithic group, however, is an easy out. Again, such laments seem to be predicated on an economic determination.

What of the well-known Hollywood "insider" or independent filmmaker with an established track record that continues making films once commercially successful and known in the mainstream? This type of filmmaker quickly tests the limits of conceptualizing independent film solely on the basis of money. When moving beyond the sole economic purview of independent film, another definition resorts to the more ambiguous idea of an "independent spirit" that pervades filmmakers regardless of their level of success or proximity to Hollywood funding. So while, as in *Outsider Features,* author Richard Ferncase espouses an almost apologetic justification for the inclusion of successful filmmakers by writing, "while most of these directors now work with studios and can no longer qualify as being truly 'independent,' all were outsiders when they made the films discussed in this book," what remains unsaid is that these directors, while having "gone Hollywood," nevertheless maintain their symbolic status as outsiders and continue to have significance to the public despite the tarnish of financial success.[9] The idea of an independent spirit animating and infusing filmmakers, regardless of where they rank in relation to the Hollywood industry, usefully expands wide enough to fit all incarnations of independents. However, when casting a net this wide, distinctions emerge within the group that only bring us back to the beginning of any attempt to make sense of the independent film phenomenon. As Ferncase notes, "the independent label, applied to all types of films, has clearly lost its meaning. A more precise term — specialty film — has been coined to describe a type of independent film that differs from the common low-budget commercial film and the exploitation feature."[10] On the surface there seems to be little overlap among the older alternative cinematic practices and the recent, more commercialized surge in independent film production.

Rick Altman's work in *Film/Genre* helps to clarify this idea for thinking about independent film. In attempting to understand how genre categories' functions and attributes have shifted over time, he explains that

> instead of utilizing a single master language, as most previous genre theoreticians would have it, a genre may appropriately be considered multi-coded. Each genre is simultaneously defined by multiple codes, corresponding to the multiple groups who, by helping to define the genre, may be said to "speak" the genre. When the diverse groups using the genre are considered together, genres appear as regulatory schemes facilitating the integration of diverse factions into a single social fabric.[11]

Altman notes that genres are not inherently stable categories, but are constantly impacted by the users of a genre. Such a conceptualization is particularly useful for considering the negotiation as they pertain to independent film as a phenomenon in relation to television. It is from this backdrop of independent film's complicated identity that the Independent Film Channel launched its attempt at stabilizing the genre through marketing and programming.

IFC Finds Its Niche

Cable conglomerate Cablevision Systems Corporation — the parent company operating Bravo, a network devoted to cultural programming since going on air in 1980 — launched the Independent Film Channel as a digital cable network on September 1, 1994. As it exists today, IFC is a vertically integrated brand that produces and distributes films under the banners IFC Films and IFC Digital Media, promotes and screens films on the IFC cable channel, and has moved into exhibition by acquiring and renovating the Waverly Theater in New York City. However, when IFC debuted, reflecting the increased competition of specialty networks, its location on a higher tier of cable channel services did not make the new channel's presence to viewers immediately felt. In order to create an identity and awareness beyond its cable channel, sister channel Bravo incorporated several strategies into its programming schedule to market the new independent film venture.

Bravo regularly has featured art films as distinct selling points to foster and identify a specific upscale demographic niche since the beginning of its operation. A Bravo advertisement appearing in *American Film* magazine typifies the network's early promotion strategy. Featuring the headline "Culture Everyone Can Turn To," the double-page advertisement included the channel's monthly programming schedule, described premiering films, and discussed in a brief column the original Bravo series, *Profile*, hosted by noted film critic Charles Champlin. By showcasing its TV schedule, Bravo pushed the notion that it was a cable destination for art lovers and art film viewers. Although not exclusively focused on film, Bravo nevertheless cultivated high art tastes by grouping together art films like *Mon oncle* (1958) with other cultural specials like *Toulouse-Lautrec* and *Silent Night with Jose Carreras*. Over time, Bravo continued to pursue its desired audience by scheduling films with an appeal that was both artistic and global. Bravo's "World Cinema" series with the slogan, "Come speak the language," and Bravo's "Five Star Cinema" series indicate the specific scheduling practices utilized by the network into the mid– and late–1990s to interpolate the "right" viewer while maintaining the network's adherence to an arts and entertainment identity. The overt cineaste address made by Bravo with promotional campaigns such as these created an atmosphere ripe for spinning off an even more specifically targeted cable network. Independent film, eluding easy definition as a category, offered a prime opportunity for filling in the blanks to construct a niche market assumed to target an audience that advertisers considered highly desirable but difficult to reach. Utilizing preview nights and commercials, Bravo was a key arena in which IFC built initial viewer consciousness of the new cable network.

As Joseph Turow explains in *Breaking Up America*, the success of branding any product occurs through the deployment of several strategies that include adopting marketing techniques such as using program bumpers/lead-ins, signature shows, and commercials. In the case of introducing a new network, Turow writes,

Creating a "branded format" then means arranging materials — songs, articles, magazines — into a package that people in a target audience would see as reflecting their identity ... media people worked with ad people to make clear whom their formats were for, whom they weren't for, and what that meant.[12]

For IFC, these techniques were critical since IFC had two obstacles to overcome from its inception. First, IFC was not Sundance, an entrenched independent film label whose film festival was already known as a significant progenitor directly linked to the contemporary ascendancy of the independent film movement. The Sundance Film Festival began as the ailing U.S. Film Festival in Park City, Utah. However, Robert Redford's Sundance organization took over the festival and launched the first festival in 1985, putting his star power to work for the out-of-the-way festival, and provided an institute to cultivate artists away from the commercial pressures of Hollywood. After the 1989 *sex, lies & videotape* success at the festival, Sundance became a regular destination for industry types and a mythological promised land for independent filmmakers struggling in obscurity. By the early 1990s, Sundance had plans to launch its own cable channel in conjunction with the premium movie channel, Showtime. Unlike Sundance Channel's obvious built-in association with its festival, the Independent Film Channel had to create its identity from scratch. Such direct competition from the outset led to IFC's second major obstacle: creating a recognizable version of independent film distinct from the one associated with Sundance.

While the task was no doubt daunting, it is important to keep in mind that promoting a new, distinct version of independent film linked to IFC was aided considerably by several factors. To begin with, the imprecise nature of independent film as it exploded through the 1980s and early 1990s offered optimism about the potential audience for such films, increasing the social and economic viability of the idea of independent cinema. Additionally, the new IFC venture was helped by the maturation of the cable industry and deregulation of media ownership laws in the mid–1990s. These government and industrial developments created a favorable business environment for entertainment companies willing to hedge their bets on highly targeted and specialized niche network endeavors in digital cable television. Further, the continuing growth of marketing techniques dovetailed with the proliferation of the Internet, resulting in a perception of limitless expansion of the potential for reaching specialized audiences. As Megan Mullen notes in *The Rise of Cable Programming*,

> Just as in the 1980s and early 1990s competition from cable helped to shape the direction of broadcast television, now the presence of the Internet is helping to shape the direction of cable.... Specialized cable channels, combined with the Internet and recent retailing and target-marketing trends, have encouraged view-

ers to select programs according to how they fit particular lifestyles rather than where they fit individuals' daily or weekly schedules.[13]

IFC's coordinated previews and promotions on Bravo, in conjunction with its website campaign, worked to situate IFC as a distinct destination for experiencing independent film.

IFC's preview night on Bravo played an important role in laying out the discursive parameters for the new channel, its audience, and independent film as a symbolic term. "IFC Fridays," featured on Bravo Friday evenings, offered an exclusive three-hour time slot showcasing IFC programming on the Bravo channel. The special lead-in introduction piece, lasting approximately one minute, worked vigorously to stake its claim to the independent film turf war. Defining the terms of IFC's version of independent film, the promo began with a pitch-black background displaying a basic white engraver's typeset as if from an old typewriter that stated "$2,000." This was followed by another caption, "out of the lab." Accompanied by a minimalist fast snare drum score, flash cuts followed of Quentin Tarantino addressing the camera with a news clipping, a scene from John Waters' *Hairspray* featuring Ricki Lake dancing, and finally Kevin Bacon, as a struggling filmmaker in *The Big Picture*, viewing a small strip of 16-mm film in a lab. The piece concluded with a voice-over announcer stating, "Whatever it takes to get it on film. Bold, provocative, hungry.... Hey, it was either groceries or one last roll of film. The best in independent filmmaking available twenty-four hours a day."[14] The commercials during "IFC Fridays" further defined the IFC independent film universe. The audience address in the commercials encompassed montages of famous independent film clips (a canon, if you will), a parody of independent filmmaking, as well as the straight celebrity testimonial. While different in style, the overall message was the same: all the formats address a privileged, cinephile viewer that is rewarded for having specialized knowledge. This strategy assumes the viewer will know the movies referenced and make the right connections to understand the scope and spirit of the channel, as well as understand the meaning of the independent film genre.

A similar strategy was deployed on the concurrent IFC website. The website's content overtly hailed the cinephile web surfer by stating on its home page, "You don't run with the box-office herd. You're an independent-minded film fan who wants everything Hollywood doesn't offer."[15] This entreaty for exclusive inclusion forms its own canon of independent directors by touting the members of IFC's advisory board that included, among others, Martin Scorsese, Steven Soderbergh, and Susan Siedelman. Interestingly, this list included only film directors, reinforcing IFC's connection to art cinema and the New Hollywood era that perpetuated the auteur theory and directorial "vision" in an American context. Analyzing the New Hollywood phenomenon of the late 1960s and early 1970s, Timothy Corrigan explains that,

> Despite its often countercultural pretensions, auteurism became a deft move in establishing a model that would dominate and stabilize critical reception for at least thirty years. The subsequent auteurist marketing of movies ... guaranteed a relationship between audience and movie in which an intentional and authorial agency governs, as a kind of brand-name vision that precedes and succeeds the films.[16]

Such a strategy benefited IFC because it enabled the channel to perpetuate connections to an already established art cinema canon, providing a depth and stability to the recent (and, to a large extent, unheard of) films offered on the new channel. This too, as Mullen notes, was a strategy known as "framing" that cued "viewers to read and understand [the network] in particular ways.... Framing not only interpolates or hails desirable audiences, it can be used to assert a narrowcast identity."[17] In essence, IFC used film history and the 1970s New Hollywood auteurs as its backbone to symbolically link the outsider/independent mythologized status of the work done in that earlier era with the programs, filmmakers, and stories to be showcased on the new channel.

From Hollywood to Indiewood

In November 1997, the *New York Times Magazine* featured as its cover story, "The Two Hollywoods," featuring Tom Hanks and Ben Affleck as symbols of the parallel universes of contemporary movie making. The feature story discussed the differences between mainstream Hollywood fare (personified by Tom Hanks) and independent fare (with Ben Affleck as its poster boy). The ascendancies of both the Sundance Film Festival and Miramax were understood as pillars of an alternate industry able to promote and sustain itself in healthy competition with the big budget, high-concept films backed by Hollywood. While this dichotomy is a false one (the use of Affleck being just one instance of the inherent problem of trying to make such neat divisions), the rhetorical device used to posit separate filmmaking spheres provided the grist for IFC to perpetuate its own branding efforts. In tandem with already circulating ideas about a quickly developing alternative "Hollywood," IFC set about promoting and establishing an "Indiewood" on its channel and magazine. With IFC staking its claim to the independent film on its website and cable network, the IFC original series, *At the Angelika*, and *IFC Rant* magazine were important tools for deploying the scope and perimeter of IFC's preferred reading of the independent film genre on the channel and beyond.

A signature show, explains Turow, "is a series created expressly for a particular programming network as an explicit on-air statement to audiences and advertisers about the personality of the network."[18] For IFC, *At the Angelika* has been a signature program since the channel's earliest days. *At the Angelika* utilizes similar promotional strategies as those deployed by "Hollywood" to create excitement about upcoming films by featuring host Alison Bailes previewing new independent films screening at the Angelika art house theater in New York City. The show intercuts Bailes's introductions and opinions with scenes from the featured films and her interviews with the film's primary participants, namely the film's director or lead actor. She particularly emphasizes the interview aspect of the program in special "wrap-up" reports from major film festivals like Sundance, Cannes, or the Independent Spirit Awards.

Regular segments of *At the Angelika,* as well as the "special reports" from annual film events, perpetuate and promote independent film as a recognizable, alternate film practice/industry distinct from Hollywood. This concept is played out in a multitude of ways in the program. For one, Bailes often highlights the films from an auteurist perspective by discussing the featured director's entire body of work and international reputation. For example, when Bailes spotlighted the latest Lars von Trier film, *Dogville* (2003), she placed the new film in context to the overall trilogy von Trier was creating as well as his relationship to Danish national cinema. Another way that von Trier's status as an artist was reinforced was by emphasizing the willingness of famous "Hollywood" names to forgo their usual fees and comforts in order to do quality work with a respected and daring foreign film director. The novelty effect of high-priced stars slumming in independent film is another trope regularly deployed in the show. For instance, Bailes introduced the film adaptation of the Michael Cunningham novel, *At Home at the End of the World*, by focusing on Irish actor Colin Farrell's role in the film. Bailes states, "Despite constantly being touted as the next biggest thing, Colin Farrell continues to work in independent film. For every *Minority Report* there's an *Intermission* or *Veronica Guerin*.... Farrell deserves his props as he continues to challenge himself in non–Hollywood fare."[19] The question concerning the decision by popular actors to work in Hollywood versus independent films only reinforces the separateness of the two arenas rather than providing the ultimate evidence that little distinction actually exists between the two. Through this framework, what becomes apparent is that actors choose their roles with a conscious eye toward moving back and forth between big and small, inside and outside, Hollywood and Indiewood, American and foreign national cinema, rather than considering all the employment opportunities as different parts of one entire industry along a continuum.

Another thematic trope utilized in *At the Angelika* that creates independent film as a distinct phenomenon is the way the series often works in direct opposition to Hollywood's behind-the-scenes promotional spots. Christopher Anderson in *Hollywood TV* considers how the television show *Disneyland* operated as a promotional program for both the soon-to-be-completed park and the Walt Disney films. Anderson concludes that

> Disney developed his own "operational aesthetic" through television, enhancing his audience's pleasure — and anticipation — by offering precious glimpses of the filmmaking process. Of course, Disney's depiction of the production process was selective; it ignored the economics of filmmaking in favor of focusing on the studio's technical accomplishments.[20]

For independent film, particularly its treatment on *At the Angelika*, the "precious glimpses of the filmmaking process" overtly state the economics of filmmaking. It may even be safe to say that the economics, as they are inextricably bound with the starving artist and true vision of authentic, artistic self-expression, are what constitutes IFC's version of independent film. The accomplishment stems from overcoming the economic adversities to tell a story in a way not necessarily encouraged by Hollywood orthodoxy. As the film director Chris Kentis offers in his talks about making *Open Water* (2003), "These days, effects are computer generated. We wanted to try something I don't think Hollywood's even interested in trying right now."[21] A film like *Open Water* offers up an example of how a filmmaker, attempting to get back to a "real" depiction between actors and their interactions with dangerous marine life, is the difference between independent film and Hollywood. While *At the Angelika*'s rhetorical address offered cues about how to read, define, and make sense of independent film as its own distinct body of work apart from (though, always in relation to) Hollywood product, ultimately the signature show's reach and significance could only extend as far as IFC's cable channel audience.

Another way IFC attempted to create brand awareness for the cable channel was through its companion magazine, *IFC Rant*. The magazine functioned as a specialized channel guide, offering a detachable section inside with all the month's film listings. While the schedule provided a pragmatic reason for audiences to subscribe to the magazine, the listings also offered evidence of the channel's eclectic range and variety of programs to the casual, non–IFC subscriber thumbing through the magazine. Whatever guideposts the listings provided metonymically for IFC's overall message and genre definition, the articles and tone throughout the rest of the magazine made explicit. As the

IFC Rant media kit states, the magazine "is the national consumer magazine that puts the future of independent film in your hands. Literally ... [it] delivers profiles of upcoming films and sought-after indie personalities and the inside buzz from the independent film world."[22] Beyond advertising on its sister channels, *IFC Rant* circulated both the channel logo and the channel's use of independent film in other arenas where preferred consumer markets congregated. The magazine, sold in book and record stores like Barnes & Noble and Virgin and offered complimentarily in selected theaters nationally such as The Seven Gables in Seattle, significantly broadened the reach of IFC beyond the cable network, reaching out to the potential cinephile who did not necessarily spend too much time watching television. By 2003, *IFC Rant* reached over 150,000 subscribers with a total estimated audience reach of 500,000.[23]

The preoccupation with defining independent film and its relationship to Hollywood films is directly approached in the *IFC Rant* debut issue. The opening "Why Rant?" discussion features the magazine's editorial board laying out its mission statement to "cover films that we think aren't being covered much in the other film magazines, the consumer ones like *Movieline* or *Premiere*."[24] Immediately, the reader is meant to interpret *IFC Rant* as something more authentic than the mere "consumer" magazines. The "Why Rant?" section offered the opportunity for the magazine's editors to assert their informed cineaste voices as arbiters of taste and distinction both in their reception of popular culture and in how they would cover this culture. What is interesting about this intent to offer something different by *IFC Rant* editors is the ironic and self-conscious opinions they bring to bear on the subject of movie programming, moviegoing, and movie tastes in general. The editors are far too savvy and self-aware to completely buy into the overall generic bifurcation between independent and Hollywood films. Instead, what comes through is the importance of the overall experience of moviegoing as a factor in film attendance. As Senior Editor Anthony Kaufman explains,

> Ultimately, I don't think most people say, "Tonight, I'm going to go see an independent film or I'm going to go see a Hollywood movie." It's more about what movie is of interest to you and then you decide, okay, this happens to be playing at a smaller theater as opposed to the one with super sound and the stadium seating with the chair rests.[25]

These remarks reveal the problem and impossibility of any final attempt to consider a place apart from Hollywood, or the mainstream, commercial cinema. Instead, what is established is the primacy of the reading strategy. Discerning independent film or "Indiewood" is about the choices the viewer makes in the selection of a movie or of a venue, and what the viewer/audience, member/consumer does with the text and experience. These choices are what activate a reading and understanding of independent film as a brand and identifiable genre.

From Virtual World to the Real World

The magazine also makes clear connections between IFC, independent film, emerging technologies, and the Internet. For instance, advertisements in the debut issue informed the reader about several digital and Internet forums for independent filmmaking. Resfest, a digital film festival, was advertised in the inaugural issue with submission information and the slogan, "The planet's turning anyhow. Move with it."[26] Another full-page advertisement announced IFC online, displaying website screen captures to highlight the broadband theater, events, and festival components available online. For the broadband theater, the ad reads, "The movie is always about to begin ... new short and feature length independent films form emerging, cutting-edge filmmakers — on demand, streamed right to your desktop."[27] These examples demonstrate the link between independent film and the technological euphoria about digital capabilities and using the Internet to bypass long-standing barriers to film distribution. This development coincided with the increasing availability of inexpensive digital video recording equipment, allowing greater access to the means of production to anyone interested in moviemaking.

Another function of the magazine is to sell the Internet. Throughout its pages, the magazine constantly refers the reader to continue the IFC experience by logging onto its website. Taglines at the end of articles, or on spotlight issues, or in the TV listings all instruct the reader that more information is available on IFC's website. This poses interesting questions about the use of the website as a center for disseminating information about the cable channel and its version of independent film. While the totality of branding independent film on IFC can be viewed as the final commodification of the idealized alternative viewpoint and practice associated with independent film, no system is ever 100 percent accounted for by this argument. And while there remains in the virtual world of ifctv.com an overt address and imperative to sell an idea (and cable channel subscription), it is ultimately a concept that presupposes an active consumer. While IFC's heavy reliance on its website to educate potential subscribers about the cable network reinforces the important role the TV channel holds in creating a space for watching independent film, the Internet website also demonstrates the increasingly symbiotic relationship cable sought with this emerging technology. Though IFC, at the first instance, is a cable channel created to package and disseminate a certain subset of filmed programming to a national audience through a satellite cable channel, the addition of the Internet as a marketing and information tool offered the opportunity for a bifurcated audience address.

An important distinguishing feature of the website was that it stood for a space where people selected to experience IFC, not just something sent from "out there" like on Bravo preview nights or in magazine advertisements. This distinction is crucial because it shaped how the ifctv.com website was constructed with a certain amount of participation assumed on the part of its audience. As Turow notes,

> Creators of online "homepages" for marketers and media firms also argued that attracting customers in cyberspace ought to go beyond simply laying out lifestyle signals, as magazine covers and cable networks tended to do. They felt that, more in the style of radio formats and promotional events, an online site should foster a sense of camaraderie among the people its creators wanted to draw in.[28]

In this regard, the IFC website, circa the late 1990s, offered its visitors the opportunity to enter in sweepstakes, keep abreast of the important events in the independent film world such as the dates for all types of film festivals and contest entry deadlines, and, finally, participate in chatboards called "Your Rants." In each of these instances, the activities enabled the website user to assume various levels of interactions with an implied independent film community connected through the virtual website. This opportunity for interaction ultimately enhances a sense of participation in and community with IFC, creating an idealized communal spirit already embedded in the myth of independent filmmaking and fostered by IFC in its website.

Linking an idealized community of independent filmmaking through IFC is most fully realized in the use of real, geographically specific theatrical exhibition venues in New York City. As Kevin Corbett argues,

> The movie theater's perseverance may be due to its symbolic importance to our culture, a symbolism that has shifted with every threat and transition the film industry has experienced. Its perseverance may also be due to industrial efforts to exploit the theater's symbolic value. As such, the movie theater as a symbolic and cultural site has frequently been a contested one."[29]

While IFC's chief competitor, the Sundance Channel, emanated from a site-specific geographic referent, IFC did not have such a home base. In contrast to Sundance, IFC sought to establish its location in a distinctly East Coast, urban setting. The push to locate independent film in the New York City anchors IFC's conceptual brand of independent film, but also introduces instability to the term. Instead of creating the definitive version of independent film, IFC, through the series *At the Angelika* and then with the acquisition and renovation of the Waverly Theater in Greenwich Village, privileged and unleashed a dynamic and more organic version of independent film. In "Walking in the City," Michel de Certeau writes,

> The panorama-city is a "theoretical" simulacrum, in short, a picture, whose condition of possibility is an oblivion and a misunderstanding of practices.... The ordinary practitioners of the city live "down below" but the thresholds at which visibility begins ... they are walkers ... whose bodies follow the thicks and thins of an urban "text" they write without being able to read ... the networks of these meanings, intersecting writings compose a manifold story that has neither author nor spectator, shaped out of fragments of trajectories and alterations of spaces: in relation to representations, it remains daily and indefinitely other.[30]

This extended quote illustrates the discrepancy and inherent fallibility of an overarching and omnipresent reading of the global landscape. Attempts to decipher a planned and predetermined meaning or map of a complex system like the city is ultimately meaningless. Instead, primacy is given to the "individual" who lives in, interacts with, and makes use of the "down below" space of the city, the movie theater, or the space in between the two.

This idea is remarkably articulated in the opening credit sequence of *At the Angelika*. The opening shot is from outer space seeing the Earth with a number superimposed over it and a small label in the lower left-hand corner that reads "very deep space." Rapidly, our "view" plummets, along with the distance meter, into the atmosphere, above the North American continent, to the Manhattan skyline all the way down to street level, and to the front door of the Angelika movie theater on the corner of Houston and Mercer, in the heart of the Soho District. While the initial point of view occurs high above the overall mapped space, this program quickly takes us "down below" and we, along with the program's host, and all those visiting the theater are to experience independent film at this theater on our own terms. The level of random interactions that are now possible by the city and the everyday are also enacted in this sequence. Spoofing *Run, Lola Run* (1998), the opening segment features *At the Angelika* host Alison Bailes in three different scenarios trying to make it through the city to a movie starting in fifteen minutes. These sequences enact the inherent random unpredictability of the viewer's understanding and reading of independent film and, by extension, the IFC brand due to the potentially infinite interactions between the filmgoer, the location, and its urban context. In short, there is no master plan. Bailes's choice of interviewing in the lobby among the theatergoing public performs a reciprocal relationship that both enhances the "specialness" of the theater since it is an elevated setting while, at the same time, fixes the essentially gossip and promotional aspects of the interview to a real, lived space. The symbiotic interaction of these spheres infuses independent film as a viable generic commodity to be experienced at all levels, from the films playing at the theater to the actual choice made to view the films at a particular theater.

This relationship is pushed further still as IFC establishes its own theater by renovating the Waverly Theater into the IFC Center. According to IFC reports, the center features three screens, post-production facilities, and a café that will "serve all consumer touch points, from people who want to see independent film in New York, to people who want to bump into a filmmaker in the editing rooms, to people who want to hang out and discuss films in the café."[31] In an age of multiplex art houses, the IFC Center stands out for also offering a place for filmmakers to work. The acquisition of the new IFC Center represents the final stage of IFC's construction of a vertically integrated brand name. Indeed, as one article reported, the renovation project gives IFC a "brick-and-mortar presence" and that "as a vertically integrated company, an IFC-backed film could have its Gotham premiere at IFC Center. It gives the company a guaranteed theatrical release—a big driver for ancillary revenue—for all its film."[32] These facts do little to counter any cultural pessimist's accusations. However, once again, the fact of the theater's location and its historical significance, while attracting IFC, prevent the theater from losing its relevance and neighborhood legibility to its patrons. For one, the Waverly Theater, located in Greenwich Village not too far from New York University, claims to be the launching pad for inaugurating *The Rocky Horror Picture Show* (1975) as *the* cult phenomenon in the 1970s. Thus, its significance as a cultural landmark and as a neighborhood theater offering alternative fare and as a witness to the cycles of theatrical exhibition surrounded the theater as a symbol. As one article noted,

> For almost 70 years the theater has mirrored transformations in the film business, in the neighborhood and in the way people watch movies. The Waverly was always able to adapt, until movies were distributed like commodities in multiplexes, and neighborhood theaters became anachronisms.[33]

Its importance to its patrons' collective memory is evident in a website devoted to movie theaters. For the Waverly, a spirited discussion on a message board contains status reports on the shuttered building, the stages of renovation, anxieties about what IFC will do to the theater, and generally what will happen if the theater is never reopened. As one respondent noted, "The Waverly is a shell inside, or at least it was when I last peeked through the entrance in late November ... but perhaps we'll finally see films flickering ... sometime soon or, heaven forbid, a new Chase branch or something similar within the next 6–12 months."[34] Another post stated, "The Waverly Theater looks like it's never going to reopen. It's been sitting there all boarded up. The letters of the marquee have fallen off. It [sic] been over two years."[35] Clearly, very different from the IFC Center public relations quotes, statements from the individuals walking through the streets bring their own meanings to the theater that will no doubt affect the way the new theater is used when it eventually opens. As de Certeau states,

> Linking acts and footsteps, opening meanings and directions, these words operate in the name of an emptying-out and wearing-away of their primary role. They become liberated spaces that can be occupied.... People are put in motion by the remaining relics of meaning, and sometimes by their waste products, their inverted reminders of great ambitions. Things that amount to nothing, or almost nothing, symbolize and orient workers' steps: names that have ceased precisely to be "proper."[36]

In this sense, the very location of the theater and the renovation of an older building with its already established meanings and history for its patrons will come to bear on the new endeavor, leaving the new IFC Center, independent film, and IFC's brand an open cluster of meanings and associations that may fall out of the preferred boundaries created by IFC. Echoing this thought, Mark Jancovich asserts that "instead of autonomous and authentic sites of meaning, every place is defined through its relation to other places."[37] So it is that the Waverly/IFC Center as a constructed three-dimensional experience for independent film can never stand alone and create understanding in a vacuum. Instead, its mystique, power, and dynamism come from the juxtapositions of the Waverly's history as a theater, its location in relation to other neighborhood theaters like the Angelika and the Landmark Sunshine, as well as its Greenwich Village address, and finally all the individuals who attend or remember the previous theater before the Center's debut. This seems to be the preference of IFC executives since plans for the theater include keeping the Waverly's original neon sign inside the lobby as a gesture to the theater's legacy.

In discussing independent film, as it exists on IFC, what becomes clear is that, procedurally at least, making sense of the current media landscape entails, more than ever before, taking in a wide range of materials. The text is uncentered and elusive. No text exists on its own; all must be read in relation to each other if any sort of meaning or understanding is to be gained. With the contemporary cable universe marked by a dizzying variety of programming and delivery options, the undifferentiated flow of images against the backdrop of constant industrial consolidation through corporate mergers often works against any optimistic possibilities for the individual voice. Even the most romanticized of individual voices — the independent filmmaker — is no longer out of reach to the commercial drives of television. However, through its dispersal across multiple platforms and distribution venues, IFC actually ends up offering a cultural space that links both regional and national audiences together and reconciles the push and pull of commercial imperatives against artistic drives. Michel Foucault's conceptualization of the heterotopia offers a useful way to understand how IFC operates across its platforms. He explains that "the heterotopia has the power of juxtaposing in a single real place different spaces and locations that are incompatible with each other."[38] This is an instructive summation for considering how the different ideas circulating about independent film through the IFC franchise work together to juxtapose commerce/art, public/private, and production/consumption. In this sense, the technological televisual networks of both cable and the Internet are a symbiotic combination for participation by the individual — a participation that is suggested by the overall project of independent film as an expressive form available to and for anybody. IFC's broad attempt to market and anchor a specific version of independent film provides an instructive instance to consider how genre comes to live and breathe in our contemporary multi-media world.

Notes

1. Steve Neale, *Genre and Hollywood* (New York: Routledge, 2000), 39–40.
2. Graeme Turner, "The Uses and Limitations of Genre." In *Television Genre Book*. Ed. Glen Creeber (London: BFI, 2001), 5.
3. Greg Merritt, *Celluloid Mavericks: A History of American Independent Film* (New York: Thunder's Mouth Press, 2000), xiii.
4. Vincent LoBrutto, *The Encyclopedia of American Independent Filmmaking* (Westport, CT: Greenwood Press, 2002), xiii.
5. Ibid., xiv.
6. Ibid.
7. Peter Biskind, *Down and Dirty Pictures: Miramax, Sundance and the Rise of Independent Film* (New York: Simon & Schuster, 2004), 21.
8. Emanuel Levy, *Cinema of Outsiders* (New York: New York University Press, 1999), 5–6.
9. Richard Ferncase, *Outsider Features: American Independent Films of the 1980s* (Westport, CT: Greenwood Press, 1996), xv.
10. Ibid., xiv.
11. Rick Altman, *Film/Genre* (London: BFI Publishing, 1999), 208.
12. Joseph Turow, *Breaking Up America* (Chicago: University of Chicago Press, 1997), 92.
13. Megan Mullen, *The Rise of Cable Programming: Revolution or Evolution?* (Austin: University of Texas Press, 2003), 192–93.
14. "IFC Fridays Introduction." Independent Film Channel, Jericho, NJ (1999).
15. The Independent Film Channel, Home page. Available at URL: <http://www.ifctv.com.>.
16. Timothy Corrigan, *A Cinema Without Walls: Movies and Culture After Vietnam* (New Brunswick, NJ: Rutgers University Press, 1991), 101.
17. Mullen, *The Rise of Cable Programming*, 163.
18. Turow, *Breaking Up America*, 105.
19. "Promotion of *At Home at the End of the World*," *At the Angelika* # 87, Independent Film Channel Productions, Jericho, NJ (2004).
20. Christopher Anderson, *Hollywood TV* (Austin: University of Texas Press, 1994), 145.
21. "Promotion of *Open Water*," *At the Angelika* # 87, Independent Film Channel Productions, Jericho, NJ, (2004).
22. "2003 *IFC Rant* media kit," Independent Film Channel, 1.

23. Ibid., 3.
24. Eugene Hernandez, "Why Rant?" *IFC Rant*, May/June (2000): 5.
25. Ibid.
26. "Resfest advertisement," *IFC Rant*, May/June (2000): 31.
27. "IFC online advertisement," *IFC Rant*, May/June (2000): 4.
28. Turow, *Breaking Up America*, 119.
29. Kevin J. Corbett, "The Big Picture: Theatrical Moviegoing, Digital Television, and Beyond the 'Substitution Effect.'" *Cinema Journal* Winter (2001): 18.
30. Michel de Certeau, "Walking in the City." In *The Cultural Studies Reader*. Ed. Simon During (New York: Routledge, 1993), 153.
31. Martin Edlund, "New York Independents Buck a Trend in Movie Theaters," *New York Sun*, May 4 (2004): 1.
32. Charles Lyons, "Marquee Attraction," *Daily Variety*, August 18 (2003): A26.
33. Julie Salamon, "Theater in Village Is Granted a New Life," *New York Times*, July 15 (2003): E1.
34. Posted by br91975. Available at URL: <http://www.cinematreasures.org/ Waverly Twin>. Accessed on 14/2/2004.
35. Posted by William. Available at URL: <http://www.cinematreasures.org/ Waverly Twin>. Accessed on 18/2/2004.
36. de Certeau, "Walking in the City," 159.
37. Mark Jancovich and Lucy Faire with Sarah Stubbings, *The Place of the Audience: Cultural Geographies of Film Consumption* (London: BFI, 2003), 16.
38. Michel Foucault, "Of Other Spaces: Utopias and Heterotopias." *Rethinking Architecture*. Ed. Neil Loach (New York: Routledge, 1997), 354.

3

"Off-Beat" as a Generic Designation in *Variety* Reviews

JASON SCOTT

In this chapter I will address the meaning and significance of a short-lived and forgotten generic designation used by *Variety*, the term "off-beat," or more commonly given as "offbeat." While this critical term derives from music and continues to be used as a qualifying term in film reviews, I will argue that in its particular uses in the trade journal *Variety* around 1963 the term became associated with a particular type of film, and developed from a generic qualifying adjective to a loose designation of genre. While this was not as clearly defined as, for instance, "meller" or "oater," horror or "romanticomedy," other commonly used generic labels from *Variety*, "offbeat" arguably achieved generic status in terms of defining an audience, and audience expectations, in relation to stylistic, formal and thematic qualities. In this sense, "offbeat" can be considered a generic term in a similar way, and to the same extent, that for example "Indie" now functions, or outside film the catch-all "alternative" music category. The use of "offbeat" within *Variety* mobilizes its figurative connotations, as unusual, unconventional or eccentric, yet the circumstances of the mid-1960s contributed to a more specific cluster of meanings. "Offbeat" was an *indigenous* term (to the time), which changed meanings and associations in the period 1963 to 1968, and then gradually lost its more specific connotations and fell out of use.[1] In this respect it differs from the related term associated with a national cinema trend, or production trend, "Swinging London," which was not an indigenous category at least at the time of earlier examples. My research considers offbeat's use as an implicit generic designation in *Variety* reviews between January 1964 and December 1968.

My account of "offbeat" addresses the notion of short-term generic designations, distinct from production trends or cycles.[2] Bordwell and Thompson define a cycle as a "short-lived fashion for certain subgenres within a genre," providing the example of '50s "adult" Westerns,[3] whereas Steve Neale defines "cyclic — confined to small groups of films made during specific and limited periods."[4] Hence, as Neale explores, a cycle need not be restricted to generic imitation. Cycles encompass the reworking or transposition of elements from individual successful films, including the narrative structure from an individual film, as in the "'one locale' setting films," or might be inspired by topical events.[5] As a notable example of a transitory cycle, Richard Maltby notes the PCA-classified "Farce-Murder-Mystery" single-season genre, with 11 films so classified in 1944, two the next year, and then none.[6] Barbara Klinger develops the notion of "local" genres to explicate a short-lived generic category.

> The studios and review establishment alike used the adult film label as a means of identifying certain films with sensationalistic content. The adult film was a "local" genre, in the sense that it was a historically specific and transitory category that gained steam during the post-war years and faded from view in its Hollywood usage after the 60s. It none the less functioned as a recognized and influential means of classifying films during this time, effectively reorganizing the field of existing genres.[7]

Within my discussion I recognize that discourses around genre can shift and the connotations for generic labels or designations can develop or vary in different contexts. Within the *Variety* reviews the term offbeat initially designates unorthodox or inventive films, and is related to British comedies and other specialty fare. However, this is distinct from art house films, and is not so commonly used to describe foreign language pictures. Instead, "offbeat" is in some ways equivalent to the more contemporary term "crossover," in terms of distinguishing product that diverges from Hollywood norms and conventions but might still appeal successfully to a wider audience. I will explore more fully the range of films and production contexts that is associated with offbeat, but it includes British films, some European art cinema, American underground and other low-budget or marginal indie production, and, later in the period, work by the new directors within Hollywood. Hence, British comedies of 1963 onwards are often identified as "offbeat," associated with their directors, and frequently criticized for their "arty" or "art house" qualities and blend of styles, as well as distinguished from Hollywood product in terms of their tone. Richard Lester's *A Hard Day's Night* (1964) is a definitive example, described as "offbeat" at three points in the review, including in the summary byline.[8]

A May 1967 *Variety* article identifies a distinction between "offbeat-imports" and Hollywood production, and primarily identifies offbeat with British films. The article opens,

> In the wake of such successful U.S. offbeat-imports as "Alfie," "Georgy Girl," and "Blow Up"—all of them financed by major U.S. distributors—many in the trade are asking the same question these days. "Why can't we make the same kind of picture here?"[9]

The article proceeds to associate offbeat with British films, albeit referencing England, but also to "the kind of 'personal' picture that comes out of Europe." However, it also quotes Sidney Lumet and Joseph Losey, "who have succeeded in making the sort of pictures we're talking about."[10]

I will concentrate on how the term "offbeat" is used in *Variety* reviews. As Maltby notes, "Reviews in *Variety* provided, as their primary function, an assessment of a new movie's box-office potential."[11] Hence, the review commonly works to identify a potential audience and identify points of appeal for the film; even within the Classical period distinguishing between rural audiences ("hicks"), neighborhood theatres and metropolitan audiences.[12] The 1950s and 1960s also saw the rise in awareness of a teenage or youth audience, with *Variety* reviews identifying "teenage appeal" or box office potential in "youth situations." The format of reviews in *Variety*, both at the time and dating back to some of its earliest film reviews, organized the review into several distinct discursive blocks, as part of an overall conventionalized discourse structure. Hence, the title is followed by optional inclusion of translated title, country of production, and color format. The date seen, if the reviewer attended a U.S. preview, precedes key credits, of production and creative personnel, concluding with selected cast. The byline follows, included for all films judged as appropriate commercial prospects, and provides a summary description of the film and its box office prospects. Beneath this is the main body of the review text, completed by the *Variety* pseudonym of the critic. The byline has a privileged status. It commonly designates a generic label, whether by means of a single generic term, "comedy," "meller," "oater," "horror" and so on, or often in terms of a conflation of terms, for instance "war meller," *Operation Bikini* (1963)[13]; "sci fi meller," *The Day of the Triffids* (1963)[14]; "romantic meller," *In the Cool of the Day* (1963)[15]; and "oater comedy," *Waterhole No. 3* (1967).[16]

In discussing the descriptive terms in use in *Variety* reviews of films in 1934, Neale distinguishes the generic and nongeneric, the more stable and specific from the loose, broad or indeterminate: "Terms like 'comedy,' 'western' and 'musical' can be found, as can films which correspond to them. But they exist alongside broader or more indeterminate ones like 'drama' and 'costume picture.'... They also exist alongside hybrids like 'comedy drama' and 'comedy ... prizefight film' and terms indicative of production and exhibition categories like 'programmer' and 'nabes' (neighbourhood theatres)," as well as terms denoting stars, cycles, series, or reference to source in the case of adaptations of novels, "legit" plays and shows.[17] While genre is a key point of reference in the byline, these other privileged features recur. The film's appeal is assessed in terms of exhibition categories and evaluation. Thus, in arguing for the generic significance of the term offbeat I will consider the extent it is used within the byline, or combined with other generic terms. I will address the extent to which "offbeat" can be considered both precise, and a generic designation, not merely a descriptive term that could be substituted by terms such as "unusual" or "unconventional." In this respect I will argue for the systematized or routinized scope of connotations for "offbeat." I also address the privileging of the term, by repetition, as in the review of *A Hard Day's Night* previously referenced, or by its positioning within the main text of the review, in the opening and closing paragraphs, for example. In this respect, and more generally, I will be analyzing the association of "offbeat" with other terms, whether through collocation or other means. I will also discuss ways in which the term is deemphasized, in terms of its combination with other terms, or substitution by alternative terms. Nonetheless, one aspect that will help organize my discussion is attention to the systematic use of the term, notwithstanding the variety of other terms it is associated or combined with, which alter its specific connotations in individual cases. I have mentioned the notion that a cluster of associations becomes tied to "offbeat," but in each use only some of these are mobilized.

I also consider the extent to which "offbeat" partially functions as an "exhibition category," at least in its use in *Variety*. While Neale notes the applicability of broader generic terms, which encompass "'the feature film,' 'the newsreel,' 'the cartoon,' 'the B film,' 'the A film' and 'the serial,'"[18] he distinguishes production and exhibition categories. However, I suggest offbeat carries generic implications as well as proposing an expected audience. While a genre can be understood as constituting a "set of expectations,"[19] implicit in this is the audience who share these expectations, what we might relate to the expected audience or "audience image": "In 1956 *Variety* suggested that along with blockbusters 'unusual, offbeat films with adult themes that television could not handle' allowed the industry to retain one section of its audience."[20] This use suggests the earlier applicability of the term, but also its looseness, qualifying films' thematic content and potential audience. I will explore the range of associations made with "offbeat," and thereafter the clustering of associations. These include genre categories: comedy, "wayout" comedy, and the self-conscious distinction "Offbeater." Associations around exhibition categories encompass specialty and art house situations, "semi-artie," and both "evolving audiences" and divided audiences. Aesthetic distinctions are premised on connotations of unconventional, experimental, and stylized, whereas production distinctions are mobilized around Godard, and low budget. Additionally, offbeat is associated with loose terms: theme, casting, characters, and locations.

Offbeat Comedy

The association of offbeat with comedy, and in particular British comedy, is central to my claim of generic significance for the term "offbeat." While the term was used in description of films of other genres, even as a qualifying adjective connected to other genres, it is the frequent use of the conflation "offbeat comedy," or coupling of offbeat with other, looser terms connoting comedy that marks out this category of films. I will address below alternative ways of characterizing this grouping. I will also note films that are defined as comedies and otherwise associated with offbeat. The designation "offbeat comedy" features most prevalently in the reviews of Rich, as well as in one review by Myro. For instance, *A Jolly Bad Fellow* (1964) was described in the byline as a "bright comedy" but the main review text began: "This is the type of witty, offbeat comedy that used to be a favourite of the old Ealing films set up," with Ealing explicitly motivated by reference to Michael Balcon as producer and Robert Hamer's script.[21] Similarly, the byline of the review of *The Knack* (1965) begins, "Offbeat comedy from Woodfall stable." This association with the British studio is repeated in the text, although not with the generic conflation, "offbeat Woodfall production, which was justifiably invited to the Cannes festival."[22] Rich characterizes *Cul-de-sac* (1966) as an "offbeat comedy drama."[23] References to offbeat associated with looser terms denoting comedy feature in the reviews of *A Hard Day's Night*, *The Wrong Box* (1966) and *Work Is a Four Letter Word* (1968) by Rich, as well as the Murf review of *Bye Bye Braverman* (1968). In particular, the review of *A Hard Day's Night* privileges the term offbeat by its inclusion in the byline as well as by repetition. Initially, the byline suggests the Beatles film "also stands up as a lively, offbeat and funny film." Within the main text of the review offbeat is associated with both eccentricity, but also dynamism and imagination: "a wacky, offbeat piece of filming, charged with vitality and inventiveness." Finally, in a later paragraph the term is used as an adjective to describe the "spiky, funny, offbeat dialog well turned to the Beatles' respective characteristics."[24] Rich relates the potential audience for *The Wrong Box* to its comedy: "This shapes up as a possible hit for audiences who like their humor slightly offbeat."[25] The American *Bye Bye Braverman* is described by Murf in the byline as an "offbeat Sidney Lumet pic," and also as a "dark comedy." This initial paragraph ends associating offbeat with its exhibition possibilities: "Offbeat pic will find what market it has ... in special, key-city situations, particularly in N.Y."[26] Finally, for *Work Is a Four Letter Word*, the "plot and 'message' are merely hooks for a series of off-beat situations, some very funny and others over-reminiscent and over-stressed." Additionally, there is an "offbeat contribution to the surrounding surrealism."[27]

There are a number of British comedies that are distinguished in similar terms to offbeat, but not labeled as such. *One Way Pendulum* (1965) is described in the byline as a "swinging film" and a "wayout comedy."[28] *Smashing Time* (1967), with its "Swinging London" background, is also described as being a "too British" comedy, with a typically British tone.[29] This corroborates the distinction made around British comedies, albeit associated with "swinging" rather than "offbeat." *Morgan!* (1966) is characterized as a "British entry" among "comedies of the same genre, which usually combine the screwball elements of the Marx Bros. anarchy with situation comedy plots."[30] *Bedazzled* (1967) is more explicitly associated with a particularly British comedy, within the opening sentence of the review: "'Bedazzled' is smartly-styled & typical of certain types of high British comedy."[31] Further examples include *Help!* (1965), with its "frantically contrived" elements, also implicitly evaluated as "ultra-clever-clever";[32] *Alfie* (1966), described in the byline as including "cheeky situations, mingled with humor, some pathos ... a curiosity draw";[33] and *Georgy Girl* (1966), labeled in the byline as "lightweight comedy."[34] Both *Alfie* and *Georgy Girl* were described as "offbeat-imports" in the 1967 article discussed previously.

Further films are defined as comedies, either explicitly or by use of some synonym, but are associated with offbeat another way. These include *Goldstein* (1964), *A Fine Madness* (1966), *The Honey Pot* (1967), *The Happening* (1967), *Divorce American Style* (1967), and *The April Fools* (1969), with *What's New Pussycat?* (1965), *Cat Ballou* (1965), *The Loved One* (1965), and *Lord Love a Duck* (1966) in the review of the latter. Hence, the review of *Goldstein* features a byline that opens with the generic designation "far out farce or satire," while later in the discussion of the story's mid–Chicago backdrop, the review describes "this fast moving unorthodox but absorbing offbeat pic."[35] Similarly, *A Fine Madness* is designated by the byline a "far-out sex comedy-drama about a non-conformist" and the main body of the review opens, "'A Fine Madness' is offbeat, and downbeat in many ways. Too heavy handed to be comedy, yet too light to be called drama."³⁶ *The Honey Pot*, another British comedy, is described by the opening of the byline as "lustily outfitted, elegantly sophisticated comedy but occasionally tedious, for discriminating audiences." Later, in the second to last paragraph of the review the term offbeat features in relation to a role: "Cliff Robertson is surprisingly good in his offbeat role as the temporary righthand man."³⁷ *The Happening* is also defined in terms of genre within the byline, as a "wacky comedy a la mode, oddly mixed and only spasmodically effective." The opening clause of the body of the review likewise characterizes the film more generally as an "intriguing offbeat item." The review subsequently uses another term that might describe comedies with a contemporary style or contemporary appeal, as "click" comedies. *The Happening* "does contain enough zany elements peculiar to click comedies today."³⁸ The term *click* is sometimes used in reviews with the sense of being successful with audiences, for instance in the review of *Accident* (1967), or "should click by touching the mood of the time" in the review of *Here We Go Round the Mulberry Bush* (1968).³⁹ Again, *Divorce American Style* (1967) is labeled in the opening words of the byline a "first rate comedy about U.S. marriage mores, including tragic overtones"; while an association with offbeat is made later in the review with respect to roles, the first paragraph ending, "Dick Van Dyke, Debbie Reynolds, Jason Robards, Jean Simmons and Van Johnson score in offbeat starring roles."⁴⁰

"Way out" Comedy

Besides "click" comedies, a number of offbeat films are identified as "way out" (or else way-out). The review of *Lord Love a Duck* is telling since it defines a corpus for the cycle of way-out comedy. *What's New Pussycat?*, *Cat Ballou*, *The Loved One*, and *Lord Love a Duck* are grouped together as offbeat. This grouping is made in the opening paragraph of the body of the review, following a byline that includes the alternative cyclic label for *Lord Love a Duck*: "Hilarious entry for current way-out cycle; carries rich exploitation." The debatable status of this cyclic label is discussed in the opening sentences of the review: "Some may call George Axelrod's 'Lord Love a Duck' satire, others way-out comedy, still others brilliant, while there may be some who ask, what's it all about. Somewhere in this wide breach lies the clue, dependent upon the viewer, but in this day when such offbeat effusions as 'What's new pussycat?,' 'Cat Ballou' and 'The Loved One' are doing boff biz — and 'Duck' fits into this category — it should reach its mark."⁴¹ This is one of the most self-conscious identifications of offbeat as a generic designation, albeit as a term associated with a cycle. However, it is complicated by the use of "way-out" as the cyclic label in question. This is not necessarily as problematic as it might initially appear. These are not the only films that are identified as "way-out" or "wayout" within *Variety* reviews. Other examples include *One Way Pendulum, Morgan!, Blow-Up, Bedazzled,* and *Work Is a Four Letter Word.* There is some justification for suggesting that the term "way-out" or "way-out" is used almost synonymously with "offbeat." Some of these other films are explicitly identified as offbeat, while they almost invariably correspond to characteristics suggested by the category of offbeat comedy. Several are British. Generic labeling of *One Way Pendulum* is featured in the byline, which characterizes the film as a "wayout comedy."[42] *Cat Ballou* is described in the first paragraph after the byline as "sparked by an amusing way-out approach."[43] *What's New Pussycat?* is described with use of the term "wayout" in its initial review. This opens after the byline, "'What's New Pussycat' is designed as zany farce, as wayout as can be reached on the screen."[44] *Blow-Up* is associated with a "way-out treatment."[45] *Bedazzled* is similarly designated within the byline as "way-out British comedy." I have already discussed the review of *Work Is a Four Letter Word,* but significantly the byline begins with "wayout comedy-fantasy." The review also references "a series of off-beat situations" and "some offbeat contribution to the surrounding surrealism."[46] Finally, *Morgan!* is associated with "way-out" rather than offbeat, within the body of the review as a "way-out pic," and defined within the byline as "zany tragic-comedy."[47]

Some *Variety* reviews of offbeat films, or those described as "way-out," feature marked use of inverted commas, to add a qualified or ironized sense to particular terms that seem salient to the cluster of associations of offbeat. Hence, the appeal of *The Gospel According to Matthew* (1964) is described as follows: "Those 'with it' will probably feel it a fascinating, even moving film, others may rate it as a crashing bore, still others may fault its unconventional approach." Hence, the audience is divided with use of inverted commas, around "with it."[48] The review of *The Happening* features a succession of distinguished terms, including in a list of the disparate elements of the film: "'in' gags, socalled [sic] 'black humor,'" and in the final paragraph reference to "'cute' effects ... to make the film truly 'different.'"[49] *Bye Bye Braverman* is similarly related to "'dark comedy,'" albeit this use of single quote marks also serves to signify a quote from the production publicity.[50] Finally, in the sixth paragraph of the review of *Work Is a Four Letter Word,* quote marks set off the message of the film; "The plot and 'message' are merely hooks."[51] An example of a related film that is not labeled offbeat, but is described with the term "with it" in speech marks, is *Help!* with the byline attributing "Many 'with it' gags and giggles."[52]

"Offbeater"

In typical *Variety* style, the noun "offbeater" features in reviews of *Masculin, feminin* (1966), *Seconds* (1966), and *Two or Three Things I Know About Her* (*Deux ou trois choses que je sais d'elle*) (1967) all by Mosk, and *Doctor Faustus* (1967) by Otta. Notably, then, two of these films are directed by Jean-Luc Godard, while three of the usages of the noun derive from one critic. Mosk discusses the mixture of elements in *Masculin, feminin*, as well as Godard's "usual personal style," within the first paragraph of his review, which also labels the film "this offbeater."[53] His *Seconds* review byline opens, "Offbeater that does not quite become a thriller, outright parable or complete suspense item." Later in the penultimate paragraph he designates "this offbeater."[54] He also labels Godard's *Two or Three Things I Know About Her*, in the initial paragraph, "Specialized outlets abroad, at best, loom for this offbeater."[55] In Otta's review of *Doctor Faustus*, the byline ends with "for very specialized appeal and related curio values which must be suitably hyped to milk maximum returns from this offbeater."[56] In addition to the association of the noun offbeater with films directed by Godard, other films described more routinely as offbeat include *Alphaville* (1965) and *Le weekend* (1968), both in reviews by Mosk, the former in his review of *Nick Carter et le trefle rouge* (1965).[57]

Offbeat, Exhibition and Audiences

Offbeat is also explicitly associated with a range of exhibition possibilities. In particular, offbeat seems to be related to "evolving audiences," a blurring of exhibition categories and distinctions between art house and other selected situations, and more general exhibition success. *La femme mariee* (1964) is judged within the final paragraph of the review as "primarily an art possibility.... It needs specialized handling but could pay off on its offbeat, outspoken attitudes and its refusal to compromise."[58] Hence, offbeat is partly endorsed as a quality that potentially lifts the film above art house or specialized exhibition. *Lord Love a Duck* is in contrast related to offbeat "doing boff biz — and 'Duck' fits into this category — it should reach its mark." However, this is qualified as "dependent upon the viewer."[59] I will consider further examples of "offbeat" films dividing the audience in due course. *Masculin, feminin* is assessed in the first paragraph of the review as "this offbeater that appears mainly for arty houses abroad." The final paragraph stresses, "This is best for arty spots."[60] The review of *The Wrong Box* also suggests a dichotomy between audiences for and against offbeat films. Hence, the third paragraph suggests,

"This shapes up as a possible hit for audiences who like their humor slightly offbeat," while the final paragraph reiterates, "'The Wrong Box' will absorb some filmgoers" but not others. The byline elides description of the film as offbeat but nonetheless confirms this assessment: "Marquee names ... ensures interest but result is spotty."[61] The *Movie Star, American Style, or, LSD, I Hate You!* (1966) review features the term offbeat in the byline to describe the exhibition possibilities of the film: "Exploitable via LSD sequence. Mainly for specialty houses, but could be an offbeat dualer."[62] Thus, offbeat again potentially improves the exhibition prospects, from specialty houses, but qualified for a dual programmer. According to its review, *Rat Pfink a Boo Boo* (1966) "might generate some offbeat excitement."[63] *Accident* is judged within the review text as "another offbeat and adventurous feature, which, with shrewd selling, should click with more adult audiences and be a rewarding and provocative talking-point among film buffs." The byline provided a more qualified assessment, beginning, "Boff item for buffs."[64] Similarly, the first paragraph of the review for *Two or Three Things I Know About Her* suggests it "appears mainly for buffs," continuing, "Specialized outlets abroad, at best, loom for this offbeater." The final paragraph restates the assessment of specialized potential: "This will be a difficult one for arty theatre chances and playoff."[65]

A further association is added in the review of *Le weekend*. Its box office opportunities are gauged in the final paragraph: "But with evolving audiences, ... his [Godard's] pix can not be ignored or passed off. His latest should arouse interest, controversy and curiosity. Thus, it looms a more potent arty entry than many of his previous pix. Right handling, plus savvy followup, might make this a solid off-beat item for foreign climes, and it should make for better biz than usual on his own grounds."[66] Hence, off-beat success is related to "evolving audiences." While *Bye Bye Braverman* was attributed "spotty b.o. potential" and judged an "offbeat pic" for "special, key-city situations,"[67] *Les biches* (1968) was described as having an "offbeat theme [that] could have this a specialized item abroad with exploitation handles rather obvious."[68] *La socrate* (*The Socratic One*) (1968) was judged in the first paragraph as "mainly for art spots and specialized use but could snag evolving audiences if properly placed." The penultimate paragraph repeated this notion that its "splintered and fragmented style" could "slant it for art chances as more evolving audiences form for the more offbeat and unusual." Finally, the last sentence associates the "offbeat" label with specialized exploitation: "So this is an offbeat, dithyrambic pic that will need careful handling for best results."[69] The offbeat audience features in a *Variety* article on original U.S. production, and the potential of the college exhibition circuit: "since the college student body is currently the most accessible audience for 'offbeat' fare."[70]

In some instances, assessment of the exploitation potential of a film is collocated in the byline with labeling as offbeat, rather than associated within a single clause. For instance, the byline of the review of *Seconds* reads: "Offbeater.... Theme and Rock Hudson name for probably okay playoff, exploitation and specialized handling." (Playoff is second and subsequent run locations.) The final paragraph suggests the film, "still has some unusual handles for specialised slotting with some word-of-mouth perhaps helping at home."[71] Similarly, the review byline for *Tell Me in the Sunlight* (1967) characterizes the film as an "offbeat romance, awkwardly made but sometimes touching.... Limited b.o. in certain situations." Subsequently, the first paragraph concludes, "pic will either strike a chord in certain semi-artie situations, or die at the b.o.,"[72] suggesting the potential niche for offbeat films, not exactly art house but with uncertain general box office appeal. Likewise, a rare example of a European film, besides British or French, that is described as offbeat, the Spanish *Peppermint Frappe* (1967) is summarized as follows: "Offbeat Geraldine Chaplin starrer has strong art house potential." Again, the byline collocates labeling the film as offbeat and assessment of art house exploitation prospects. Perhaps it is significant in this case that an otherwise unheralded Spanish film is warranted a byline, and hence the byline is required to concisely explicate this. The first paragraph of the review reiterates this judgment: "It should do excellent art house business and might even have a market in more general situations."[73] Murf again suggests the divided audience for offbeat films in his review of *The Swimmer* (1968); despite the film's "sleeper potential," later in the same review he notes, "A lot of people are not going to understand this film; many will loathe it; others will be moved deeply."[74]

Further examples of offbeat films were assessed as suitable for art house or specialized situations: *Goldstein, Who's Crazy?* (1965), *Doctor Faustus, Bedazzled, Adelaide* (1968), *Rachel, Rachel* (1968), and *Wonderwall* (1969).[75] Notably, *Wonderwall* was related to a specific exhibition site in London, as "the kind of offbeat pic that should find a ready home at Cinecenta, the new West End four-theatre complex designed to give a showplace to some films at which the two big circuits would probably look askance."[76] Other offbeat films that were deemed to have likely appeal among adult, selective or discriminating audiences are *The Knack, A Fine Madness, Cul-de-sac, Mister Buddwing* (1966), and *The Honey Pot*.[77]

Experimental/Unconventional Productions

Offbeat is also used to describe films as being experimental, inventive, or imaginative. Notably, Ronald Gold's article on "offbeat-imports" addresses the issue of experimentation, distinguishing between opportunities and traditions in Europe, and too "far out" U.S. experimenters.[78] The connotations of offbeat thus extend beyond description of comedy. Hence, *Dr. Strangelove* (1964), "a funny comedy," has a screenplay that is "imaginative and contains many an offbeat touch."[79] *A Hard Day's Night*, while established as "funny" in the byline, is described as "a wacky, offbeat piece of filming, charged with vitality and inventiveness."[80] Similarly, Lester's *The Knack* is attributed as having "considerable invention."[81] The review of *Who's Crazy?* without a byline, opens with "narrow gauge film expanded to 35m [sic]: this offbeat, inventive, semi-improvised feature" and hence associates offbeat with invention, as well as nonstandard, or low-budget format.[82] Similarly, the review byline of *Rat Pfink a Boo Boo* reads, "An off-beat low-low budget pix that occasionally presents some clever cinematic devices." The review proper begins, "As an experimental film 'Rat Pfink' has its interesting moments and cinematic devices."[83] Besides these two low-budget films identified as offbeat, there are other examples of low-budget films, or those produced outside Hollywood, that are likewise designated as offbeat, including *Hallelujah The Hills* (1963), a "witty, comic offbeat non–Hollywood pic" according to the byline, and also described as having "inventive visual comic flair";[84] the "Yank indie pic with an inventive drive" *Goldstein*;[85] and *Rachel, Rachel*, an "offbeat, low-budget drama" according to the byline.[86] In addition, in the review of *Hallelujah The Hills*, the production group is also described as offbeat, the main review text opening with "formerly this offbeat N.Y. film-making group."[87] A variety of films with non–Hollywood production context are identified as offbeat, including independent American, and foreign, but most frequently British production within the period 1963 to 1968; yet offbeat predominantly connotes the unconventional style or form often associated with non-mainstream production.

Offbeat is also associated with new styles; sometimes pejoratively in terms of incongruous styles, gimmicks or over-direction. Examples include the "slickly lensed"[88] *A Hard Day's Night* and *The Knack*'s "witty style."[89] The "confused style" of *Mickey One* (1965) is attributed to Arthur Penn, with the film's style, sequences and narrative also confusing or obscure.[90] *The Wrong Box* review notes "conflicting styles" in the byline,[91] whereas that for *Mister Buddwing* notes in conclusion, "direction offbeat." The remainder of the review elaborates this, with reference to "arty cinematics" and direction "with an eye to the offbeat."[92] More pejoratively, *The Happening* is criticized for "over-direction" and "'cute' effects."[93] "'Bedazzled' is smartly-styled."[94] *La socrate* is attributed "a shrewd compendium of avant garde techniques that get fresh life," and "overall coherence in its splintered and fragmented style.... If it uses more proven avant garde aspects rather than the newer kinds, it also has its bows to hippy outlooks and the essay-like readings and asides incorporated in the new styles of filmmakers."[95] Style is privileged in the review byline of *The Swimmer*: "Offbeat, stylized and excellent film." The opening paragraph reiterates, "The stylized, episodic, moody film..."[96]

Conclusion

In terms of the numbers among this selective analysis of *Variety* reviews, offbeat is predominantly associated with comedy as a genre at least within the period 1964 to 1968. This association is commonly further specified with British comedies. The term is also alternatively associated with experimental or unconventional films, or films with specialized appeal. While other genres do feature offbeat, they are exceptional, at least until the later 1960s, so the term could be understood as a genre qualifier, or a subgeneric designation. A genre qualifier might accumulate subgenre status, or even that of a genre. While Leutrat distinguishes between the adjectival use of Western, which "mostly enabled one to be more precise about a traditional generic term,"[97] and its later promotion to noun status, it is arguable exactly when a generic qualifier becomes fixed in its meaning, at least in particular contexts. Is it when the generic noun is first used, when it becomes more recognized and widespread, or can an adjectival term connote a recognized subgenre, or "local" genre? This clearly suggests an important question. How do generic designations, or generic distinctions, come into being and develop? As Neale suggests, "For a genre's history is as much the history of a term as it is of the films to which the term has been applied."[98] So the origins and the diffusion of a term are significant, as are any transformations of its meanings or additional connotations. In the case of offbeat, this is a descriptive term that is used more widely, and only gains a more particular cluster of associations during this short period, specifically in *Variety*. These associations coalesce, establishing a generic qualification, which also determines a subgenre of comedy — unconventional, with "evolving audience" appeal. This provides one account of how a genre might develop, with the consolidation of connotations around a genre qualifier, but in this instance the influence of the term is limited, primarily restricted to *Variety*.

Some generic designations are restricted to use in trade journals, and do not diffuse to wider use, either through promotional materials, or through popular criticism. Likewise, terms for cycles, production trends and exhibition categories significantly aid the characterization of a film by the trade press, in routinized and systematic ways, but do not necessarily cross over into wider use. Yet in considering the generic status of individual films, particularly in their historical context, we need to consider these indigenous terms: generic labels, generic qualifiers, and production and exhibition categories. If a generic distinction was organized around a particular term, or even a number of related terms as with way-out and offbeat, this is salient to the significance of these films at the time, even if some were later categorized according to a production trend, as Swinging London films.

Offbeat is used in a routinized way, with a cluster of associations. Those uses that are variant, which do not mobilize one or more of these associations, are usually explicable. Barbara Klinger suggests that "adult films" functioned as a recognized and influential category of films, and hence constituted a "local" genre.[99] Offbeat, as a generic designation, is recognized, at least in *Variety*, and influential as a term, albeit primarily in *Variety*. Offbeat is used in relation to a self-conscious discussion of a generic cycle, albeit this is defined as the "current way-out cycle."[100] Notably, this group of films is the only corpus of offbeat films provided in *Variety* reviews. However, in Ronald Gold's article on offbeat-imports he exemplifies these with reference to *Alfie*, *Georgy Girl*, and *Blow-Up*. He also proceeds to reference *Seconds*, which some might recognize "as a genuine and successful effort in the 'European' genre."[101] Offbeat is also used as a noun, "offbeater," although without such a consistent meaning. This is associated with Godard, and his inventive approach, as well as the generic uncertainty of *Seconds* and the esoteric art house appeal of *Doctor Faustus*. A short-lived or local genre might share some similarity with a cycle, or even a production trend, yet we need to maintain the distinction. In contrast to the more immediate influence of individual films, or elements of successful films, within the cycle, and the broader shifts inherent in the production trend, the local genre signifies the relationship of films suggested by reception and marketing. In the case of offbeat, the term also designates those films that correspond to a perceived audience trend.

Genres are partially defined in terms of stability, but by considering the initial development of a genre that is then cut short, we can engage with the way genres are consistently open to repositioning and redefinition. With established genres this repositioning remains bounded, both due to the widespread awareness of canonical films within the genre, and to the continuity of generic images and use of generic labels in promotion, as well as in criticism. Yet this stability around the definition of a genre is probabilistic, not a matter of certainty. It is a matter of degree, how consolidated a genre is, as a label, as an image, as well as in terms of the films that constitute the genre in recognized ways. And this process of consolidation can become undone, the generic label "fading out" of use, or becoming anachronistic, whether in the case of the adult film, apropos the introduction of the ratings, or offbeat, with the expanded experimentation of Hollywood in the late 1960s. Yet, for the short period within the mid–1960s, offbeat does designate the "European genre" with cross-over appeal.

Offbeat is associated with exhibition prospects from early in the period, while it is also later identified with an audience trend, "evolving audiences," particularly in 1968. Hence, offbeat films are initially assessed as appealing to selective or art house audiences, but this becomes expanded to include a different audience for offbeat films, an audience that appreciates offbeat humor, or at least an audience for whom offbeat films might "click." Particularly in 1967 and 1968, as well as later, offbeat films are identified with the potential to divide audiences, and have the potential to appeal to semi-artie or more general audiences, but this is not guaranteed.

Within the period 1964 to 1968, inventive and stylized comedies are identified as offbeat, particularly British films. Offbeat was used at the time to explain the difference between Hollywood and European films, and to explore the changing circumstances for "Hollywood financed experimentation."[102] Ronald Gold suggested that British films benefited from snobbism: "This means not only that an offbeat property from England has a better chance to be accepted than a similar U.S. script, but often that 'art' pictures which do get made here are sold short."[103] Clearly, this omits important considerations, particularly in relation to the audiences for offbeat films, aside from production finance. Gold characterizes the anti-establishment approach of offbeat films: "All, or almost all, the offbeat imports knock or make fun of the establishment,"[104] suggesting that this is predominantly the British establishment, which audiences find more acceptable to knock. From 1967, as the counter culture seemed to take hold of the young audience in America, an opening arose for "Hollywood offbeat," while an American "directors" cinema adopted innovative aesthetics. So the term lost its significance. A search in the web archive of *Variety* reviews throws up only two examples, including only one relevant use in the review of *Work Is a Four Letter Word*. Whereas the term was frequently included in the byline for reviews at the time, it has now been excised as irrelevant, a forgotten generic designation.

Notes

1. Steve Neale, *Genre and Hollywood* (London: Routledge, 2000), 41.
2. Richard Maltby and Ian Craven, *Hollywood Cinema* (Oxford: Blackwell, 1995), 111; Tino Balio, *Grand Design: Hollywood as a Modern Business Enterprise, 1930–1939* (New York: Scribners, 1993), 179.

3. David Bordwell and Kristin Thompson, *Film History* (New York: McGraw Hill, 1994), 820.
4. Neale, *Genre and Hollywood*, 255, n. 2.
5. Ibid., 237–238.
6. Maltby, *Hollywood Cinema*, 111.
7. Barbara Klinger, "'Local' Genres: The Hollywood Adult Film in the 1950s." In *Melodrama: Stage Picture Screen*. Ed. Jacky Bratton, Jim Cook, and Christine Gledhill (London: BFI, 1994), 135; also the notion of "local" genres is cited in Maltby, *Hollywood Cinema*, 111, n. 13 with reference to Klinger's conference paper on "'Local' Genres: The Hollywood Adult Film in the 1950s."
8. *Variety*, 15/7/64.
9. *Variety*, 10/5/67: 3, 32.
10. Ibid., 3.
11. Maltby, *Hollywood Cinema*, 415.
12. Neale, *Genre and Hollywood*, 235.
13. *Variety*, 10/4/63.
14. *Variety*, 1/5/63.
15. *Variety*, 15/5/63.
16. *Variety*, 4/10/67.
17. Neale, *Genre and Hollywood*, 234–235.
18. Ibid., 31.
19. E. D. Hirsch, *Validity in Interpretation* (New Haven: Yale University Press, 1967), 74, cited in Neale, *Genre and Hollywood*, 23.
20. "Sticks No on 'Hick Pix' Kick," *Variety*, 5/12/56: 1, cited in Klinger, "'Local' Genres," 136. See also Maltby, *Hollywood Cinema*, 137.
21. *Variety*, 13/5/64.
22. *Variety*, 19/5/65.
23. *Variety*, 8/6/66.
24. *Variety*, 15/7/64.
25. *Variety*, 1/6/66.
26. *Variety*, 7/2/68.
27. Variety, 12/6/68.
28. *Variety*, 27/1/65.
29. *Variety*, 27/12/67.
30. *Variety*, 13/4/66.
31. *Variety*, 13/12/67.
32. *Variety*, 4/8/65.
33. *Variety*, 30/3/66.
34. *Variety*, 13/7/66.
35. *Variety*, 6/5/64.
36. *Variety*, 4/5/66.
37. *Variety*, 22/3/67.
38. *Variety*, 29/3/67.
39. *Variety*, 22/2/67; *Variety*, 24/1/68.
40. *Variety*, 7/6/67.
41. *Variety*, 19/1/66.
42. *Variety*, 27/1/65.
43. *Variety*, 12/5/65.
44. *Variety*, 23/6/65.
45. *Variety*, 21/12/66.
46. *Variety*, 12/6/68.
47. *Variety*, 13/4/66.
48. *Variety*, 16/9/64.
49. *Variety*, 29/3/67.
50. *Variety*, 7/2/68.
51. *Variety*, 12/6/68.
52. *Variety*, 4/8/65.
53. *Variety*, 4/5/66.
54. *Variety*, 25/5/66.
55. *Variety*, 5/4/67.
56. *Variety*, 25/10/67.
57. *Variety*, 22/12/65; *Variety*, 10/1/68.
58. *Variety*, 16/9/64.

59. *Variety*, 19/1/66.
60. *Variety*, 4/5/66.
61. *Variety*, 1/6/66.
62. *Variety*, 17/8/66.
63. *Variety*, 14/9/66.
64. *Variety*, 22/2/67.
65. *Variety*, 5/4/67.
66. *Variety*, 10/1/68.
67. *Variety*, 7/2/68.
68. *Variety*, 10/4/68.
69. *Variety*, 24/4/68.
70. *Variety*, 10/5/67: 3.
71. *Variety*, 25/5/66.
72. *Variety*, 12/4/67.
73. *Variety*, 6/9/67.
74. *Variety*, 15/5/68.
75. *Variety*, 6/5/64; *Variety*, 11/8/65; *Variety*, 25/10/67; *Variety*, 13/12/67; *Variety*, 1/5/68; *Variety*, 21/8/68; *Variety*, 15/1/69.
76. *Variety*, 15/1/69.
77. *Variety*, 19/5/65; *Variety*, 4/5/66; *Variety*, 8/6/66; *Variety*, 14/9/66; 22/3/67.
78. *Variety*, 10/5/67: 32.
79. *Variety*, 22/1/64.
80. *Variety*, 15/7/64.
81. *Variety*, 19/5/65.
82. *Variety*, 11/8/65.
83. *Variety*, 14/9/66.
84. *Variety*, 15/5/63.
85. *Variety*, 6/5/64.
86. *Variety*, 21/8/68.
87. *Variety*, 15/5/63.
88. *Variety*, 15/7/64.
89. *Variety*, 19/5/65.
90. *Variety*, 8/9/65.
91. *Variety*, 1/6/66.
92. *Variety*, 14/9/66.
93. *Variety*, 29/3/67.
94. *Variety*, 13/12/67.
95. *Variety*, 24/4/68.
96. *Variety*, 15/5/68.
97. Neale, *Genre and Hollywood*, 44, his translation of J. L. Leutrat, *Le western: Archeologie d'un genre* (Lyon: Presses Universitaires de Lyon, 1987), 127–128.
98. Neale, *Genre and Hollywood*, 43.
99. Klinger, "'Local' Genres," 135.
100. Whit, *Variety*, 19/1/66.
101. *Variety*, 10/5/67: 32.
102. *Variety*, 10/5/67: 32; *Variety*, 10/5/67: 3.
103. Ibid., 32.
104. Ibid., 32.

PART TWO

Textual Negotiations

4

Film Noir as Male Melodrama

The Politics of Film Genre Labeling

JANET STAIGER

When film scholars think of melodrama, likely an image such as one from Douglas Sirk's 1957 film *Written on the Wind* comes to mind in which the family doctor meets Kyle Hadley (played by Robert Stack) in the local drugstore and breaks the news to him that tests "show a ... well, let's call it a weakness." Kyle isn't sterile, but more tests are needed. Kyle's hand tightens around his soda glass (he's recently overcome alcoholism with the help of a good woman played by Lauren Bacall), music begins and then rises in volume, and Kyle walks out the front door, past a small boy riding a mechanical horse. The message about Kyle's interior thoughts and feelings is quite explicit and excessive by gesture, music, and iconography.

Although numerous accounts of what constitutes melodrama exist, a standard one in film studies is Christine Gledhill's description in which she follows Peter Brooks in seeing melodrama as "the degeneration of bourgeois tragedy" in which "tragic action was increasingly internalized as individual error."[1] Moreover, "the notion of 'poetic justice'" produced "a new moral mission for the theatre.... The theatre took on an educative role through the power of example and appeal to the 'sympathetic emotions' of what was understood to be an essentially benevolent human nature."[2] Aesthetically, plots were constructed as crisis after crisis; the world was dichotomized; coincidences revealed a moral allegory; and "gesture, music, and iconography"[3] presented subjective character information, usually highly emotional in content.

All these features exist in the scene from *Written on the Wind*: another crisis, a black-and-white world — at least from Kyle's perspective, coincidences that are proof of a deep social order, and "gesture, music, and iconography" revealing character and textual meaning.

Gledhill notes that in the late 1800s, realism appeared. In contrast with romantic melodrama in theater, its aesthetic presentation of subjective character information occurred through "dialogue, character analysis, and naturalized performance"[4] and was quickly associated with "a re-masculinisation of cultural value": "Realism came to be associated with (masculine) restraint and underplaying. It eschewed flamboyant characterization in favor of psychological analysis."[5] Other scholars also have pointed out that perhaps less well known is that at least in the 1800s, melodramas often articulated a radical progressive agenda toward national and social politics, an ideology also taken up by many realistic and naturalistic texts.[6]

In the case of Hollywood cinema, Gledhill and other feminist scholars have considered the strands of nineteenth-century melodrama within films associated with female protagonists. For instance, Lea Jacobs's work on the melodramatic formula of the fallen woman is a touchstone. Jacobs describes the formula but points out that, in the early 1930s, a spate of fallen-women films indicates that narratives in which fallen women sacrifice their virginity for men and children increasingly trouble the standard proscription of sexual chastity for melodramatic heroines. This sacrifice motif questions the traditional social mores of sexual purity in favor of proposing a higher code of personal morality.[7] Eventually, the Hollywood Production Code and regulatory boards negotiate ways to try (sometimes rather unsuccessfully) to secure traditional morality for female protagonists in these narratives.

In considering the fallen-woman formula, I have concurred with Jacobs but have also stressed that twentieth-century Hollywood ideology requires that an individual have choices and *recognize* social rights from wrongs. Individualized agency replaces the nineteenth-century's attribution of causality to inherent good or evil. That is, in the early 1800s, texts represent people as born bad and good, villains and victims. In the early 1900s, the moral allegory played out on the grounds of psychologized personal choice, and bad women are those who persist in making wrong choices. This is still melodrama, but ideologically reconfigured. Moreover, twentieth-century melodrama might display subjective character either through its nineteenth-century romantic melodramatic form via "gesture, music, and iconography" or through late nineteenth-century realism via "dialogue, character analysis, and naturalized performance."[8]

Now it would seem strange that only females are faced with such dilemmas of choice. And, in fact, obviously since Hollywood cinema has been a very male-centered medium, I believe that Hollywood narratives also place male protagonists into this plot trajectory and these aesthetic modes. However, when men face social and moral choices, film scholars have called this drama. Or action, or thrills, or suspense. To date, film studies has only flirted with recognizing that male protagonists might be parallel with females, that some films might well be described as displaying a "fallen-man" formula and being a male-centered melodrama.

However, if we made this analogy, the fallen-man formula would be described as one in which plot devices lure a man into wayward paths because of his lack of control. These lures may be drink or gambling or even blind ambition; they are often sex, perhaps motivated as derived from a femme fatale tricking, seducing, or forcing the man into his wayward path.[9] The narrative focuses on the man's lack of self-mastery, his fall from proper manhood (and often proper masculinity); it analyzes the man's pathology; and it critiques his moral decline. In such films, as for the fallen woman, the male protagonist may be able to redeem himself, and depending on the era,[10] he may escape significant punishment, or, with more traditional melodrama, he is rewarded elsewhere: in moral heaven.

I have now used the word "melodrama" to describe films normally labeled by scholars as drama or by a specific generic term (science fiction, thriller, horror, etc.). The point of this essay is to argue that much of Hollywood drama might well be called "male melodrama,"[11] a point Gledhill notes briefly and a fact that contemporaneous film industry practitioners saw, as Steve Neale has argued in his "Melo Talk."[12] Neale points out that the U.S. film trade papers did *not* use the term "melodrama" for romances or women's films but for "war films, adventure films, horror films, and thrillers, genres traditionally thought of as, if anything, 'male.'"[13] Additionally, the trade papers did not use the term pejoratively when they labeled much of Hollywood's output as "melodrama"; a film could be evaluated as a good or bad melodrama (i.e., well done or not). I have also noted previously that the Hollywood industry liked to label films by many terms, hoping to attract viewers who preferred certain sorts of formulas and emotional and aesthetic experiences; poly-generic labeling and re-labeling has a long history.[14] It has been academic scholars who have been more committed to trying to put films into only one (correct) category.

In re-labeling many Hollywood male-centered dramas as melodramas of the fallen man, I intend only to point out some useful analogies and features with this terminological change. I do not mean to ascribe to these films a penchant for "low-cultural values" or that they are merely "action" movies.

In fact, as I shall stress below, some reason exists to claim just the reverse since the films are arguing for what constitutes appropriate moral and social behavior. What I do want to point out is that these films are a formulaic exploration of an individual's relations to other people and to social and moral conventions of right behavior, which justifies labeling them melodramas. Moreover, while following one melodramatic formula, their aesthetics range from "romantic" to "realism" to "modernist." And, as I shall point out in the conclusion, likely academic film scholars would have seen this earlier had the politics of genre labeling not been so infused with gender associations.

To make this argument, I want to focus on films categorized as film noir,[15] although this formula is quite alive in contemporary action and superhero films. I believe that conceptualizing film noir as one cycle of male melodrama provides much clarity to the textual features of (many of) these (and other) Hollywood films.[16] I specifically choose film noir because scholarship in the last ten years has flirted with making this observation for these films but then backed away. If we view film noir as containing a large number of fallen-men films and think of the formal and stylistic features as variable means of expressing subjective character, then we will be more in harmony with how Hollywood at the time perceived these films, and we will be better able to explain these texts formally, stylistically, and ideologically. No reason exists that we need cement the cycle into this terminology, but the vocabulary also allows us to connect these films to predecessors and successors, and to explain the continuing production of neo-film noirs and other male melodramas. For the fascination with fallen men continues unabated.

Film Noir and Its Labeling

In an excellent analysis of masculinity in the films of post World War II film noir, Frank Krutnik refers to film noirs as having features akin to women's melodrama and heroes who are "fallen men." In fact, Krutnik states that these films might be a form of "masculine melodrama."[17] He writes, "these films tend to be obsessed with lapses from, and failures to achieve ... a position of unified and potent masculinity."[18] He notes that "the investigative narrative serves simultaneously as a means by which the male's 'fall' can be measured, and as a strategy by means of which his 'fall' can be recuperated."[19] In most of these films, the spectator is positioned not as a witness to the superior detective, as a Dr. Watson surprised by the deciphering of a puzzle, but as a bystander to the hapless protagonist: "the spectator's superiority of knowledge and viewpoint is accompanied by powerlessness, for he or she is, of course, unable to intervene, to warn the hero, or to change the course of events."[20] In my opinion, this positioning of the audience as helpless in the face of the protagonist's wrong choices is symptomatic of melodrama's masochistic aesthetic that both Gledhill and Neale argue creates pathos and the tears that result.[21] Krutnik even observes, "'splashy visual set-pieces' which punctuate these thrillers tend to occur at, and explicitly serve to accentuate, such moments of impairment, danger and confusion, where the hero's Oedipal trajectory is most threatened."[22] Despite all this, Krutnik identifies the movies and labels the chapters "tough thriller" and "criminal-adventure thriller."

I am not going to speculate about why Krutnik cannot bring himself to step over the line and actually identify film noirs as male melodramas. However, more recent work by Neale and James Naremore takes a broad perspective on this set of films and how film scholarship has approached them. Neale stresses that the common film industry tag for these and many other action movies was "melodrama." "The terms used most regularly [in contemporary reviews] to mark [film noir] were terms like 'psychological drama,' 'psychological melodrama' and 'psychological thriller.' ... The term used to describe nearly all the films subsequently labeled *noir* ... was melodrama."[23] Neale underlines that it is 1970s film studies scholarship that associated "melodrama" with "women and the woman's film."[24]

Film studies was not alone in creating such a connotation to the term, "feminizing" it. As Andreas Huyssen has observed, social commentators in the twentieth century have envisioned middle-class mass culture as feminine against radical modernist high art that is, by contrast, masculine.[25] This constructed homology plays itself out through aesthetic dynamics. Naremore convincingly argues that during the 1920s through 1940s, high modernism has an interest in violence and criminality, against mass culture that is soft. "By midcentury ... serious art was expected to create an atmosphere of toughness, darkness, and alienation."[26] Naremore goes on to assert that the pulp fiction sources for much of film noir should be re-conceptualized as modernist, and he notes the radical progressive agenda of many of the original writers and the filmmakers attracted to producing these adaptations. Naremore does mention that Graham Greene has described film noir as "blood melodrama,"[27] and for the *classicus locus* of film noir, *Double Indemnity* (1944), Naremore states, "[Billy] Wilder's melodramatic allegory could not be more obvious."[28] Still, Naremore does not explore the possible contradictions between declaring these films to be both modernist and melodrama.

I have less trouble with this because, as Richard Dyer and Linda Williams have argued,[29] the scholarly attitude toward melodrama needs to be recognized as one likely related to larger hierarchies of taste that view emotion as inferior to reason. As they note, melodrama is a genre exploiting emotional responses, and, hence, it has developed connotations of lower status. Yet, I have pointed out that Hollywood constructed a narrative mode that combines and oscillates between (higher status) realism and romantic melodrama. By 1915, classical Hollywood's ideology has redefined "'bad' ... as the failure to act in the right way even upon recognizing the proper choice.... Such a morality, which fits neatly with Christian theology as well as [turn-of-the-century] reformism, easily works into a narrative plot of the classical three-act formula. Plot points are moments of character decision in relation to events. Additionally, tremendous weight is given to character psychology and development — manifested either through external means (the older melodramatic practices) or through internal ones (such as in realist practices)."[30] Thus, built into the classical Hollywood system is the *option* of romantic or realist melodramatic constructions of character and theme, an option often taken by its filmmakers.

Moreover, as Naremore suggests, twentieth-century modernist aesthetics may also be marshaled to service. Naremore's tracing of the individuals involved in the production of these films is an extremely valuable contribution to the context for the films. In particular, the aesthetic choices seem modernist in the complexity of the narrative form and the offering of intense individual or multiple subjectivities such as innovated by James Joyce, Virginia Woolf, William Faulkner, and John Dos Passos. Yet the protagonists' toughness, the stoicism, for instance, in voice-over narration from doomed men, also mimics modernist writers such Ernest Hemingway and F. Scott Fitzgerald. As Sarah Kozloff discusses, the increasing use of voice-over narration and flashback structures after 1939 in Hollywood can be attributed to the influence of radio narration (especially Orson Welles's Mercury Theatre on the air literary adaptations), documentary and newsreels, the employment of prestigious screenwriters who appreciated the value of the word (more exploitable through extravagant voice-over narration), and the narrational voice and stream-of-conscious narration of important modernists.[31]

To notice the fallen-man formula and variable aesthetic choices in film noir is not to assert that these observations "explain" these films. The films variously argued to be film noir continue to display complexities of representing women, sexual orientation, race, and class; to use other formulas besides the fallen-man one; and to evince contradictions, schisms, and structuring absences. Yet, noticing this may have some value. What does happen when we see film noir as one cycle of male melodrama (as commentators of the period saw these films)? Do any advantages accrue?

The Enactment of Male Melodrama

To consider this, I begin with *Double Indemnity* because so many scholars consider it as a, if not the, core instance of the cycle. As Neale predicts, the trade papers describe *Double Indemnity* as melodrama:

- "based on a sensational murder of the '20s, [*Double Indemnity*] has become an absorbing melodrama in its Paramount adaptation" (Kahn, *Variety*)
- "the season's nattiest, nastiest, most satisfying melodrama" (*Time*)
- "a pretty good murder melodrama" (John Lardner, *New Yorker*)
- "the most neatly machined movie since 'The Miracle of Morgan's Creek' and the meanest one since 'The Maltese Falcon' (without being as good as either), is a murder melodrama called 'Double Indemnity'" (Manny Farber, *New Republic*).[32]

Double Indemnity opens with Walter Neff (played by Fred MacMurray) careening in his car in the middle of the night to his insurance agency building, stumbling into his office, and beginning a Dictaphone account of recent events for his boss, Barton Keyes (Edward G. Robinson), as he nurses his left shoulder where he has been shot. His opening statement is that his boss had it right: that the Dietrichson death was murder, but he asserts immediately that Keyes had the wrong man. Instead, Neff asserts that he did it, for money and a woman. The film then begins cross-cutting between Neff dictating the story and flashbacks of Neff meeting Phyllis Dietrichson (Barbara Stanwyck), being enchanted by her, plotting the "perfect" murder of her husband, and so forth until the climax when he confronts her about whether she was playing him as a sucker for another man, she shoots him, and then he shoots her.

If I match this story against the requirements for the option of classical Hollywood fallen-person melodrama, I would note that in terms of the plot, this is a story of a man whose ego interfered with him controlling his morality. In *Double Indemnity*, the lures are two: money and sex.[33] Neff is, from the start of the plot, a wounded man so his "fallen" nature is iconically signified immediately. Subsequently, the narrative is a self-revelation of his individual error, a confession of his egotism, and, ultimately, his justified punishment. The first plot point focuses on the two lures: Phyllis Dietrichson's ankles and the potential insurance payout. The second plot point reinforces his erroneous choices that produce his final emasculation: he turns from Dietrichson because he believes she has cuckolded him with another lover.

If the plot is a classical fallen-person plot, so is the narration. The plot of *Double Indemnity* is not a detective story; or rather, the puzzle to be solved is not *who* did it, but how did Neff fall?[34] What is the lesson to be learned? How can we account for the coincidences except for some superior moral force? Indeed, the narration creates melodramatic anxiety and suspense. Multiple times, editing and shot choices result in superior knowledge for the spectator. For instance, the narration reveals that Dietrichson is arriving at Neff's apartment while Keyes is still there. Thankfully, Neff's door opens out into the apartment building's hallway so she can hide behind it as Keyes heads to the elevator. Later, when Neff is approaching Dietrichson's home to confront her, the narration switches to her preparations for his visit, including putting a gun under her chair cushion. In these high suspense moments, however, the audience is an immobilized bystander. Moreover, since the opening scene has already established Neff's culpability, any identification established with Neff is bound to produce a futility of any happy outcome and the "too-late-ness" of melodramatic masochism.[35]

Aesthetically, *Double Indemnity* is replete with romantic and modernist choices as well as realism. In terms of romanticism, the moral allegory is pervasive. Many critics focus on the plot relation between Neff and Keyes as a latent homosexuality mostly because of a symbolic motif of Neff repeatedly lighting Keyes's cigar and saying, "I love you."[36] In the final scene, Keyes stands over Neff and lights his cigarette, metaphorically illuminating the shift in male dominance. Moreover, dialogue has established that Keyes's smaller stature may appear to be deceptive. In this final scene, the physical relations are reversed as well.

If moral allegory via *mise-en-scène* is prevalent, so is "gesture, music, and iconography" to create character subjectivity. The final scene wallows in this. Beyond the cigarette lighting, as Neff attempts to leave, the music rises in scale and volume, until Neff collapses at the front door, as Keyes predicted. At this point the main musical instrument, a violin, mimics Neff's physical movement by going down the scale, and volume declines as well. As the cigarette-lighting/love scene proceeds, the music rises up in scale and volume again, until it reaches its crescendo and climax as Keyes flicks the match lit and the scene ends in black. Thus, gesture, music, blocking, and lighting articulate character interior emotions rather than relying only on realism's dialogue or naturalistic acting to explicate character.

In terms of modernism, Neff is an archetypical tough, observing narrator akin to Nick Carraway (*The Great Gatsby*) and Jake Barnes (*The Sun Also Rises*). Although the narration is channeled through a single subjectivity (Neff), it shifts back and forth from the wounded Neff sitting in his office, spilling out the story into the Dictaphone, to images of the events as he recalls them. The focalized narration is faithful to his point of view; it almost never shifts away to information to which he was not privy.

Ideologically, this film appears to present a traditional ideology: cheating insurance companies and murdering husbands will lead to emasculation and moral degeneration although Naremore argues rather convincingly that the film criticizes much of modern Los Angeles, urbanity, and capitalism.[37] Scholarship about the variable possible endings of the film considered by Paramount Pictures, including one showing Neff's execution in a gas chamber, indicates that the Hollywood Production Code with its "moral justice" restrictions controlled much of the agenda for the film. Surprisingly, director Billy Wilder wanted the scene; Paramount and the Production Code thought it unduly gruesome.[38] Where the film exists in ideological discourses is debatable; its condemnation of Neff's choices is explicit, reinforcing a melodramatic formula.

Nor is it easy to see a radical politics for a film often intuitively thought to be part of the film noir cycle but sometimes difficult to fit in: the 1941 *The Maltese Falcon*. Classical Hollywood cinema almost always uses a romance subplot no matter what is occurring in the main plot. In the case of *The Maltese Falcon*, Sam Spade (Humphrey Bogart) has an overt option to fall, failing to uphold the code of being a good partner to his slain coworker and the law in general and, instead, following after his desires for the criminal Brigid O'Shaughnessy (Mary Astor). However, this film presents the proper moral outcome for the plot. Sam turns her in to the police. Yet, in doing this, Sam loses in the romance subplot and is thus emasculated there, producing the strong ambiguity at the ending of the film and a sense of melodramatic masochism as well. For, had Sam not chosen the wrong woman to desire, which he did, no individual error would have produced his ultimate dilemma. Thus, *The Maltese Falcon*'s protagonist makes the proper choice in terms of social behavior although even his minor stumble in the love plot produces punishment elsewhere as well: like the woman, the Maltese falcon that he and the others seek turns out to be fake. A nice enactment of divine retribution.

Likewise, thinking of the 1942 *Casablanca* as a male melodrama in the 1940s fallen-man cycle shows just how conservative and widespread the formula might be.[39] Notice that at the beginning of *Casablanca* American expatriot Rick Blaine (Humphrey Bogart) is represented as weak and morally shady. He is trapped in a foreign country and not doing his patriotic duty of fighting in the war. What is the cause? As with *Double Indemnity*, a flashback explains this. Rick fell in love and then his ego was crushed when Ilsa (Ingrid Bergman) didn't meet him to leave Paris. *Casablanca* ends happily, however, when Rick recognizes his patriotic duty, stops wallowing in his own problems for the good of the group, and rejects the lure of love of—perversely here, even a good!—woman for the homosocial bonding with Louis Renault

(Claude Rains) as they head off to father a free nation. After the war, good men may end up with good women.

This narrative of fallen men, narration of coincidence and melodramatic suspense and anxiety, and aesthetics of romanticism's gesture, music, and iconography; realism's dialogue, character analysis, and "naturalistic" acting; and modernism's "objective" subjectivity and complex multiple subjectivities to create characters and thematic discourse occur throughout classical film noirs. Film noir plots usually construct some sort of sympathetic features for the fallen man to induce a modicum of pathos, if not identification, by the audience. Raymond Borde and Étienne Chaumeton assert, "It is the presence of crime which gives film noir its most constant characteristic."[40] If crime pervades these films, the fallen man will be associated with those criminal acts, but almost always some redeeming feature attaches to the protagonist. So, for instance, in *This Gun for Hire* (1942), Raven (Alan Ladd) may be a passionless hired killer, but he likes cats and even hits a maid who tries to push his cat out the window. This narrative information comes early in the film; only later does the good woman (Veronica Lake) pull out of him that his mother abused him, producing the behavior he now exhibits. Often, if the film is using voice-over narration, the fallen man asserts after the fact his own stupidity, creating the "too-lateness" of the mode. Michael O'Hara (Orson Welles) begins *The Lady from Shanghai* (1947) with voice-over, stating, "When I start out to make a fool of myself, there's very little can stop me." Richard Wanley (Edward G. Robinson) in *The Woman in the Window* (1944) and Johnny Forbes (Dick Powell) in *Pitfall* (1948) are middle-aged professionals with a midlife crisis; both men are married with children and bored with their lives. Very few films offer protagonists utterly lacking in complexity. One example is *Brighton Rock*'s (1947) Pinkie Brown (Richard Attenborough). Another is Arthur Montgomery (Robert Ryan) in *Crossfire* (1947) who is motivated only by hating Jews and publicly humiliating his fellow soldiers.

As in tragedy, in melodrama, some character flaw propels the protagonist into an adventure.[41] Unlike tragedy, twentieth-century classical Hollywood melodrama often provides overt signals through dialogue that the protagonist has a choice. This dialogue can come from other characters or from the protagonist (often through voice-over analyzing his own actions in a clinical tone). Numerous characters warn Steve Thompson (Burt Lancaster) in *Criss Cross* (1949) that Anna Dundee (Yvonne DeCarlo) is leading him into trouble, but Steve declares, "I'm going to do what I want." Sometimes the choice is represented as subjective premonition: Rip Murdock (Humphrey Bogart) in *Dead Reckoning* (1947) says of the femme fatale, Coral Chandler (Lizabeth Scott), "If I'm wrong about you, I'm dead."[42] Although too late in

The Killers (1946), the "Swede" Pete Lund (Burt Lancaster) declares, "Once I did something wrong."

A moralistic resolution and assumed lesson work best if characters have at least one chance to correct their errors. This takes an obsessive form in *The Woman in the Window*. Professor Richard Wanley unwisely answers the call of the "siren of adventure" and finds himself drinking in Alice Reed's (Joan Bennett) living room when a jealous lover comes in and attacks them. In self-defense, Richard kills him. Then fearing the police will not believe such a story, Richard dumps the body in a suburban park. That is his first wrong choice — or second if having a drink with Alice is the first. He repeats this pattern of lack of trust of public officials when he counsels Alice to try to poison a blackmailer, again, rather than turning to officials to solve the problem. The film might have ended with his suicide[43] except that the narrative discourse obsessively needs to be sure the point is made. Richard wakes up from a nap: this was all a dream. Then, as he leaves the club where he has been sleeping, he returns to the start of the dream's adventure, the store window where a beautiful woman's portrait had first entranced him. Another woman appears, as if to create the narrative again. Richard flees, avoiding the siren.[44]

Hence, coincidences do not matter in this formula, any more than they do for other more fantastical formulas. For example, in *Detour* (1945) Al Roberts (Tom Neal) picks up the same hitchhiking woman (Ann Savage) as Charlie Haskell (Edmund MacDonald) did. Or even more improbable, Ballin Mundson (George Macready) marries Johnny Farrell's (Glenn Ford) ex-wife (Rita Hayworth) in *Gilda* (1946). One highly incredible event is a record sticking at the end of *Brighton Rock* so that Rose Brown (Carol Marsh) believes that Pinkie loved her; this is, of course, highly ironic, however, since belief in his love means she will not repent.

In melodrama, the narrative focus is not on explication of the crime but resolution of the character's choice making. As Mary Ann Doane puts it, "Film noir, instead, constitutes itself as a detour, a bending of the hermeneutic code from the questions connected with a crime to the difficulty posed by the woman as enigma (or crime)."[45] While I see the woman as merely one of several lures to test the character's self-control, Doane's central observation is that many of these films seem to detour from standard detection plots to character analysis. Or, it might be said that the primary plot is the fallen-man plot; the crime is the subplot, explaining the common critical objection to some of these film noirs that it is occasionally difficult to figure out who did what to whom.[46]

Dead Reckoning is a good example. Although Rip is a war hero and self-admittedly a ladies man, Coral seems to knock him off course. Although he is seeking his soldier buddy Johnny (William Prince) and then his buddy's murderer, he detours from the crime/detection course to assist Coral who is losing large sums of money gambling. This detour results in his being drugged and framed for a waiter's death. Rather than head to the police (numerous of the causes for falls are due to egos — the protagonist thinks he can resolve the problem rather than turn to the police), Rip proceeds on his own, producing his error (egotism, conceited self-assurance) while lured by the woman. The detection of Johnny's death recedes as resolving his relation with Coral moves to the foreground (although we suspect that the resolution of the latter will also produce solution of the former). The film warns about focusing on Rip's choice making in the first scene: Rip is fleeing from the police and turns to a priest to tell him, "I'm not doing anything wrong." The film then moves into Rip's flashback in which he recounts events up to another confrontation with Coral in which he tries to deduce what is going on and whether she knocked him out while he was searching for a letter. Eventually, a longish expository scene occurs in which one villain unravels the mystery of Johnny's death and other events, but the film still needs to complete the fallen-man plot. Shot at as he leaves the villain's nightclub, Rip is offered a choice again. This time, he heads to the cops. He also makes, from the film's discursive point of view, another better choice: while Rip admits he loved Coral, "That's the tough part of it. I loved [Johnny] more."

At any rate, preferably, the resolution of the fallen-man story is morally unambiguous. During the era of the Production Code, resolutions had to fit conservative norms of moral justice rather than any principle of likely reality. In no case in the some twenty film noirs that I reviewed for this essay[47] did a protagonist escape from his actions after losing self-control. For fallen men who make the wrong choice, and fail to shift course or redeem themselves, some sad or bad ending occurs. In the instance of Dix Steele (Humphrey Bogart) in *In a Lonely Place* (1950), his violent temper results in the loss of the girl (Gloria Grahame). Occasionally, if the fallen man has committed a crime, the justice system arrests him (e.g., *Detour*). More often, the police kill him (*Crossfire*). Or worse, his own error in trusting the wrong person results in his death: *The Killers, Criss Cross,* and *Out of the Past* (1947) (although Jeff Bailey [Robert Mitchum] redeems himself at the last minute by calling the police).

For fallen men who make the right choice, the reward is sometimes the good woman: *Gilda* (or at least Gilda is not as bad as Johnny thought she was), *The Dark Corner* (1946), *Pitfall,* and *Kiss Me Deadly* (1955). Or just release from the situation: *Dead Reckoning, The Lady from Shanghai,* and *The*

Third Man (1949). The reward may even presumably be moral heaven as in the case of *This Gun for Hire* in which Raven dies but knows that he has done the right thing in helping finding the saboteurs, receiving the good woman's approval as he dies.

Perhaps the stress or accentuation on the moral in this cycle of fallen-men melodramas is why stories often portray the protagonists as doomed, with events commonly told in flashbacks and deaths as "normal." While some of this is likely related to late 1940s existentialism, as Robert G. Porfirio contends,[48] it also eliminates overarching narrational suspense, reinforces the moral allegory, and produces the pathos, the "too-lateness" of melodramatic masochism.[49] If only Raven in *This Gun for Hire* had met a good woman earlier; if only Al in *Detour* had called the police; if only Holly Martins (Joseph Cotten) in *The Third Man* had seen through Harry Lime's (Orson Welles) façade during their college days and reported him for cribbing then; if only Dix in *In a Lonely Place* had controlled his temper.

Melodrama Aesthetics and the Film Noir Style

The fallen-man formula may use romantic, realist, or modernist aesthetics or all of these. If romantic, choices in lighting, blocking, acting style, camera movements and distances, editing, and music may be motivated as symbolism to reveal the moral allegory or character subjectivity.[50] If realist or modernist, the motivation beyond character revelation may additionally be photographic realism in an urban setting, etc. In all cases, also possible causes for non-normative stylistic choices are intertexuality (other films in this cycle look like this) and "pure" aesthetic expression (high contrast photography is beautiful, nearly abstract at times). Here I particularly agree with David Bordwell who remarks that film noir, constructed ex post facto as "particular patterns of nonconformity within Hollywood," while a minority practice, still adheres to classical norms of character and story unity while it offers "new realistic and generic motivation."[51]

Within the romantic aesthetic, symbolism often occurs in these films. The pathetic fallacy produces rain at times (and also cinematographic tour de forces). In *Brighton Rock*, as Pinkie is warning Rose not to say anything about what she knows, thunder crashes (and the music increases in loudness). Thunder and rain return at the climax. *Dead Reckoning* uses a repeating non-diegetic insert to symbolize masculine courage in the face of possible death. Rip tells his story to an army chaplain known for parachute jumping with the men, but the first visual representation of this occurs when Rip is knocked out and then endures a beating. It returns at the conclusion when Coral, whom Rip has nicknamed "Mike," is dying. Rip says as she is going that it is just like jumping, and the film concludes with a shot of a parachute opening. Paul Kerr agrees with Janey Place and Lowell Peterson that men may be shot in a nonstandard style of soft-focus "signifying feminine decadence" while bad women were "often photographed in harsh, unflattering and undiffused light with wide angle distorting lenses."[52]

The Lady from Shanghai is one of the most florid of these films in this regard. Symbolism occurs in the dialogue with Michael comparing Elsa Bannister (Rita Hayworth), her husband, and her husband's partner to sharks that are so whipped into an eating frenzy that they devour each other and themselves. The yacht on which they sail and Michael crews is the Circe. The carnival location through which Michael both escapes police and attempts to track Elsa, to find the gun that would prove his innocence, is not merely a "crazy" house but is surreal and intertextual, with some sections echoing the décor in *The Cabinet of Dr. Caligari* (1919). The voice-over narration, given solely to Michael, is nearly poetry: "When I start out to make a fool of myself, there's very little can stop me. If I'd know where it would end, I'd never have let anything start. If I'd been in right mind, that is. But once I'd seen her, once I'd seen her, I was not in my right mind for quite some time." Of course Michael has pretensions to being a writer, as one character remarks.

Place and Peterson also observe that "complementary to the *noir* photographic style among the better-directed films is a mise-en-scène designed to unsettle, jar, and disorient the viewer in correlation with the disorientation felt by the noir heroes."[53] Within classical Hollywood film, such a symbolic aesthetic is not the best explanation for mise-en-scène that deviates from the norm, but in the case of a romantic melodramatic aesthetic, such an interpretation makes sense within its motivations. The most blatant example is *The Third Man*, with all of its canted and odd-angled shots, only some of which are motivated as point-of-view or even eyeline matches. *Kiss Me Deadly* produces similar sorts of shots, particularly of Mike Hammer (Ralph Meeker) traveling up and down excessively long lengths of stairs.

Dialogue conveys not only character information but also symbolic motifs. In *Out of the Past*, Jeff often speaks during his extended flashback in voice-over narration (one value to voice-over narration is its ability to "rise" beyond realistic motivations). Speaking of his first encounter with Kathie Moffat (Jane Greer) he says, "Then I saw her coming out of the sun." That alone has a sort of literary quality to it. However, fairly soon in the narrative, he says, "Then she walked in out of the moonlight, smiling." And to feel the power of rhyme, the phrase occurs once more: "Then I saw her walking up the road in the headlights." In each case, Kathie is associated with a sudden appearance, a source of light, and a sort of visionary experience for Jeff. However, although Jeff's enchantment is growing, by the third version, an alert spectator might notice the shift from natural to manmade sources of illumination (and generic conventions and reading competence should alert us anyway as to the possible inauthenticity of Kathie's existence).

Music creates symbolic commentary. In *The Killers*, music composed by Miklos Rosza, violins comment on the pathos of the opening scenes in which the Swede waits passively to be killed and explains to Nick Adams (Phil Brown), "Once I did something wrong." In one of the final scenes, as Kitty Collins (Ava Gardner) powders her nose after telling part of her story to the insurance investigator Jim Reardon (Edmond O'Brien), two killers enter the bar to shoot Reardon, but cops expect the trap and fire back. On the soundtrack two musical themes "battle" each other in a very dissonant moment.[54]

As melodrama with a presumption of moral certitude, conflicts may be black and white — literally. Paul Schrader notes, "Because film noir was first of all a style, because it worked out its conflicts visually rather than thematically, because it was aware of its own identity, it was able to create artistic solutions to sociological problems."[55] Whether these films are politically progressive or conservative, both sorts of discourse envision a dichotomous political and social scene. Articulating the conflict in binaries makes ideological and aesthetic sense.

However, the extensive use of voice-over narration in fallen-man film noirs belongs mostly to the realist and modernist aesthetics in which voice-over narration from one of the characters in the film provides access to the interiority of the character who objectively, and usually unemotionally, analyzes his[56] situation.[57] Voice-over narrators may speak in the present and "tell" the entire film, or at some point in the film they may enter to narrate or exit from an extended flashback with the rest of the film finishing without voice-over.[58] Karen Hollinger argues, "In film noir, first-person voice-over narrators, in fact, frequently offer their confessions to patriarchal authority figures within the film text or to the film audience itself who seem to be asked to grant a kind of absolution and to act as a curative force."[59] This is the case in *Double Indemnity*. In any event, when voice-over narration occurs, it is usually from the fallen man who both details (as in a confession) but also analyzes his behavior.[60] In the film noirs that I reviewed, in no case did other characters or the image undermine the voice-over narration of a fallen-man protagonist. The voice-over narrator is often (justifiably) hard on himself. Michael in *The Lady from Shanghai* calls himself stupid; Johnny in *Gilda* says he should have had better instincts.

Two films did have multiple subjective narrators with flashbacks from their points of view. In *Crossfire*, police ask Montgomery what happened, and a flashback provides Montgomery's version of the events. Ironically, his version shows Montgomery belittling his colleagues and speaking derogatorily about Jews. However, since Montgomery is not aware of the "fallen" nature of his bigotry, his narration is fairly accurate as far as it goes; he does not describe the murder he commits. Keeley (Robert Mitchum) also provides an account of the events via a flashback. While the film is not quite yet a *Rashomon* sort of story (that film is released in the U.S. in 1950 and *Crossfire* comes out in 1947), it borders on a sort of variable-subjectivities' proposition.

Another multiple-narrator film is *The Killers*. Likewise, it doesn't breach the variable-versions-of-reality criterion. Rather it is very much like *Citizen Kane* (1941) in that the film begins with the central figure's death, the killing of the Swede; the insurance investigator attempts to solve the mystery of the Swede's death, and flashbacks from multiple people involved in the Swede's life piece together the story of the fallen man.

Conclusion

Whether constructed ex post facto (as the term film noir was) or used at the time (as the label *melodrama* was), the critical function of using categories is to see things perhaps not otherwise visible. In conclusion, then, thinking about film noir as male melodrama with a fallen man formula has three advantages for scholars. One is that this explains the stylistic excesses yet variations among the films "felt" to be part of the cycle. In many cases the narrative formula adopts the older romantic aesthetics of playing out the moral allegory in mise-en-scène, music, and metaphor. In other cases, a realistic and modernist aesthetic controls the film. Thus, distinguishing between plot formulas and historically valid aesthetic options in Hollywood might permit explanations for the sort of diversity that has troubled scholarship on genre and on film noir for decades. And, the melodramatic romantic aesthetic explains the stylistic anomalies that created troubles for film scholars in categorizing the film generically.

Additionally, recognizing that the focus in these films is on men and their agency (not a surprise) might explain Doane's observation that the femme fatale in film noir seems to have an "evacuation of intention."[61] I have not closely considered the films with which Doane is working for the function of the women. However, if her observation is the case, then the representation of the femmes fatales of the 1940s film noirs may be a reversion to early nineteenth-century representational systems of character explanation (they are just born bad), which would be understandable and also worthy of note. Understandable in that the woman is not (and in Hollywood *often* is not) the center of the moral story to be told and is almost always the bearer (not the maker) of meaning. Worthy of note in that the scriptwriters and directors have regressed to much earlier means of representing character motivation for a set of films that clearly are very specific to their current historical circumstances, dealing with war and business in the 1940s and parenting in the 1950s. Is this a nostalgic move providing symptomatic evidence of conservativism or a modernist "detached objectivism"?

Finally, considering film noir as male melodrama foregrounds the politics of gendering genres. Melodrama is linked in film studies' (but not the industrial) imagination with the low feminine. Thrillers, especially film noir, are associated with the high masculine. Failing, even refusing, to see the melodramatic fallen man formula in film noir, indeed in much of Hollywood "drama," is a consequence of cultural hierarchies permeating academic discourse. Messing this up, even returning film noir to its original generic label, is the job of the cultural studies critic, and I am glad to do it.

Acknowledgments

Special thanks for their feedback on earlier drafts of this paper go to Walter Metz, the University of Texas Film Faculty Group (Jim Buhler, Sabine Hake, Tony Hilfer, Joe Kruppa, David Prindle, and Nancy Schiesari), the 2004 Cultural Studies Association of America conference participants, and several classes of graduate students at the University of Texas at Austin.

Notes

1. Christine Gledhill, "The Melodramatic Field: An Investigation." In *Home Is Where the Heart Is: Studies in Melodrama and the Woman's Film*. Ed. Christine Gledhill (London: BFI Publishing, 1987), 16.
2. Ibid., 17.
3. Marcia Landy, "Introduction," In *Imitations of Life: A Reader on Film and Television Melodrama*. Ed. Marcia Landy (Detroit, MI: Wayne State University Press, 1991), 15; see also Steve Neale, "Melodrama and Tears." *Screen* 27.6 (1986): 6.
4. Gledhill, "The Melodramatic Field," 27.
5. Ibid., 34.
6. Michael Hays and Anastasia Nikolopoulou, "Introduction." In *Melodrama: The Cultural Emergence of a Genre*. Ed. Michael Hays and Anastasia Nikolopoulou (New York: St. Martin's Press, 1996), xiii–ix.
7. Lea Jacobs, *The Wages of Sin: Censorship and the Fallen Woman Film, 1928–1942* (Madison: University of Wisconsin Press, 1991), 6–9.
8. Janet Staiger, *Bad Women: Regulating Sexuality in Early American Cinema* (Minneapolis: University of Minnesota Press, 1995), 83–85.
9. Notice here how the femme fatale can be used as a projection for guilt. From the man's point of view, if the woman who seduces him is irresistible, then his lack of control is explained. Thus, the

femme fatale, although apparently threatening, is actually necessarily so to justify to the man his own behavior. She is a handy fantasy.

10. During the era of the Production Code, the insistence on proper endings to these stories is much more intense.

11. Here I agree with Linda Williams that melodrama pervades the classical Hollywood cinema, see "Melodrama Revisited." In *Refiguring American Film Genres: History and Theory*. Ed. Nick Browne (Berkeley: University of California Press, 1998), 42–88. However, I disagree with her position that this observation jeopardizes the arguments in David Bordwell, Janet Staiger, and Kristin Thompson, *The Classical Hollywood Cinema: Film Style and Mode of Production* (London: Routledge & Kegan Paul, 1985). Our point is that Hollywood cinema secures a "classicism" in its production of form and style: its principles "rely on notions of decorum, proportion, formal harmony, respect for tradition, mimesis, self-effacing craftsmanship, and cool control of the perceiver's response" (3–4). These principles of creation may differ from expectations for audience effect, which may well be hopes for outcomes of high emotional response secured by action, thrills, and even melodramatic excess.

12. Gledhill, "Melodramatic Field," 12–13 and 33–36; Steve Neale, "Melo Talk: On the Meaning and Use of the Term 'Melodrama' in the American Trade Press." *The Velvet Light Trap* 32 Fall (1993): 66–89. Also see John Mercer and Martin Shingler, *Melodrama: Genre, Style, Sensibility* (London: Wallflower, 2004), 4–9 and 85–87.

13. Neale, "Melo Talk," 69.

14. Janet Staiger, "Hybrid or Inbred: The Purity Hypothesis and Hollywood Genre History." *Film Criticism* 22.1 Fall (1997): 5–20.

15. Good discussions of the impossibility of deciding what film noir "is"—a genre, a style, a cycle—and what films are or are not in the category are in Frank Krutnik, *In a Lonely Street: Film Noir, Genre, Masculinity* (London: Routledge, 1991), 15–29 and Steve Neale, *Genre and Hollywood* (London: Routledge, 2000), 151–54. I am inclined to agree with Robert G. Porfirio's view that *Citizen Kane* is a major immediate filmic source of film noir; see "No Way Out: Existential Motifs in the *Film Noir*" [1976] rpt. in *Film Noir: A Reader*. Ed. Alain Silver and James Ursini (New York: Limelight Editions, 1996), 78 and 80. However, Paul Kerr's discussion of the industrial contexts, Krutnik's of general sources, and Naremore's on modernism are probably the best broader explanations for the films. See Paul Kerr, "Out of What Past? Notes on the B *film noir*." [1979], rpt. in *Film Noir*, 107; Krutnik, *In a Lonely Street*, 33–72; James Naremore, *More than Night: Film Noir in Its Contexts* (Berkeley: University of California Press, 1998), 40–95.

16. Thinking of film noir as male melodrama will not be all that needs to be said about this cycle of films. However, I believe it can provide an important foundation that explains many features previously noticed and gathers together films felt to be part of the cycle but that do not always fit with other methods of classification. As I shall also note, not all films usually categorized as film noir are male melodramas so I am not providing a solution to the long-standing debate about what is film noir.

17. Krutnik, *In a Lonely Street*, 164. The only other uses of this term that I have found are Henry Jenkins' "'...Never Trust a Snake': WWF Wrestling as Masculine Melodrama." *Out of Bounds: Sports, Media, and the Politics of Identity*. Ed. Aaron Baker and Todd Boyd (Bloomington: Indiana University Press, 1997), 48–78; Dave Kehr, "The New Male Melodrama." *American Film* 8.6 April (1983): 42–47; Deborah Thomas, "Film Noir: How Hollywood Deals with the Deviant Male." *CineAction!* 13/14 Summer (1988): 18–28; Florence Jacobowitz and F. Jacobowitz, "The Man's Melodrama: Woman in the Window and Scarlet Street." *CineAction!* 13/14 Summer (1988): 64–73; and Mercer and Shingler, *Melodrama*, 89 and 98–99. Jenkins' discussion of WWF wrestling indicates that it seems to operate in the older nineteenth-century mode of melodrama: the shows provide no explanations for the characters' actions, and gesture and iconography are key to its representational style. Jenkins is dealing specifically with "masculinity"; I am implying masculinity but also looking broadly at male-centered texts. Kehr assumes melodrama is family or emotion centered. Focusing on *Kramer vs. Kramer* (1979) and several other films in that period, he argues that the male protagonists replace the females of the melodramas of the 1940s and 1950s, feminizing the men as they deal with taking over the nurturing and perpetuation of the family. I would suggest that the story of the threatened family is another formula within the larger melodramatic field. For this later set of films Kehr notices as well the influence of Ingmar Bergman's and other art films in creating what I am calling a modernist style for this "new male melodrama." He remarks that these films evince a "studious objectivity"; "[t]he narration of *Ordinary People* is detached and dispassionate" (46). Certainly overlap between the fallen man and the threatened family formulas may exist, although in some of the most classic fallen-man narratives, the male's error is what threatens the family. That is not the problem for the films Kehr is considering (unless one postulates that the man had not been attending to the family adequately until the crisis is before him). Finally, Mercer and Shingler's excellent synopsis of the critical discus-

sion of melodrama points out that Linda Williams considers 1980s male-centered action films as melodramas.
18. Krutnik, *In a Lonely Street*, 93.
19. Ibid., 128.
20. Ibid., 130.
21. For a good discussion of the argument by Gledhill and extension by Neale, see Mercer and Shingler, *Melodrama*, 79–81.
22. Krutnik, *In a Lonely Street*, 131–132.
23. Neale, *Genre and Hollywood*, 169, 175. This is a revision of his "Melo Talk" essay.
24. Ibid., 184; on this critique see also Gledhill, "Melodramatic Field," and Mercer and Shingler, *Melodrama*.
25. Andreas Huyssen. *After the Great Divide: Modernism, Mass Culture, Postmodernism* (Bloomington: Indiana University Press, 1986).
26. Naremore, *More than Night*, 47.
27. Ibid., 45.
28. Ibid., 89.
29. Richard Dyer, "Coming to Terms: Male Gay Porn." *Jump Cut* 30 (1985): 27–29; Linda Williams, "Film Bodies: Gender, Genre, and Excess." *Film Quarterly* 44.4 Summer (1991): 2–13.
30. Staiger, *Bad Women*, 83.
31. Sarah Kozloff, *Invisible Storytellers: Voice-Over Narration in American Fiction Film* (Berkeley: University of California Press, 1988), 33–35, 40. Also see Dana Polan, *Power & Paranoia: History, Narrative and the American Cinema, 1940–1950* (New York: Columbia University Press, 1986), 45–87.
32. Kahn, "'Double Indemnity,'" *Variety*, April 26 (1944): 12; "The New Pictures," *Time* 44.2 July 10 (1944): 94; John Lardner, "The Current Cinema: Blood and Premiums." *The New Yorker* 20.31 September 16 (1944), 53; Manny Farber, "Hard-as-Nails Dept." *The New Republic* 111.4 July 24 (1944), 103. I want to stress that my concern is not to claim that film noir should be labeled melodrama because the industry uses that term; rather, I want argue that film noir is melodrama within film scholars' current sense of the concept.
33. I agree with Krutnik who, following Parker Tyler, argues that Neff's transgression isn't the money or the woman but "the very desire to transgress"; see *In a Lonely Street*, 139. A "lure" is not the character flaw, which is what is being investigated in a fallen-man plot.
34. Paul Arthur notes that deaths often start noir narratives and that plots are seldom "'whodunits'"; see "Murder's Tongue: Identity, Death, and the City in *Film Noir*." In *Violence and American Cinema*. Ed. J. David Slocum (New York: Routledge, 2001), 161.
35. This past tense also creates a sort of passivity to the male protagonist's character, effectively placing him in the traditional position of the female melodramatic victim's narrative role since he cannot do anything now about his mistakes in the past, reinforcing the pathos and too-lateness of the melodramatic sensibility.
36. See Krutnik, *In a Lonely Street*, 142–47, who is following Claire Johnston. On the general representations of homosexuality or undercurrents of it, see Charles Higham and Joel Greenberg, "Noir Cinema" [1968], rpt. in *Film Noir*, 28–30; Mary Ann Doane, *Femmes Fatales: Feminism, Film Theory, Psychoanalysis* (New York: Routledge, 1991), 99–118; Richard Dyer, *The Matter of Images: Essays on Representation* (New York: Routledge, 1993), 52–72; Naremore, *More than Night*, 98–99; Robert Lang, "Looking for the 'Great Whatzit': *Kiss Me Deadly* and *Film Noir*." *Cinema Journal* 27.3 Spring (1988): 32–44.
37. Naremore, *More than Night*, 91–95. He also argues that noirs are related to the "social melodramas" of the 1930s and "the coalition of liberal and socialist interests" of the 1930s and World War Two (103–107, 123–35).
38. Naremore, *More than Night*, 81–82, 91–95.
39. Scholars note the misogyny of these films. I would argue this is another instance of an articulated preference in Hollywood cinema to exclude women from the narrative world. Carol Flinn argues the same in "Sound, Woman and the Bomb: Dismembering the 'Great Whatsit' in *Kiss Me Deadly*." *Wide Angle* 8.3–4 (1986): 115–27. Also see the essays in *Women in Film Noir*. Ed. E. Ann Kaplan (London: BFI Publishing, 1980). Walter Metz notes that *Casablanca* becomes the intertext for so many recent action-hero films (e-mail to author, 18 July 2005).
40. Raymond Borde and Étienne Chaumeton, "Towards a Definition of *Film Noir*" [1955], rpt. in *Film Noir*, 19. Paul Schrader disagrees: "A film of urban night life is not necessarily a *film noir*, and a *film noir* need not necessarily concern crime and corruption"; see "Notes on *Film Noir*," [1972], rpt. in *Film Noir*, 54.
41. Films may start with the fallen man positioned to fall or with him already fallen. In the latter case, usually the plot structure includes a flashback to the man prior to the fall. Examples of this

latter form with a flashback to pre-fallen state include *Casablanca, Detour, The Killers, Dead Reckoning, Out of the Past,* and *Criss Cross.*

42. However, although he is wrong about her, he is also wrong about ending up dead.

43. The Production Code in 1944 would have prohibited this ending.

44. This woman is not the beautiful and elegant Alice but a floozy, making the choice a bit less compelling.

45. Doane, *Femmes Fatales,* 102.

46. Several films considered film noir do not seem to me to be fallen-men melodramas — specifically from the group reviewed: *Laura* (1944), *The Blue Dahlia* (1946), and *D.O.A.* (1950). *Laura* seems to be a crime investigation with a romance subplot; *The Blue Dahlia* is the same. While I could work to make the detective Mark Pherson (Dana Andrews) or the husband Johnny Morrison (Alan Ladd) into fallen men, neither of them exhibits more than semi-illicit desires: to secure Laura (Gene Tierney) or to hit Helen (Doris Dowling). Neither of them actually acts on his desires. In the case of *D.O.A.,* as Frank Bigelow (Edmond O'Brien) says, all he did was notarize a sale. While he does decide to travel to San Francisco because he is unsure of his commitment to Paula Gibson (Pamela Britton) and he does party with other women, the killer could just have well poisoned him in his hometown. I am not claiming that these films are, therefore, not film noirs. I am only indicating that many film noirs are fallen-men melodramas. Certain parts of the aesthetics of these fallen-men melodramas can appear in other formulas, justifying the inclusion of non–fallen-men plots within the category of film noir.

47. I looked at films commonly discussed in the literature on film noir. I did include two British-produced films: *Brighton Rock* and *The Third Man.* Obviously, some of the specifics related to the Hollywood context do not apply to these movies.

48. Porfirio, "No Way Out," 89.

49. On masochism in these films, see Tony Williams, "*Phantom Lady,* Cornell Woolrich, and the Masochistic Aesthetic" [1988], rpt. in *Film Noir,* 131; Krutnik, *In a Lonely Street,* 102 and 112. Both Williams and Krutnik use the work of Gaylyn Studlar on a masochistic aesthetic, and Krutnik extends it to explain why some protagonists are emasculated and good women appear in the films.

50. Notice as well that in *Written on the Wind* the doctor tells Kyle that his possible sterility is a sort of weakness, producing the clinched fist and face, a rise in the music's volume, and a coincidental encounter with a young boy on a horse — just what the man fears he will not be able to produce. Gesture, music, and iconography are choreographed to express subjectivity. Although *Written on the Wind* is usually grouped in with family melodrama because of the transfer of power between generations, it, too, is probably better considered as fallen-man melodrama.

51. David Bordwell, et al., *Classical Hollywood Cinema,* 75.

52. Kerr, "Out of What Past?" 111; Janey Place and Lowell Peterson, "Some Visual Motifs of *Film Noir*" [1974], rpt in *Film Noir,* 64 and 66.

53. Place and Peterson, "Some Visual Motifs," 68.

54. An excellent analysis of sound aesthetics in *Kiss Me Deadly* is in Flinn, "Sound, Woman and the Bomb."

55. Schrader, "Notes on *Film Noir,*" 63.

56. As fallen-man melodramas, these voice-over narrations are almost always from a male point of view. Flashbacks may come from female characters and, occasionally, these flashbacks are introduced with the woman's voice-over narration. However, this is very rare. In only one case does a female's voice-over control the film's narration. In this instance, *Mildred Pierce* (1945) becomes a fallen-woman melodrama. See the valuable analysis of the film in Pam Cook, "Duplicity in *Mildred Pierce.*" In *Women in Film Noir,* 68–82.

57. Although most people discuss melodrama as a mode that must speak all, Peter Brooks devotes a full chapter to the trope of muteness. He asserts that gestures become signals to abstract concepts but also that theatrical conventions included banners, flags, and conventional symbols to convey these ideas. Importantly, in these films the protagonists cannot speak in the diegesis; voice-overs seem to function as did the banners, etc.; see *The Melodramatic Imagination: Balzac, Henry James, Melodrama, and the Mode of Excess* (New Haven, CT: Yale University Press, 1976), 56–80.

58. Most flashbacks begin with some voice-over narration even if the character has been speaking in the diegesis. Voice-over narration can occur without flashbacks, of course; and vice versa.

59. Karen Hollinger, "*Film Noir,* Voice-Over and the Femme Fatale," [1990 and 1995], rpt. in *Film Noir,* 244. Hollinger continues that in some films what the character says does not match with what is shown to the audience, which "encourage[s] a perception not only of the text's structural contradictions but also of a social failure that lies beneath them" (247). In such cases, the moral discourse is still expressed but perhaps more subtly.

60. This is literally the case in *The Postman Always Rings Twice* (1946) when Frank Chambers

(John Garfield)'s voice-over ends with his prison confession to a priest. Exceptions to this in the films I reviewed were two. In *Laura*, the film shows Waldo Lydecker's (Clifton Webb) narration to be incomplete although nothing he states is a lie; while Lydecker is a criminal, the film is not part of the fallen-man formula (see above). Major Calloway (Trevor Howard) opens *The Third Man* with a voice-over narration but does not continue to comment on the plot as the film continues. Incidentally, Steve in *Criss Cross* provides a voice-over narration, although he dies in the final shot. Eventually, we have a dead voice-over narration in *Sunset Boulevard* (1950).
  61. Doane, *Femmes Fatales*, 2.

5

Beyond the Valley of the Classical Hollywood Cinema

Rethinking the "Loathsome Film" of 1970

HARRY M. BENSHOFF

Performance is one of that new breed of movies that do not try to win you over by wit, seriousness, humor, plot, characterization, logic, dialogue, or any other such outmoded paraphernalia. Instead, the film is built up — if anything so slapped together can be said to be built — from shocks piled on shocks. Not surprises, which are a time-honored device; not titillations, equally established though somewhat less honorable; and not even shocks in the sense of bouts of honest-to-goodness imagination. Rather, the film progresses by what I imagine a series of electroshocks to be like, but a shock treatment administered not by a therapist but by a misprogrammed computer. The genre can only be called the Loathsome Film.
— John Simon (film critic)[1]

The Loathsome Film (an excellent title, and one I hope you will hang on to) is an attempt by some filmmakers to reflect artistically what is happening to the world socially. Almost all the filmmakers who enjoy making them are participating happily in what they believe will rid the silent majority of its complacency and resistance to change. To talk about "morality," whether a film is "immoral" or "amoral," to criticize it by middle-class standards, which by virtue of that standpoint are effete artistically, is to miss the point completely.... Loathsome Films are, from the point of view of their makers, a reflection of joy not hate, a new artistic freedom that the movie business has been lacking and badly needs.
— Michael Sarne (film director)[2]

In August of 1970, in a special review of *Performance* published in *The New York Times*, film and theatre critic John Simon described the film as "Loathsome," a term he had been using for several years to describe films that he felt were "promiscuous and amoral," "indescribably sleazy, self-indulgent, and meretricious," all "mindless intellectual pretension and pathologically reveled-in gratuitous nastiness [signifying] nothing."[3] Among the other films Simon singled out as Loathsome were: *Boom!* (1968), *Secret Ceremony* (1968), *Candy* (1968), *End of the Road* (1970), *Something for Everyone* (1970), *Myra Breckinridge* (1970), and *Beyond the Valley of the Dolls* (1970). Simon's comments on *Performance* started a small controversy within the pages of *The New York Times*, as other film reviewers, filmmakers, and everyday moviegoers contributed to the debate in special response pieces and letters to the editor. The critical controversy Simon started was not an isolated one, either to the pages of *The New York Times* or to the film *Performance*, for heated debate over many of the films Simon had labeled Loathsome had already begun or was beginning to take place. As early as 1965, Pauline Kael was blaming an influx of foreign and independent American films for the "structural disintegration" of the American filmgoing experience.[4] Audience tastes were changing, and the Hollywood industry was struggling — sometimes in quite bizarre ways — to remain au courant.

Loathsome films (and films like them) proliferated in the late 1960s because of the cultural and industrial crises besetting the American film industry. As countercultural audiences — who generally preferred foreign, independent, and avant-garde films to Hollywood fare — continued to grow, studio revenues dwindled. Many Hollywood studios were on the verge of bankruptcy, and several allowed themselves to be bought out by larger corporate entities.[5] New studio leaderships adopted an almost "try anything" approach to winning back their audiences. Younger, foreign, and/or countercultural filmmakers were hired in an attempt to reach younger, foreign, and/or countercultural audiences. Their efforts were abetted by the dissolution of the Hollywood Production Code and the institution of the MPAA Ratings system in 1968, a move that afforded Hollywood filmmakers the chance to exploit greater degrees of nudity, violence, and other assorted "adult topics." As such, many Hollywood films of this era (including the films John Simon considered Loathsome) contain stylistic elements and subject matter "borrowed" from foreign, avant-garde, and/or (s)exploitation cinemas. Many of them are critical of the formal and thematic imperatives of classical Hollywood cinema, and a few of them mount sustained critical attacks on not just the Hollywood film industry, but on the nation as a whole. Arguably, they are among the most radical films that the Hollywood industry has ever produced.

Hollywood may have been undergoing a "nervous breakdown" during these years, but the films it produced and the controversies they created are at the nexus of ongoing political debates about artistic form, content, and industrial control. As the following analysis hopes to demonstrate, Loathsome films created controversy because of their generic hybridity, stylistic experimentation, and queer content. The backlash to them was an attempt by critics, filmmakers, and moviegoers to renegotiate the form, content, and meaning of Hollywood film — to rewrite the "laws of the market" in order to stifle a specific "mode of expression." The weapon in this battle was the concept of "aesthetic taste," but the goal of the war was ultimately the exclusion of certain forms and content from the sphere of Hollywood filmmaking. Speaking of the relationship between taste and social control, Pierre Bourdieu has argued that "art and cultural consumption are predisposed, consciously and deliberately or not, to fulfill a social function of legitimating social differences.... Social subjects, classified by their classifications, distinguish themselves by the distinctions they make, between the beautiful and the ugly, [or between] the distinguished and the vulgar."[6] Films that critics dubbed Loathsome films — ones that in many cases attempted to expand the syntax and meaning of Hollywood filmmaking — became instead the "bad objects" of a critical crusade that sought to purge Hollywood filmmaking of foreign, countercultural, and/or queer influences.

The Films

The eight films briefly introduced below (including *Performance*) are those singled out as Loathsome by John Simon in 1970. In general, Loathsome films were highly publicized and featured major Hollywood stars. However, none were directed by Hollywood studio filmmakers, and most were shot abroad and/or had foreign financing. All but one of them (*Performance*) were adapted from preexisting sources (plays, novels, and the film *Valley of the Dolls* [1967]).

Boom! was a U.S.–British coproduction directed by Joseph Losey. A baroque adaptation of Tennessee Williams's play *The Milk Train Doesn't Stop Here Anymore*, the film was shot on location in Sardinia. It stars Elizabeth Taylor as the richest woman in the world, who, now that she is dying, is visited by a failed poet (played by Richard Burton) who may or may not be the Angel of Death. Noel Coward, playing a character called the Witch of Capri, drops by for dinner and some bitchy bons mots. Liz and Dick discuss mortality while modeling outrageous costumes and headdresses.

Secret Ceremony was another Joseph Losey film made abroad and released by a major Hollywood studio (Universal). It exemplifies Losey's auteurist interest in class relations, role-reversal, and the performativity of identity. In it, a prostitute (Elizabeth Taylor) whose daughter has drowned develops a strange surrogate relationship with a rich girl (Mia Farrow) whose mother has also died. A murky psychological drama, the film dabbles in "psychosis, incest, lesbianism, murder, [and] suicide."[7]

Candy was a U.S.-French-Italian coproduction directed by Christian Marquand, and adapted by Buck Henry from the book by Terry Southern and Mason Hoffenberg (itself loosely based on Voltaire's *Candide*). The film follows a beautiful blond teenaged girl through a series of satirical sexual escapades. Her suitors are played by a variety of leering pop culture icons including Marlon Brando, Richard Burton, Charles Aznavour, John Huston, and Ringo Starr.

End of the Road, based on the novel by John Barthes, was directed by film editor Aram Avakian and released by Allied Artists. A black satire on the insanity of postwar American culture, the film features Stacy Keach as a college professor searching for meaning and identity in the modern world. He survives bizarre psychological treatments administered by Dr. D (James Earl Jones), and begins an affair with Rennie, a colleague's wife (Dorothy Tristan). At the end of the film, a botched abortion kills Rennie, and the doctor and the professor dump her body into a lake.

Beyond the Valley of the Dolls was directed by sexploitation filmmaker Russ Meyer for 20th Century–Fox, who had planned the film as a sequel to the studio's 1967 hit *Valley of the Dolls*. However, with the aid of a script written by film critic Roger Ebert, Meyer turned the film into a satire of the Hollywood melodrama. In it, a three-girl band and their manager travel to Hollywood where they encounter the "oft times nightmarish world" of the entertainment industry, including a psychotic transsexual record producer.

Myra Breckinridge, directed by Michael Sarne and released by 20th Century–Fox, was based on Gore Vidal's controversial novel about a transsexual dynamo who travels to Hollywood to tear down American gender roles. Postoperative Myra is played by Racquel Welch, preoperative Myron is played by film critic Rex Reed, and John Huston and Mae West appear as characters representative of classical Hollywood filmmaking. In the film's most notorious scene, Myra uses a strap-on dildo to sodomize a cowboy actor.

Something for Everyone was shot in Bavaria by stage director Harold Prince. Based on the novel *The Cook* by Harry Kressing, the film stars Michael York as a young opportunist who insinuates himself into an aristocratic family headed by Angela Lansbury. Via murder, mayhem, double crosses, and various seductions of both men and women, York's character is successfully integrated into the family structure.

Performance was a collaboration between cinematographer Nicholas Roeg and portrait artist Donald Cammell. It was shot in England in 1968 and (reluctantly) released by Warner Brothers two years later. In it, James Fox plays a sadistic gangster on the run who hides out in the decaying London mansion of a retired rock star (played by Mick Jagger). Sex, drugs, and rock and roll ensue, and personalities begin to melt and merge. At the end of the film, it is unclear who is left for dead and who survives.

Critical Reception

Loathsome films were seen by many mainstream critics (besides John Simon) as the harbingers of a moral and aesthetic breakdown in American cinema. Most of them did not merely receive negative or dismissive reviews — they were seen as part of a concerted disturbing trend and thus attacked with vicious fervor. For example, in his review of *Performance*, Arthur Knight in *Saturday Review* commented that the contemporary movie "screen seems afflicted with a kind of cinematic halitosis."[8] Renata Adler in *The New York Times* described *Secret Ceremony* as part of a trend towards a "colored genre of sick, ritual films."[9] Especially egregious to most critics were *Beyond the Valley of the Dolls* and *Myra Breckinridge*, two X-rated films released by 20th Century–Fox in June of 1970. *Variety* called *Beyond the Valley of the Dolls* the "most derisible, most hootable film made by a major studio in years ... as funny as a burning orphanage."[10] *Time* magazine opined that *Myra Breckinridge* was "contemptible," "grotesque in the extreme," "about as funny as a child molester," and "so tasteless that it represents some sort of nadir in American cinema."[11] *Newsweek* called it a "lavishly tasteless masturbation fantasy,"[12] and even Andy Warhol's *Interview* called it a "murky piece of horse dung."[13] Charles Champlin in *The Los Angeles Times* declared that 20th Century–Fox had "fouled its own nest" and suggested that studio moguls Darryl and Richard Zanuck, "man and boy, ought to have their studio washed out with soap."[14] Even (supposedly objective) medical professionals got involved in the fray: a review of *Myra Breckinridge* in *Medical Aspects of Human Sexuality* called it "unspeakably vulgar" and "repulsive."[15]

Just two months after Fox released *Myra Breckinridge* and *Beyond the Valley of the Dolls*, Warner Brothers released *Performance*, which was again savaged by most mainstream critics. Richard Schickel in *Life* proclaimed it "the most disgusting, the most completely worthless film I have seen since I began reviewing."[16] *Newsweek* placed it "among the ugliest, most contrived, and most self-indulgent films of the year,"[17] while the *Saturday Review* said it was "perversion exploited for its own sake ... the nadir of tastelessness."[18] Charles Champlin called it "pretentious and repellent,"[19] and even the reviewer for the gay newspaper *The Advocate* called it "an example of degrading putrescence."[20] However, *Performance* was not universally derided upon its initial release, and a few critics dared to champion it. Comparing it favorably to *Petulia* (1968) and *Muriel* (1963), *The Hollywood Reporter* said that *Performance* was "as great and disturbingly mature a work of art that we're likely to witness in 1970: the most compelling, mesmerizing visual experience of the year."[21] It was also warmly received in Great Britain.[22] Of all the Loathsome films, *Performance* has been the one most critically "rehabilitated" over the years, a fact perhaps best attested to by its recent inclusion in the BFI Film Classics series of monographs.

Similarly, several other Loathsome films received widely divergent reviews. While *The Hollywood Herald Examiner* found *End of the Road* to be "appalling ... one of the most repellent films I can remember,"[23] *The Wall Street Journal* called it "wildly funny and profoundly sad.... [it ranks] among the most impressive and most important American films."[24] Other Loathsome films inspired far less vitriol. *Boom!* and *Secret Ceremony* were generally dismissed as pretentious art films by an expatriate director, while *Candy* was judged by most to be a bland sex comedy. Of all the films, *Something for Everyone* received the most positive reviews from mainstream critics (excepting Simon). Even the usually quite conservative *Hollywood Citizen News* called it "one of the best films of the past few years."[25] This is possibly due to the fact that — despite its subject matter — *Something for Everyone* is the one Loathsome film that most clearly adheres to classical Hollywood style, creating a unified diegetic space via continuity editing, plausible characterization, and cause-and-effect storytelling. Other Loathsome films were far more experimental in style, and only succeeded in alienating mainstream critics.

Form and Content, Genre and Tone

Loathsome films *were* scandalous to many critics of their era because of their content. Many of them feature nudity and fairly frank (for their era) representations of sexuality. *Candy* is a slick heterosexual sex comedy, and *End of the Road* features a gruesome abortion scene. *Something for Everyone, Beyond the Valley of the Dolls, Myra Breckinridge,* and *Performance* all feature gay, bisexual, and/or transgendered characters. Homosexuality was an increasingly public issue in 1970, one year after the Stonewall Riots and their subsequent media coverage. Hollywood had been tentatively exploiting the topic ever since the 1961 Production Code Amendment, but after the Code fell, queer characters seemed to be everywhere, giving fright to Hollywood homophobes. Even *Boom!*, a film without explicit sexual acts, was understood by many critics as homosexual, and several made snide comments (using the era's euphemisms for homosexuals) about author Tennessee Williams's "gothic menagerie of the decadent, the deformed, and the diseased."[26]

Yet, the answer to why Loathsome films were singled out for a moral crusade over other films of the era (even those with explicit queer content such as *Boys in the Band* [1970] or *The Christine Jorgensen Story* [1970]) has as much to do with their style as it did their subject matter. Many Loathsome films set out to subvert the formal (as well as thematic) imperatives of classical Hollywood filmmaking. They foreground and critique aspects of classical Hollywood form such as film genre, the star system, linear narrative, and continuity editing. As such, critics weaned on classical Hollywood style were confounded by what they saw, and decried the films' "ambiguous symbolism" and "flashy technique" as much as (if not more than) their content.[27] As Bourdieu notes, "A work of art has meaning and interest only for someone who possesses the cultural competence, that is, the code into which it is encoded.... A beholder who lacks the specific code feels lost in a chaos of sounds and rhythms, colours and lines, without rhyme or reason."[28] As such, critics could only see the films' attempts at formal experimentation as "artistic disorientation and commercial diarrhea."[29] As another critic put it about *End of the Road*, "It's supposed to be unsophisticated to expect that a movie will show some concern for the characters, action, and theme of the novel it is based upon [but] everything is dumped into a whirlpool of photographic tricks."[30]

Specifically, many Loathsome films employ dialectical montage rather than continuity editing to make their points. Both *End of the Road* and *Myra Breckinridge* make extensive use of extradiegetic film clips in counterpoint to the stories they tell. In the case of *Myra Breckinridge*, the film is punctuated with clips from classical Hollywood films, setting up a dialectical confrontation between Hollywood as it imagined itself in its heyday and an antithetical critical position embodied by Myra herself. This device fractures the diegetic unity of traditional Hollywood narrative and creates a meta-level of spectatorial involvement that comments ironically upon the action. For example, in the film's infamous dildo rape scene, Myra/Myron is figured as both filmic actor and cinematic spectator, simultaneously part of the diegesis but also figured as an observing critic. Traditional Hollywood genres (including the horror film, musical, and western) are invoked in order to suggest how they might be rewritten or reunderstood in light of Myra's sexual terrorism and her oft-stated goal: "the destruction of the American male in all its particulars." As the sequence plays out, classical Hollywood icons are reimagined in new contexts, and the sexual euphemisms of classical style (the knight's lance, the battering ram, the dam bursting) are all made explicit through the cross cutting. *Time* magazine was especially horrified that "in the context of *Myra*, Laurel and Hardy are made to look like fags."[31] Indeed, the juxtaposition of Laurel and Hardy clips within the uber-queer space of the dildo rape scene allows the spectator to recognize the latent homosexual core of the famous comedic buddies, in effect de-repressing decades of queer invisibility.

Another thing that confused and angered critics about these films was their generic instability. Reviewers were often perplexed about the exact type of film they were reviewing, and thus what their "proper" response to it should be. *Performance*, for example, combines elements of the gangster film, the musical, the drug film, and the European art film. *Something for Everyone* was variously described as "a sort of black horror-comedy,"[32] a "black comedy fairy-tale drama for adults,"[33] and a combination of *The Sound of Music* (1965) and *The Damned* (1969).[34] *The Los Angeles Herald Examiner* dubbed *Beyond the Valley of the Dolls* a "musical horror sex comedy," and *Secret Ceremony* was received by many critics as an art-house horror film. This mixture of high and low genres was an affront to many critics, who decried the mixture of sexploitation scenes and high art pretension within the commercial cinema. *End of the Road* was condemned as a "peculiar combination of chichi, opportunistic avant-gardism and calculating commercialism [that] makes it far more offensive than the crassest products from either Hollywood studios or the underground."[35] As Bourdieu has again noted, "The most intolerable thing for those who regard themselves as the possessors of legitimate culture is the sacrilegious reuniting of tastes which taste dictates shall be separated."[36] In other words, while there may be separate cultural spaces for avant-garde, sexploitation, and Hollywood film practices, they should definitely not exist in the same movie. Summing up many critical evaluations of such hybridizations, *Newsweek* simply said of *Myra Breckinridge* that "the mixture of styles is poison."[37] Similarly, *Something for Everyone* was described as "an innocent seeming piece of Bavarian chocolate that has been vitriolized by hypodermic injection."[38]

As part of their generic hybridity, most of the Loathsome films also feature an unstable tone of address and extreme fluctuations in mood — they tend to veer from comedy to horror, and from atrocity to absurdity. For example, in *Beyond the Valley of the Dolls*, a sex and drug orgy segues into a proto-slasher movie wherein secret transsexual "Superwoman" brutally beheads "Jungle Boy" as the 20th Century–Fox logo theme music plays on the soundtrack. Some reviewers did decode *Beyond the Valley of the Dolls* as it was intended — as a satire of Hollywood's melodramatic clichés — but many others were confused over whether it was meant to be taken seriously or not. One critic seemed to get the joke and called it "the best awful movie I've ever seen," but still objected to the film's horror-violence, which was judged to be overdone in conjunction with the film's satire.[39] Even the reviewer for *The Advocate* had trouble knowing if the film was meant to be a "put-on" or not, demonstrating the fact that younger, countercultural, and/or queer critics could also miss the point of these films: "For the first 90 minutes it is unclear whether you are watching a bad movie or if it is intentionally bad."[40] Mistaking send-up for sincerity, the reviewer went on to chastise screenwriter Roger Ebert for "ideas of homosexuality [that] appear to have been formed when he viewed *Tea and Sympathy* [1955]."[41]

Similarly, some reviews of *Candy* objected to the film's violence in conjunction with its humor, while others were unsure if the film was meant to be a sex film or a *parody* of a sex film. Some suspected that the film's parodic elements were merely the "alibi" for releasing an outright sex film, noting that "spoofing sex is a way to make a sex show and get away with it."[42] Still others saw *Candy* as a moral parable. According to a story in *The Hollywood Reporter*, one daring minister from New Mexico was using the film as a teaching tool, comparing teenage nymphet Candy to Jesus Christ in his Sunday sermons.[43] Conversely, in small-town Mississippi, a print of *Candy* was seized and theatre personnel were arrested on obscenity charges.[44]

Yet, the form and content of the Loathsome film were not condemned by everyone. Occasionally, a critic would praise a Loathsome film precisely because of its audacious hybridity. The *Boston After Dark* critic said that *Something for Everyone*, "with its combination of innocence and immorality, is a delightfully perverse film. There will not be another film like it for some time to come."[45] Others noted that generic and formal hybridization could and did produce interesting work. In the initial positive review of *Performance* that ran in *The New York Times* (to which John Simon's piece was a rebuttal), Peter Schjeldahl praised the generic hybridity and collaborative efforts of filmmakers Donald Cammell and Nicholas Roeg, arguing that the very act of collaboration could and did produce a new and very interesting type of film.[46]

Thus, battle lines were drawn between younger critics and countercultural filmgoers who appreciated the way Loathsome films expanded notions of film art, and older, more establishment-oriented critics who did not. As *Variety* commented about *End of the Road*, "Its audience potential seems limited to the weirdo trade.... [the film is] a muddled 'now' anti–Americana which will find its greatest audience enthusiasm in the pseudo-intellectual and other offbeat circles."⁴⁷ Similarly, *Newsweek* called *End of the Road* an example of the "provocative confrontation film that is so popular now, particularly among young moviegoers."⁴⁸

Loathsome films were increasingly described by their enthusiasts not as mere films but as "trips" or "experiences" that could be best appreciated while under the influence of drugs.⁴⁹ *Boston After Dark* compared *End of the Road* to LSD films like *Yellow Submarine* (1968), *2001: A Space Odyssey* (1968), *Fellini Satyricon* (1969), and the re-release of *Fantasia* (1940), seeing them all as "part of a new (at least in popular terms) and developing aesthetic — art — especially film art, as experience."⁵⁰ Paul Krassner in *Cavalier* put it quite bluntly when he exhorted his readers to "get stoned with some friends you love and go see *End of the Road*."⁵¹ The advertising copy for *End of the Road* also exploited the film's "heady" quality, promising audiences that the film would be "a trip without drugs."⁵² And while "head trip" might have been a positive review to younger, hipper critics, the same concept was used in negative terms by old-school critics such as Charles Champlin, who warned his readers that *Performance* was "a tale I think only the stoned can see unless forewarned."⁵³

Camp

In addition to their generic and tonal instability, most Loathsome films are also camp. The era's broadening mainstream — as opposed to subcultural — awareness of the "camp sensibility" was tied to the publication in 1964 of Susan Sontag's "Notes on Camp."⁵⁴ In that essay she described how camp — initially a reception strategy used by urban gay men to negotiate heterocentrist cultural artifacts — was becoming a more mainstream pop phenomenon. Sontag's essay differentiated between naïve camp (the camp of "failed seriousness" created when spectators mock what was intended to be taken seriously) and deliberate camp (a comedic campiness intentionally encoded into a text by its creators). By the late 1960s, countercultural audiences of all sexualities were snickering at the clichés and banalities of Hollywood's usual fare. Thus, when *Valley of the Dolls* was received by audiences as an exquisite piece of naïve camp, filmmakers began to produce deliberately campy films such as *Candy*, *Myra Breckinridge*, and *Beyond the Valley of the Dolls*. Unlike films that might be called naïve camp, films that are deliberately campy are self-consciously aware of their "bad" acting, "cheesy" dialogue, and over-the-top plotting. Thus, in *Beyond the Valley of the Dolls*, when wheelchair-bound Harris miraculously regains his ability to use his legs at a climactic moment, audiences are expected to laugh at the Hollywood cliché being quoted. *Beyond the Valley of the Dolls* also makes use of "soap opera organ" music during some of its more outlandish scenes, another clue to its deliberate over-the-top campiness.

Yet, while many critics of Loathsome films invoked the concept of camp in their reviews, there was little critical consensus as to exactly what the term meant. A few even acted as if they didn't know what camp was: for example, *The Hollywood Citizen News* reviewer feigned confusion when "the 20th Century–Fox publicity department told [him] the film [*Beyond the Valley of the Dolls*] is high camp"; missing the point entirely, he then preceded to chastise the film for its bad acting and dialogue.[55] For most reviewers, however, the term *camp* was invoked as a way of describing something frivolous, apolitical, and ultimately meaningless. For critics like John Simon, dedicated to the high moral seriousness of film art, the flippancy of camp was enough to categorize any such films as debased. For example, almost all the reviews of *Boom!* referred to it as camp because of its hammy actors loudly declaiming bad dialogue amid baroque settings: "Movie Star vaudeville team [of Elizabeth Taylor and Richard Burton] has become one of the greatest camps of our time."[56] *Time* magazine opined that Liz and Dick "display the self-indulgent fecklessness of a couple of rich amateurs hamming it up at the country-club frolic, and with approximately the same results."[57] Yet, it is part of *Boom!*'s ambiguous tone that one is never quite sure if its campiness is deliberate or naïve. Some critics noted that while Burton and Taylor appeared to being playing their roles "straight" (and thus producing a naïve camp effect), "Mr. Coward, who knows a disaster when he sees one, gives a brilliant display of self-parody, as if he were telling the audience 'My dears, I *know* how ridiculous all this is, but the joke is on you — you *paid* to see it!'"[58]

If *Boom!* represents the frivolity and stylistic excess of much pop camp, then other Loathsome films (especially *Myra Breckinridge* and *Beyond the Valley of the Dolls*) exemplify a more critical queer camp, i.e., camp intended to critique dominant notions of gender, sexuality, and in many cases, film form itself. In his introduction to *The Politics and Poetics of Camp*, Moe Meyer argues that queer camp always contains a deconstructive charge, whereas pop camp — the mainstream commodification and incorporation of queer camp — tends to elide or downplay such a critical project.[59] For example, the Loathsome sex comedy *Candy* might best be understood as pop camp — it derives its effects from self-aware generic parody and over-the-top acting without significantly challenging the premises of hetero/sexist culture or film form. Comparatively, *Myra Breckinridge* and *Beyond the Valley of the Dolls* might best be considered examples of deliberate queer camp — they intentionally set out to call into question Hollywood film form and its complicity in creating social stereotypes about gender and sexuality. Yet, the relationship between pop camp and queer camp is never quite severed: as Meyer argues, even pop camp artifacts maintain a trace or residue of queer camp's deconstructive charge, forcing "the bourgeois subject of Pop camp [to] assume a queer position in order to account for these dispossessed objects.... Pop camp becomes the unwitting vehicle of a subversive operation that introduces queer signifying codes into dominant discourse."[60]

Not surprisingly, few reviewers praised these films on those grounds, although a rare few did allow that camp and social commentary could coexist. *Boston After Dark* commented that "*Something for Everyone* is an odd movie, at times pointed towards suspense, at times balanced on the edge of camp, at times almost pushing towards social comment.[61] *Boom!* was praised within the pages of the closety gay British film journal *Films and Filming* (it is "the second best thing [Liz] has done in her whole career ... the movie remains a brilliant occasion"[62]) and in more recent years it has become (along with many of the other Loathsome films) a camp classic celebrated within queer subcultures. *Films and Filming* also opined that "*Myra Breckinridge* is everything it sets out to be, a kind of Pop-Art movie, bizarre and extravagant: a cartoon-strip of allegorical grotesques, brashly exhibited in a wild, camp, uninhibited and outrageously funny romp which, under Sarne's direction has evolved into a brilliant and irreverently vicious attack on an America crumbling under the hypocrisy of its social and moral values."[63] Indeed, beneath the contempt and vitriol Simon and his ilk heaped upon the Loathsome film was a larger issue, one that pitted old straight Hollywood's traditional form and content against a younger, queerer, countercultural aesthetic. Not only was the legitimacy of the films at stake, but also that of their filmmakers and audiences.

The Battle for "Morality"

Although they did not have the vocabulary to name it as such, the subversive charge of deliberate queer camp was noted by some critics of the Loathsome film, many of whom did make a link between the films' campiness and homosexual "taste." Invoking the homophobic euphemisms of his day, Charles

Champlin's diatribe against *Beyond the Valley of the Dolls* called it "a treat for the emotionally retarded, sexually inadequate and dimwitted. It is a grievously sick mélange ... a totally degenerate enterprise which tries to ameliorate its rottenness by pretending to be camp."[64] In an op-ed piece he wrote for the *Sunday Calendar* a few days later, Champlin's homophobic agenda is more clearly stated: both *Myra Breckinridge* and *Beyond the Valley of the Dolls* "make a major studio ... and by extension the industry as a whole — look as corrupted and venal as the filmmakers and exhibitors who cater to the sad, select clienteles for stag and gay films."[65] Similarly, in his press release denouncing Jack Valenti and his new MPAA Ratings System, former 20th Century–Fox executive Paul Monash lambasted the X rating, which he felt was "a total disservice to the entire film industry. Hollywood used to cater to the tastes of the country: now it is pandering to the sick fantasies of the perverted."[66]

These comments are reflective of the "pink mafia" conspiracy theory, the paranoid belief that homosexuals in the entertainment industry were (or still are) attempting to destroy American morals by promoting both overt and covert pro-homosexual themes. Simon himself forthrightly invoked the homosexual conspiracy theme in his review of *Something for Everyone*, seeing it as "a prime example of disguised homosexuality at its distorting worst." He continued: "What is objectionable is the covert slanting of the film toward making heterosexual relations unappetizing, and toward turning moral values upside down.... I submit that the entire film exemplifies a kind of vengeance on the heterosexual world ... anything that the so-called normal world considers healthy and decent — and some if it, so help us, *is* healthy and decent — is systematically trodden underheel."[67] Similarly, a reviewer for *The Motion Picture Exhibitor* noted, "The many scabrous subjects that have been loaded into *Performance*, including sadism, lesbianism, and transvestitism, represent something of a victory over morality."[68]

Even when the homosexual bogeyman was not so directly invoked, many reviews of Loathsome films made use of apocalyptic verbiage. Charles Champlin bemoaned the cultural ramifications of "scandalous" public art like *Beyond the Valley of the Dolls*: "What the existence and nature of this movie says about the present and the future of this society is in fact appalling to contemplate.... Its message is simply that nothing in the world has meaning, value, worth or dignity.... No success is worth the damage inflicted on the human spirit by this garbage."[69] When plans to film *Myra Breckinridge* were announced in 1968, one critic rhetorically asked of 20th Century–Fox: "What motivates you in attempting to transfer this sickening sick, obnoxious and viciously obscene book to the screen?"[70] That same columnist was also outraged that *Candy* was a Christmas release.[71] Then, during the post-production musical scoring of *Myra Breckinridge*, the second bassoonist walked out, claiming, "I want no part in this picture. I'm a church going American and I'll not contribute to the demoralization of the country."[72] *Secret Ceremony* was also attacked on moral grounds: "There is no one normal or wholesome in the story"[73] bemoaned the *Film TV Daily*, while *Newsweek* was disturbed that the film's "moral implications are quite fuzzy."[74]

However, many Loathsome filmmakers were just as concerned with "morality" as were their films' critics. Although they employed various modes of stylistic excess (including dialectical montage, generic hybridity, and camp), Loathsome films remained firmly engaged with the era's countercultural politics, questioning the morality of postwar America's institutionalized racism, (hetero)sexism, and class warfare. Occasionally, a sympathetic critique would acknowledge that fact: "*End of the Road* is a shocking, abrasive motion picture that penetrates the malaise of a sick era, individually prescribed, but nationally indicated."[75] Another called *End of the Road* "a radical, anarchist critique of society"[76] and yet another "a two hour paroxysm ... against the pervasive violence in America."[77] Indeed, its empty bourgeois characters and madhouse setting serve as apt metaphors for postwar American culture, and the film's dialectical inserts of great American achievements constantly speak a bitter irony. Anticipating that the film would become a symbolic battleground, female lead Dorothy Tristan noted in a pre-release interview that "A lot of people will hate the film. They'll think it's a desecration of the American flag — and it's just the opposite. It's a cry to the American people — a cry in the dark."[78] Fulfilling her worst expectations, the critic from the *Motion Picture Herald* said the film's "satirical stabs at the Establishment and the American Way of Life" were just as "repellent and nauseating [as] any sadistic display yet put on the commercial screen."[79]

Ultimately, most of the Loathsome films were committed to invoking social change, as well as a change in classical Hollywood aesthetics. *Life* magazine noted that "*End of the Road* will add impetus to the already lively youth rebellion. And, if members of an older generation should happen to attend a screening of the film, it just might end their apathy."[80] Similarly, as Michael Sarne, director of *Myra Breckinridge* put it in his rebuttal to John Simon's review of *Performance*, "Whether the establishment likes it or not, there is a revolution going on in the cinema, music, poetry, and in the minds of young people.... Loathsome Films will increase in the way that social revolution is growing more violent and radical."[81] Loathsome films were situated on the cutting edge of the 1960s counterculture, a remarkable political position for films made within and/or released through the major Hollywood studios.

Conclusion

"Taste classifies the classifier," as Bourdieu has said, and thus when John Simon wrote, "You do not have to be a drug addict, pederast, sado-masochist or nitwit to enjoy *Performance*, but being one or more of those things would help,"[82] he was indirectly telling his readers that he was none of those things. More directly, he was also implying that if one actually liked the film, the chances are you *were* a hippie, a homosexual, a pervert, a criminal, or just a plain old idiot. Under the guise of film criticism, John Simon and "cultural hygienists" like him were policing the line not only of permissible film practice, but also permissible social existence.[83] The labeling of these films as Loathsome blurred into the process of labeling their creators and supporters as being themselves Loathsome — or at least un–American — and thus less worthy than their establishment counterparts. As part of the larger mainstream backlash to countercultural ideals, the campaign to smear Loathsome films was mostly successful. Stylistic experimentation and queer (or even leftist) content ebbed from Hollywood filmmaking throughout the 1970s, and films critical of American genres and/or institutions were replaced by nostalgic Hollywood blockbusters such as *Jaws* (1975), *Rocky* (1976), and *Star Wars* (1977) — films that reinscribed classical Hollywood form and content for a new generation of moviegoers.

Still, the creation and reception of Loathsome films are more than just an interesting anecdote in film history. They dealt with "themes — aesthetic, political, philosophical and sexual — which still dominate our intellectual and emotional lives."[84] Is it nostalgic or appalling to know that, following protests by Christian activists, a screening of *Beyond the Valley of the Dolls* was canceled by the AMC Theatre chain as recently as 1997?[85] In many cases, Loathsome films embodied techniques, ideas, and concepts that in recent years have been theorized under postmodern, postcolonial, feminist, and queer rubrics, while their activist stance and stylistic hybridity look ahead to the films of New Queer Cinema. Occasionally, a critic of the Loathsome film hinted at some of those ideas. "Lurking somewhere deep in the muddled and mind-boggling display of optical tricks and garish color effects [of *Performance*] is perhaps some kind of theme about the search for identity and the 'thin line' that separates masculinity from femininity.... The corollary would seem to be that unisex is a good thing."[86] Concurring, *The Motion Picture Exhibitor* said that *Performance* "attests that all opposites (opposite sex genders, opposite time periods, and opposite social roles) are all ultimately reversible."[87] More recent critics, having Judith Butler and other feminist and queer theorists to draw upon,[88] have argued that "the whole emphasis of the film is to banish representation in favor of performance, a performance in which the spectator is a key actor."[89] Indeed, most of the Loathsome films might in some way be seen as being about the performative roles — racialized, sexualized, classed — that each of us has been conditioned to play. Via campy posturing that ruptures and questions Hollywood form (as in *Boom!, Candy,* and *Beyond the Valley of the Dolls*) and/or more explicit narrative thematics (as in *Myra Breckinridge, Secret Ceremony, End of the Road* and *Performance*), Loathsome films raise questions about the role dominant Western cultural institutions (and especially Hollywood cinema) continue to play in the legitimization of personal and social identity.

Notes

1. John Simon, "The Most Loathsome Film of All?" *The New York Times* August 23 (1970), Section 2, 1D, 5D. Reprinted in John Simon, *Movies into Film* (New York: Dial Press, 1971), 363–367. Future references to this essay will be given as page numbers from the book.
2. Michael Sarne, letter, "Movie Mailbag: Who's Right about *Performance?*" *The New York Times* September 20 (1970): 14.
3. Simon, "The Most Loathsome Film of All?" 364–367.
4. Pauline Kael, "Zeitgeist and Poltergeist, or Are the Movies Going to Pieces." In *I Lost It at the Movies* (Boston and Toronto: Little, Brown, 1965), 14.
5. For an overview of these issues, see Jon Lewis, *Hollywood v. Hard Core: How the Struggle Over Censorship Saved the Motion Picture Film Industry* (New York: New York University Press, 2000), 135–229.
6. Pierre Bourdieu, *Distinction: A Social Critique of the Judgement of Taste.* Translated by Richard Nice (Cambridge, MA: Harvard University Press, 1984), 6–7.
7. Richard Gertner, "[Rev. of] *Secret Ceremony.*" *Motion Picture Herald* October 23 (1968). Page number missing. Copies of this and all film reviews quoted below are on file at the Margaret Herrick Library at the Academy of Motion Picture Arts and Sciences, Los Angeles.
8. Arthur Knight, "*SR* Goes to the Movies." *Saturday Review* August 22 (1970).
9. Renata Adler, "[Rev. of] *Secret Ceremony.*" *The New York Times* October 24 (1968), 55:1.
10. Murf., "[Rev. of] *Beyond the Valley of the Dolls.*" *Variety* June 18 (1970).
11. Unsigned, "[Rev. of *Myra Breckinridge*] Some Sort of Nadir." *Time* July 6 (1970).
12. Paul D. Zimmerman, "X-Rated Mind." *Newsweek* July 6 (1970).
13. Robert Weiner, "Seeing Double." *inter/VIEW* 1.9 (1969) [sic].
14. Charles Champlin, "Sexploiteer Hitchhikes on *Dolls*' Title." *The Los Angeles Times* June 18 (1970).
15. Rev. of *Myra Breckinridge, Medical Aspects of Human Sexuality* 4.8 August (1970): 49.
16. Richard Schickel, "*Life* Movie Review: A Completely Worthless Film." *Life* October 2 (1970).
17. Paul D. Zimmerman, "Under the Rock [Rev. of *Performance*]" *Newsweek* August 17 (1970).
18. Knight, "*SR* Goes to the Movies."
19. Charles Champlin, "Mick Jagger Stars in *Performance.*" *The Los Angeles Times* August 5 (1970).
20. Allan Leopold, "*Performance*? What Is It?" *The Advocate* Aug–Sept (1970): 14.
21. Larry Cohen, "*Performance*: Brilliant Disturbing Work of Art." *The Hollywood Reporter* August 3 (1970).
22. Colin MacCabe, *Performance* (London: BFI Publishing, 1998), 64.
23. Winfred Blevins, "Tristan Strength of *End of Road.*" *Hollywood Herald Examiner* April 18 (1970).
24. John J. O'Connor, "Antonioni and Avakian Surprise." *The Wall Street Journal* February 12 (1970).
25. Leo Guild, "*Something for Everyone*: Excellent Black Comedy." *Hollywood Citizen News* August 20 (1970).
26. Paul D. Zimmerman, "Under the Rock [*Rev. of Boom!*]" *Newsweek* June 3 (1968).

27. Richard Gertner, "*End of the Road,* Rated X!" *Motion Picture Herald* February 18 (1970).
28. Bourdieu, *Distinction,* 2.
29. Robert Colaciello, Rev. of *Performance, inter/VIEW* 1.9 (1969) [sic], 20.
30. Blevins, "Tristan Strength of *End of Road.*"
31. Unsigned, "[Rev. of *Myra Breckinridge*] Some Sort of Nadir."
32. Murf., "[Rev. of] *Something for Everyone,*" *Variety* July 22 (1970).
33. Unsigned, "[Rev. of] *Something for Everyone.*" *Boxoffice* August 3 (1970).
34. Richard Cuskelly, "*Something for Everyone:* Stunningly Innovative." *Los Angeles Herald Examiner* August 19 (1970).
35. Unsigned, [Rev. of] *End of the Road.*" *Time* February 23 (1970).
36. Bourdieu, *Distinction,* 56–57.
37. Paul D. Zimmerman, "X-Rated Mind." *Newsweek* July 6 (1970).
38. Greg, "[Rev. of] *Something for Everyone.*" *Motion Picture Exhibitor* August 5 (1970).
39. Richard Cuskelly, "Beyond the Valley — A Funny Parody." *Los Angeles Herald Examiner* June 18 (1970).
40. Harold Fairbanks, "Beyond *Dolls*— How to Make Worse Out of Bad." *Los Angeles Advocate* July 8–21 (1970): 13.
41. Ibid., 15.
42. Rev. of *Candy, Saturday Review,* January 11 (1969).
43. Chuck Mittlestadt, "Albuquerque Reverend Plugs *Candy, Graduate, Attic.*" *The Hollywood Reporter* February 12 (1969).
44. "High Court Gets Theatre Appeal on Obscenity," *The Hollywood Reporter* April 30 (1970).
45. Deac Bossell, "Prince Makes New Debut." *Boston After Dark* August 25 (1970).
46. Peter Schjeldahl, "One Emerges a Little Scorched, But..." *The New York Times* August 16 (1970).
47. Spil., "[Rev. of] *End of the Road.*" *Variety* January 28 (1970).
48. "The Independent" [Rev. of *End of the Road*], *Newsweek* March 16 (1970): 100.
49. For an overview of the era's LSD films, see Harry M. Benshoff, "The Short-Lived Life of the Hollywood LSD Film." *Velvet Light Trap* 47 Spring (2001): 29–44.
50. Larry Peitzman, [Rev. of *End of the Road*], *Boston After Dark* April 29 (1970).
51. Quoted in Peitzman.
52. Referenced in Richard Gertner, "[Rev. of] *End of the Road.*" *Motion Picture Herald* February 18 (1970).
53. Charles Champlin, "Mick Jagger Stars in *Performance.*"
54. Susan Sontag, "Notes on Camp." *A Susan Sontag Reader* (New York: Vintage Books, 1983 [1964]), 105–119.
55. Leo Guild, "*Dolls* Costly, Tedious Bore." *Hollywood Citizen News* June 18 (1970).
56. Stanley Kauffmann, "Stanley Kauffmann on Films: Booms and Busts." *New Republic* June 8 (1968).
57. Unsigned, "Cinema: New Movies: *Boom!*" *Time* May 31 (1968).
58. Unsigned, "[Rev. of]*Boom!*" *Glamour* September (1968).
59. Moe Meyer, "Introduction: Reclaiming the Discourse of Camp." *The Politics and Poetics of Camp.* Ed. Moe Meyer (London and New York: Routledge, 1994), 1–22.
60. Ibid., 13.
61. Bossell, "Prince Makes New Debut."
62. Gordon Gow, "[Rev. of] *Boom!*" *Films and Filming* March (1969).
63. Michael Armstrong, "[Rev. of] *Myra Breckinridge.*" *Films and Filming* April (1971).
64. Charles Champlin, "Sexploiteer Hitchhikes on *Dolls'* Title." *The Los Angeles Times* June 18 (1970).
65. Charles Champlin, "Breakthrough or Breakdown in Film Standards?" *Los Angeles Times,* Calendar Section, July 5 (1970): 1, 22–23.
66. Mary Murphy, "Valenti Blasted for Condoning *Myra.*" *The Los Angeles Times* June 26 (1970).
67. John Simon, "[Rev. of] *Something for Everyone.*" *Movies into Film,* 160–162.
68. Greg, "[Rev, of] *Performance.*" *Motion Picture Exhibitor* August 19 (1970).
69. Charles Champlin, "Sexploiteer Hitchhikes on *Dolls'* Title." *The Los Angeles Times* June 18 (1970).
70. Abe Greenberg, "Voice of Hollywood." *Hollywood Citizen News* November 6 (1968). *Myra Breckinridge* had been a hot topic in gossip columns ever since it became a bestselling novel in 1968. According to some sources, Vanessa Redgrave, Jeanne Moreau, Carol Channing, Barbra Streisand, and Anne Bancroft were all interested in playing the title role, as were a few authentic transsexuals and female impersonators; Vernon Scott, "More on Vidal's Myra: Mia's Not Interested." *Los Angeles Herald-Examiner* April 8 (1968).

71. Abe Greenberg, "Voice of Hollywood: Sexsational *Candy* to Be Public's Yuletide Gift?" *Hollywood Citizen News* October 30 (1968).
72. Joyce Haber, "Raunchy *Myra* Scene Protested." *The Los Angeles Times* June 4 (1970).
73. Mandel Herbstman, "[Rev. of] *Secret Ceremony*." *Film TV Daily*, circa October (1968).
74. Raymond A. Sokolov, "Style and Surface." *Newsweek* November 4 (1968).
75. Dale Munroe, "[Rev. of] *End of the Road*." *World Cinema* April 17 (1970).
76. Larry Peitzman, "[Rev. of *End of the Road*]." *Boston After Dark*, April 29 (1970).
77. Richard Meryman, "A Cinematic Assault." *Life* November 7 (1969): 65.
78. Quoted in Meryman, "A Cinematic Assault," 67.
79. Richard Gertner, "[Rev. of] *End of the Road*."
80. Munroe, "[Rev. of] *End of the Road*."
81. Sarne, letter, "Movie Mailbag: Who's Right about *Performance*?," 14.
82. Simon, "The Most Loathsome Film of All?," 363.
83. The apt phrase "cultural hygienist" is used by Jeff Sconce to refer to those who would seek to keep the canon free of disreputable works. For a similar discussion of the politics of film taste, see Jeff Sconce, "'Trashing' the Academy: Taste, Excess, and an Emerging Politics of Cinematic Style." *Screen* 36.4 Winter (1995): 371–93.
84. MacCabe, *Performance*, 78.
85. "Roger Ebert Flick Gets Thumbs Down." *Press-Telegram* August 19 (1997): A2.
86. Richard Gertner, "[Rev. of] *Performance*." *Motion Picture Herald* August 12 (1970).
87. Greg, review, *Motion Picture Exhibitor* August 19 (1970).
88. For an introduction to queer theories of gender and sexuality, see Judith Butler, *Gender Trouble: Feminism and the Subversion of Identity* (New York: Routledge, 1990) and *Bodies That Matter: On the Discursive Limits of "Sex"* (New York: Routledge, 1993).
89. MacCabe, *Performance*, 76.

6

Rethinking the History of European Horror

Television, La porta sul buio *and* Historias para no dormir

ANDREW WILLIS

Horror in recent times, as Mark Jancovich has pointed out,[1] has moved from an object on the periphery of academic genre study to one of the major focuses of contemporary critical writing and teaching. As the subject of film studies has shifted and changed over the past twenty years, and as the discipline has established itself within the academy, horror cinema has become an increasingly important and central area within genre studies, a fact reflected by the rapidly expanding list of books devoted to various aspects of the analysis of horror films. However, while low budget, American independent horror films are now regularly studied alongside more mainstream Hollywood studio offerings and horror movies produced within a range of international contexts, there still remain a number of areas that have not yet hit the critical and academic radar. Of course, if we are to fully understand the historical development of the genre, then these still under-explored areas must be placed into the critical spotlight, and a process of reassessment regarding their place within the genre's history undertaken.

One such area is horror productions made for television, and in particular their shifting relationship to horror cinema. Indeed, if horror television remains an under-explored area, then programs made outside the United States have received almost no attention. In order to address both these issues, in this chapter I want to discuss the place of horror television in Italy and

Spain during the late 1960s and early 1970s. I have selected these countries as they are two nations with strong reputations for horror film production during this period. I also want to argue that, while acknowledging the distinct formal codes and conventions of each, the links between film and television in each case were significant and have been grossly overlooked due to a concentration on horror films at the expense of television.

Popular Genres on Television

As television sets became more prevalent in people's homes in the 1950s, and the output of the industry more attractive and appealing to general audiences, popular film genres began to be translated for the small screen with increasing regularity. The most obvious and consistent transfer from cinema to television was the domestic melodrama. This popular genre, as Lynne Joyrich argues, found a clear transfer from the big screen into the television soap opera. She states, "Both the daytime and prime-time soap opera, for example, seem to employ many of the characteristics of the film melodrama."[2] However, to simply suggest these characteristics did not need adaptation would be to ignore the narrative and visual differences between the two mediums.

Another of the most significant transfers from the big screen to the small in this period was the western, and this format clearly highlights the difference between the appearance of a genre on film and on television. Landmark series such as *Wagon Train*, *Rawhide* and *Gunsmoke* all attracted extremely large and faithful audiences in the late 1950s and 1960s. However, as Edward Gallafent has observed, most television westerns might best be read in relation to other genres. Discussing *Rawhide*, he suggests that "the episodes were essentially anecdotes, set in the western context, but borrowing elements of their structure from other generic models, such as the family melodrama or even on occasion the horror story."[3] Therefore, it is vital that the shift from one medium to another is not seen as straightforward and seamless, but rather as a more complex translation. The emphasis on the melodramatic elements present in *Rawhide* indicates that those making westerns for television were drawing out the elements from the genre that were, as Joyrich suggests, most suitable to television. The large-scale landscapes that provided the backdrop for so many western films were replaced by the more restrictive and domestic towns and camps of the television western.

Like these genres, horror also made the transfer from cinema to television during this period and similarly one can argue that the codes and conventions of the horror film also had to be adapted to the newer medium. Indeed, unlike other genres, the possible limits of horror needed to be identified, which was one of the greatest challenges to those attempting to make horror television and revealed the thematic constraints of the medium. These limitations for the most part exist institutionally, and are often based on the perceived access to television by the general population.

Horror onto Television

By the mid–1960s, horror film production in Europe had assumed a significant place within the film industries of many countries, including Great Britain, Italy, France and Germany, with Spain following by the end of the decade. The success of these films produced in Europe, alongside those imported from the United States, indicated that there was an audience for horror stories in all these countries. The success of U.S. television imports, such as *The Twilight Zone* and *Alfred Hitchcock Presents,* revealed that these audiences would also watch horror, and horror-related, television, particularly those "twist in the tale" style stories. It was therefore a logical move for television companies in these countries to latch onto this potential popularity and make their own horror-tinged television products. I now want to turn my attention to two of these instances in Italy and Spain.

Dario Argento, Italian Television and La porta sul buio

Throughout the 1960s, from Mario Bava's *La maschera del demonio/Mask of the Demon* (1960) to Dario Argento's *L'uccello dalle piume di cristalle/The Bird with the Crystal Plumage* (1970), horror films had slowly become a significant part of the Italian commercial film industry.[4] By the late 1960s directors also introduced more explicit horror imagery into the murders contained in the mystery or "whodunit" films known collectively as *Gialli*. The Giallo film genre had originally acquired its name from the publishing world. As Mary P. Wood has observed, "The word *giallo* entered the popular vocabulary to denote mystery stories from 1929 when the publisher Mondadori launched detective fiction in yellow covers. The word has come to be used both as a shorthand term for any type of detective fiction and, more widely, as a generic term for stories with a mystery element."[5] This mystery and suspense, that became central to this type of film, made the giallo an appropriate genre for translation into Italian television when producers came to consider what horror stories might be suitable for the small screen.

From its first official broadcast on January 1, 1954, Italian television, like that of Spain, was a monopoly controlled by the state broadcasting company — in this case, *Radiotelevisione Italiana* (RAI). This situation existed until 1974 when a private sector developed, resulting in many local channels appearing. While for the most part television was conceived as a public service in Italy, as Stephen Gundle argues, it was not averse to utilizing already existing popular formulas. These were usually developed from U.S. models. For example, Gundle cites *Lascia o raddoppia? (Double or Quit?)*, which he argues was a local version of the American *The $64,000 Question*. Gundle also states that such shows "were invariably heavily adapted, however, to take account of different tastes and expectations,"[6] in this case those of the Italian public. The adaptation of popular U.S. television programs and styles quickly became as staple a part of Italian television as it already was for the Italian film industry.

The giallo series *La porta sul buio* is a good example of a television program that was on one level a localized version of an American model, but also clearly drew on particularly Italian generic inflections. In this case, the American influence seems to be internationally popular anthology series such as *Alfred Hitchcock Presents*. Here, the program replaced Hitchcock, who had provided introductions to each episode of that series, with the young Italian film director Dario Argento. While today when anyone considers the Italian horror film the name of Dario Argento looms large, at that time he was just beginning to become more widely known to the general public. Now, of course, he is one of the few European directors specializing in the horror genre whose name is known beyond the confines of fan culture. The place of the series in establishing Argento as a public figure in his home country is important and offers an often ignored explanation for his continued association with the giallo in the Italian public's imagination.

Dario Argento began his association with film as a critic before moving on to become a screenwriter for a number of popular gangster films and westerns,[7] most famously contributing to Sergio Leone's landmark *C'era una volta il west/Once Upon a Time in the West* (1968). He made his directing debut in 1970 with *L'uccello dalle plume di cristallo/The Bird with the Crystal Plumage* taken from his own script. Since then he has directed around seventeen theatrical feature films, as well as producing a number of works by young directors and continuing to contribute to screenplays that have been made by others. Most of these works have been within established popular genres, most often the giallo and the horror film, and occasionally producing works that blurred the line between the two styles. However, very little attention has been paid to Argento's television work, particularly by those arguing for his auteur status. Strangely, *La porta sul buio* has been widely overlooked given the pivotal role it played in making him a recognizable public figure.

La porta sul buio was first broadcast by RAI in 1972. It was made up of four one-hour-long films, each made specifically for television: *Il vicino di casa/The Neighbour*, *Il tram/The Tram*, *La bambola/The Devil* and *Testimone oculare/Eyewitness*. While he did not direct all the episodes, the series made an important contribution to the establishment of Argento's public persona through his on-screen introduction to each episode. When the series was broadcast he had made three successful feature films. His debut had been followed in 1971 by *Il gatto a nove code/The Cat o'Nine Tails* and *4 mosche di velluto grigio/4 Flies on Grey Velvet*. However, while his name may have become better known following their release and box-office success, in Italy the broadcast of the television program would play an important role in solidifying his growing reputation as a horror director. In addition, the direct address introductions he contributed to each episode ensured his face became an important part of that public persona, something quite rare for all but the most famous film directors. As Chris Gallent has observed, the director "gave brief introductions ... more or less following the blueprint of *Alfred Hitchcock Presents*"[8] to each episode. It was these introductions that helped make Dario Argento a household name in Italy, his distinctive face recognizable to many of the population, and furthermore, one who would thereafter be closely associated with the horror genre in their minds. As Gallent further argues, "Aside from the inherent vanity of such an exercise, these utterances by the author's voice have performed the function of consolidating Argento's position as a public figure, branding his product whilst also encouraging an awareness of his identity and control beyond the fiction."[9]

The introduction to the first episode begins with a shot of a door that slowly opens, allowing the camera track into the darkness beyond. The title *La porta sul buio* appears followed by the credit "di Dario Argento." There is then a cut to a shot of Argento sitting among lights and television studio cameras mounted on tripods. Looking directly at the viewer he says that the shows will cause "fear, anguish, unease," before going on to suggest that they will give those watching a chill. The opening sequence then cuts to Argento standing on the road next to his car with the hood open. He again looks directly into the camera and tells those watching that the car has actually broken down. Another passing car stops and a couple within offers him a lift. They tell him they are going to stay in the country, but that the girl is nervous and a little afraid. Argento tells them nothing ever happens in the country and that they should not be afraid. They then drop him off and as they drive off we realize that the story has already begun, as they are the couple who will be at the center of episode one, *Il vicino di casa*. The inventiveness of the introductions, and, in particular, the way in which Argento becomes the bridge between the institutional world of the production company and their studio and the fictional world of the episode makes him an enormously powerful presence. It is not therefore surprising that with these appearances he made such an instant, and long-lasting, impact on Italian audiences.

The centrality of television to the process of his ascendance to the position of public auteur is something that is mostly ignored by those who have written about Argento's films and career. For the most part they create his status as auteur exclusively through his cinematic output, choosing to ignore the place of television within his body of work.[10] However, as television materials and archives become more widely available to those interested in the history of the horror genre, and key figures within it, this oversight can be addressed and the place of television reassessed. For example, Luigi Cozzi, who worked on the program, claims that when the series was first broadcast it attracted almost 30 million viewers in Italy alone.[11] This figure attests to both the importance of RAI in this period, but also to the amount of impact the name and image of Dario Argento suddenly had in Italy at that time. Ignoring this would seem to be a significant oversight, but of course television must be considered as different from film; it is, after all, a different medium with distinctive demands on the horror director and one in which important constraints on Argento caused him to produce slightly different work. It would simply be inappropriate to judge his film and television work as interchangeable, and the specificity of the latter must be remembered.

La porta sul buio is clearly a series constrained to a certain extent by the limits of television. The scripts for the show had to be passed as acceptable by the RAI producers and from the outset they were concerned about the potential levels of violence that may have been contained in the individual episodes, particularly after the success of *The Bird with the Crystal Plumage* and Argento's subsequent association with the increasingly violent Giallo. This meant that when they were conceptualizing the show, those working on it were aware that to please the RAI producers they would have to see *La porta sul buio* as "an attempt to create a suspense thriller without showing too much violence on the screen ... both to avoid censorship and to show that there is more than one way to create suspense."[12] Argento himself would state in his introduction to the first episode, "These are Gialli, but a new kind. They are different." One of those differences would be the level of explicit violence allowed on screen. Television as a medium was much more heavily restricted in what it could show than cinema. Therefore, the transition of this style to television was much more difficult than that of more "classic" horror tales and the simple "twist in the tail" stories that had been at the heart of other television anthology series. For example, Cozzi recalls that the script of *Il tram* caused concern for the RAI producers who were anxious that the killer was described as one who would wield a thin knife, something of a typical weapon for a giallo assassin. The producers felt its visual appearance would be too phallic and after some discussion agreed that a hook would be more suitable. Argento shot the episode with that implement, which is arguably much more brutal when one considers the physical damage it might cause.[13]

Although *La porta sul buio* only ran for four episodes, it is important to place it within the wider context of both Argento's career and Italian popular culture of the period. In the first instance it reveals the way that television played a vital role in establishing Argento as the leading horror director of the time, at least in the public's imagination. Significantly, this is something that an analysis of just his films does not acknowledge. Secondly, the popularity of the program reveals that home-grown horror and gialli had a wide audience in Italy, and were not just one of the peripheral genres within Italian popular cinema as they are occasionally portrayed. It also shows that audiences did not reject horror television as something that was a poor relation to the "real" horror found on cinema screens.

Narcisco Ibáñez Serrador, Spanish Television and Historias para no dormir

In the late 1960s, horror film production in Spain began what was to become an unprecedented boom, which lasted until the mid–1970s. The 1967 release of *La marca de hombre lobo/ The Mark of the Werewolf* suggested that a domestic audience was available for Spanish horror and the huge box-office success of both *La residencia/ The Finishing School* (1969) and *La noche de walpurgis/ The Werewolf's Shadow* (1970) confirmed it. While the director of *La noche de walpurgis*, Leon Klimovsky, was to contribute another nine horror-related titles to this boom, Narcisco Ibáñez Serrador, director of *La residencia,* spent most of his subsequent career in television making only one further feature, *Quién puede matar a un niño?/ Who Can Kill a Child?* (1975).

The fact that Ibáñez Serrador, arguably the most important and overlooked contributor to the Spanish horror boom of the 1960s, was working in television perhaps explains his critical neglect. If the horror genre is still marginalized within writing about Spanish cinema,[14] then the history of Spanish genre television is even more neglected. However, to understand the roots of the horror revival and subsequent boom within Spanish cinema I would argue one has to look outside the narrow confines of film production and include a wider consideration of horror on television before 1967, in particular, the hugely successful series *Historias para no dormir/Stories to Keep You Awake*.

Narciso Ibáñez Serrador had originally developed his ambitions to make a series of horror-style stories for television when he was based in Latin America. In 1958 he had been involved in an anthology series called *Obras maestras del terror/Masterpieces of Horror* for Argentine television, writing and directing a number of episodes. A key element of that program was the presence of his father Narciso Ibáñez Menta, an actor who was very much associated with the horror genre in Argentina and Latin America more generally. Many of the episodes of *Obras maestras del terror* involved adaptations of, broadly speaking, horror stories written by the likes of Edgar Allan Poe, Robert Louis Stevenson, Gaston Leroux and the more contemporary Ray Bradbury. A significant number of these scripts were undertaken by Narciso Ibáñez Serrador himself under his writing name Luis Peñafiel. The program ran for two successful years and was adapted for the cinema as *Obras maestras de terror* in 1960, and directed by Enrique Carreras from scripts by Peñafiel. This series provided Ibáñez Serrador with a successful blueprint he would revive in Spain a few years later as *Historias para no dormir*.

Spanish television had begun to broadcast in 1956 with the state-run TVE. By 1966, when the first episode of *Historias para no dormir* was shown, there were two channels operated by the state broadcasting company, TVE2, starting in 1965. Therefore, as in Italy, the impact of television programs on the popular imagination could be quite enormous. This certainly seems to have been the case with *Historias para no dormir*. Antonio Lázaro Reboll quotes Sara Torres, who was part of a celebration of Spanish horror produced in conjunction with the San Sebastian horror film festival, that to "the vast majority of Spanish television spectators who are now in their forties and fifties, the name Chicho Ibáñez Serrador is inevitably linked to horror stories."[15]

Much of this is due to the fact that *Historias para no dormir* was a wildly popular television series across Spain in the mid–1960s. On reflection, its influence has been sorely overlooked, both in terms of its bringing horror to the Spanish mainstream and the way it wetted the appetite of a large audience for home-grown horror products, giving them credibility in the process. The brainchild of director, writer, producer and even sometime actor, Narcisco Ibáñez Serrador, the series began production in 1965 and consisted primarily of suspense and horror stories, although there were occasional forays into science fiction and some of the episodes were difficult to categorize. The impact of the program has led Lázaro Reboll to argue that "any account of

Spanish television history must include the horror-suspense series *Historias para no dormir*."[16] Indeed, if it were not for the problematic low cultural status of much horror within Spanish culture, in combination with that of television, the series would probably be much more widely regarded as, what it certainly is, a landmark in the history of not only Spanish broadcasting but of European television. Lázaro Reboll argues that the negative critical reception in Spain for Narciso Ibáñez Serrador's first feature film, *La residencia*, was largely due to his being closely associated with the television medium.[17] The difference between the cultural status of film and television at this time had also been behind Dario Argento's decision to direct his own contribution to *La porta sul buio*, *Il tram*, under the pseudonym Siro Bernadotte. According to Luigi Cozzi, Argento was well aware of the different cultural status of the two mediums and felt it would undermine his theatrical reputation if he worked in television.[18]

The popularity of *Historias para no dormir* with domestic audiences in Spain should not be seen in isolation. It is fruitful to link it to the horror film boom that began in the late 1960s, particularly in terms of its enormous cultural impact on Spanish society. By 1969 and the release of his debut feature, the association of the name Narciso Ibáñez Serrador with the horror genre would have undoubtedly enticed audiences to consider going to see a film bearing his name. In that year they had the opportunity with the release of *La residencia*. With his introductions to each episode of the television series he had created a public persona for himself that was closely linked to the horror genre. Unlike most other television production staff at TVE at the time, a mainstream popular audience knew who he was and would even recognize him in the street. This was in no little part due to the preamble to each episode, which set the scene for each week's program, working to assist the audience in how to approach the material. Such an introduction was vital due to the variety of programs on offer across the series. Ibáñez Serrador became very important to the audience and their expectations, his introductions indicating the tone of what was to follow. Sometimes it would demand a weighty, even philosophic introduction, while others were more comedic and suggested a lighter story for that week. Certainly, the models for these introductions were once again those of popular U.S. shows such as *The Twilight Zone* and *Alfred Hitchcock Presents*, and as in those instances, they brought the same level of public awareness of Narciso Ibáñez Serrador as a home-grown horror maestro, even if he had been imported from Latin America.

The variety of approaches accommodated across the episodes of *Historias para no dormir* were one of its major strengths, and the series allowed the production team working on the program to utilize a wide range of styles.

While some were quite naturalistic, others operated in a more clearly anti-illusionist mode. However, at the heart of the show was Ibáñez Serrador's commitment to the Gothic literary heavyweights and the accepted classics of the horror genre, something that had been maintained from the Argentine original. Matt Hills argues that the idea or concept of "Gothic TV" was something that enabled the creation of a distinction between acceptable and unacceptable forms of television. As he puts it, "those producing, publicizing and writing about television can also produce cultural distinctions, suggesting that 'Gothic TV' is superior to devalued (or culturally inappropriate) TV horror."[19] Hills suggests, as does Helen Wheatley,[20] that "gothic" allows for a connection with literature and the associated middle-brow respectability that horror is usually denied. In the case of *Historias para no dormir,* the gothic stories may be seen as the more "respectable" episodes that made space for the more challenging and original stories that the show also produced.

It is therefore not surprising then that *Historias para no dormir* often adapted works by well-known writers with established gothic reputations. For example, in 1966 the first series included *El pacto,* which was taken from "The Facts in the Case of M. Valdemar" by Edgar Allan Poe. It was Poe's work that also provided the original story that was the source of the episode *El tonel,* and it was also the base for *El trapero,* which was made in 1966 and remade in 1982. In 1967 it became Poe himself who was the subject of an episode with *El cuervo.* The work of another established literary figure, Henry James, was adapted for the *El muñeco* episode in 1966, and W. W. Jacobs' famous story *The Monkey's Paw* appeared as *La zarpa* in 1967. The sources of these episodes of *Historias para no dormir* were significant, as they provided it with a foundation clearly drawn from the already acceptable literary tradition within the genre. The importance of the cultural capital provided by these established works was a vital component to the acceptance of the series within the rather conservative institution of Spanish television at the time. It is also likely they helped the program reach the culturally snobbish middle-class Spanish audience usually resistant to the fiction output of the television medium.

However, while many of the episodes of *Historias para no dormir* were conventional adaptations of horror "classics" as the Argentine originals had been, perhaps the most memorable were those that were the most formally challenging. Such episodes stretched the boundaries of how television told stories at the time. For example, *El asfalto,* which was broadcast in 1966, might on reflection best be described as almost experimental. Taken from a story by Carlos Buiza, the episode opens with a man who has his right leg in plaster walking along the street on a hot day. He crosses the road and finds that the tarmac is melting in the sun and his feet and walking stick are sticking. When he next tries to cross the road he becomes totally stuck and as the sun heats up begins slowly sinking. The plot then unfolds as he attempts to engage a number of people to assist him, most of whom ignore his pleas. Slowly he becomes more and more desperate as he sinks farther and farther into the melted road surface. As with most episodes of the program, *El asfalto* is completely studio bound. However, it makes a virtue of this fact by creating a completely theatrical rather than naturalistic setting for the story. The street, the sun and the cars that pass are all conceptualized as if parts of a set for a music hall performance, and the acting styles of those involved further enhances this non-naturalistic feel. Narcisco Ibáñez Menta, who plays the increasingly desperate lead, is made up as if for the stage or silent screen and his expansive performance style further reflects this. The music used for the episode is also like that commonly associated with the accompaniment of popular theatre or silent cinema. The episode as a whole shows how the series could be innovative as well as traditional. Once again, detailed examination of each series will allow for a fuller realization of the impressive and groundbreaking nature of *Historias para no dormir,* and of the career of Narcisco Ibáñez Serrador.

Revival in the 1980s: Nostalgia and Horror in Spain

Ibáñez Serrador's horror reputation was sustained in the 1970s by a series of short story collections and comic books bearing his name. In the 1980s he hosted a television season of thirty-two classic horror films from across the globe under the umbrella title, *Mis terrores favoritos.* The films were broadcast from October 12, 1981, to May 17, 1982, on TVE and helped maintain his position as Spain's premiere television horror personality. The series also made a significant intervention in the reclamation of Spain's forgotten horror film history with its inclusion of works from the 1960s and 1970s boom period. This was accomplished in particular by placing Claudio Guerin Hill's *La Campana del infierno/ The Bell of Hell,* Eugenio Martin's *Pánico en el transiberiano/ Horror Express,* Jorge Grau's *No profanar el sueño de los muertos/ The Living Dead at the Manchester Morgue* and his own *La residencia* alongside accepted classics of the genre such as *Psycho* (1960), *Dracula* (1931) and *The Mummy* (1932). Through their inclusion he made a bold statement regarding his opinion on the status and importance of Spanish horror productions. Such programming clearly argued for these Spanish films to take their rightful place within the genre's international canon.

Historias para no dormir itself was also revived in the 1980s, further revealing the lasting potential of the format and its creator. The revival revisited the basic concept of the 1960s series, television adaptations of classic and original horror stories. Once again, Ibáñez Serrador offered an introduction to each edition and once again genre stalwarts were adapted such as *El trapero* from the work of Edgar Allan Poe. Representative of a significant new trend in this version of the series, the remaking of earlier episodes proved popular with the public. This approach reveals that the producers were well aware of the place of *Historias para no dormir* in the popular Spanish imagination. Indeed, this may well indicate that TVE, who commissioned the series, was aware that in the politically charged, post–Franco Spain, there was already a stirring of nostalgia for the simpler, entertainment television of the past. While the reimagined series was less well critically received than the originals it still found an audience. The lasting power of the *Historias para no dormir* concept was to reveal itself once again almost twenty years after the 1980s' version.

Into the 21st Century: 6 Peliculas para no dormir

However much it might still be ignored by critics, writers and academics studying the histories of Spanish film and television, the horror genre remains an important part of the Spanish film industry. In August 2004 John Hopewell reported in *Variety* that Filmax, one of Spain's major film production companies, was in the process of making a series of horror films for television. They were to be known collectively as *6 Peliculas para no dormir/6 Films That Won't Let You Sleep*.[21] A name that would, as I have argued, have great resonance for many people in Spain. Significantly, not only had Filmax taken the name of Ibáñez Serrador's legendary television series, they had also hired the aging producer to oversee the operation and direct one of the films, *El ser*, himself. The influence of Narciso Ibáñez Serrador and *Historias para no dormir* on a generation of Spanish directors is further reflected by the impressive roster of established figures who have contributed to the latest incarnation of the series. These include top directors such as Alex de la Iglesia, Jaume Balagueró, Enrique Urbizu and Paco Plaza. In light of this high profile revival of the *Historias para no dormir*, it is certainly about time that those writing the histories of Spanish cinema and popular culture woke up to the enormous impact of the format. More precisely, it should be acknowledged as a key European horror text whose influence is still undoubtedly ongoing.

Conclusions

Considering the level of interest in horror among audiences, fans and academics, and given the particular social, political and economic circumstances of European film and television in the late 1960s and early 1970s, it is surprising that its horror output remains such an under-explored area. Why might that be so? There remains something of a critical orthodoxy regarding the popular cinema and television of Europe from the early 1970s, much of which is based on the potential for such products to be read simply in relation to national identity. Horror, perhaps due to many of the films being international coproductions (like the western) and the television series not appearing in English-language versions, has fallen outside this.

Horror itself has appeared much more widely than most histories of the genre acknowledge, and when reevaluating generic canons one must be aware of the importance of mediums not always instantly associated with particular genres. Such works help inform our understanding of genre in a more complex way, acknowledging the specificity of the medium. Television horror in the 1960s and early 1970s could not operate within the boundaries laid out by its cinematic counterparts, and those producing it found their own ways of telling horror stories specifically for the medium. In the cases of *La porta sul buio* and *Historias para no dormir* these proved highly popular with the audiences of the day, challenging the assumption that small-screen horror was in some way a poor relation to the more explicit cinematic offerings of the period. More archival work needs to be done on horror on television, as it will help scholars break out of the slowly solidifying canons of the genre. It will also assist in acknowledging the wider realities of the inter-linked horror production across film and television in Europe during the 1960s and early 1970s. On a number of levels television played a key role in cultivating horror audiences in countries such as Spain and Italy and their contribution should be more widely acknowledged.

Notes

1. Mark Jancovich, "General Introduction." In *Horror, The Film Reader*. Ed. Mark Jancovich (London: Routledge, 2002), 1.
2. Lynn Joyrich, "All That Television Allows: TV Melodrama, Postmodernism, and Consumer Culture." In *Private Screenings: Television and the Female Consumer*. Ed. Lynn Spigel and Denise Mann (Minneapolis: University of Minnesota Press, 1992), 229.
3. Edward Gallafent, *Clint Eastwood: Actor and Director* (London: Studio Vista, 1994), 13.
4. For more on Italian horror cinema see Leon Hunt, "A (Sadistic) Night at the Opera: Notes on the Italian Horror Film," *Velvet Light Trap* 30 Fall (1992), 65–75.
5. Mary P. Wood, *Italian Cinema* (Oxford: Berg, 2005), 53.

6. Stephen Gundle, "Television in Italy." In *Television in Europe*. Ed. James A. Coleman and Brigitte Rollet (Bristol: Intellect, 1997), 62.
7. For full details see Chris Gallant (ed.), *Art of Darkness: The Cinema of Dario Argento* (Goldaming: FAB Press, 2001), 301–307.
8. Ibid., 52.
9. Ibid.
10. See for example Maitland McDonagh, *Broken Mirrors/Broken Minds: The Dark Dreams of Dario Argento* (New York: Citadel Books, 1994).
11. Luigi Cozzi interviewed on *Door into Darkness* DVD, Dragon Film Entertainment (2004).
12. Ibid.
13. Ibid.
14. There is very little mention of the horror boom in such key overviews as Nuria Triana Toribio, *Spanish National Cinema* (London: Routledge, 2003).
15. Antonio Lázaro Reboll, "Screening 'Chicho': The Horror Ventures of Narciso Ibáñez Serrador." In *Spanish Popular Cinema*. Ed. Antonio Lázaro Reboll and Andrew Willis (Manchester: Manchester University Press, 2004), 155.
16. Ibid., 152.
17. Ibid., 153.
18. Cozzi Interview.
19. Matt Hills, *The Pleasures of Horror* (London: Continuum, 2005), 119.
20. Helen Wheatley, "*Mystery and Imagination*: Anatomy of a Gothic Anthology Series." In *Small Screens, Big Ideas: Television in the 1950s*. Ed. Janet Thumim (London: I. B Tauris, 2002), 165–180.
21. John Hopewell, "Hot Helmers Set to Roll on Vet's Horror Wheel." *Variety*, July 26 (2004).

7

Can Rock Movies Be Musicals?

The Case of This Is Spinal Tap

ANDREW CAINE

This Is Spinal Tap (1984) depicts the backstage intrigue of a fictional British heavy metal band's American tour. The film focuses on the three main personalities of Spinal Tap, the band, Nigel Tufnel (Christopher Guest), David St. Hubbins (Michael McKean) and Derek Smalls (Harry Shearer), concentrating on their musical path from the 1960s to the 1980s and their relations with key members of their entourage, Jeanine Petitbone (June Chadwick), David's girlfriend, and the group's manager, Ian Faith (Tony Hendra). Shot in documentary, or rockumentary, style by fictional director, Marti Di Bergi, portrayed by the movie's actual director, Rob Reiner, *This Is Spinal Tap* comprises a mixture of backstage humiliations, interviews with the principal characters, concert performances and imaginary archive footage.

As a film about a rock 'n' roll band, featuring musical interludes for a significant proportion of the movie's short running time (82 minutes), *This Is Spinal Tap* undoubtedly represents a production about musicians and the music business. However, should the film be considered a musical? In film reference books, such as *1001 Movies to See Before You Die* and *The Time Out Film Guide*, it is described as a comedy, drama or rock movie rather than as a musical.[1] Considering that *This Is Spinal Tap* revolves around a critique of the entertainment industry, such satirical realism would seem incompatible with the popular reputation of the musical for fantasy and escapism. As a study in failure, despite the band's triumphant comeback at the end of the film, it hardly exemplifies a genre that Richard Dyer states "offers the image of 'something better' to escape into, or something we want deeply or that our day-to-day lives don't provide."[2] The *Virgin Encyclopedia of Stage and Screen Musicals* omits Reiner's film, even though documentaries that inspired *This Is Spinal Tap*, such as *Gimme Shelter* (1970) and *The Last Waltz* (1978), are included.[3]

Such classification not only poses questions about how rock movies relate to issues of genre, but also raises questions about how and why audiences, critics and producers associate films with particular generic categories. This chapter details two key concerns. First, it examines why *This Is Spinal Tap* is rarely interpreted as a musical by critics and audiences. Second, it negotiates the uneasy historical relationship between rock movies and the musical, using *This Is Spinal Tap* to illustrate the links between these two types of production.

To achieve this task, the chapter divides into four components. First, information about audience and critical perceptions of the musical are mentioned. A discussion of *This Is Spinal Tap*'s historical context follows next, with particular emphasis on the film's links to contemporary trends within comedy. The third and fourth elements critique the rock movie's relationship with the musical, suggesting differences and similarities between *This Is Spinal Tap* and the backstage musical tradition.

Audiences, Genre and This Is Spinal Tap

Audiences play a crucial role in shaping how particular films are marketed and interpreted. According to Rick Altman in *Film/Genre*, Hollywood's economic interest lies with mentioning a film's hybrid or multi-generic status: *This Is Spinal Tap* can legitimately be described as a musical, comedy, drama, buddy film, mock documentary and rock movie.[4] However, as Altman argues, "the perceived nature and purpose of genres depend directly and heavily on the identity and purpose of those using and evaluating them."[5] Therefore, if viewers recognize a film as being primarily associated with one particular genre they may not recognize its hybrid status.

Several examples of this tendency emerged in a Channel Four program on *The 100 Greatest Musicals* broadcast at Christmas 2003.[6] This chart listed the British public's choice of the one hundred best musicals, complete with commentaries from critics and celebrities. Several choices, especially the *Buffy the Vampire Slayer* special, "Once More with Feeling" and the Eminem vehicle *8 Mile* (2002) met with disbelief from commentators, not used to such productions being described as musicals. Renowned rock movies, such as *This*

Is Spinal Tap and *A Hard Day's Night* (1964), failed to make the countdown, as did rock documentaries. Such results, and the reactions raised to the unexpected inclusion of *Buffy* and Eminem, indicate that not only is generic status indicative of an individual's perception about specific cultural products, but also that consensus regarding the contents and formation of genres may not exist among different consumer groups.

My own experience teaching *This Is Spinal Tap* as a contemporary musical illuminates this point. In two institutions, I showed students how the film demonstrated similarities with the backstage musical tradition. They remained unconvinced, assuming that *This Is Spinal Tap*'s recognized status as a comedy classic meant that the film did not deserve the tag of musical. This position possibly resulted from the fact that many contemporary audiences have particular assumptions about the musical genre. While the editors of *Musicals and Beyond* extend the genre's parameters to include any film dependent upon music for dramatic effect, Martin Rubin distinguishes the traditional musical from those, primarily realist, films that merely include musical numbers.[7] The latter category, in which Rubin would presumably include *This Is Spinal Tap*, are not musicals due to their realist preoccupations, while the traditional musical "is a film containing a significant proportion of musical numbers that are impossible."[8] Steven Cohan elaborates this point, explaining how the past classics of the genre often fail to meet the expectations of contemporary audiences:

> To them musicals are an odd species of entertainment: the plots seem not only escapist but hackneyed, recycled from film to film, the characters lack psychological depth and their passions are corny, chaste beyond belief; the Tin Pan Alley songs are out of synch with contemporary musical styles, the big production numbers are too over-the-top to be taken seriously. Most alienating of all, the convention of a character bursting into song or dance with inexplicable orchestral accompaniment, the hallmark moments in any movie, occasions laughter rather than applause because, it breaks with cinematic realism.[9]

This Is Spinal Tap is a film about music, but the impact of dance within the movie appears negligible. Indeed, dance has contained relatively little significance within the rock movie since the 1950s. Apart from the elaborate MGM style routines based on the classic musical tradition, such as the Cliff Richard vehicle *Summer Holiday* (1962) and Elvis Presley's dramatic choreography accompanying the title song to *Jailhouse Rock* (1957), dance proved to be marginal in the rock movie from its inception. By the time of mid–1960s films, such as *Help!* and *Catch Us If You Can* (both 1965), dance barely featured in rock movies; when it did, the source of inclusion usually involved novelty value, indicated by the routines of go-go dancer Candy Johnson in American International Pictures' beach movie cycle.

This Is Spinal Tap mocks the idea of dance and putting on the show, through its dissection of the band's artistic pretensions, exemplified by the fiasco of the "Stonehenge" performance. For Nigel Tufnel, "Stonehenge" represents the apex of Spinal Tap's act, their most powerful and dramatic song. The scene not only reveals the band's idiocy, as Nigel fails to differentiate between feet and inches, and lofty pretensions, but also demonstrates the limitations of music and dance in contemporary cinema. It culminates in abject ridicule for Spinal Tap, as their hopes for a grand performance are destroyed by the small design of the Stonehenge model, the result of Nigel's mathematical error, and through the sudden arrival of two dancing dwarves in pixie dress, accompanied by the sound of pan pipes, midway through the song. By having the band's performance interrupted in this way, *This Is Spinal Tap* parodies the idea of a singing and dancing musical. Much to their consternation, the routine becomes a "comedy" number. By laughing at the group's stupidity and misfortune, the viewer not only enjoys the debunking of Spinal Tap's artistic credentials, but also, however unconsciously, recognizes the apparent artificiality of all musical numbers in which characters suddenly burst into song and dance.

The other great characteristic of the traditional musical is romance. Invariably, the studio era musical involved a union of the male and female protagonists into some form of romantic partnership, perhaps best exemplified by the Fred Astaire and Ginger Rogers films produced at RKO during the 1930s. For critics such as Altman and Jane Feuer, the emphasis on heterosexual romance formed perhaps the vital characteristic of the genre. Altman's *The American Film Musical* even utilizes romance as the catalyst for the various plot and narrative devices of the genre, to the extent that he almost excluded *The Wizard of Oz* from his survey.[10] Rock movies often aimed at teenage audiences (it was feared that girls would be alienated by romantic rivals to their favorite male stars), explaining why romance did not feature in many such films including *A Hard Day's Night* and *Help!* Indeed, several of Presley's earliest films, such as *King Creole* (1958) and *Wild in the Country* (1961) do not culminate with romantic union, while *Love Me Tender* (1956) and *Flaming Star* (1960) climax with the deaths of his characters.

In *This Is Spinal Tap,* the only romance allowed to flourish belongs to the platonic, brotherly love between the band's two founders, Nigel and David. They are seen as almost brothers because they have known each other from early childhood, and they have worked together throughout their adult lives. Their shared object of devotion lies with the band. Apart from David, none of the other band members appears to have a stable relationship, while behind the scenes in hotels and on the tour bus, Spinal Tap indulge their sexual cravings upon groupies. Such lust accounts for the herpes sores prominent on several members' lips at various points of the film.[11]

Women are shown as being destructive upon the group's creativity, particularly through the character of Jeanine. She plays a crucial role in the departures of Nigel and Faith from the group's coterie; instead of a partnership between old friends, she wishes to make her man, David, the center of attention. Rows between Nigel and David cause acrimony in the studio, while the growing physical and social distance between the two men becomes visible at the airport where Nigel sits away from the band. Jeanine's influence proves disastrous; the "Stonehenge" fiasco occurs as Nigel tries to avoid the prospect of performing in her astrologically inspired costumes. Jeanine tries to manage the band after Faith's departure, making bad bookings at a zoo and airforce base, respectively. She forms a destructive influence upon band unity "not only because she is a female who demands power in this boy's club," as Carl Platinga argues, "but because she is secretive, scheming and utterly humorless."[12] The film's climax restores Nigel and Faith to their previous roles in the band's organization, after they achieve an unexpected hit single in Japan. During the shots of the triumphant Japanese tour, Jeanine appears a subdued figure, literally reduced to an insignificant spectator, albeit with the misogynist bully Faith standing over her shoulder with his trademark cricket bat. *This Is Spinal Tap* therefore apparently reverses the classical Hollywood musical through stressing that romantic love can destroy creativity and friendship. Only when Nigel is restored, at Jeanine's expense, can the vindication of Spinal Tap as successful musicians occur.

The music contained within the film also represents the antithesis to that popularly associated with the Hollywood musical. As I explain later, rock movies have possessed an ambiguous relationship to their musical parent genre since the first rock 'n' roll movies in the mid–1950s. Moreover, as hinted earlier, popular music moved into styles alien from the Broadway tradition of Cole Porter, Rodgers and Hammerstein and Irving Berlin that dominated the studio era musical. It is difficult to think of two popular music icons as dissimilar as Astaire and Ozzy Osbourne, probably the most famous representative of heavy metal, the musical genre inhabited by Spinal Tap.

Heavy metal emerged in the late 1960s, emerging from a combination of rhythm and blues, psychedelic and rock music influences. The key progenitors of the early British heavy metal bands were acts such as the Rolling Stones, The Who, Cream, the Jimi Hendrix Experience and The Yardbirds. All these artists symbolized the emergence of rock music, as distinct from pop, during the mid–1960s. Originating from rhythm and blues or jazz backgrounds, such acts wanted to challenge the hitherto rather cozy arrangement between show business and popular music. Unlike earlier pop artists, such as Presley and Pat Boone, they did not wish to become all-round entertainers, equally adept at dancing, singing or acting. Combined with increasingly sophisticated instrumentation and studio technology, pop began to shift into the more confrontational rock music, typified by singles such as the Stones' "(I Can't Get No) Satisfaction" and The Who's "My Generation." The aggressive musical stance, outrageous behavior and lyrical misogyny of acts such as the Stones and Hendrix paved the way for many of the stereotypes associated with heavy metal: loud music, sexist lyrics and a chaotic sex, drugs and rock 'n' roll lifestyle.

As British pop veterans from the 1960s, Spinal Tap's history places them within the tradition of rhythm and blues turned hard rock acts of this era. The fictional Spinal Tap first achieved success in the mid–1960s as a Mersey-beat style combo, the Thamesmen, before jumping upon the psychedelic bandwagon with "(Listen to the) Flower People" and changing to their more familiar name. Similar developments were made by actual bands of the early heavy metal era such as Led Zeppelin, Deep Purple and Black Sabbath, who all moved from blues-based music to hard rock.

There are other inter-textual links between Spinal Tap and British rhythm and blues/hard rock veterans of this era. The Electric Banana club, where Marti Di Bergi first saw Spinal Tap in 1966, takes its name from an album by the Pretty Things.[13] There are parallels in the relationship between fictional schoolfriends Nigel Tufnel and David St. Hubbins and that of Stones frontmen Mick Jagger and Keith Richards. Besides their friendship since school days, Nigel and David possess reputations for rock 'n' roll debauchery and latent sexism, similar to the reputations of their possible real-life inspirations. The Stones effectively established the hard rock motif, through a combination of repetitious guitar riffs and lyrical misogyny, thanks to songs such as "Under My Thumb" and "Bitch," while they supposedly flirted with the occult with material like "Sympathy for the Devil."

Such masculine aggression became synonymous with heavy metal. Whitesnake, a heavy metal act of the 1970s and 1980s, became renowned for record sleeves featuring naked women in position of distress in the vein of Spinal Tap's *Smell the Glove*, even naming one of their albums *Slide It In*. Guns n' Roses, a metal band of the post–Tap era, changed the original artwork to their *Appetite for Destruction* album after protests about its depiction of a robot raping a woman, while Iron Maiden's biggest hit gloried in the title of "Bring Your Daughter to the Slaughter."[14]

Marketing and Promotion: This Is Spinal Tap *as a Comedy*

On the DVD of *This Is Spinal Tap*, in a trailer produced at the time of the film's release, Reiner stated that his film was "a comedy about a British rock 'n' roll band." Television adverts for the film included such statements as "One of the funniest movies ever!" (Steven Schafter, *US Magazine*) and "The funniest movie ever about Rock 'n' Roll" (*Newsweek*).

Such information provides valuable material for considering *This Is Spinal Tap*'s generic status. At the time of its release, adverts and trailers attempted to position the film as a comedy centered on a heavy metal band rather than as a musical. Altman argues that critics "regularly treat genres as watertight, unproblematic categories," while, for Steve Neale, "reviews nearly always contain terms indicative of a film's generic status."[15]

The original material on *This Is Spinal Tap* tried to limit the generic appeal of the film, by limiting its hybridity while stressing both the movie's musical and comic dimensions. The publicity material emphasized the film's links to rock 'n' roll, yet the comedy connection appeared more significant. Reiner's persona also contains relevance. Like the other key cast members and scriptwriters, Guest, McKean and Shearer, Reiner's reputation lay as a comedy actor rather than as a musician. The director appeared in the successful American sitcom *All in the Family* during the 1970s, while Guest, McKean and Shearer had varying connections with *Saturday Night Live*. Tony Hendra was the cofounder of another comedy institution, *National Lampoon* magazine.[16] Casting has long associated particular stars with specific genres since the silent era. Altman rightly argues that "the use of familiar stars usually makes them predictable on the basis of the title and credits alone." For example, the likes of John Wayne and Gene Kelly arouse audience preconceptions about the Western and musical genres respectively.[17] Considering the cast's comedy roots, the heavy metal theme and the unfashionable status of the musical during the 1980s, the decision to promote *This Is Spinal Tap* as a comedy appears logical.

The links to *Saturday Night Live* are revealing in understanding *This Is Spinal Tap*'s position as a comedy. The American television show and the *National Lampoon* magazine/films became associated with a particular kind of "gross out" humor. Epitomized by films, such as *National Lampoon's Animal House* (1978) and *Porky's* (1981), and performers including John Belushi and Chevy Chase, for William Paul, throughout the late 1970s and early 1980s, "there arouse a series of comedies and an apparent desire to push the boundaries of good taste."[18] Such films feature characters defined "in terms of their sexual desire." The likes of Bluto Blutarsky (Belushi) in *National Lampoon's Animal House* are celebrated "by the extent to which they have embraced their animal natures."[19] For example, the fun-loving Bluto and his associates at Delta House with their food fights, toga parties and sexual cravings are more positive than the repressive and staid Omega House. In "animal comedies," the emphasis largely lies upon an ensemble cast, concentrating upon a group of friends rather than individuals, while they are often based around a random or fragmented plot before the triumph of the animal fraternity.[20]

This Is Spinal Tap shares numerous characteristics of the gross-out/animal style of comedy. The band members and their entourage are constantly swearing, while the band is shown as juvenile, animalistic and grotesque through their sexual obsession. On his temporary departure from the band, Faith attacks the group's "adolescent fantasy world." Nigel boasts that the group's popularity with teenage boys results from the "armadillos in our trousers," while Derek describes "Sex Farm" as "a sophisticated ... view of the idea of sex." The link between penile power, masculine posturing and musical status reaches its apogee when female customs women stop Derek at an airport check. An inspection reveals the bassist's attempts to enhance his masculine prowess by placing a cucumber wrapped in foil down his trousers. Just as college boys in *National Lampoon's Animal House*, *Porky's* and *Fast Times at Ridgemont High* (1982) lustfully crave pneumatic women, the members of Spinal Tap remain unaware of their own childishness with regard to sex. They are thirty-something musicians who are still adolescents with their views on women; Nigel sees no difference between "sexist" and "sexy."

Spinal Tap's immaturity becomes obvious near the start of the film, when they run into difficulties regarding the cover art to their latest album *Smell the Glove*. According to PR executive Bobbi Flekman (Fran Drescher), the sleeve depicts "a greased naked woman on all fours with a dog collar around her neck and a leash and a man's arm extended out up to her holding on to the leash." Although Platinga regards Bobbi as "a relatively positive character," for the band, as with Jeanine later in the film, she represents a threat.[21] Bobbi denounces the mentality of a band stuck in the 1960s in their social attitudes. Her complaints about the cover art not only demonstrate the extent to which Spinal Tap are rooted in the past, but also that her role as a record company executive gives Bobbi power over the band's male chauvinists. Through her vocation, she denies Spinal Tap much-needed publicity, which contributes to the failure of their tour. The reluctance to sell and advertise *Smell the Glove* by supermarkets is matched by the indifference of the hierarchy at Polymer records. Spinal Tap's tragedy lies with their inability to realize the consequences of their "non-too-subtle celebration of animal masculinity" that connects "sexual relations to animal drives and strutting sexual display."[22]

As a film centered on a rock band, *This Is Spinal Tap*, like the other examples of "animal comedy" mentioned above, primarily functions as an ensemble piece. The mock documentary style also enables the movie to show the culminative effect of a series of failures on the tour, such as Derek getting stuck in a pod during "Rock 'n' roll Creation" and the band getting lost backstage, poor ticket sales and deteriorating personal relationships. Following Nigel's departure, things get so dire that they resort to performing Derek's tuneless "Jazz Odyssey" when billed below a puppet show. However, with the return of Nigel and Faith, *This Is Spinal Tap* transforms itself from a survey in failure to a study of how persistence and friendship yield rewards. Despite their idiocy and musical mediocrity, by the end of the film, according to Platinga, most viewers "nonetheless cheer for what may be their final triumph," due to the group's lasting friendship, strength in adversity and their personalities as "likable fools, quite boyish and gentle despite their macho posing and tough lyrics."[23]

Although *This Is Spinal Tap* shares numerous similarities with the "animal comedy" cycle, it contains a significant difference. With the possible exception of *Fast Times at Ridgemont High*, much of the humor in "animal comedy" stemmed from physical pranks, such as the toga party and food fight in *National Lampoon's Animal House,* rather than verbal putdowns. In *This Is Spinal Tap*, although visual comedy is evident, witness Derek's cucumber problems or his incident with the pod, much of the humor results from the verbal humiliation that the band receive. When Marti Di Bergi's interviews mention that reviewers have called their *Shark Sandwich* album a "shit sandwich," complaining that the band are "treading water in a sea of retarded sexuality and bad poetry," such comments reveal great detail about Spinal Tap's attitude to women, childishness and evident musical incompetence.

To this extent, the film emphasizes the satirical origins of *National Lampoon* and *Saturday Night Live.* For example, *Monty Python* member Eric Idle's spoof of the Beatles, *The Rutles: All You Need Is Cash,* was shown in the United States on *Saturday Night Live,* arguably serving as a prototype for *This Is Spinal Tap.* Like Reiner's film, it features a reporter/director investigating the history of a famous fictional rock band. Stylistically, both *All You Need Is Cash* and *This Is Spinal Tap* combine songs with interviews and fake archive footage, although the Rutles' production featured actual documentary footage from the 1960s.[24] In the case of *This Is Spinal Tap*, the film's mix of satirical documentary and humor succeeds because it brutally exposes the pretensions and the "pathetic reality" of the heavy metal band.[25] This task is achieved through the movie's use of the style and traditions of the rock movie, which in turn borrows heavily from its parent genre — the musical.

Rock Movies and the Musical

With the advent of rock 'n' roll in the mid–1950s, film studios sought to exploit the boom by integrating the new music into feature films. Elvis Presley's long and lucrative, if not creatively satisfying, film career began with *Love Me Tender*, while the likes of Bill Haley and His Comets, Little Richard and Chuck Berry saw screen action in vehicles such as *Rock Around the Clock*, *The Girl Can't Help It* and *Rock, Rock, Rock* (all 1956). Throughout the first decade of the rock movie, the sub-genre largely met with critical indifference and occasional hostility. Publications such as *Sight and Sound* attacked rock movies not only for their commercialism in pandering to the latest teenage tastes, but also for their perceived dilution of cinema's artistic potential. Low-budget, poorly plotted films, often revolving around a televisual style revue format, to the critical elite such production represented a form of "anti-musical": films about pop music, or starring pop stars, that did not live up to the expected standards and artistic codes of the MGM musical.[26] Rick Altman offers similar judgements, connecting the decline of the musical to the rise of the rock film:

> From family entertainment, the musical rapidly becomes the fief of the youth crowd. It may have an operational value for that section of the population, but the limiting of the audience clearly limits the overall effect. What's more as we can see from the recent break-dancing craze, the tendency is toward increasingly idiosyncratic and spectacular dance forms. Where once every new dance was aimed at enticing more couples onto the dance floor, now the new dances simply multiply the number of spectators. If we sometimes feel that the soul has disappeared from the musical in recent years, it is surely in part because of the genre's revised relation to the process of music and dance productions.[27]

Considering that the rock musical emerged as a means of attracting teenager customers, the form has always occupied a hybrid status. For example, *Love Me Tender* is a western, romance, musical and teenpic. The early history of the rock movie is inseparable from the rise of the teenpic, a largely realist genre that sits uneasily with the fantasy and escapism ingrained within many musicals. Thomas Doherty states that the teenpic incorporates "a certain verisimilitude into the stylistic and cultural rites of the moment, notably the inside-dope details of the vernacular, fashion and music."[28] Gritty social commentary figured alongside music in some teen-centered films, most notably *King Creole*, with the pessimistic nature of such films representing a retreat from fantasy. The rock movie married the musical more comfortably in traditionalist productions such as *Summer Holiday*, the Pat Boone vehicle, *April Love* (1957) and Presley's beach movies, typified by *Blue Hawaii* (1961). These films incorporated the gloss and professionalism associated with the studio-era musical through their use of color photography, lush locations and escapism. By the mid–1960s, such productions appeared increasingly dated thanks to a combination of changing teenage audience tastes, the transition from pop to rock, with the accompanying distrust of traditional show business, and the decline of the musical genre.

This Is Spinal Tap belongs to a trend evident within rock movies that dates back to the form's earliest days. The likes of *Rock, Rock, Rock* and *Rock Around the Clock* were revue movies that linked a succession of guest musicians, often depicted in televisual style, with flimsy plots. In this sense, they looked back to the earliest days of the film musical when revue productions dominated the genre, while simultaneously relating the rock movie to the current threat of television. Moreover, by recording musical performances without extensive choreography, set designs or dancing, such ventures offered a stripped-down reality. The emergence of the rock documentary in the mid–1960s, with *The TAMI Show* (1965) and *Don't Look Back* (1967) merely extended a trend evident since the very earliest days of the rock movie. *The TAMI Show*, a concert film depicting a jamboree in 1964, included performances from James Brown, the Supremes, the Beach Boys and the Rolling Stones. It dispensed altogether with the romantic plots evident in the likes of *Rock, Rock, Rock*; instead the film recorded the concert as it happened.[29] *Don't Look Back* provided a cinema verité account of Bob Dylan's 1965 British tour. Besides showing Dylan performing, it portrayed an image of the singer-songwriter backstage. The viewer sees the star confronting journalists, his anger when a bottle is thrown from his hotel room and assorted joking around with his associates, as well as glimpses of fans assembling for concerts and business meetings.

The backstage rock documentary thrived throughout the 1960s and 1970s, with such landmarks as *Woodstock* (1970), *Gimme Shelter* and *The Last Waltz*. In the case of *Woodstock* and *Gimme Shelter*, the music sits alongside glimpses of the festivals at Woodstock and Altamont in 1969. *The Last Waltz* offers an insight into the history of the Band at their farewell performance, with interviews interspersed during the concert performances.

This Is Spinal Tap borrows from such previous rock documentaries. An uncharitable observer could remark that the worst aspects of Spinal Tap's music appears evident in the self-indulgence and virtuoso posturing apparent in several acts performing at Woodstock. Marti Di Bergi's persona owes a debt to Martin Scorsese, the director of *The Last Waltz*, particularly with his Italian-American origins and his tendency to show himself interviewing the Band. *This Is Spinal Tap* utilizes the same structure as Scorsese's film, with the nostalgic account of the group's history being mixed with the present.[30] Several recollections contain a rather *Tap* quality, most notably Robbie Robertson recollecting stories about shoplifting and one-arm go-go dancers. Nigel Tufnel's demonstration of his guitar collection, complete with amplifiers extended to "11" mirrors the scene in which Rick Danko shows Scorsese around the Band's studio/clubhouse, which previously operated as a "bordello." In *Gimme Shelter,* Mick Jagger describes his plans for the Altamont concert as "creating a sort of microcosmic society, which sets an example to the rest of America, as how one can behave in large gatherings." *This Is Spinal Tap* features such cosmic rambling from the Jaggeresque David St. Hubbins, who wears a Saturn jumper, made by Jeanine, in the tour bus, while he endorses her plans to forecast the band's future with horoscopes. Ian Faith resembles Albert Grossman, Dylan's bullying and rude manager in *Don't Look Back*. When informed about a complaint concerning the noise emanating from his client's room, Grossman insults the hotel worker as "one of the dumbest assholes and most stupid persons" that he has encountered, threatening to punch the man "in the goddamn nose." Such threatening behavior comes naturally to the foul-mouthed and abrasive Faith, who insults hotel receptionists, record company executives and Jeanine with impunity, while also demonstrating a fondness for wrecking hotel rooms with his cricket bat.

This Is Spinal Tap *and the Backstage Musical Tradition*

Although the rock documentary, as a form that records a version of reality, appears distinct from the musical, it shares similarities. Jonathan Romney writes:

> Backstage moments in film promise not only to initiate us into closely guarded arcana of the music biz in general, but also to reveal the star as he or she really "is," with the motley off, the dance moves temporarily dropped. They offer us a fantasy "Access All Areas" pass, one of those areas being the artist's truth, for backstage is imagined as a far more "real" space than the stage on which the artists do their work—which is supposedly to provide a spectacular, ritualised display of their very being.[31]

Moreover, Romney acknowledges that the rock documentary, despite its realism, owes a debt to "the backstage musical, and to every film that makes a virtue of displaying, performance and a complex unnatural negotiation."[32] The links between *This Is Spinal Tap*, or the lack of them, to such staples of the music as dance and romance were demonstrated earlier. However, the film undoubtedly represents a movie about entertainment. As such, it becomes profitable to consider the film in terms of its relationship to the backstage musical.

During the 1950s, one of the major trends within the MGM musical, best demonstrated by *Singin' in the Rain* (1952) and *The Band Wagon* (1953), saw an increasing self reflectivity and awareness evident within the film text. Scripted by Betty Comden and Adolph Green, these films satirized the nature of entertainment in order to reinvigorate the musical tradition. Nostalgia for the past could only strengthen the musical in the present, whether by detailing the transition to sound (*Singin' in the Rain*) or the triumphant comeback of a veteran performer (*The Band Wagon*). Jane Feuer describes such techniques as "conservative reflexivity," a process that involved "an unveiling and re-veiling of entertainment's mystique."[33] She details the "myth of entertainment" displaying a process of "demystification and remythicization."[34] Audiences receive insight into the workings of entertainment, but successful entertainers are then remythicized. Only those workers who fail as entertainers have their talent and credentials fully exposed. For instance, in *The Band Wagon*, Tony Hunter effectively stands as a surrogate for the film's star, Astaire. Both Hunter and Astaire are song-and-dance men whose greatest success, at the time of the film's release, lay in the past. They share not only the same iconic symbols, top hat, cane and tails, but also each have an uncanny knack to entertain with the resources available. It is through Hunter's initiatives that the show can eventually triumph in the face of adversity.

This Is Spinal Tap shares the nostalgic self-reflexive mood of *The Band Wagon* and *Singin' in the Rain*. Like these MGM classics, *This Is Spinal Tap* concerns protagonists who are associated with, and happier living in, the past. As stated earlier, these veterans of the sixties prove incapable of adapting to the modern world with regards to their attitude towards women. They are also evidently happier talking about their past, whether through discussing the misfortunes suffered by former drummers, past musical glories and the childhood reminiscences of Nigel and David. Ironic cheers from the two frontmen appear when they hear a Thamesmen song from 1965, "Cups and Cakes," on the radio. What the band proves unable to understand is that they are now perceived as an oldies act, residing in the "Where are they now?" file. Fake archive footage of 1960s hits, "Gimme Some Money" and "(Listen to the) Flower People," enhances the film's nostalgic feel, parodying television shows such as *Ready, Steady, Go* and *The Ed Sullivan Show*. It is not insignificant that a heavy metal version of "Gimme Some Money," the band's first hit, features in the rehearsals. The tuneless noise that we hear not only exposes the band's relative lack of musical ability, but also shows that they still wish to play 1960s material albeit in a form disparate from the song's original Freddie and the Dreamers/Gerry and the Pacemakers model. Spinal Tap desire to play oldies, but they recognize that to play the songs in their original style would effectively acknowledge their musical irrelevance. Hence, they continue along their own musical path, blinding themselves to their own limitations and that of their work.

The film's analysis of nostalgic entertainment therefore appears superficially critical. However, any critique of the band's failure must acknowledge that their failures are balanced by the film's climax. If *This Is Spinal Tap* constituted a truly deconstructionist rock movie, it would not willingly endorse the concept of entertainment. The band are entertainers; their adult lives have been spent recording and touring — music represents their raison d'être. This objective is obvious from the beginning of the film, when Marti Di Bergi's introduction declares, "Let's boogie," i.e., let's get down to entertainment via rock 'n' roll. Significantly, Spinal Tap begin and end the film with "Tonight I'm Gonna Rock You Tonight," the item in their repertoire that testifies to their existence. Although the song refers to sexual encounters with "an under-aged object of desire,"[35] the "rocking" metaphor should surely be interpreted as a call to rock the crowds through music. With this anthemic and bombastic feel-good song, Spinal Tap provide their signature tune rather on the lines of similar offerings such as Queen's "We Are the Champions." This explains why the song opens the show, while also appearing during the band's triumphant return in Japan.

"Tonight I'm Gonna Rock You Tonight," like many of the songs in *This Is Spinal Tap*, serves a crucial narrative function. The music perfectly complements the dramatic action, specifically, the characters of the band. "Big Bottom" with its explicit references to sexual relations, informs viewers that this band sees women as only being worthy of potential conquest.

While such euphemisms reveal cogent information into the band's personalities, the song lyrics also explain *This Is Spinal Tap*'s status within the musical genre. According to Feuer, the "myth of entertainment" principally revolves around three concepts: "the myth of spontaneity," "the myth of integration" and "the myth of audience."[36] The use of music in *This Is Spinal Tap* illustrates how the "myth of integration" can be utilized to examine contemporary films featuring musical performance. Integrated musicals often concern those films in which the music directly links to character and plot. As the example of "Big Bottom" confirms, *This Is Spinal Tap* features songs that subscribe to the integrated musical tradition. For Feuer, integration does not simply relate to the connections between song, character and plot. She writes that "successful performances are intimately bound up with success in love, with the integration of the individual into a community or a group, and even with the merger of high art." This statement contains value for studying films such as *The Band Wagon* in which Tony Hunter moves "from isolation to the joy of being part of the group."[37] He overcomes isolation by the spontaneity of musical entertainment, which eventually manages to incorporate ballet dancer Gabrielle Gerard (Cyd Charisse) and pretentious theatre impresario Jeffrey Cordova (Jack Buchanan). Meanwhile, this artistic success coincides with Tony and Gaby's growing personal relationship, as she ditches her choreographer boyfriend who snobbishly refuses to back the plans for the new musical, thereby excluding himself from happiness amid the group.

In *This Is Spinal Tap*, the romantic side of "the myth of integration" is actively downplayed. Indeed, as stated earlier, the film appears decidedly anti-romantic. However, the film's climax stresses the importance of integrating Faith and Nigel back within the group's circle. Spinal Tap's artistic success results from the artistic and personal chemistry within the group, which supersedes the personal union of David and Jeanine. The film contains no successful attempts at linking high and popular art. Derek compares Nigel and David as the "visionaries" of the band, in the vein of Byron and Shelley, but David makes gormless comments such as describing the original St. Hubbins as "the patron saint of quality footwear." Nigel may describe his piano piece as a combination of Bach and Mozart, but the fallacy of his lofty aspirations become obvious when he names the piece "Lick My Love Pump."[38]

Spinal Tap's eventual triumph represents a return to traditional rock 'n' roll values. The film vindicates them for doing what they do best: performing intuitively and enjoying each other's company. In this sense, the reprise of "Tonight I'm Gonna Rock You Tonight" supplies an energetic reaction to the failures of disastrous and pretentious schemes. This aspect of the film coincides with "the myth of spontaneity," performances that look natural, yet which in reality result from years of dedication and rehearsals. At the end of the film, Spinal Tap can suddenly boogie and entertain again, when Nigel rejoins, because his talent, and vital role within the band over many years, means that he only has to walk on stage with a reenergized Spinal Tap for the band's creativity and popularity to reemerge.

Similar developments occur in *Singin' in the Rain* in which the industrious, charming song-and-dance man, Don Lockwood (Gene Kelly), survives the transition to sound. His talent as a stage performer and dancer bequeaths him the ability to adapt to the new Hollywood scene through reinventing himself as a musical star. Dance and music come naturally to Lockwood, as demonstrated by the famous routine with the umbrella in the pouring rain during the "Singin' in the Rain" routine. This contrasts with the talentless and manipulative Lina Lamont (Jean Hagan), Lockwood's co-star, who fails to show the ingenuity and flexibility to succeed in the sound era. Lina's broad New York twang makes her voice unsuitable for sound cinema, which, combined with her arrogance in believing her own self-organized publicity, leads to her eventual public humiliation.

Audiences play a crucial role in shaping ultimate success in *This Is Spinal Tap*, just as they did in studio-era musicals. In both *The Band Wagon* and *Singin' in the Rain*, the audience's rejection of a flawed performance leads to a reawakening of entertainment via Tony Hunter and Don Lockwood. A similar process occurs in *This Is Spinal Tap*. The sign that the band has sacrificed any kind of spontaneity and audience appeal occurs when, following Nigel's departure, they are reduced to playing Derek's "Jazz Odyssey." Although jazz is associated with such concepts as improvisation and self-expression, there exists a long-standing mutual suspicion with rock 'n' roll. In the 1950s, numerous jazz critics denounced the new music as commercialized and debased, while rock musicians, such as John Lennon, disliked jazz.[39] Even today, among rock critics there exists an association between jazz and snobbishness, pretentiousness and elitism.[40] Such characteristics emanate from Derek who denounces Spinal Tap's old oeuvre as "mind numbing, head banging bullshit," despite the audience's rejection of his jazz opus. Here, the largely empty crowd for "Spinal Tap Mark II" literally gives the tuneless, bass-dominated improvisations the thumbs down. In all three films, the audience rejection reminds the performers of their need to entertain. Without receptive customers, the purpose of entertainment becomes futile: they must revert to what they know best to succeed in the future.

Conclusion

This Is Spinal Tap illustrates several key trends concerning hybrid films in the post-studio era. First, it belongs at the end of a historical cycle of "gross out" comedies, while also demonstrating thematic links with the classical Hollywood musical. The film situates itself in the traditions of both *National Lampoon's Animal House* and *Singin' in the Rain*. Second, the film can be read in terms of the subsequent careers of its stars. *The Simpsons*, which includes Harry Shearer as a key voice actor, shares the same kind of satirical knowingness mixed with verbal and visual humor evident in *This Is Spinal Tap*. The mock documentary has continued to thrive, not least in other films associated with *This Is Spinal Tap*, such as the Christopher Guest directed *Best in Show* (2000) and *A Mighty Wind* (2003).

Whether *This Is Spinal Tap* deserves classification as a musical remains an open debate, probably dependent upon who answers the question. It seems strange to list rock documentaries in reference books on musicals, but not a fictional film that contains palpable links with the genre. Possibly, cultural expectations have precluded any comprehension of the film as a musical. Alternately, after a history of fifty years, perhaps it is time to celebrate the half-century of the rock movie by declaring the form as a genre in its own right. It contains inseparable links to other genres, such as the musical, comedy, drama and the teenpic, yet it remains a cultural medium with its own idiosyncratic history and canon.

Notes

1. Steven J. Schneider (ed.), *1001 Movies You Must See Before You Die* (London: Cassell, 2004), 14; Tom Milne (ed.), *The Time Out Film Guide* (Harmondsworth: Penguin, 1993), 938.
2. Richard Dyer, "Entertainment and Utopia." In *Hollywood Musicals: The Film Reader*. Ed. Steven Cohan (London: Routledge, 2002), 20.
3. Colin Larkin, *The Virgin Encyclopedia of Stage and Screen Musicals* (London: Virgin Books, 1999).
4. Rick Altman, *Film/Genre* (London: BFI Publishing), 18.
5. Ibid., 98.
6. *The 100 Greatest Musicals*, broadcast in the UK on Channel Four on December 26 and 27 (2003).
7. Bill Marshall and Robynn Stillwell, *Musicals and Beyond* (Exeter: Intellect Books, 2000); Martin Rubin, "Busby Berkeley and the Backstage Musical." In *Hollywood Musicals: The Film Reader*, 57.
8. Ibid., 57.
9. Steven Cohan, "Introduction." In *Hollywood Musicals: The Film Reader*, 1.
10. Rick Altman, *The American Film Musical* (Bloomington: Indiana University Press, 1987), 16–27 and 104–105; Jane Feuer, *The Hollywood Musical* (London: Macmillan, 1993), 71–72.
11. Carl French, *This Is Spinal Tap: The Official Companion* (London: Bloomsbury, 2000), 158–159.
12. Carl Platinga, "Gender, Power and a Cucumber: Satirizing Masculinity in *This Is Spinal Tap*." In *Movie Music: The Film Reader*. Ed. Kay Dickinson (London: Routledge, 2003), 159.
13. Colin Larkin, *The Virgin Encyclopedia of Popular Music*, 4th ed. (London: Virgin Books, 2002), 1000.
14. Ibid., 1324.
15. Altman, *Film/Genre*, 127; Steve Neale, *Genre and Hollywood* (London: Routledge, 2000), 39.
16. French, *This Is Spinal Tap*, 176, 184, 207, 228 and 248.
17. Altman, *Film/Genre*, 25.
18. William Paul, "The Impossibility of Romance: Hollywood Comedy, 1978–99." *Genre and Contemporary Hollywood*. Ed. Steve Neale (London: BFI Publishing, 2002), 117.
19. Ibid., 117.
20. Ibid., 119–120.
21. Platinga, "Gender, Power and a Cucumber," 159.
22. Ibid., 158.
23. Ibid., 161.
24. French, *This Is Spinal Tap*, 126; see also Eric Idle's commentary on the DVD special edition of *The Rutles: All You Need Is Cash*.
25. Platinga, "Gender, Power and a Cucumber," 156.
26. Andrew Caine, *Interpreting Rock Movies: The Pop Film and Its Critics in Britain* (Manchester: Manchester University Press, 2004), 89–98.
27. Altman *The American Film Musical*, 359.
28. Thomas Doherty, *Teenagers and Teenpics: The Juvenilization of American Movies in 1950s* (Philadelphia, PA: Temple University Press, 2002), 207.

29. The precise title of *The TAMI Show* depends upon which prints are utilized. Its original cinema title in Britain was *Teenage Command Performance*, while the DVD edition, *That Was Rock*, cuts several numerous numbers, integrates material from another concert film, *The Great TNT* (1966) and includes jarring introductions for each artist by Chuck Berry.
30. French, *This Is Spinal Tap*, 199–200.
31. Jonathan Romney, "Access All Areas: The Real Space in Rock Documentaries." In *Celluloid Jukebox: Popular Music and the Movies Since the Fifties*. Ed. Jonathan Romney and Adrian Wooton (London: BFI Publishing), 84.
32. Ibid., 86.
33. Feuer, *The Hollywood Musical*, 91.
34. Jane Feuer, "The Self-Reflective Musical and the Myth of Entertainment." In *Hollywood Musicals: The Film Reader*, 32.
35. French, *This Is Spinal Tap*, 271.
36. Feuer, "The Self-Reflective Musical and the Myth of Entertainment," 32.
37. Ibid., 35.
38. In *Running with the Devil,* Robert Walser reviews the debt to classical technique evident in numerous metal musicians. For further information, see *Running with the Devil: Power, Gender and Madness in Heavy Metal Music* (Hanover, NH: University Press of New England, 1993), 57–107.
39. Caine, *Interpreting Rock Movies*, 42–48, 54–60; Phil Thompson, *The Best of Cellars: The Story of the World Famous Cavern Club* (Liverpool: Bluecoat Press, 1994), 59.
40. For example, see the rock section by Ben Edmonds in Jenny Bulley (ed.), *The MOJO 1000: The Ultimate CD Buyers Guide* (2001): "It infuriates jazz snobs when I say this, but rock 'n' roll is the greatest of all modern music" (np).

8

"A Most Historic Period of Change"

The Western, the Epic and Dances with Wolves

JAMES RUSSELL

The epic western *Dances with Wolves* opened in the United States on November 9, 1990. Despite its relatively average $18 million budget, the film went on to gross $184.2 million at the domestic box office, and a further $240 million overseas, making it the third highest grossing release of 1990.[1] It also won seven Academy Awards, including Best Picture and Best Director. The film can therefore be viewed as an exemplary "sleeper" hit. Few within the industry had expected *Dances with Wolves* to generate much in the way of public interest, and some had labeled Costner's film "Kevin's Gate," in ironic homage to the film that bankrupted United Artists in 1980, Michael Cimino's *Heaven's Gate*.[2] Patterns of success and failure at the box office during the previous decade seemed to justify such dismissals. Throughout the 1980s, western and epic films remained highly marginal in contrast to their predominance during prior periods of Hollywood history.

However, the success of *Dances with Wolves* appeared to contradict negative preconceptions of epic and western films. In subsequent years the major Hollywood studios initiated a range of related productions, each designed to capitalize on the success of Costner's unexpected hit. In many cases, the formal and thematic qualities of these related productions were dependent on an interpretation of *Dances with Wolves*' generic status. Had audiences responded to the film because it was an epic, a western, an ecological drama, or a Native American historical saga? This chapter traces the application of two competing generic labels, "western" and "epic," from conception and production, through to marketing and reception. The "western" qualities of the film dominated during the early stages of this process, but I will show how these features were eventually superseded by a focus on the film's "epic" qualities following its release. To this end, I begin by defining some of the terms I shall be using, and placing these terms in a historical context. I then look at the intentions of the filmmakers and studio executives, at the narrational and thematic qualities of the film, and at *Dances with Wolves*' impact on the film marketplace. I will argue that the attachments and associations that accumulated around generic terms such as "epic" and "western" during earlier periods of Hollywood's history have had a profound, but uncontrolled, impact on *Dances with Wolves*, and contemporary film culture more generally.

"Epics" and "Westerns"

Throughout this chapter, I adhere to recent conceptions of genre that originate with Richard Maltby, Steve Neale and Rick Altman.[3] In different works, all these scholars argue that Hollywood films are best understood as entries in short-lived, interconnected cycles of production, to which generic labels are applied by producers, marketing departments, critics and viewers in a scattershot, ad-hoc fashion. Genres are shared ideas about particular stories, whereas films are commercial products that make reference to these ideas. For Altman, the widespread popular adoption of a generic label comes to act as "proof" of its existence as a viable descriptive category, while Neale argues that the only means to establish generic credentials available to scholars is detailed investigation of the terms used to describe a film.[4] In either case, popular conceptions of particular genres are invariably based on the features of earlier cycles. Therefore, as Neale puts it, the generic label of "historical epic" is

> essentially a 1950s and 1960s term. It was used to identify, and to sell two overlapping contemporary trends: Films with historical, especially ancient world settings; and large scale films of all kinds which used new technologies, high production values and special modes of distribution and exhibition to differentiate themselves from both routine productions and from alternative forms of contemporary entertainment, especially television.[5]

Neale observes that the content of the epic was marked by "a dramatic and thematic concern with political and military power, political and military rule, and political and military struggle [which] found articulation on national, international and sometimes global and cosmic scales."[6] Furthermore, these epics can be distinguished from other films with historical settings by a narrational focus on "world historical events, the distant myths or more recent turning points of the culture [which] must be treated with resources of cinematic style ... connoting grandeur and overwhelming cultural significance," in the words of Bruce Babington and Peter William Evans.[7] The epic cycle was initiated by the success of Cecil B. DeMille's *Samson and Delilah* in 1948, consolidated by Mervyn LeRoy's *Quo Vadis* in 1951, associated with emergent "big screen" technologies with *The Robe* (1953), and achieved greatest critical and commercial success in *Ben-Hur* (1959). Although many epics were set in the ancient world, other epics dealt with a range of different historical periods. However, the cycle (or, more accurately, group of cycles) declined massively after 1968, following a period of overproduction.[8] Historical epics then remained marginal throughout the 1970s and 1980s, when occasional releases such as *The Last Emperor* (1987) failed to achieve commercial success despite critical appreciation.

Alternatively, the thousands of films set on the American frontier after 1860, which effectively constitute the "western," arguably form the most long-lived and least representative, of Hollywood genres. Although they may appear to constitute a coherent genre, with thematic ebbs and tides that reflect broader social and cultural shifts, as John Cawelti, Will Wright and others have all argued, such conceptions invariably fail to acknowledge the diverse range of subtly different western cycles that have coexisted throughout Hollywood's history.[9] The western is not so much one century-long storytelling tradition, as a mass of coexisting cycles, all designed to capitalize on presumed audience preference. Of these cycles, Sheldon Hall has noted that "epic westerns are generally the most conscious of the genre's basis in an actual, as opposed to mythic, past," but, with the exception of *How the West Was Won* (1962), very few "westerns of authentically epic scale and ambition" have ever been released.[10] Significantly, Kevin Costner repeatedly cited *How the West Was Won* as the key influence on *Dances with Wolves*.

While the epic effectively vanished by the 1970s, westerns remained an important part of American film culture. David A. Cook has identified four different western cycles that dominated during the 1970s. Aside from the "Traditional Western," the 1970s also saw the emergence of "Vietnam Westerns," "Modernist or Anti-Westerns," and "Comic or Parodic Westerns."[11] As the labels suggest, these films often attempted to revise the history of the west that had featured in earlier cycles of the western movie.[12] A case in point is Arthur Penn's *Little Big Man* (1970), which Margo Kasdan and Susan Tavernetti claim "inverts the common mythologies of the American frontier usually presented in the western film genre," by presenting the Indians as "victims of malevolent treatment by the United States Army."[13] In *Little Big Man*, the Indians are heroes and the Americans are murderous invaders, a theme that resonates in *Dances with Wolves*. However, as Kasdan and Tavernetti note, Penn's film is more "comic and ironic" in tone than Costner's stately, tasteful and more recognizably epic approach.[14] As the 1970s wore on, westerns seemed to decline in popularity and production.

The death knell for epics and westerns was finally sounded in 1980 by the catastrophic box office performance of Michael Cimino's *Heaven's Gate*, which Stephen Prince claims was "widely regarded by the industry as [a] test of the genre's viability and [its] fate was interpreted as evidence of an exhausted market."[15] *Heaven's Gate* told the story of a clash between landowners and cattle ranchers in 1890s Wyoming. It cost $35 million to make and $6 million to market, but it received disastrous reviews, and by 1983 it had only returned $1.5 million.[16] The loss effectively destroyed United Artists as a film distributor, and it entirely discouraged other studios from bankrolling expensive epics or westerns for some time. According to Stephen Prince, "The eighties were a terrible decade for fans of the genre.... The western had seemingly lost its cultural force [and] the production rate that characterized the genre in earlier times was over."[17] Recent work by Neale has shown that Prince's conclusions are a little overstated. Westerns did continue to be made for cinemas and TV during the 1980s, but the majority failed commercially.[18] However, the success of the ABC television miniseries *Lonesome Dove* in 1989 suggested that audiences may not have vanished entirely.[19] This minor reignition of interest may have helped popularize *Dances with Wolves*, but Costner had begun work on his epic western some time before, when there were no related cycles in production, and when both epic and western movies were associated with box office failure. Consequently we should ask: how and why did the film get made?

Constructing Dances with Wolves

Kevin Costner's love of western movies has defined his career as a star and as a director. He has claimed, "I can remember as a ten year old watching *How the West was Won* and certain moments made me tingle with the magic of it."[20] On the set of Lawrence Kasdan's 1986 commercial failure, *Silverado*, Costner apparently spent his days reenacting scenes from the westerns he had watched in his youth, and while publicizing the film he told the press, "I waited my whole life to be in a western," dedicating his performance to "everyone who ever dreamed of being in a western."[21] David Thomson has described Costner's later career as "the most blatant example in screen history of an actor following his own fantasies — at enormous cost sometimes, but doggedly, like some lone scout mapping the far northwest."[22] Early reviews of *Dances with Wolves* emphasized and sometimes mocked Costner's commitment to the western. For instance, J. Hoberman wrote in the *Village Voice*, "Who even admits liking westerns, let alone raising $18 million to make one? More garrulous than the old Gary Cooper ever was, Costner has let it be known that the 1962 roadshow *How the West Was Won*, the *Ben-Hur* of the horse opera, is among his favourites."[23] Recently, Costner's profile has diminished, but he has continued to star in, and direct, westerns, including his performance in the title role of Lawrence Kasdan's unsuccessful *Wyatt Earp* (1994), and his 2004 directorial effort *Open Range*. In the introduction to the "making of" book that accompanied the release of *Dances with Wolves*, Costner wrote, "There is little doubt I will make other movies, but if I could not *Dances with Wolves* would complete the picture I have had of myself since I was a little boy. It will forever be my love letter to the past."[24] Costner's comments exhibit a deep attachment to the defunct Hollywood western, and *Dances with Wolves* can therefore be understood as the fulfillment of a childhood dream. Furthermore, Costner never distinguishes between different western cycles, and his nostalgic view seems to erase or elide the more pessimistic, revisionist westerns of the 1970s. In fact, *Dances with Wolves* seems to present revisionist sentiments (which critique the expansion of whites into "Indian territory") as part of a "classic" western narrative, suggesting that Costner's highly nostalgic conception of the Hollywood western differs radically from critical accounts. This highly subjective nostalgia informed both the film's production, and its narrative.

The origins of *Dances with Wolves* can be traced back to the early 1980s. In 1981, Kevin Costner starred in a low-budget gambling drama called *Stacy's Knights* (released 1983), which was directed by Jim Wilson, and written by Michael Blake. Wilson, Blake and Costner became friends, and at some point Costner suggested that Blake turn one of his movie ideas, about a cavalry officer on the American frontier, into a novel.[25] Blake, a journalist turned screenwriter, completed the novel in 1986, and the trio quickly set about reconfiguring it as a movie. Later, Costner would claim that "Michael managed to forge all the elements most attractive to me — simplicity, dignity, humor and poignancy" into both the story and the character of John Dunbar.[26] At this point Costner was becoming visible as a star, with roles in Kevin Reynolds' *Fandango* (1985), Lawrence Kasdan's *Silverado*, and the lead in Brian DePalma's *The Untouchables* (1987). With the proceeds from this acting work, Costner employed Blake to work on the script adaptation.[27] The novel, meanwhile, was published in 1987.

Even with a script completed, the major studios were understandably reluctant to green-light *Dances with Wolves*. The legacy of *Heaven's Gate* effectively ensured that the project would remain in "development hell" until Costner, fresh from the success of *Field of Dreams* (1989) decided to raise funding for the project independently. Costner and Jim Wilson set up their own company, Tig Productions, and, after a series of failed deals, brought in renowned dealmaker Jake Eberts, who raised enough capital to commence pre-production by selling overseas distribution rights.[28] Two weeks before production was due to start, Costner, Wilson and Ebert convinced the mini-major Orion Pictures to put up the remaining $9 million of an estimated $15 million budget, in return for domestic distribution rights. As part of the deal, Kevin Costner had "final cut" as producer, director and star.[29]

According to cofounder Mike Medavoy, Orion Pictures had been conceived of as a "director-friendly" studio "where filmmakers could realise their visions without interference from executives."[30] The company had been formed by departing United Artists executives in 1978, who envisaged a studio devoted to interesting, relatively highbrow product — an equivalent to the failing UA dream. Throughout the 1980s Orion enjoyed critical and commercial success with Oscar-oriented films such as *Amadeus* (1985) and *Platoon* (1986), as well as exploitation-type productions like *Bull Durham* (1988) and *Robocop* (1987).[31] The studio was one of many independent distributors to emerge in the 1980s, as the growing video market increased demand for product, and opened up opportunities for studios other than the established majors to prosper.[32] However, by the end of the decade Orion was mired in financial difficulties, and although two of the films it initiated at this time went on to become massive hits, *Dances with Wolves* and *The Silence of the Lambs* (1991), the studio filed for bankruptcy in 1991.

Despite Orion's "hands off" mandate, Costner clashed with executives several times during filming, and at least one decision may have exacerbated Orion's financial difficulties in the long run. When Costner started to go over budget, Orion insisted that he forfeit his salary in favor of a share of the gross. Costner agreed, and $3 million was channeled away from the star and back into the film. The movie eventually came in at $18 million, a scant 5 percent over its projected costs. Although Orion executives were apparently unhappy with Costner's three-hour cut, the deal that Costner had arranged meant that they were obliged to release his version of the film.[33] Therefore, the film can be read as Costner's highly personal attempt to revisit the epic western tradition, in defiance of commercial wisdom or interference, and Costner can be understood as the dominant creative contributor.[34] The next section will demonstrate that Costner's nostalgic desire to return to the popular genres of

Hollywood's past was also integral to the thematic and narrational organization of the film itself.

The Cinematic Past in Dances with Wolves

The title, *Dances with Wolves*, is intentionally multifaceted. It is the name that John Dunbar adopts at the moment he becomes accepted as a Lakota Sioux warrior; it is a key point of transition in the narrative, when Dunbar is spotted by the Indians performing a war dance in the company of his pet wolf; and finally, it is an allegory for the film itself. Dunbar finds himself alone on the frontier, surrounded by people he has been trained to think of as violent savages — wolves of a sort. He chooses not to fight these "wolves" but to enter into a more benign relationship. He "dances," with all the implications of submission and sensuality that the term suggests. This dance leads him to an ancient and, the film implies, spiritually purifying existence. Through his encounters with the Sioux, the Union soldier Dunbar is redeemed. However, the way of life that he encounters is passing, and the film is riddled with nostalgia for a better, older way of life. Arguably, this nostalgia echoes Kevin Costner's attempt to revisit, and revive, the epic western tradition.

The film begins with an injured and dispirited Dunbar attempting to commit suicide on a Tennessee battlefield in 1863. His attempt to end his life by charging Confederate lines inadvertently allows his Union compatriots to mount a surprise attack, and rout the enemy. Dunbar is declared a hero, and is offered the posting of his choice as a reward. He elects to head out to the western frontier, away from the fighting, but also away from the modern world. His first stop is Fort Hays, the last functioning Union outpost before the frontier. There he is given his orders by an obviously insane Major Fambrough, who tells him, "I am sending you on a knight's errand, you will report to Captain Cargill at the furthermost outpost of the realm, Fort Sedgewick." After Dunbar departs, Fambrough cries out, "To your journey and to my journey!" and shoots himself in the head. Dunbar is guided by Timmons (described by Fambrough as a "peasant"), a lewd, dirty man about whom Dunbar writes in his diary (a device that initially justifies the voice-over), "Were it not for the company, I would be having the time of my life." Despite the presence of Timmons, at this point the film begins to focus on the beauty of the landscape. Wide, epic shots introduce the unspoilt west. Dunbar then arrives at Fort Sedgewick to find it abandoned and polluted by its previous occupants, but decides to stay nonetheless.

All the Anglo-American characters in this opening section, except Dunbar, are shown to be dirty, destructive and demented. The fighting in Tennessee is chaotic, and lacks any stated ideological purpose, while Fort Hays has driven Fambrough to mental collapse. In both places, a central character attempts suicide as a means of escape. Timmons exhibits little appreciation for the beauty that surrounds him as he travels west, and is killed by an Indian raiding party as he heads home. An extended cut of the film, released in Europe a year after the film's theatrical release, and subsequently screened on American television, shows the original occupants of Fort Sedgewick driven to despair, and eventually fleeing east. However, when Dunbar crosses the frontier, he moves back in time, away from the corrupt, violent present of 1863, towards an ancient and, the film suggests, ennobling form of existence. As a result of his suicide attempt, Dunbar is able to literally escape into the distant past, prompting Native American critic Edward D. Castillo to suggest that the bulk of the film should be read as a posthumous fantasy, a "dream quest" in which Dunbar dies, and then uncovers his true identity.[35]

At Fort Sedgewick Dunbar cleans the camp and maintains routine patrols. As time passes he finds himself drawn to the local Sioux. In direct contrast to the Anglo-American characters in the film, the Sioux Indians inhabit an enviable world of familial harmony and contentment. We see them discussing what to do about the white man, and they decide, in eminently democratic fashion, that Dunbar is a man with whom treaties can be arranged. Gradually, Dunbar comes into closer contact with the Sioux. He saves a white Sioux adoptee, Stands with a Fist (Mary McDonnell) from committing suicide (the third suicide attempt in the film) and brings the anxious Sioux news of an approaching buffalo herd. In time, he learns the Sioux language, Lakota, becomes close friends with Kicking Bird (Graham Greene) and falls in love with Stands with a Fist. In the process Dunbar is transformed into Dances with Wolves. However, when Dunbar returns to Fort Sedgewick to collect his journal, he is captured by Union soldiers. Dunbar refuses to speak to his captors in English, or acknowledge the person he had been, and as a result, he is tortured. Eventually, the Sioux are able to rescue him, but Dunbar returns knowing that the Sioux are doomed, and that westward expansion of white civilization cannot be stopped. He tells Kicking Bird, "You always ask me about the white people. You always want to know how many more are coming. There will be a lot, my friend. More than can be counted, like the stars. It makes me afraid for all the Sioux." Now a fugitive, Dunbar and his wife decide that they must go back to Anglo civilization and defend the Indian nations. A postscript informs us, "Thirteen years later, their homes destroyed, their buffalo gone, the last band of free Sioux submitted to white authority. The great horse culture of the plains was gone and the American frontier was soon to pass into history."

Throughout the film, the equality and moral integrity of the Sioux stands in stark contrast to the depiction of Anglo characters. In part this depiction was closely allied to a burgeoning "new age" movement, which merged Indian cultural practices and trappings such as buckskin, dreamcatchers, sweat lodges, homeopathic healing and communal living, with ecological concerns and an eastern spirituality emphasizing self-enlightenment.[36] As cultural historian Philip J. Deloria has observed, these simplistic conceptions of the Native American lifestyle and culture were offered as remedies to the social ills of suburban, corporate America.[37] Popular writing such as Ed McGaa's *Rainbow Tribe: Ordinary People Journeying the Red Road*, the work of Lynne Andrew, and James Redfield's *The Celestine Prophecies: An Adventure* presented the Native Northern and Central Americans as ecologically and spiritually harmonious figures with much to teach the contemporary United States.[38] *Dances with Wolves* can certainly be understood in this context. Indeed, the press book used self-consciously "spiritual" terms to sell the film, describing it as "the extraordinary journey of one hero's search for humanity in the ultimate frontier — himself."[39] However, by valorizing the distant past over the present, the film also reflected a very different tradition of debate about the role of the media in contemporary American society.

Shortly after its release, *Dances with Wolves* won Best Film at the Independent Spirit Awards, an event designed to honor independently produced movies. In his acceptance speech, Costner lambasted the "typical Hollywood movie" as "an incomplete, half-thought-out piece of shit."[40] He was by no means alone in his belief that there was something wrong with mainstream contemporary filmmaking. In 1992 Michael Medved published the bestselling *Hollywood Vs. America: Popular Culture and the War on Traditional Values* in which he argued that Hollywood had become "an all powerful enemy, an alien force that assaults our most cherished values and corrupts our children."[41] Medved claimed to speak for the "silent majority" of Americans, and quoted surveys suggesting that over 80 percent of Americans believed there was too much violence and profanity in the movies, and that the situation was getting worse.[42] Medved's criticisms resulted from an ongoing conflict between conservatives (often those with evangelical religious agendas) and more liberal forces that has informed American social and political life since the 1960s, and is sometimes known as the "culture wars."[43] Medved's dismissal of Hollywood movies for their violence and profanity was very similar to Costner's dismissal of Hollywood movies at the Independent Spirit awards.[44] In different ways Costner and Medved were both arguing that the quality and moral integrity of Hollywood filmmaking had diminished during the 1970s and 1980s, and were appealing for a return to the more overtly edifying productions of their youth. Indeed, Jim Collins has argued that the "old fashioned" nature of Costner's film is an attempt to escape the challenges and uncertainties of a postmodern media environment.[45] Although Costner would likely have described his project differently, it is certainly the case that *Dances with Wolves* was an act of nostalgic recuperation, and Dunbar's journey can be read as a useful allegory of Costner's intentions.

Like the film's title, the significance of Dunbar's voyage into the past can be interpreted in several ways. Certainly for Kevin Costner, and perhaps for older viewers with fond memories of westerns and epics, the film offered an opportunity to regress to boyhood. When he arrives at the frontier Dunbar finds himself relying on the sorts of survival tactics familiar to boy scouts across the world. At times, the fort resembles nothing less than a mature version of the sort of summer camps (often with "Indian" names) that remain popular with American children today. When the Sioux appear, Dunbar becomes part of an adult game of "Cowboys and Injuns," albeit one in which the main participant decides to switch sides halfway through. With *Dances with Wolves*, Costner presided over a western, but he was also able to participate in one. Just as Dunbar was able to escape a troubling present, so Costner had sought to escape a filmmaking climate in which westerns had virtually vanished, by returning to the cinematic terrain of his youth. This journey was closely associated with symbolic images of death and suicide, which embody a thematic preoccupation with death and rebirth. For many of the film's characters, suicide attempts prefigure a profound personal transformation. Costner's agenda as a filmmaker can be understood in similar terms. He was attempting to reinvigorate film culture, by presiding over the rebirth of the western (and, to a lesser extent, epic) movies that had defined his childhood. By repeatedly stressing that the past is more enriching and edifying than the present, *Dances with Wolves* championed a long-defunct tradition of epic and western films. As Dunbar voyages into the past, he enters the iconographic and narrational terrain of the epic western.

Consequently, the chaos and violence of the east acts as a metaphor for film culture at the end of the 1980s. Violence was a key concern of commentators such as Medved, who perceived an "addiction to graphic ... and sadistic violence" in many Hollywood films.[46] Medved identified films from the late 1980s and early 1990s such as *Lethal Weapon 2* (1989), *Batman* (1990) and *Total Recall* (1990) as examples of a growing predilection for amoral violence. Such claims were not limited to conservative figures. Even *Variety* lamented *Total Recall*'s "heedless contribution to the accelerating brutality of its time."[47] In fact, Costner's previous film, *Revenge* (1989), had been heavily criticized for its extreme violence and brutality. The redemption that Dunbar finds among the Sioux can therefore be read as equivalent to the redemption that Costner was seeking by producing the film. As a star and a filmmaker, he was moving away from his perceived misdeeds in a violent present, exactly like Dunbar.

The hopeless voyage that Dunbar makes back into Anglo-American society can therefore be read as a metaphor for Costner's journey as a filmmaker. Dunbar took a suicidal risk in fighting for the Sioux, in order to bring about a greater understanding of and tolerance for, the dying inhabitants of the American past. By making *Dances with Wolves*, Costner was offering the epic western as a cure for the ills of the modern age, and, effectively, fighting for its survival (perhaps "suicidally" sacrificing his popularity in the process). However, Orion's marketing department and movie critics presented the film in a slightly different light, and as a result, its impact on film culture was not quite what Costner had intended.

Critical and Commercial Responses

> During one promotional interview, Costner claimed:
>
> I never saw it as a political film about the plight of the Indians. I'm aware that it has a political feeling and that there are other, harder stories to tell, but I was attracted to its humanity and to the sense of humour I felt I could bring to it. Also, I like its epic quality: *Silverado*, *The Untouchables* and *Field of Dreams* had that too. I like big movies. I like it when there's a lot at stake. I like big casts. I think the longer a movie is the better.[48]

The writer Michael Blake has said that he had always envisaged *Dances with Wolves* as "an epic movie.... I felt that the only way we could present the book in movie form was as an epic, something larger than life."[49] Although Costner was clearly motivated by an obsession with westerns, the film he produced was epic in scope. The fact that Costner was so keen to link *Dances with Wolves* and *How the West Was Won* is particularly telling in this regard.[50] As Sheldon Hall has observed, in the epic western, as in the historical epic, the depiction of pivotal moments in history is a primary thematic concern, and Costner's film was ultimately concerned with the end of Native American civilization, rather than the more mythic terrain of the conventional western.[51] Through Dunbar, the audience experiences what historian Hugh Brogan has called "the white conquest of the continent" from the position of the conquered.[52] As a result, the marketing and critical reception of Costner's film played a pivotal role in reestablishing the cultural (and financial) capital of the term "epic." Both Altman and Neale assert that the use of generic terms plays an important role in establishing new cycles. By examining the use of key terms, it is therefore possible to trace *Dances with Wolves'* impact on production trends.

Although Orion had not been able to exert much influence on Costner during production, the studio was able to control the film's marketing. Fearful of having its already dubious box office appeal further tarnished by association with the apparently unfashionable western, Orion chose to market the film as an epic.[53] *Dances with Wolves* was a prestigious historical film set in the American west, but, Orion attempted to assure audiences, it was *not* a western. Considerable linguistic somersaults were employed to describe the film in the accompanying press book. Here it was presented as "an epic set in America's most historic period of change — the 1860s."[54] The description is notable for the way that mention of the west or the western is steadfastly avoided. Meanwhile, the "making of" book that accompanied the film's release was entitled *Dances with Wolves: The Illustrated Story of the Epic Film*. Again, the term "western" was never used. Orion's marketing department appeared to believe that epics were saleable, but westerns were not. Therefore, Orion's marketing campaign seemed to contradict Costner's earlier agenda — to revisit and revive the epic Hollywood western.

Nevertheless, many critics understandably chose to label *Dances with Wolves* a western despite Orion's efforts. Roger Ebert described it as "one of the best Westerns I've ever seen," and the *New York Post* went so far as to claim that "Kevin Costner has single-handedly brought back the Western."[55] The film also won the National Cowboy Hall of Fame's Western Heritage Award.[56] However, other reviewers clearly interpreted the film as an epic. The *Los Angeles Times* claimed that "it's impossible to call it anything but epic" and compared it favorably with *Lawrence of Arabia* (1962).[57] Reviews in *New York* magazine, the *Christian Science Monitor* and *Newsweek* used similar terminology.[58] This was also visible in the United Kingdom, where one reviewer wrote, "Long devalued by being thrown at anything longish with a big budget, the word 'epic' is rescued by Kevin Costner's sweeping, moving and engrossing study of the American frontier."[59] When *Dances with Wolves* became a critical and commercial hit, these reviews offered those in the film industry a vital means of interpreting the film's appeal. Repeatedly, reviewers expressed admiration for Costner's daring attempt to mine Hollywood's generic heritage. The film's exceptional box office performance suggested that this act of nostalgic recuperation had resonated with audiences across the world. As a result, *Dances with Wolves* inspired a diverse range of related productions, which all incorporated and emphasized different aspects of Costner's movie in accordance with the rules of what Rick Altman describes as the "producer's game."[60] According to Altman, the production of generically marked movies can described by a simple set of rules, which expose how production schedules are designed to exploit the generic characteristics of prior hits:

1. From Box Office information, identify a successful film.
2. Analyse that film in order to discover what made it successful.
3. Make another film stressing the assumed formula for success.
4. Check box-office information on the new film and reassess the success formula accordingly.
5. Use the revised formula as the basis for another film.
6. Continue the process indefinitely.[61]

To understand the effect of *Dances with Wolves* on Hollywood, one must play the producer's game, and search for releases clearly designed to capitalize on its success.

Neale has identified 41 western movies, television series and documentaries that appeared between 1990 and 1995, including *Dances with Wolves*.[62] He argues that this cycle was related to a broader revitalization of "'New Western' culture," with distant links to the "New Age" movement, but also to a burgeoning country music industry that was becoming increasingly popular with mainstream listeners. Furthermore, we can safely assume that it usually takes somewhere between two and three years for a film to go from the earliest stages of conception through to final release. Therefore, the noticeable increase in mainstream production of westerns in 1992 and 1993 must be attributed to the success of *Dances with Wolves*. In 1992, Clint Eastwood's *Unforgiven* won four Academy Awards, including Best Picture, but despite greater critical acclaim, Eastwood's film was nowhere near as commercially successful with audiences as *Dances with Wolves*. *Unforgiven* made $101.2 million in domestic receipts, and $58 million overseas, not even a third of *Dances with Wolves*' takings.[63] The success of *Dances with Wolves* had made Eastwood's western seem like a viable financial investment, but audiences did not respond so well to the film. Box office returns generated by other westerns steadily diminished until the disappointing performance of *Tombstone* (1993) and *Wyatt Earp*, which grossed $56 million and $25 million respectively in the North American market, brought the limited cycle of westerns to an end.[64] The western has since reassumed the marginal position it occupied during the 1980s. Occasional attempts to revive the western do continue, but are usually personal projects produced at the margins of the industry, as in the case of *Open Range*. Despite Costner's best efforts, the cycle of western movies he sought to initiate had stalled and died within a period of less than five years.

Dances with Wolves also inspired a limited cycle of what might be termed

"Native American" movies. These included *Geronimo: An American Legend* (1994) and *Black Robe* (1991), as well as *Thunderheart* (1992), a contemporary thriller set on an Indian reservation. On television, Ted Turner, another western aficionado, produced a series of TV movies under the "Native Americans" banner for his TNT network. These were historical biopics such as *Squanto: A Warrior's Tale* (1994). Meanwhile, Costner himself hosted a documentary series about American Indian history called *500 Nations* (1994). None of the films achieved particular success at the box office, or in the television ratings, and this cycle also quickly died out.

Several obviously epic films also appeared in the wake of *Dances with Wolves*. Michael Mann's *The Last of the Mohicans* (1992) combined elements of the swashbuckler, romance and epic in a story about Indian trappers fighting in the Franco-Indian War. The emphasis on Native American customs, and whites learning the ways of Indians clearly resembled Costner's film. By revisiting the classic novel by James Fenimore Cooper and a 1936 film directed by George B. Seitz, Mann, like Costner, was looking to reinvigorate a popular story from Hollywood's past. Although the film wasn't a flop, it only performed adequately at the box office, making $75.5 million domestically.[65] The same was true of Ron Howard's *Far and Away* (1992) and Ronald F. Maxwell's *Gettysburg* (1993). Howard's film was a romantic tale of Irish settlers in the American West, budgeted at $60 million and released by Universal. It grossed $58.9 million domestically, and $78.9 million overseas.[66] Maxwell's was a star-studded reenactment of the famous civil war battle that had originally been intended for television (on TNT) but that had grown in scale during production, and eventually received a limited release with the independent distributor New Line.[67] Other independently minded filmmakers, often with overt political agendas, were also able to find funding for epic projects of their own, such as Spike Lee's *Malcolm X* (1992), and Oliver Stone's *JFK* (1993) and *Nixon* (1995). These films generated huge volumes of media comment, thus contributing to a climate in which big budget historical films could be considered increasingly viable. As a result, the studios were increasingly willing to green-light epics, including two enormous successes, Steven Spielberg's *Schindler's List* (1993), and Mel Gibson's *Braveheart* (1995). In every case, these films had originated with committed individuals who had expressed particular interest in the defunct epic tradition, much like Costner. Retrospectively then, it is clear that the primary impact of *Dances with Wolves* on film genre was not to bring about a revival of the western, but rather to initiate the emergence of a new cycle of highly successful historical epics, which has included *Titanic* (1997), *Saving Private Ryan* (1998) and *Gladiator* (2000).[68]

Dances with Wolves had its origins in Kevin Costner's childhood exposure to, and fascination with, genres that had dominated earlier periods of Hollywood's history. He was able to revisit this cinematic terrain, as he understood it, but he was motivated by more than simple nostalgia. Costner viewed the epic and western as inherently valuable cinematic institutions, and *Dances with Wolves* was an attempt to revive those traditions. At an allegorical level, the narrational preoccupation with death and rebirth, past and present, was a clear reflection of Costner's agenda. Dunbar's commitment to the enriching yet vanishing world of the Sioux mirrored Costner's commitment to the western. The generic labels applied to the film in the wake of its release offered viewers, reviewers and Orion's marketing department an opportunity to interpret this project, but in turn, these terms took on a life of their own, opening a space for the unlikely revival of the Hollywood historical epic.

For Costner, terms such as "western" and "epic" clearly invoked a powerful web of associations, memories and beliefs. The production and impact of *Dances with Wolves* demonstrate how such intimate and conceptual generic categories can have a direct influence on the more economically motivated cycles of film production. Much recent work on genre has argued, rightly in my view, that greater scholarly emphasis should be placed on production cycles, and on the use of generic terms by producers, critics and audiences. However, we should not forget that this approach is dependent on a "shared-yet-subjective" circulation of ideas about what a genre *is*. Genres such as the western and the epic may not be real or circumscribable in the manner that critics once claimed, but popular ideas and assumptions about genre, however misconceived, can have a genuine impact on the economic realities of filmmaking. As *Dances with Wolves* demonstrates, ideas about genres can sometimes lead to unexpected developments in film culture.

Notes

1. Financial data from Box Office Mojo, <http://www.boxofficemojo.com/?movies?id=dances with wolves.htm>.
2. Mike Medavoy and Josh Young, *You're Only as Good as Your Next One: 100 Great Films, 100 Good Films and 100 for Which I Should Be Shot* (New York: Atria, 2002), 160.
3. Richard Maltby, *Hollywood Cinema* (London: Blackwell, 2003), 74–110; Steve Neale, *Genre and Hollywood* (London: Routledge, 2000); and Rick Altman, *Film/Genre* (London: BFI Publishing, 1999).
4. Altman, *Film/Genre*, 66 and Neale, *Genre and Hollywood*, 253.
5. Neale, 85.
6. Ibid.
7. Bruce Babington and Peter William Evans, *Biblical Epics: Sacred Narrative in the Hollywood Cinema* (Manchester: Manchester University Press, 1993), 4.
8. See James Russell, "Debts, Disasters and Mega-Musicals: The Decline of the Studio System." In *Contemporary American Cinema*. Ed. Linda Ruth Williams and Michael Hammond (London: McGraw-Hill, 2006), 50–52.
9. John Cawelti, *The Six Gun Mystique* (Bowling Green: Bowling Green University Press, 1970);

Will Wright, *Sixguns and Society: A Structural Study of the Western* (Berkeley: University of California, 1975). For a critique of these studies, see Maltby, *Hollywood Cinema*, 85.
    10. Sheldon Hall, "*How the West Was Won*: History, Spectacle and the American Mountains." In *The Book of Westerns*. Ed. Ian Cameron and Douglas Pye (New York: Continuum, 1996), 255.
    11. David A. Cook, *Lost Illusions: American Cinema in the Shadow of Watergate and Vietnam, 1970–1979* (Berkeley: University of California Press, 2002), 173–182.
    12. One good overview of these cycles can be found in Michael Coyne, *The Crowded Prairie: American National Identity in the Hollywood Western* (London: I.B. Tauris, 1997).
    13. Margo Kasdan and Susan Tavernetti, "Native Americans in a Revisionist Western." In *Hollywood's Indian: The Portrayal of the Native American in Film*. Ed. Peter C. Rollins and John E. O'Connor (Lexington: University Press of Kentucky, 1998), 121.
    14. Ibid., 122.
    15. Stephen Prince, *A New Pot of Gold: Hollywood under the Electronic Rainbow, 1980–1989* (Berkeley: University of California Press, 2002), 309.
    16. Ibid., 37. See also Steven Bach, *Final Cut: Dreams and Disaster in the Making of Heaven's Gate* (New York: Morrow, 1985).
    17. Prince, *A New Pot of Gold*, 314.
    18. Steve Neale, "Westerns and Gangster Films since the 1970s." In *Genre and Contemporary Hollywood*. Ed. Steve Neale (London: BFI, 2002), 27–47.
    19. For further details of epic and western-themed TV miniseries at this time, and the relationship of these productions to cinematic cycles, see chapter three of James Russell, *The Historical Epic and Contemporary Hollywood* (New York: Continuum, 2007).
    20. Todd Keith, *Kevin Costner: The Unauthorised Biography* (London: Ikonprint, 1991), 19.
    21. Quoted in ibid., 63.
    22. David Thomson, *The New Biographical Dictionary of Film* (London: Little, Brown, 2002), 181.
    23. J. Hoberman, "[Rev. of] *Dances with Wolves*," *Village Voice* November 20 (1990): 69.
    24. Kevin Costner, "Introduction." In *Dances with Wolves: The Illustrated Story of the Epic Film*. Kevin Costner, Michael Blake and Jim Wilson (New York: Newmarket, 1990).
    25. See Keith, *Kevin Costner*, 130; Orion Pictures, *Dances with Wolves* Press Kit, held at the BFI Library, London: 3; and Costner, Blake and Wilson, *Dances with Wolves*, viii.
    26. Costner (et al.), *Dances with Wolves*, vii.
    27. Kelvin Caddies, *Kevin Costner: Prince of Hollywood* (London: Plexus, 1995), 77.
    28. Medavoy and Young, *You're Only as Good as Your Next One*, 159.
    29. Ibid., 95.
    30. Ibid.
    31. For more on the history of Orion see Yannis Tzioumakis, "Major Status, Independent Spirit." *New Review of Television Studies* 2.1 May (2004): 87–135.
    32. See Justin Wyatt, "The Formation of the Major Independent: Miramax, New Line and the New Hollywood." In *Contemporary Hollywood Cinema*. Ed. Steve Neale and Murray Smith (London: Routledge, 1998), 75 and Justin Wyatt, "Independents, Packaging, and Inflationary Pressure in 1980s Hollywood." In *A New Pot of Gold*, 142–159.
    33. For details of Costner's relationship with Orion, see Keith, *Kevin Costner*, 136 and Medavoy and Young, *You're Only as Good as Your Next One*, 163.
    34. Because he controlled so many aspects of the production process, Costner can be understood as a "vertically integrated auteur," in the manner outlined in Warren Buckland, *Directed by Steven Spielberg: Poetics of the Contemporary Hollywood Blockbuster* (New York: Continuum, 2006), 15.
    35. Edward D. Castillo, "Dances with Wolves." *Film Quarterly* 44 (1991): 16.
    36. See Shari M. Huhndorf, *Going Native: Indians in the American Cultural Imagination* (Ithaca, NY: Cornell University Press, 2001), 162–198.
    37. Philip J. Deloria, *Playing Indian* (New Haven, CT: Yale University Press, 1998), 183.
    38. Ed McGaa, *Rainbow Tribe: Ordinary People Journeying the Red Road* (San Francisco: HarperCollins, 1992); Lynn Andrews, *Medicine Woman* (New York: Harper and Row, 1981); James Redfield, *The Celestine Prophecies: An Adventure* (New York: Warner 1993). For more information on this trend see Dirk Johnson, "Spiritual Seekers Borrow Indian Ways." *New York Times* December 27 (1993).
    39. *Dances with Wolves* Press Book, BFI: 1.
    40. Quoted in Keith, *Kevin Costner*, 147.
    41. Michael Medved, *Hollywood vs. America: Popular Culture and the War on Traditional Values* (New York: HarperCollins, 1992), 3. Although Medved's book was published two years after the release of *Dances with Wolves*, he had been working as a movie critic for a long time, and we can thus assume that his views had been part of popular debate about the movies throughout the late 1980s.
    42. Ibid., 4.

43. For a detailed discussion of this phenomenon, see Charles Lyons, *The New Censors: Movies and the Culture Wars* (Philadelphia: Temple University Press, 1997) and William D. Romanowski, *Pop Culture Wars: Religion and the Role of Entertainment in American Life* (Dower's Grove, IL: Intervarsity, 1996).

44. In fact, Medved was strongly critical of *Dances with Wolves*, which he viewed as unpatriotic. See Medved, *Hollywood vs. America*, 226.

45. Jim Collins, "Genericity in the Nineties: Eclectic Irony and the New Sincerity." In *Film Theory Goes to the Movies*. Ed. Jim Collins, Hilary Radner and Ava Preacher Collins (London: Routledge, 1993), 257.

46. Medved, *Hollywood vs. America*, 183.

47. Undated, anonymous *Variety* review, quoted in John Walker (ed.), *Halliwell's Film, Video and DVD Guide 2004* (London: HarperCollins, 2004), 884.

48. Kevin Costner, quoted in Geoff Andrew, "Indian Bravery." *Time Out* January 9 (1991): 16.

49. Michael Blake, quoted in Syd Field, *Four Screenplays: Studies in the American Screenplay* (New York: Dell, 1994), 256.

50. Hall, "*How the West Was Won*: History, Spectacle and the American Mountains," 255.

51. Ibid. For a more elaborate extrapolation of the epic film's thematic "work," see James Russell, "Foundation Myths: DreamWorks SKG, *The Prince of Egypt* (1998) and the Historical Epic Film." *New Review of Film and Television Studies* 2.2 November (2004): 240–241.

52. Hugh Brogan, *The Penguin History of the USA* (London: Penguin, 1999), 70.

53. See Greg Evans, "Orion Creates Epic Pitch for *Dances with Wolves*." *Variety* November 5 (1990): unpaginated clipping; "*Dances with Wolves* file," Margaret Herrick Library, Academy of Motion Picture Arts and Sciences, Los Angeles.

54. *Dances with Wolves* Press Book, BFI Library: 1.

55. Roger Ebert, "[Rev. of] *Dances with Wolves*," *Chicago Sun-Times* November 9 (1990): 20, and Jami Bernard, "[Rev. of] *Dances with Wolves*," *New York Post* November 9 (1990): 35.

56. Details of this were presented on a press release from Orion Studios, dated January 30 (1991). Obtained from the *Dances with Wolves* clippings file, PARC.

57. Sheila Benson, "[Rev. of] *Dances with Wolves*," *Los Angeles Times* November 9 (1990): Calendar, 1.

58. David Denby, "[Rev. of] *Dances with Wolves*, *New York* November 19 (1990): 107; M. S. Malone, "[Rev. of] *Dances with Wolves*," *Christian Science Monitor*, December 7 (1990): 12; and David Ansen, "[Rev. of] *Dances with Wolves*," *Newsweek* November 19 (1990): 67.

59. Shaun Usher, "[Rev. of] *Dances with Wolves*," *Daily Mail* February 8 (1991): 28.

60. Altman, *Film/Genre*, 35.

61. Ibid., 38.

62. Neale, "Westerns and Gangster Films since the 1970s," 33.

63. Financial data from Box Office Mojo, <http://www.boxofficemojo.com/?movies/?id=unforgiven.htm>.

64. Financial data from Box Office Mojo, <http://www.boxofficemojo.com/?movies/?id=tombstone.htm and http://www.boxofficemojo.com/?movies/?id=wyattearp.htm>. See also Neale, "Westerns and Gangster Films since the 1970s," 33.

65. Financial data from Box Office Mojo, <http://www.boxofficemojo.com/?movies/?id=lastofthemohicans.htm>.

66. Financial data from Box Office Mojo, <http://www.boxofficemojo.com/?movies/?id=far and away.htm>.

67. Financial data from Box Office Mojo, <http://www.boxofficemojo.com/?movies/?id= gettysburg.htm>.

68. For a sustained overview of this cycle, see *The Historical Epic* (2007).

9

"A Term Rather Too General to Be Helpful"

Struggling with Genre in Reality TV

SU HOLMES

> I sit there and people don't comment on me, I am completely left out. I should not have to be nasty to get noticed.... I know it's a game, but I *refuse* to diminish my character to survive. People are just performing — if they wanted to be in *EastEnders* or *Coronation Street*, then fine, go and do it. But *this* [pause] this is *Reality* TV.
> — Craig Coates, *Big Brother*, June 2, 2005.

As this example suggests, much of Reality programming has been characterized by a highly self-conscious awareness of Reality TV itself — its conventions, mediation and the cultural debate surrounding it. Craig's speech became a rather famous (and amusing) moment in the *Big Brother* of 2005 (UK), but it is also notable for suggesting how the self-reflexive nature of Reality TV often intersects with issues of genre. In *Big Brother*, discourses on genre are activated, negotiated and contested all the time. In the first UK version (2000) for example, one of the greatest crimes of "Nasty Nick"— dramatically expelled from the house after seeking to influence nominations — was surely his flat insistence that any "strategy came into play before I entered the house. It was a game show." This was met with a raised eyebrow from host and interviewer, Davina McCall, as contestants are always expected to validate the sense that the "experience" of *Big Brother* is more meaningful than traditional generic categories might imply. At the same time, the contestants have often sung "It's only a game show, it's only a game show" when the intensity of eviction nights becomes too much, aiming to downplay the relative power of both producers and viewers in shaping their fate ("It's *only* a game show so we don't care"). Yet contestants are also quick to deny the game show referent ("this is not *just* a game — the relationships I have made in here are real"),[1] or the link with soap opera ("if they wanted to be in *EastEnders*...") when shoring up the reality credentials of the show and the "special" exclusivity of its experience.

These are examples of how Reality TV juggles its generic hybridity in complex ways, "strategically activating and denying" generic roots as needed.[2] On the one hand, it has been mooted as the ultimate example of postmodern genetricity, rendering any residual notion of "pure" generic forms outdated.[3] Yet on the other, Reality TV has emerged as a key focus of debate about television genre, as the concept circulates between broadcasters, critics, contestants, fans or academics. Using examples from the British context, I want to explore this debate here, while also reflecting on its implications for the study of genre and television more widely.

"Assumptions of Genre"

The concept of Reality TV, and the debate surrounding its generically hybrid roots, is the product of broader shifts in the use of the factual moving image in television. John Corner influentially coined the term "post-documentary culture" to conceive of television's "new diversity of ... popular uses of recorded reality." Corner does not mean that documentary is now dead or gone, but his term points to "the scale of its relocation as a set of practices, forms and functions" in the contemporary television environment.[4] The term is also intended to indicate the crisis of definition — and indeed survival — that documentary now faces. Within this context, Reality TV's playful approach to generic hybridity, and its relations with the documentary, the soap opera, the talk show or the game show, were debated self-consciously in the initial academic work in the field.[5] This debate also had significant implications for issues of methodological approach: this was a time of considering whether critical or theoretical frameworks associated with documentary, soap opera or other genres were to be of any use.[6] But this self-consciousness appeared to recede quite quickly, with the concept of "Reality TV" often being treated as a self-evident category, and regularly referred to as a "genre." Given that generic hybridity is far from new and does not in itself invalidate the idea of generic categories, ambiguities here only in part relate to the self-conscious mixing of generic referents. More significant is the fact that the term *Reality TV* has been applied to a vast range of television programming, whether emergency services or "real crime" TV (*Blues and Twos, Police, Camera Action!*), docusoaps (*Airline, Driving School*), reality-game shows (*Big Brother, Survivor, The Apprentice*), reality talent shows (*Pop Idol, Fame Academy*), reality dating shows (*Joe Millionaire, The Bachelor*), or makeover programs (whether these involve making over the home, the self or the life).

The fact that we immediately need subcategories to describe the field clearly hints at the rather broad currency of the term. But these groups are of course in themselves somewhat arbitrary: there are shows that would not fit easily into any of these categories, while many would slide between them. Furthermore, we only need to look at the considerable range of terms used by the industry, the press or academics to see the proliferation of categories that are at work here. Some terms aim to label the entire phenomenon, such as "light factual," "reality entertainment" or "unscripted drama," while others aim to speak to sub-categories, whether the "formatted documentary," the "episodic reality soap," "reality game show," the "gamedoc," the "reali-com," "historical reality documentary series," "Therapy TV" or "celebrity challenge series." This may simply confirm Graham Barnfield's suggestion that over the last decade, such a wide range of productions have been positioned under the umbrella of Reality TV "that one wonders if the term is too general to be helpful."[7] The apparently "natural" drive to delineate more specific categories may indeed confirm his argument, but while the problems here speak to the advent of Reality TV, they also have their roots in wider debates about television's relations with genre.

Despite what Jason Mittell describes as the "virtual omnipresence"[8] of generic categories in television, from television scheduling and listings, channel branding, everyday talk to academic study, the complexity of the medium's relations with genre have rarely been subjected to sustained analysis. This is particularly so when compared to literature or film. John Caughie has observed "the pervasiveness of *assumptions* of genre in writing and thinking about television, and ... the simultaneous difficulty in identifying where the theoretical grounding of these assumptions lie [original emphasis]."[9] This ambiguity is in part shaped by the fact that, while it is often assumed, the conceptual status of genre remains more contested in television studies. Approaches to genre were initially transferred from film studies, without sufficient consideration of their theoretical and methodological implications.[10] A key effect of this was that it made for a primary emphasis on television's narrative and fictional genres, leaving the applicability of the concept to non-fiction television particularly ambiguous.[11] Others suggest that television has historically employed a greater degree of generic hybridity — although these arguments inevitably then downplay the ongoing significance of these debates to film. Jane Feuer aimed to raise the issue of televisual specificity when she observed that, while television has always employed program types, they "do not operate as discrete texts for the same extent as movies; the property of 'flow' blends one program unit into another."[12] Feuer ultimately suggested that television exhibits a greater tendency toward horizontal combination, the move to "recombine *across* genre lines."[13]

Others have approached the issue from an economic and industrial perspective. Graeme Turner has suggested that "there is not much evidence that the term 'genre' or any equivalent abstraction is actually used in [the] ... industrial process [of production]."[14] Turner foregrounds the production category of the format, a concept referring to the range of items that can be included in a licensing agreement in exchange for financial return.[15] Peter Bazalgette, Creative Director of Endemol UK, appears to confirm this view when he suggests that "trying to come up with a term or genre to describe *Big Brother* is like going down a blind alley.... It's just *Big Brother*."[16] We might also note that television producers have little economic interest in aligning their product with one particular category (as has of course also been observed of the film industry).[17] Within this context, Frances Bonner has suggested that moves "both popular and academic" have been "away from using the term 'genre' to talk of television,"[18] and Bonner's *Ordinary Television*—which ambitiously ranges across Reality TV, lifestyle television, chat shows and quiz/game shows — may well be evidence of this. While to pinpoint a recognizable move *away* from genre may at present be overstating the case, Bonner astutely observes that even *The Television Genre Book* (2001) begins with an essay by Steve Neale foregrounding the uneasy conceptual coexistence of genre and television.

Jason Mittell's *Genre and Television: From Cop Shows to Cartoons in American Culture* is the most recent and concerted attempt to really investigate this relationship. Mittell is primarily interested in a discursive approach to genre, and is quick to criticize the "textualist assumption" of previous approaches, particularly those used in literary and film studies. To be fair, film studies pursued the discursive route some time ago, as initially most associated with the work of Neale and Rick Altman. Neale famously argued that genres do not simply consist of films, but are activated by audience expectations and the circulation of the "intertextual relay," the various industrial, journalistic and other media texts that define a film for consumption.[19] It was through this approach that Neale drew attention to the gulf that may exist between, on the one hand, industrial or historical definitions, and on the other, the theoretical categories adopted by scholars and critics.

As this suggests, Neale's emphasis on a discursive approach to genre was in large part driven by the desire to *historicize* genre studies: to foster examination of the array of genres in circulation at any one time. In comparison, and in a Foucauldian sense,[20] Mittell's paradigm points us toward the political function of generic categories. As he expands, we "should focus on the breadth of discursive enunciations around any given instance, mapping out as many articulations of genre as possible and situating them within larger cultural *contexts and relations of power* [my emphasis]."[21] Mittell's aim is to draw attention to how "studying *television genres* is distinct from studying *genre television* [original emphasis]."[22] In other words, scholarly interest in television studies might be better invested in examining how generic categories develop, shift and interact with their broader cultural contexts, and studying genre texts is only one part of this process.

This approach seems useful when faced with the vast range of programs that have been labeled "Reality TV," and the question as to whether there are any common textual attributes that link them. Some occupy self-enclosed episodes, while others adopt an ongoing serial structure, or more of a series form. Not all adopt a similar low-grade reality aesthetic, and some make greater use of the hand-held camera, montage sequences and musical cues. Not all pivot on the spectacle of placing the self under pressure in a mediated environment (real crime TV aims to follow, rather than directly precipitate action, and retains a distance from its subjects), and the nature of this invariably differs between daytime and prime-time programs. Not all formats involve the symbiotic relationship between interactivity and eviction, fostering a Machiavellian combination of cooperation and competition between contestants and handing part of the narrative control to the audience. Lastly, not all are based around the claim to display the experiences of "ordinary" people.

At the same time, we may be unwilling to agree that the category of Reality TV is simply a discursive effect, insisting that some form of textual criteria must come into play. If a soap opera or sitcom, filmed in television studios, and based on actors and scripts, were billed as "Reality TV," we would surely object. Is it not the case that Reality TV must at least make a claim to be "unscripted" — as the term "unscripted drama" would imply? Yet in the cultural debate surrounding it, this has of course been one of the most contested aspects of Reality TV. Always used in a disparaging sense, the terms "casting," "scripting" and "characters" rapidly entered the public debate around Reality TV, expressing an unease about the use of the factual moving image (however tenuously defined) as primarily entertainment, while simultaneously dismissing its claim to the real. In the discursive circulation of Reality TV as a cultural category, the idea of unscripted action occupies a place on a sliding continuum with that of fiction, mapping a difference of degree, rather than a tangible boundary.

James Friedman's suggestion that what "separates the spate of contemporary reality-based television ... [is] the open and explicit sale of television programming as a representation of reality,"[23] would support the argument that it is best recognized as primarily a discursive, rather than textual category. In fact, from a different angle, Nick Couldry has argued that it is vital to *retain* the breadth that structures this definition, and to narrow the conception of Reality TV, or even debate its parameters, "is not necessarily helpful."[24] For Couldry, it obscures the "flexibility inherent to 'reality TV' as a ritual category."[25] Couldry refers here to how the media constructs and maintains a symbolic hierarchy between the media and ordinary worlds, presenting itself as the privileged "'frame' through which we access the reality that matters to us as social beings."[26] This is what he terms the "myth of the media centre," fostering the notion that mediated space is both "special" and significant, and that to enter it — or even briefly pass through it — is to receive a form of symbolic validation in contemporary society. From this perspective, the emergence of something called "Reality TV" only dramatizes this mediated myth in a more explicit and urgent form.

Couldry willingly acknowledges that much of the public debate surrounding Reality TV has focused less on validating than *contesting* its claim to the "real," contributing to the greater cultural skepticism about television's presentation of reality.[27] At the same time, he justifiably observes that "such sophistication is a long way from a *general* loss of belief in television's *underlying* status as our privileged access point to social 'reality.'"[28] None of the programs challenge the underlying myth — however self-reflexive they are about manipulation, construction and performance — that it is possible to read "human reality" into spaces that are constructed and monitored for television.[29] For Couldry then, the term *Reality TV* is evidently not "too general to be helpful,"[30] insofar as he explores its ideological use value in legitimating the media's symbolic power.

It is perhaps no coincidence that the approaches offered by both Couldry and Mittell widen, rather than narrow, the parameters of "generic" definition. Indeed, they both emerge from disciplinary contexts that have had uneasy relations with the idea of generic canons. The reasons for this are multiple and complex, ranging across television's traditionally ephemeral nature, the suspicion of value judgments (and television and cultural studies' greater struggle to establish their subject matter as worthy of academic attention), and the extent to which the idea of "judgment" here has traditionally focused on ideological, rather than aesthetic, concerns.[31] Where the idea of the canon has had the most currency is in the field of television drama — the sphere in which television displays its closest relations with film or literature. Nevertheless, forms of canon making appear everywhere in television, whether in the medium itself (the current obsession with tracking the "Top Ten" or "The Best 50"), or in academic teaching and scholarship (the organization of modules and books, from *Fifty Key Television Programmes* [2004] to *The Television Genre Book*).[32] The impetus behind such categories is necessarily evaluative, even when it aims to encompass a broad range of popular television.

This is not to imply that it is desirable (or even possible) to evacuate the idea of judgments. For over a decade, there has been a steady call from certain television scholars — and one not always taken up — to recognize the importance of evaluation.[33] This is particularly so in relation to developing aesthetic criticism in television, or enabling students and academics to enter into debates about television policy, for example. But scholarly work on Reality TV has arguably occupied a particularly ambivalent relationship with this debate, perhaps understandably so given that its derided cultural status has been so central to its circulation. Even while aspects of despair or derision might enter the analysis in either explicit or implicit form,[34] scholars often feel compelled to comment on this derision, before letting the "real" analysis commence. The impetus behind attempts to define Reality TV are indeed less articulated in terms of canonical debates (its derided cultural value indeed making this a rather incongruous image), than they emerge from the bid to negotiate a space for the "rationality" of intellectual analysis in a rather unwieldy textual field. But this could arguably be interpreted as clouding the status of our own role in relation to the cultural circulation of Reality TV as it moves through press, industry and indeed academic discourse, particularly where issues of categorization, terminology and genre are concerned.

This is because, as scholars have previously recognized, genre definitions are inextricably tied to practices of evaluation, and by extension, notions of "taste."[35] In other words, particularly as linked to the articulation of social identity, genres can also be articulated as categories of distinction,[36] whether in relation to viewers, critics or academics. Lacking the clear functionality of film and theatre reviews, press commentary on television, particularly in the broadsheet press, represents what Christine Geraghty calls a "matter of humour and condescension,"[37] and it largely functions to showcase the personality and expertise of the reviewer.[38] In this respect, it is often the most explicitly evaluative form of commentary. To analyze this sphere is clearly to privilege the voices of critics, and the cultural capital upon which they draw: critics are viewers, but they are not "ordinary" viewers. But there are two important points to make here. First, while it may find expression in different spaces, viewers are clearly no less likely to articulate conceptions of genre as a mode of evaluation. As Mittell comments, "hierarchies between programs and genres are one of the primary ways in which television viewers situate themselves in relation to media texts and their own social locations."[39] To examine the critical reception of Reality TV is not to suggest a picture in which "powerful" critics use their discursive power to trample on the pleasures and tastes of the mass audience, as they too may subscribe to the same criteria, even if it is articulated in different ways. Second, while the television trade press (publications such as *Broadcast, Television* or *Televisual*) evidently perform a different function to that of the broadsheet press, there is also a blurred line here where the discussion of Reality TV is concerned: the press is one of the main ways in which the definitions/discourses of producers find their way into the wider media sphere. But what I am suggesting is that it is the explicitly evaluative rhetoric of critical discourse that makes it worth revisiting here, particularly in illustrating the difficulty of divorcing ourselves from these debates, and the impossibility of offering an objective definition of Reality TV.

What's in a Name?

In approaching Reality TV as a cultural category that circulates within relations of power, a starting point is that reactions to its generic hybridity have drawn on highly traditional intrageneric hierarchies of taste. Shaped by discourses of cultural value, and their relations with wider cultural categories such as class and gender, this of course exemplifies why television and cultural studies have been suspicious of such hierarchies. Reality TV has regularly been invoked as the exemplary focus in broader concerns over the "tabloidization" of television, and as critics have noted, these debates (whether applied to television or the wider media context) rely on barely disguised gender hierarchies: a melodramatic, private, subjective and above all "feminine" sensibility is seen to have invaded the rational, detached and public territory of "masculine" culture.[40] Lisbet Van Zoonen has argued that Reality TV is in part derided and controversial because it flagrantly challenges the traditionally bourgeois hegemony of public/private domains, and its basis in discourses of class and gender.[41] Indeed, the binaries above have slipped neatly onto an opposition between popular factual programming and the longer heritage of documentary — with the latter imagined as subject to threat and invasion by the feminine influence of the soap opera (narrative structures, characterization, emotional display) and the apparently "innate" frivolity of the game show.

With their propensity for stylistic excess, these genres share a climate of critical hostility,[42] although the political impetus behind their denigration (or alternatively, their audience associations) differs between national contexts. In America, both were historically aimed at a daytime, and thus primarily female audience. In the UK, it is the working-class associations of the game show that loom large, while soap opera has for some time enjoyed a widening, prime-time appeal. It is needless to say that these generic referents operate at a highly abstract level in the debate surrounding Reality TV, in which traditional hierarchies are painted with a very broad brush. While John Fiske referred to game shows as "the lowest form of television,"[43] this role may well have been "usurped" by Reality TV ("Trash TV") at the level of public debate. But it is precisely their merging, the incursion of these genres into the domain of factual television, that produces a product that offends a range of aesthetic and cultural sensibilities.

This emerged most visibly around the year 2000-2001, which saw a number of popular Reality formats emerge (*Big Brother, Survivor, Popstars*). While there was no consensus about how to define them, both the press reception and academic commentary saw these shows as marking a shift away from the earlier docusoaps (such as *Airline, The Cruise* or *The Clampers*) in their desire to stage arenas formatted entirely for television. It was in this period that there was a particularly self-conscious groping for generically hybrid terms ("docusoap-cum-interactive gameshow"), as well as a more pronounced reaction to the aesthetic and cultural hierarchies at stake. At the same time, this was evidently prefigured by the emergence of the docusoap in the late 1990s. Largely perceived to be a journalistic invention, the term almost became a "form of abuse."[44] Although rapidly adopted by the TV industry, it is little wonder that television schedulers and announcers still invited us to consume "fly-on-the-wall documentaries" for some time.[45] The invocation of fiction, but particularly soap opera, as a form of dismissive critique accelerated with the subsequent Reality formats. In the press discussion of the BBC's millennial project, *Castaway 2000* (2000), which claimed to offer "a unique social experiment" by depositing a group of people to build a community on the remote Scottish island of Taransay, this became something of an obsession, with critics delighting in describing the "soapily suds-spattered castaways," or comparing it to Channel 4's more youth-orientated *Shipwrecked*: "Alex Garland's *The Beach* starring the cast of [teenage soap] *Hollyoaks* in designer bikinis."[46] In comparison, academic comment quite rapidly adopted the use of the term "gamedoc" to describe formats such as *Big Brother* and *Survivor*. While this could be interpreted as embracing the playful entertainment ethos of such shows, there is equally the issue of abstracting academic categories from the contexts in which the programs circulate: the term did not appear to have a currency in either press or industry circles, and there also seemed to be little academic discussion regarding the justification for, or implications of, this move.

Yet the implications of foregrounding particular generic referents was made clear by the initially contrasting terms circulated by public service and commercial broadcasters, while acknowledging that these lines can no longer be drawn with firm distinction.[47] Those producing for the BBC insisted on the (rather tautological) term "formatted documentary,"[48] while ITV1 was apparently quite happy with the notion of the "Episodic Reality Soap" (ERS)[49] — each privileging different generic referents in their conception of the form. The role of public service broadcasters is particularly interesting here given that, because of documentary's historical positioning as a public service genre, Reality TV has been a key site upon which the status, strategies and future of such channels have been debated in the multi-channel environment.

Susan Murray and Laurie Ouellette's American collection, *Reality TV: Remaking Television Culture* (2004), defines Reality TV as "an unabashedly commercial genre united less by aesthetic rules ... than the fusion of popular entertainment with a self-conscious claim to ... the real."[50] While this complements discussion about the difficulty of defining shared textual characteristics, this nevertheless also involves the use of unexplored criteria. The fact that Reality TV is "unabashedly commercial" is taken for granted here (as well as in the cultural debate surrounding the form). While this perspective may be particularly naturalized from the American perspective, how exactly is this "measured" or defined? It is this commercial status, for example, that is negotiated, and in to some degree contested, by broadcasters inhabiting the historical contexts of public service. From the start the BBC claimed that their charter would shape their use of Reality TV in particular ways. Controller of BBC1, Lorraine Heggessey, claimed in 2000 that any Reality show on the BBC would have to "have a point," and that *Big Brother* would not have been brought to the channel as they would have "spoilt it," underpinning it with "some informational content of some kind."[51] In BBC's programs such as *Castaway 2000* or *The Heat Is On* (2001) (which stranded a group of people in the Peruvian jungle), there was a tendency to deactivate the referent of the game show by replacing the concept of a monetary prize with the reward of personal growth and development. The opening titles of *The Heat Is On* explain how we will see "14 people with a point to prove to themselves and their critics.... Individual glory or personal failure is their prize." Stretching right back to the early days of radio, the BBC's negotiation of prize giving in the game show has a long and complex history. The offer of financial reward was seen as the antithesis of public service, the ultimate in commercialism (what they termed "buying the audience"), and most definitely aligned with the worst "excesses" of American commercial broadcasting.[52] In fact, Jeremy Mills, the executive producer of *Castaway 2000*, described how when the series was broadcast in America he was continually asked: "What there's no prize at the end of this? You mean they do this for nothing?" prompting him to qualify "No because for some of the people [in the program] this is some sort of spiritual journey."[53] (As hinted at the start of this article, this can also be claimed by *Big Brother* contestants — albeit with less lofty overtones — when the game show referent fails to adequately capture the apparent uniqueness of the mediated "experience"). While the institutional identity and programming strategies of the BBC have of course changed substantially between these periods, the suspicion of game show, and its association with frivolity, commercialism and greed, lingers on. This history shapes both critical responses and issues of definition, as suggested by such comments as *Castaway 2000* was their "own version of *Survivor* ... [but] being the BBC, it's less a game show ... and more a documentary about their exploits."[54]

Particularly since ITV's effective withdrawal from the field, both the BBC and Channel 4 have carried the primary responsibility for offering what Kilborn refers to as a more "balanced diet of factual/documentary programming,"[55] their success in this role remaining somewhat contested. As the UK home of *Big Brother*, Channel 4 (C4) is also a public service broadcaster, but one where the remit traditionally rested on the bid to cater to minority audiences, and to innovate in content and form. Debates have raged as to what *Big Brother* suggests about the channel's current and future institutional identity, and it is now often remarked that C4's most recognizable feature is simply its more marked address toward a younger, aspirational audience. Yet despite their differences, as well as changing interpretations of public service, both channels have shown a particular interest in what has been described in both the press and television viewing guides as "the historical reality series." With more of an apparently middle-class address, these have ranged across *The Edwardian Country House* (C4, 2002), *The 1900 House* (C4, 2000), *The Trench* (BBC2, 2002), *The 1940's House* (C4, 2001), *The Frontier House* (C4, 2002), *Pioneer House* (C4, 2005), *Destination D-Day* (BBC1, 2004) and *The Ship* (BBC2, 2002).[56] On *The Ship*, the aim was to reconstruct the experience of 18th-century sailors on Captain Cook's *Endeavour*. Deactivating the reality referent, the executive producer, Laurence Rees, claimed that "*The Ship* is a fresh new concept in the history documentary genre which ... will make compelling viewing, not only for those already fascinated by history, but also those new to the genre."⁵⁷ (The program was also produced for BBC2 in association with the History Channel, forming part of its branding.) According to Rees, what unites this "genre" is the impetus less to try and replicate the past, but to consider "how the past can illuminate the present and vice versa."⁵⁸

This use of generic terminology exemplifies here how, both textually and intertextually, there has been more of a discursive bid to align "public service" Reality TV with the province of documentary enquiry: it claims to maintain more of a link with exploring "a historical truth"—quite literally imagined *as history* here—which has a presence "out there" beyond "the boundaries of the television screen."⁵⁹ It is precisely this claim, and returning us to Murray and Ouellette's emphasis on "the commercial," that has then been subject to scrutiny in the critical reception of many of these shows. They have certainly not been the focus of such damning critiques as other Reality programs, and some have in fact received a certain degree of critical acclaim. But press critics have debated the extent of their textual, ethical or political difference from other Reality shows, arguing that "all are best seen as Reality game shows," and that all "are praying for the same result—sex, arguments and big, big ratings."⁶⁰ While the reference to "sex" is perhaps overstating the case, the key point here is that those critical of the shows, and particularly their potential relationship with public service values, are apt to *categorize* them in ways that reinforce arguments about the homogenization of channel provision in the multi-channel landscape. *The Edwardian Country House* is "*Big Brother* meets *Gosford Park*"⁶¹ or *Survivor* "dipped in an *Edwardian Marinade*,"⁶² while *Castaway 2000* was retrospectively described as a "pagan-shaped and titillation-by-turnip-planting *Big Brother*."⁶³ Categorization here is shaped by wider discourses relating to institutional authority and power, and the perceived tension between public service and commercial values. Clearly such comments also express a longstanding distaste for what are perceived as the formulaic products of mass culture, in which aesthetic creativity plays little role. The "*Big Brother* meets *Gosford Park*" comment is directly reminiscent of *The Player's* (1992) "*Out of Africa* meets *Pretty Woman*" line, forming part of its now famous satire on the commercial machinations of Hollywood cinema. At the same time, this does not straightforwardly support the significance of genre here. The idea of genre is implicit, but its currency is subservient to exemplary textual examples and the desire to replicate their success.

In terms of Reality TV, many may find themselves in sympathy with the suggestion that any differences here amount to a form of superficial packaging. But it is questionable whether this is productive at the level of analysis. As Mittell has observed, it would be useful to "see more voices complicating the blanket condemnation of a homogenous notion of reality TV, noting the crucial cultural, political, and ethical differences" between formats.[64] It is here that we clearly confront the different impetuses behind the academic discussion of Reality TV (with the primary aim to analyze), and that found in the press. The creation of internal, intellectual categories (the "gamedoc") may seem to be an analytic necessity when public discourse blurs rather than sharpens, the object of study. But I am not convinced that these spheres are necessarily antagonistic. Discursive attempts to discuss "public service" Reality TV should not be taken at face value, and differences at the level of channel/institutional remit may not necessarily be the best way to explore the distinctions between formats to which Mittell refers. At the same time, that is not to suggest that it is a form of categorization that doesn't repay attention. For example, the talent show *Fame Academy* (BBC, 2002), following in the steps of ITV's *Popstars* (ITV1, 2001) and *Pop Idol* (ITV1, 2001, 2003), probably came in for the most visible criticism where the BBC's bid to chase the popularity of Reality TV was concerned. But while undoubtedly similar to its precursors, I have argued elsewhere that it does pivot on different ideologies of stardom, selfhood and authenticity as a way of negotiating the perceived "commerciality" of the Reality tag.[65] The academic categorization of Reality TV as "unabashedly commercial,"[66] then, might find it productive to examine how the programs, and their intertextual circulation, negotiate this ethos to varying degrees.

"What Is It?: This ... *Is Reality TV"*

The discussion so far suggests how there invariably emerges a highly problematic invocation of documentary in these debates. As Corner has argued, particularly when used to make comment on the contemporary factual landscape, the term "documentary" carries with it too many "assumptions and idealisations.... The term needs pressing back towards the broader category of 'documentation' from which it initially sprang. In doing this we are going from narrowness to breadth, and we are being descriptive rather than evaluative."[67] But while a useful conception in other respects, we again see here the call to absent ourselves from wider cultural debates that are deliberately and *explicitly* evaluative. For example, this dynamic is clear in the *Daily Mail*'s review of the first series of ITV's *Hell's Kitchen* (2004) in which the notoriously bad-tempered celebrity chef Gordon Ramsay ran a specially constructed celebrity restaurant with the help of ten celebrity cooks. The review, entitled "It's Hell Watching!," adopted a perspective familiar in press discussion of Reality TV: that the "failure" of the show under discussion suggests that the popularity of Reality TV is about to come to an end. The initial ratings for *Hell's Kitchen* were not as high as ITV had hoped, and critic Neil Lyndon gleefully prophesized that it might signal the moment when television executives "must stop assuming their audiences are entirely composed of zombies who will cheerfully go on swallowing the mindless gruel they serve up."[68] He aimed to support his position on *Hell's Kitchen* by drawing on a textual comparison with another show:

> Ramsay can be ... as proved in this recent series [*Ramsay's*] *Kitchen Nightmares* on Channel 4, a gifted television performer — sympathetic, engaging and inspiring. But that series was not, in fact, "reality TV." Carefully researched, thoroughly prepared, superbly directed and edited, *Kitchen Nightmares* had all the qualities of the best documentary traditions of British television. It was full of drama, suspense, unpredictability and subtle interplays of character.[69]

Alternatively, in his article "Pap — or Porn with a Purpose?" James Robinson pondered issues of categorization in *The Observer*, this time in relation to the successful format, *Wife Swap* (C4, 2003–present). He quotes from other sources to explain how:

> "Channel Four argues that *Wife Swap* is serious factual programming that examines social issues," says one industry source. "In fact, it's 'Reality'—salacious tabloid crap." But even here, opinions may vary. *The New Statesman* described *Wife Swap* as "the most important documentary series of the decade."[70]

What immediately emerges here is the sense that it is far easier to say what Reality TV *isn't* than what it actually "is," while it also exemplifies how genre categories can be used in such a way as to reject the text as an object of media consumption.[71] Like all generic categories, definitions are to a large degree negotiated via an internal, intertextual dynamic — in relation to other texts — as the "*Big Brother* meets *Gosford Park*" description has already suggested. *Ramsay's Kitchen Nightmares* (C4, 2004–present) was broadcast in self-contained, weekly episodes, and saw Ramsay enforcing his tyrannical rule over ailing restaurant businesses with the intention of turning their fortunes around. The highly successful format combined the personality appeal of the celebrity chef, with the structural conventions of the makeover show (the business is literally made over at the level of organization and interior space), while it also nodded to the fascination with workplace conflict familiar from the docusoap.

In the mapping out of the qualities that connect to "the best documentary traditions of British television," we are of course left with a rather intriguing ambiguity. Whether at the level of production ("thoroughly prepared, superbly directed and edited"), or form and aesthetics ("full of drama, suspense, unpredictability and subtle interplays of character"), the emphasis is on characteristics that are just as easily, or in fact more immediately, associated with fiction. Of course, much of documentary criticism has emphasized its status as a constructed artifact that shares many formal and aesthetic links with fiction, and I do not rehearse these debates here.[72] But it is also perhaps deceptive to claim that this ambiguity has simply been heightened by the advent of Reality TV. Despite the coherence with which it is treated in discussions of Reality TV, documentary has never had an unproblematic status as a genre. This is linked not only to the diversity of texts associated with the term, but because it can be used to imply a genre, a style, or a particular mode of filmmaking. As with other genres, there is also the question as to how to conceptualize the defining or anchoring factors here — the intentions of the filmmaker, a repertoire of textual elements, or the conceptual framework employed by the audience.[73] Even Bill Nichols observes that the "distinguishing mark of documentary may be less intrinsic to the text than a function of the assumptions and expectations brought to the process of viewing the text,"[74] and Kilborn and Izod go on to argue that documentary has always depended on multiple points of reference for its generic definition, including scheduling, listings, trailing, reviewing and presentation. In short, the *contexts* in which its communicative acts take place.[75]

But this may then present us with a rather tautological loop, while foregrounding a key in a discursive approach to genre. The reviews are contributing to this process of contextual definition in relation to *Hell's Kitchen/Kitchen Nightmares* or *Wife Swap*. Once we have situated generic categories on the slippery slope of discourse, is it feasible to object to the distinctions others want to make? Confirming Corner's argument about the dispersal of the documentary category across the schedules, it is certainly true that the term "documentary" is used interchangeably with a range of other terms that signify the expanding uses of recorded reality. Television listings are a case in point here. To simply take one example, the program *Poor Little Rich Girls* (ITV1, 2004) appears in the article section of a TV magazine under "Reality TV" ("the idea behind *Poor Little Rich Girls* is to get spoilt young madams to swap lifestyles for ten days with someone from the opposite end of the learning scale"),[76] in the listings as a "fly-on-the-wall series," and it is referred to in a later article in the same magazine as "a real-life documentary series." The next week a critic in the same publication then explains how "I suppose the premise is similar to a game — who can adapt and conquer? Like in a game show these people are challenged to face difficulties, only here it is real life."[77]

With a largely promotional function, viewing guides do not feel obliged to make the openly evaluative assertions we find in the particularly broadsheet press,[78] although there is still a hierarchical balancing of genres above, with the game show seen as lacking the external referentiality that is used to anchor the show's appeal. Television listings may well contribute to the process of cueing generic expectations, suggesting, as Andrew Tolson argues, "how to consume [the] ... text ... in appropriate ways."[79] At the same time, at least when it comes to frameworks of viewing, it would seem problematic to place too much importance on these categories in such a highly fluid and playful discursive context. Otherwise, the example above might imply a decidedly confused viewer, effacing how such shows assume an audience that is highly literate in the manipulation of generic boundaries. With respect to *Poor Little Rich Girls,* might the viewer not be attracted by, or "cued to respond," to the program because they recognize that the lifestyle swap, particularly that based around the "clash" of class codes, is already familiar from shows such as *Wife Swap, Faking It* (C4, 2001), *Holiday Showdown* (ITV1, 2003), or *Ladette to Lady* (ITV1, 2005)? Yet this would clearly return us to a *textual* explanation, which has provided little certainty where defining Reality TV as a genre is concerned. More significantly, it may point us back to Bonner's suggestion that "it cannot be claimed that genre is ... all that fruitful a term for critical work on television, especially for work on programmes other than fictional ones."[80] As she expands, "it is much rarer for a question about genre to be asked popularly of television," and the very open "'what is it?' is more likely."[81] The trouble here is that this might be met with the simple reply, as *Big Brother*'s Craig reminds us, that *"this ... is Reality TV."*

Conclusion

This examination of Reality TV has worked under the premise that there may be much to gain from exploring the *processes* and practices of categorization, rather than simply mapping a textual category in itself.[82] Conceiving of Reality TV as a discursive category is useful in emphasizing how there is no objective way to define the phenomenon, and this in practice refers to critics, viewers, broadcasters *and academics.* The main framework shaping categorizations is clearly cultural value, something at least suggesting that, while we might wonder whether the category of "Reality TV" is "helpful" at an intellectual level,[83] we need to recognize that generic recognitions are *always* functional and useful for those articulating them.[84] But in line with arguments calling for a greater self-reflexivity about how we deal with evaluation, my point is not simply that we "tut tut" at the generic hierarchies that are at work in the critical circulation of Reality TV, before moving on to commence the "real" business of analysis in whichever field we choose. The point is that they direct us to examine in more detail *the categories and terms that we are using* and to reflect on where their basis might lie, particularly when Reality TV seems to have been so quickly accepted as an identifiable "genre." But lest we absent ourselves as simply observers, seemingly outside the generic processes at work,[85] it should of course be noted that the concept and category of "Reality TV" is useful to *us*, for what Jonathan Bignell has described as "an occasion for certain kinds of academic study."[86] How and why should be a topic for further debate.

It should also be noted here that many of the questions raised point to the *audience*—the formation of generic expectations, the perception of differences between shows, and the relationship between the cultural debate surrounding Reality TV and the processes of viewing. Clearly, audiences can and do make continual value judgments about Reality TV in ways that are not reducible to, but are often shaped by, the cultural debate that has surrounded it.[87] Yet emerging empirical audience research on Reality TV has not really tackled the rather elusive question of generic discourses — in all their myriad of contexts.[88] It hardly needs noting here that the audience also remains one of the most neglected areas of genre study in general.

At the same time, in reflecting on the implications of this for wider approaches to television and genre, I feel that I am left with many questions unanswered. First, we might note the relations between research and teaching here. From seminar rooms to essays, students eagerly explore the generic attributes of a particular text or corpus, and are certainly able to reflect on the complexities of generic categorizations. But the framework I have considered speaks to genre as a much more diffuse, ongoing and multifaceted process.[89] Certainly, in the age of the Internet in particular, press reviews on any given show, as well as the discourses of fan forums and industry publications, are available at the click of the mouse, and such material can be dissected in the teaching context. Nevertheless, the feeling that this approach in part showcases academic fancy footwork remains.

But none of this should imply an opposition or antagonism between the *textual* study of genre, and the study of its circulation as a discursive, intertextual process. (Mittell's own approach does not ignore the text, nor indeed the audience.) As the example from *Big Brother* at the start of this chapter makes clear, the unfolding of the program *participates* in this discursive process, and should remain central to its reconstruction and analysis. But it would be a matter of debate as to whether the approach explored here truly addressed the specificity of *television's* relations with genre more than it does other media forms.[90] Its disciplinary foundations are perhaps most obvious in its suspicion of canonical (hierarchical) approaches to textual classification, and its related and politicized emphasis on regimes of cultural power.

Notes

1. Craig Coates, *Big Brother* July 14 (2005).
2. Jason Mittell, *Genre and Television: From Cop Shows to Cartoons in American Culture* (London: BFI Publishing, 2004), 198.
3. Ibid.
4. John Corner, "Documentary in a Post-Documentary Culture? A Note on Forms and their Functions" (2001). Available at URL: http://www.lboro.ac.uk/research/changing.media/John%20Corner%20paper.htm [accessed January 22, 2002].
5. See Jon Dovey, *Freakshow: First Person Media and Factual Television* (London: Pluto, 2000); Jane Roscoe, "*Big Brother* Australia: Performing the Real Twenty-Four Seven." *International Journal of Cultural Studies* 4.4 (2001): 473–488.
6. Su Holmes and Deborah Jermyn (eds.), *Understanding Reality TV* (London: Routledge, 2004), 17.
7. Graham Barnfield, "From Direct Cinema to Car-wreck Video: Reality TV and the Crisis of Content." In *Reality TV: How Real Is Real?* Ed. Dolan Cummings (Oxford: Hodder and Stoughton, 2002), 49.
8. Jason Mittell, "A Cultural Approach to Television Genre Theory." In *The Television Studies Reader*. Ed. Robert C. Allen and Annette Hill (London: Routledge, 2004), 171.
9. John Caughie, "Adorno's Reproach: Repetition, Difference and Television Genre." *Screen* 32.2 Summer (1991): 127.
10. See Jane Feuer, "Genre Studies and Television." In *Channels of Discourse: Reassembled*. Ed. Robert C. Allen (Chapel Hill: University of North Carolina Press, 1992), 138–161 and Mittell, *Genre and Television*.
11. Steve Neale, "Genre and Television." In *The Television Genre Book*. Ed. Glen Creeber (London: BFI Publishing, 2001), 3–4.
12. Feuer, "Genre Studies and Television," 157.
13. Ibid., 158.
14. Graeme Turner, "The Uses and Limitations of Genre" and "Genre, Format and 'Live' Television." In *The Television Genre Book*, 5.
15. Albert Moran, *Copycat TV: Globalisation, Program Formats and Cultural Identity* (Luton: University of Luton Press, 1998), 17.
16. Peter Bazalgette, personal interview with author, August 14 (2002).
17. Rick Altman, *Film/Genre* (London: BFI Publishing, 1999), 57.
18. Frances Bonner, *Ordinary Television* (London: Sage, 2003), 10.
19. Steve Neale, "Questions of Genre." *Screen* 31.1 (1990): 49.
20. This clearly reflects Foucault's conception of discourse — the construction of specific frameworks of thinking that take place within wider systems of social and cultural power.
21. Mittell, "A Cultural Approach to Television Genre Theory," 174.
22. Mittell, *Genre and Television*, 201.
23. James Friedman, *Reality Squared: Televisual Discourse on the Real* (New Brunswick: Rutgers University Press, 2002), 7.
24. Nick Couldry, *Media Rituals* (London: Routledge, 2003), 10.
25. Ibid., 103.
26. Nick Couldry, "Teaching Us to Fake It: The Ritualized Norms of Television's 'Reality' Games." In *Reality TV: Remaking Television Culture*. Ed. Susan Murray and Laurie Ouellette (New York: New York University Press, 2004), 58.
27. Couldry, *Media Rituals*.
28. Ibid., 107.
29. Couldry "Teaching Us to Fake It," 64.
30. Barnfield, "From Direct Cinema to Car-wreck Video," 49.
31. See Christine Geraghty, "Aesthetics and Quality in Popular Television Drama." *International Journal of Cultural Studies* 6.1 (2003): 25–45.
32. John Ellis, "Importance, Significance, Cost and Value: Is an ITV Canon Possible?" In *ITV Cultures*. Ed. Catherine Johnson and Rob Turnock (Berkshire: Open University Press, 2005), 36–56.

33. See Geraghty, "Aesthetics and Quality in Popular Television Drama."
34. See Dovey, *Freakshow*.
35. Mittell, *Genre and Television*, 101.
36. Compare to Pierre Bourdieu, *Distinction: A Social Critique of the Judgement of Taste* (London, Routledge, 1986).
37. Geraghty, "Aesthetics and Quality in Popular Television Drama," 31.
38. Charlotte Brunsdon, *Screen Tastes: Soap Opera to Satellite Dishes* (London: Routledge, 1997), 137.
39. Mittell, *Genre and Television*, 101.
40. See Graeme Turner, "Tabloidization, Journalism and the Possibility of Critique." *International Journal of Cultural Studies* 2.1 (1999): 59–76.
41. Lisbet Van Zoonen, "Desire and Resistance: *Big Brother* in the Dutch Public Sphere." In *Big Brother International: Formats, Critics and Publics*. Ed. Ernest Mathijs and Janet Jones (London: Wallflower, 2004), 23.
42. William Boddy, "The Quiz Show." In *The Television Genre Book*, 79.
43. John Fiske, "Women and Quiz Shows: Consumerism, Patriarchy and Resisting Pleasures." In *Television and Women's Culture: The Politics of the Popular*. Ed. Mary Ellen Brown (London: Sage, 1990), 134.
44. Dovey, *Freakshow*, 137.
45. Holmes and Jermyn, *Understanding Reality TV*, 7.
46. Kathryn Flett, "Shipwrecked — review." *The Observer* January 23 (2000): 14.
47. I also acknowledge here that ITV has always been a hybrid institution, effectively a commercially funded public service broadcaster.
48. Jeremy Mills, personal interview with author, June 5 (2002).
49. Maureen Paton, "Come Back Docusoap — All Is Forgiven." *The Times* January 28 (2000): 28.
50. Murray and Ouellette, *Reality TV: Re-Making Television Culture*, 2.
51. *Panorama: Life on TV*. BBC1, November 21 (2000).
52. Su Holmes, "'The Question Is — Is It All Worth Knowing?': The Cultural Circulation of the Early British Quiz Show." *Media, Culture & Society* 29.1 (2007): 53–74.
53. *Panorama: Life on TV*.
54. "Invasion of the Reality Shows." *Dateline* September 13 (2000). Available at URL: http://www.eskimo.com [accessed August 25, 2005].
55. Richard Kilborn, *Staging the Real: Factual TV Programming in the Age of Big Brother* (Manchester: Manchester University Press, 2003), 41.
56. The comparison with the American context above was not intended to function as a simple contrast, as it is notable that when *The 1900 House* was screened in America, it appeared on the public service channel PBS.
57. BBC Press Release, "South Sea Adventure in the Wake of Captain Cook." July 31 (2002). Available at URL: http://www.bbc.co.uk/print/pressoffice [accessed August 26, 2005].
58. Ibid. Although what Rees does not note here is that this has also structured far more playful and youth-orientated shows such as *Bad Lad's Army* (ITV1, 2003) (recreating the experience of National Service for young male offenders), *That'll Teach 'Em* (recreating the experience of 1950s and 1950s education) (C4, 2003, 2004) and *Wakey Wakey Campers!* (C4, 2005) (recreating the experience of a 1960s holiday camp).
59. Mills, personal interview with author.
60. *The Times*. January 7 (2000): 19.
61. *The Times*, supplement. May 4 (2002): 13.
62. *Radio Times*. May 6 (2002): 44.
63. *The Guardian*. July 23 (2002): 35.
64. Mittell, *Genre and Television*, 200.
65. Su Holmes, "'Thank you, Voters': Approaching the Audience for Music and Television in the Reality-Pop Phenomenon." In *Sound and Music in Film and Visual Media: A Critical Overview*. Ed. Graeme Harper (London and New York: Continuum, 2008).
66. Murray and Ouellette, *Reality TV: Re-Making Television Culture*, 2.
67. Corner, "Documentary in a Post-Documentary Culture?: A Note on Forms and Their Functions."
68. Neil Lyndon, "It's Hell Watching." *The Daily Mail* May 27 (2004): 13.
69. Ibid.
70. James Robinson, "Pap — Or Porn with a Purpose?" *The Observer* July 18 (2004): 18.
71. Mittell, *Genre and Television*, 99.
72. Bill Nichols, *Representing Reality: Issues and Concepts in Documentary* (Bloomington and Indi-

anapolis: Indiana University Press, 1991); Richard Kilborn and John Izod, *An Introduction to Television Documentary: Confronting Reality* (Manchester, Manchester University Press, 1997).

73. Kilborn and Izod, *An Introduction to Television Documentary*, 15.
74. Nichols, *Representing Reality*, 24.
75. Kilborn and Izod, *An Introduction to Television Documentary*, 14.
76. *What's on TV.* May 22–28 (2004): 22.
77. *What's on TV.* June 29–July 4 (2004): 22.
78. Andrew Tolson, *Mediations: Text and Discourse* (London: Arnold, 1996), 99.
79. Ibid., 96.
80. Bonner, *Ordinary Television*, 11.
81. Ibid., 9.
82. Mittell, *Genre and Television*, xvii.
83. Barnfield, "From Direct Cinema to Car-wreck Video," 49.
84. Brunsdon, *Screen Tastes*, 133.
85. Altman, *Film/Genre*, 29.
86. Jonathan Bignell, "What Are We Talking About, and Why Does It Matter?" Symposium paper delivered at "Reality TV: Contexts, Debates, Future," University of Surrey, Roehampton, May 22 (2004).
87. Hill, *Reality TV*, 84–85.
88. See Janet Jones, "'Show Your Real Face': A Fan Study of the UK *Big Brother* Transmissions." *New Media and Society* 5.3 (2003): 400–421.
89. Mittell, *Genre and Television*, xii.
90. Although this point cannot be pursued in further detail here, Mittell *does* see his paradigm as addressing this. He introduces it as "a television-specific genre theory" (*Genre and Television*, xii), arguing that many of the discursive sites, channel branding, scheduling, as well as television's movement across fiction/non-fiction have no real parallels in film.

Part Three

Heritage, History and Memory

10

Repackaging Generation One

Genre, Fandom, and The Transformers *as Adult/Children's Television*

LINCOLN GERAGHTY

This chapter examines the rebirth and repackaging of *The Transformers* (1984–1987) and related toy franchise, establishing the extent to which the role of the adult collector has influenced the continued popularity and lifespan of a 1980s children's toy and television series in the early years of the twenty-first century.[1] *The Transformers* has undergone a generic shift between children's TV and adult TV. Fans that once played with the toys as children now collect the originals (retroactively called Generation One and first released in 1984) and their specially marketed reproductions; in so doing, their memories of *The Transformers* as a multimedia text become integral to the creation and perpetuation of an online fan community. In addition, special DVD box sets of the original American Saturday morning cartoon series are big sellers in U.S. and UK high street stores, as fans remember their love for the show and seek to reclaim some part of their childhood. Collecting the entire range of toys from Generation One up until more modern versions such as Transformers: Cybertron (2005), and having the original episodes on DVD, becomes an important part of Transformers fandom. In highlighting the establishment of a fan canon in the children's television fan community, and how those discourses contribute to the creation and fragmentation of fan identity and culture, I argue that the series has become a site of experimentation for individual and personal exploration. Fan affection and memory join the more familiar visual characteristics of the series — poor animation, poor dubbing, obvious commercialization — and become additional generic signifiers of a well-loved, but not atypical, children's animated television series. My analysis ultimately suggests that notions of genre and genre boundaries are becoming blurred as films, television and toys originally aimed at children are now being collected and traded by adults keen to relive their youth.

A recent article in the UK's *Radio Times* drew attention to the relationship between children's television shows and toy merchandising. The word "toyetic," according to David Butcher, is Hollywood "parlance for a film or TV show that has the potential for spin-off merchandise." Series that have toyetic characters are potential money-spinners, not only for the companies concerned but also the networks, as specific toys become associated with particular channels. Overall, this short article is wary of the seemingly dangerous threat toyetic programming offers to the UK's children — in the case of Channel Five's *Fifi and the Flowertots* (2005–present) Butcher wonders whether the intended young female audience will like it as much as the network hopes, or even if they have a choice in the matter. It is clear that television critics see little entertainment value or any cultural worth in the product-based television shows that supposedly crowd the schedules.[2] However, merchandise and spin-off series inspired by blockbusters such as the *Star Wars* films have not only produced large profits for the movie industry but also helped create and sustain fan cultures that actively collect, trade, and compare products. For example, Justin Wyatt sees *Star Wars* as a high-concept franchise, the first to really use toy merchandising to increase its market appeal. High-concept films are conceived as highly marketable, and therefore highly profitable, as well as being visually striking and stylistically innovative. Such films are different through their "emphasis on style in production and through the integration of the film with its marketing."[3] In terms of *The Transformers* cartoon series, the films (both past and future) and associated toys, we might also describe them as "high concept" since they comprise what Wyatt labels "the look, the hook, and the book": "The look of the images, the marketing hooks, and the reduced narratives."[4]

The fictional worlds of science fiction and fantasy seen in such examples as *Star Wars* and *Star Trek*, that have kept children and adults alike engrossed for years, also have underlying marketing advantages: They can grow as new characters, and therefore, new toys are added to fit in with the mythology surrounding the overall franchise narrative.[5] The infinite potential for expansion keeps the toys popular as children continue to watch and re-watch the movies and play within their own "mythological" make-believe worlds. Similarly, children's animated television such as *The Transformers*,

Teenage Mutant Ninja Turtles (1987–1996 and 2003–present), and *He-Man and the Masters of the Universe* (1983–1985, 1990–91 and 2002) — with their relentless potential for remarketing and rebirth — have shown, through market diversification into areas such as live-action film, animated series, associated toy lines and online fan clubs, that they are capable of offering adults their own make-believe worlds where "affective play" and narrative are combined in a sustainable two-way relationship.[6] However, as I shall first outline in the next section, the fictional world that *The Transformers* originally offered to children has also been heavily criticized for its banal storylines and close links with the global toy industry.

The Banality of Children's Television

For several cultural critics, "most animated programs were little more than poorly drawn, glorified half-hour commercials for action figures and video games" flooding the children's toy market in the early part of the 1980s.[7] Widely regarded as one of the poorer cartoon imports in the Saturday morning TV schedule, itself "characterised by animation which was uninspired and aesthetically redundant,"[8] critics of *The Transformers* saw it as an obvious attempt by toy manufacturers to take advantage of an already open global market by producing "the big hit with a promotional toy."[9] Timothy Burke and Kevin Burke, in their nostalgic look back at the cartoons and Saturday morning TV shows they watched when growing up, see the series as just one out of a myriad of cartoons that tried to cash in on the merchandising market. For them toy companies like Mattel and Hasbro, through series such as *He-Man*, *She-Ra* (1985), *The Care Bears* (1985–1988), and *M.A.S.K.* (1985–1986), were merely trying to copy the success of Kenner's *Star Wars* action figures by establishing and sustaining a market in which the TV show acted as an extended commercial for the range of figures, robots, plush dolls and toy sets that were being produced cheaply in Asia and being sold in America.[10] Although I wish only to highlight the view that *The Transformers* was a banal by-product of the wider market concerns of the global toy industry, it is important to stress that despite the series' unpopularity in some academic circles the series was extremely popular with children. So much so that, as I will be looking at in closer detail in later sections, those children who grew up watching and collecting the transforming robots in the 1980s continue to watch and collect them as adults in the 2000s. In fact, even though the series has been continually blamed for contributing to the increased commercialization of childhood, it can be asserted that many adults who deride the series are actually fans and enjoy poking fun at the toys and characters that used to keep them entertained as children. The defining characteristics of the children's animated television genre — the badly dubbed and drawn animation, the blatant commodity tie-ins, the poor stories — become an essential part of what it means to be a fan of the series; in effect, those who remember the series in such ways see themselves as fans because of and not in spite of them.

Part of the success of *The Transformers* can be ascribed to the fact that it was a joint project, in which American Sunbow Productions and Marvel Productions were able to take advantage of the cheaper production costs in Japan and then flood the television market back in the United States with dozens of cheaply made cartoons that could be endlessly rerun in syndication.[11] David Hubka sees the coproduced success of series like *The Transformers* as evidence of the new developments in the production and distribution of animated television in the 1980s and 1990s in which global markets had to be reached and networks had to find suitable material to fill air time.[12] However, these developments were largely seen as negative since, as Stephen Kline notes about the genre, critics continually saw the problems associated with "letting businessmen decide the fate of children's culture ... not only in the banality and violence in the programming but also in the growing commercialization of the children's cultural industries, wherein artistically sophisticated, intellectually demanding and socially relevant" kid's TV competed for audiences "with cheaply produced low-quality entertainment."[13] Furthermore, American children's television as a genre was slowly transformed from a period during which cheap entertainment was important to one in which its sole purpose was "to serve the marketer's promotional needs and not those of the children."[14] As part of a calculated success story, *The Transformers* phenomenon in the mid to late 1980s, just like the more modern animated series *Pokémon* in the late 1990s, created a "false need" that could only be satisfied through consumption; in the process it prevented other forms of children's culture — that might have been more dangerous or subversive — from existing.[15] Bob Dixon sees this "false need" most evident in the example of *The Transformers*' Optimus Prime:

> Optimus Prime, a leading figure in the Transformer concept, was so much in demand for Christmas 1985 that supplies ran short. Nevertheless, by early 1986 it had already been decided to replace the figure by Ultra Magnus, in accordance with the tactic of killing off toys when they reach a sales peak. This, it can be said, is catering for children's *wants* (which are created by advertising and publicity). But then these wants are displaced by other wants (artificially created again) the whole operation being designed to set up a puppet-like consumerism, and a condition of endless dissatisfaction.[16]

Clearly then, the successes of both *The Transformers* and *Pokémon*, being made in Japan and transferred to the American market, epitomizes the continued consumerism and dumbing-down of American youth culture (where cartoons are merely adverts) and the over-simplification of narrative in the genre of children's animated television (the only memorable thing being a catchphrase, e.g., "Robots in Disguise" or "Gotta Catch 'em all").[17]

However, even though the quality of animation suffered as a result of the genre's emphasis on low-cost production and local television audiences were exposed to homogenized global products made in Japan and shipped to the U.S., Kline intimates that children's television is important since it serves as potential space for child growth and development. Unfortunately, the arguments from critics so far outlined, about the quality and industry of Saturday morning television, often overshadow the important debates surrounding the genre as latent narrative storyteller — in fact, for Kline the medium "has become the great storyteller of post-modern culture."[18] The problem lies with those companies who place profit over story and the risk they run in upsetting the potential for children's television to act as a social guide during a child's formative years. Children "internalise and use the social knowledge conveyed in these cartoons," therefore critics should be aware of not just how they were produced and marketed but also how they are used and adapted by their key demographic.[19] After all, *The Transformers* should not be singled out as the first children's cartoon to be used as the focus of a merchandising campaign; Stefan Kanfer's *Serious Business* (1997) rightly points out the historical links that Disney's Mickey had with early retailers such as Woolworth's and how "the spinach industry credited Popeye for increasing its sales some 33 percent."[20] As David Hubka also maintains, to get a full understanding of these programs' cultural impact we must examine the audiences at which they were aimed and acknowledge that although they may simply be children's cartoons, part of an industry, children, like adults, "consume television programs in ways that articulate their own social relationships and identities."[21] In the next section I want to address some of the concerns raised in Hubka's article by looking in detail at one episode from *The Transformers*, "Child's Play" (1985). Despite the poor quality animation and its obvious marketing angle designed to get kids to go out and buy the latest robot, this episode highlights a rather more sophisticated narrative that promotes childhood identity and empowerment. Placing *The Transformers* in the contexts of narrativization and play, so important in the cultural development of children, animated television can be seen as a didactic genre in which individuality and ingenuity are emphasized over the negative associations it has with global markets and industrial profits.

"More Than Meets the Eye": The Narrativization of Child's Play[22]

Dan Fleming sees the popular effect of spin-off action figures and toys as being part of what he calls "narrativisation," whereby toy versions of TV and movie characters, such as the Lone Ranger and Tonto, informed playing with the toy: "Throughout the 1960s the toy industry became increasingly dependant on cinema and, especially, on television for play-worthy objects that could borrow the popularity of a screen character or story. Such objects then came with a narrative attached."[23] Narrativization helps children interact with fictional reality, or make-believe, during play. This creates what Fleming terms "a semiotic space" where toys can act as transitional objects, a term first used by Donald Winnicott,[24] allowing children to experiment with their own developing identities and understand the adult world.[25] Although animated television series from the 1980s have been derided for their quality, it can be argued that they still provided children with a valuable semiotic space in which the toys were not only signifiers of the mass market but also transitional objects through which children could engage with the real world.

Despite the dubious nature of commercialized merchandise and syndicated animated television, David Buckingham and Julian Sefton-Green see the more recent *Pokémon* phenomenon in a more positive light than most critics. They feel that the "catch 'em all" ethos that inspires children to buy also encourages children to create and learn the value of friendship, important in the formation and development of adult relationships in the future. Instead of teaching children to be lazy—staying indoors or simply buying everything they can to be the most popular kid in the playground—the activities of watching, collecting, trading, and playing with the cards, toys and related merchandise makes children active participants in the fictional world of *Pokémon*. While this may be terrible for some, Buckingham and Sefton-Green see the mythical world where kids must collect and train "pocket monsters" as a didactic one, where children are encouraged to embark on a "hero's quest."[26] "The narrative tropes and themes" of this quest, most obviously located in the associated cartoon series and video games, "are characteristic of the role-playing games and fantasy literature favoured by boys slightly older than the average Pokémon fan," yet, as Buckingham and Sefton-Green point out, this only serves to indicate how sophisticated the toy range actually is. Using Henry Jenkins' work on the virtual spaces of the computer game, the authors see *Pokémon* has having provided children "a very extensive space ... a self contained universe [informed by the fictional narrative of the main characters and the signature Pokémon, Pikachu] with its own unique geography and cosmology, that can only be mastered through active exploration."[27] As well as being a form of "'consumer training—a means of inducting children into" our commercially driven culture, it can also be seen as "partial training ... as a means of developing in children the 'multiliteracies' that are now essential for democratic participation."[28] This idea of training can also be linked to the specificity of the medium itself, as John Hartley sees television as a "paedocratic regime" that not only tells the viewer how to watch television but also how to enjoy it.[29] In the following analysis of "Child's Play," a typical *Transformers* episode, a similar reading can be made of the animated television genre in the 1980s—children were "trained" to consume but also "pretrained" in the difficulties of adulthood.

At the beginning of "Child's Play" the Autobots stop Megatron and the Decepticons from destroying a baseball stadium; in the resulting chaos Optimus Prime and his fellow Autobots Perceptor, Inferno, Bumblebee, and Smokescreen are trapped in the Decepticon space bridge, which violently transports them across the galaxy along with the Decepticons Starscream, Soundwave, Thrust and Ravage. This rapid introduction to the continuing conflict between the Autobots and Decepticons emphasizes the embedded nature of the warring giant robots; trapped on Earth, millions of light years from their home planet of Cybertron, they are forced to live side-by-side with humans—of course the Autobots are happy to do this, becoming adopted guardians, whereas Megatron sees himself as ruler instead of servant. Throughout this sequence, Megatron is positioned as dominant figure controlling the fight, teasing the fleeing humans, and even briefly participating in the baseball game he interrupts. The message of this episode from the outset is that play is important, but only the right sort of play since the delight the Decepticons get in watching humans suffer intimates that they like being the center of attention; as an advert for the toys this episode shouts: "Play with us, not sports!"

After landing on an alien world, the Transformers awake to find themselves confronted by Earth-like toys: balls, building bricks, a jack-in-the-box, and various models. Everything is considerably bigger than they are (significant considering they are giants back on Earth) and as a gigantic hand picks Starscream up they realize that they are in fact trapped in a boy's bedroom, on a planet where the aliens are giants and they are no bigger than the toys strewn across the floor. Erin, the alien boy, collects the "mini" Decepticons and puts them away just as any child would with the real Transformer toys. The Autobots, hiding in the giant Lego-like building, watch as Erin's parents walk in and challenge him to reveal what he has found in his bedroom. In terms of narrative, this episode seemingly replicates the experiences many children had when trying to convince their parents of the inherent value in the Transformers toys. Erin's parents blame him for the mess he made in the room, they will not believe his story that the Decepticons (his newfound toys) made the mess and that the Autobots (his newfound friends) were helping him to clean it up. The parents' response is to warn the child of the dangers of dabbling in make-believe, they don't like him making up stories and would rather see him read or go outside instead of staying in his room and playing with "useless" robots. The imaginary world created by Erin, ironically brought to life by the arrival of the Transformers, is not one that adults understand. His parents prove their ignorance further by taking the "toys" to a scientist so that they can be opened up and dissected to see what makes them "tick"—in other words, what makes them so "popular" with children.

Throughout the series attention is constantly drawn to the dual nature of the Transformer robots (robot heroes and toy robots): in "Child's Play" they become part of Erin's own space; he at first plays with them as toys and then interacts with them as people—Perceptor is keen to remind him, "Be careful, we are extremely fragile!" In a later episode, "Forever is a longtime coming" (1986), the Autobots themselves point out the dramatic irony of their fictional origins when meeting their robotic creator Alpha Trion for the first time (incidentally never released by Hasbro as a toy); the Arielbots inquire, "Where did this dinkoid come from? A toy store?" Nevertheless, as both real toys and fictional companions in "Child's Play," Optimus Prime and the Autobots stand for loyalty and friendship—things that have been recently lacking in Erin's life. After he rescues the Transformers from the scientist's laboratory he runs into the school bully who has been teasing him about the "childish" toys he plays with. Thanks to a renewed faith in himself, brought about by the Transformers he has befriended, Erin is able to counter the bully's jibes and proudly shows off his new toys, only now they are not toys to him but real people. Erin has fulfilled a dream and become part of something important, an integral component in a significant, real-life mission. To help get the Autobots back to Earth he must use his own ingenuity; he has a role to play (similar to the role-playing games outlined earlier) that comes with great responsibility. The arrival of the Transformers has allowed Erin to develop skills required in learning to grow up and mature; being able to take on more responsibilities despite his parents' lack of faith in him and their distrust of playing with toys. By the end of the episode Erin has not only helped the Autobots escape but he also provides them the toy rocket ship that Perceptor turns into their emergency transport back to Earth. As Erin waves good-bye from his bedroom window, Optimus Prime's farewell message, "Every time you look through your telescope at the stars you'll know that your friends are out there," reminds him, and the children watching, that their imaginary world — enhanced by the "narrativization" provided by the Transformers' individual characteristics and personalities — is an optimistic one; altogether more affirming and comforting than the world that Erin's parents assume the toys represent.

More than a mere thirty-minute advert, this episode, and the series as a whole, suggests that *The Transformers* narrative was both supportive and educational. Its moral message was that children should not be afraid to stand out from the crowd and stand up for what they believe in. Some might say this message simply follows the dominant ideology of the toy manufacturers, who wanted children to persuade their parents to buy their products, but one can see a more subversive message coming through in this episode that lays emphasis on the power of the individual and corresponds to a political ideology running throughout this period in American culture. For Tom Engelhardt, toys and the animated spin-off genre in the 1980s, a decade in which America's political agenda was set by President Reagan's nostalgic use of Puritan imagery and expansionist rhetoric, represented an end to what he terms "victory culture." "War play as a feel-good activity for children" became the norm as America struggled to come to terms with its defeat in Vietnam and political scandals at home.[30] The toys were objects of resilience set against the background of futuristic war; in this manufactured and industrially led world America could still emerge victorious and live up to Ronald Reagan's vision of national destiny.[31] I mention here the political contexts of *The Transformers* only to emphasize the narrative complexities of the animated television genre at this time.[32] It is clearly evident in "Child's Play" that the cost of producing these types of series was kept to a minimum; for example, at one point Erin's entire body disappears from the animation cell, colors change, and the lines of his pet cat's head appear to overlap and sit awkwardly on top of the toy rocket ship, yet these series remained popular despite their amateurish mistakes. What made them so well-loved then, and continues to appeal to adult fans now, is that the series offered more than just transforming robots — although they were attractive. It offered a semiotic space where children could perhaps discover answers to some of the problems affecting them in their childhood (or, according to Engelhardt, even problems affecting America in the 1980s), and it offers fans today that same semiotic space where nostalgia and long-suppressed feelings of kinship and camaraderie can be revived in more modern times.[33] As the fans have grown up, *The Transformers* as part of the animated children's television genre has also changed; a transformation (if you can excuse the pun) that signals the blurring of genre boundaries as the films, television series and toys originally aimed at children are now being collected and traded by adults keen to relive their youth.

Transforming Genres of Animated Television

On the one hand the concept of genre in television studies is a useful one; it is clear from some programs — comedy, soap opera, quiz shows, news — that generic conventions are easily identifiable and that networks are keen to capitalize on the potential audiences that watch these shows. Yet, on the other, critics are keenly aware of the difficulty in trying to apply genre theory to television since networks also organize viewing patterns around time-slots and "a traditional division between 'fiction' and 'faction.'" This means that while some viewers will specifically choose to watch science fiction shows or solely factual programming such as documentary and the news, others will "channel-hop" across a whole range of material: "They may watch a range of different genres as an evening's package on one channel, or they may pick out specific programs or genres (including feature films previously shown in cinemas) across channels."[34] However, this does not mean we cannot try to define the genre of Saturday morning children's television; the previous two sections have been an attempt on my part to point out that previous (negative) scholarship on the animated series from the 1980s, particularly *The Transformers*, has in itself highlighted a series of codes and conventions that can be used to help define the genre. As well as being located within a specific time period, when the growth of the cable networks and their industrial relationships with toy manufacturers helped create a market for cheap toys and associated spin-offs, children's animated television was distinguished by its precise location in the Saturday morning schedules.

In creating a time and a place for viewing (usually the lounge before parents woke up), children were given the opportunity to pick and choose (channel-hop) between their favorite programs — depending on their favorite toys etc. — thereby establishing a particular cultural and historical time frame in which the specific programs were interpreted by their audiences. As well as studying the obvious visual and audio markers that help discriminate between good quality animation and cheap imports — the dubbing, stories, artwork, one-dimensional characterization — it is important to remember that all genres, including animated television, can also be studied "as socio-historical actualities, as thematic and *ideological* constructions deriving from history."[35] As I begin to address the changing audience of *The Transformers* in the next section, it is important to keep in mind the flexible generic qualities of the series and its relationship with the freedom offered by television schedules. Also, as new forms of recording and viewing technology enter today's market, it is possible for fans to recreate the specific conditions of the original Saturday morning schedule (watching the episodes on DVD) on Saturdays, or any other day of the week for that matter. Although the historical conditions may have changed since childhood, the physical location and form in which audiences now watch the series may not have changed at all since the 1980s. However, while the visible generic "qualities" of the animated Saturday morning series may still be enjoyed again and again, the cultural contexts in which they were watched have changed — *The Transformers* has changed and evolved alongside its historical contexts and the personal contexts of the fans that continue to watch it.

According to Rick Altman, genres "serve what we might call a *memorial* purpose; that is, they recall a society's collective experience, by rehearsing the stories, characters and topics that the culture deems important." Failing to "serve as a memorial both to a collective past and to a current collectivity" means the genre is not fulfilling its role.[36] In terms of series like *The Transformers*, part of the animated Saturday morning television genre, the historically specific experiences that are required for it to act as a memorial are things like its use of familiar cultural narratives, its animation, the contexts of viewing and the associated merchandise. Traditionally, for Altman, "in order to provide the mutual reinforcement on which genres depend, social and generic structures" such as those outlined above had to be "carefully aligned" so that unified audiences could recognize the genre.[37] Now that genres are routinely aimed at diverse and disunited audiences, Altman sees them as being unable to act as "collective memorials" and instead only act as "pseudo-memorials" in which certain genres evoke familiar practices or force audiences to recollect specific experiences. This new reliance on the memory and intertextual experience of the audience means that genres no longer act as communal historical markers but as personal indicators of "the experience of the culture and its assumptions, rules and myths, as well as experience of other genre texts."[38] I would maintain, with regard to *The Transformers*, those fans that now collect the toys and rewatch the cartoons are doing so because they are taking part in the pseudo-memorialization of their long-lost youth. The series, and therefore the genre from which it originates, is now no longer historically specific, to the extent that it recalls the politics of the 1980s, but rather it has shifted to become a genre of universal narrative intertexts and personal fan contexts.

It is particularly significant for the purposes of the last section, and the chapter overall, that, as Altman suggests, "the rise of consumerism and the mass media, along with the extraordinary proliferation of narrative entertainment that they have brought, have tilted the typical generic mix of life experience/textual experience radically towards the experience of previous texts."[39] The experience of *The Transformers* and other childhood series of the 1980s as previous texts is an integral component of what it means to be a fan in today's Transformer collecting community. Memories of watching the series on Saturday mornings, getting that all too rare and expensive Optimus Prime for Christmas, or trading stickers in the playground to complete your sticker album, are important experiences and memories that are both shared and unique experiences that individual fans confess as part of their membership within the Transformer community. Just as Altman sees genres today performing "a pseudo-memorial function" counting on "spectator memory to work their magic," the continued popularity and affection that fans show towards series like *The Transformers* is part of the same trend in contemporary popular culture.[40] In what P. David Marshall calls an "intertextual matrix," the result of various media such as film, music, video, websites, television, and licensed products being "elaborately cross-referenced in the contemporary entertainment industry" through magazines, papers, and news programs, *The Transformers* as television show and Transformers as objects of adult play have also become "new intertextual commodities" that can be learned about and understood by audiences through their relationships with other cultural forms.[41]

"Robots in Disguise": Adult Toy Collecting and Fan Memory

For Kendall Walton, as children grow up, their props (transitional objects) within their fictional world of make-believe, dolls, hobbyhorses, toy trucks, and teddy bears are transformed as part of adult life: "The forms make-believe activities take do change significantly as we mature. They become more subtle, more sophisticated, less overt."[42] Therefore, for children growing up imagining themselves part of *The Transformers* universe, the toys are integral props in the make-believe relationship they have with that fictional world. Playing with and collecting the toys affirm and bring *The Transformers* story to life. Consequently, those adults that used to play with the robots begin to have a more complex relationship with the toys they collected as children. They are no longer seen as objects of play but as markers of their personal memories of childhood, as well as symbols of subcultural capital, that can be bought and traded within a fan community. There are multiple readings to be made about the playing with, and collecting of, *The Transformers* related merchandise, the most significant now being that adult fans are collecting them as part of their own search for personal memory. Art historian Michael Camille views collecting as "a socially creative and recuperative act," in which the identity of the collector is self-fashioned through the accumulation of collectibles.[43] The following extracts from a range of fan websites, blogs, and fan-produced merchandise highlight the ways in which *The Transformers* has for some fans become an integral part of personal memory, and how a child's television show and toy have remained a valuable asset in modern-day life.

On the reverse of the episode guide booklet, supplied with *The Transformers* Season 2 Part 1 DVD box set released in 2003, Daz Jamieson — a self-confessed lifelong fan and collector — reminisces about the series.[44] Along with his own personal opinions on a range of episodes in the set, Jamieson paints a picture for readers of the world that he inhabited as a child when the series was new and the toys were at the center of his universe. The two booklets from subsequent box sets follow this pattern, reminding fans that they were once part of an important cultural phenomenon and still are members of a unique family in which Generation One Transformers are intrinsic objects of affection and value. I quote at length from the first booklet to show how important nostalgia and community are both within *The Transformer* fandom and the creation of adult-orientated, repackaged media merchandising:

> The Transformers cartoon takes us all back to that special time, when life was simpler, pop bands were funkier and jeans were tighter. Timmy Mallet would introduce each episode on Wac-A-Day with an infectious smile that just wouldn't fade. Thankfully we don't have to watch the episodes in five parts, over the period of a week anymore, or sit through another round of Mallet's Mallet just to find out whether Grimlock betrayed the Autobots or not. No, now we've got DVD, and the first twenty-four episodes from season two are here in all of their unedited glory....
>
> The Transformers cartoon stands out today as a classic of animation, and features one of the finest collections of voice talent ever assembled for a series, headed up by the legends Frank Welker and Peter Cullen. With complex characters, great action sequences and a bad guy who turns into a gun, The Transformers remains one of the coolest cartoons of all time. Now let us all play that game where we try to transform our Transformers as they transform in the episodes, you know you want to.
>
> 'til all are one![45]

Jamieson weaves an attractive path through a mosaic of media memories that are designed to enthuse fans and reintroduce them to a world that they have long forgotten. Not only do we see that the DVD set is aimed at fans specifically located in the UK through the region 2 packaging, but also by Jamieson's recollection of his own viewing practices. As I previously mentioned, regarding the importance of television schedules and child viewing habits, Jamieson recollects how he (therefore the audience) watched the series as part of Timmy Mallet's own television show and how one episode was cut into five so that it could be spread across five days (part of TV-A.M.'s half-term or summer holiday morning entertainment schedule for children). Fans are given a nostalgic frame of reference to begin reimagining their own viewing practices and episode memories. Jamieson, both as a fan and fan/producer, seemingly contextualizes *The Transformers* by describing the decade as a "special time" personified by funkier pop bands and tighter jeans. This not only sets the series within a specific time frame but also highlights his own personal memories of Britain in the 1980s.

In terms of the arguments I have previously discussed, surrounding the series' lack of quality and commercial links with the toy industry, Jamieson appears to counter these claims by describing the series as a "classic of animation." Not only are its Japanese production roots missed out, the series is located as an original through Jamieson's description of the voice artists Frank Welker (Megatron) and Peter Cullen (Optimus Prime). Their voices in particular make the series legendary and are aspects of fan experience that should be emphasized and remembered — a point further underscored by talk surrounding the recent live-action film in which producers assured fans that all living original voice cast members would reprise their roles (retaining voices does not make a difference to new fans of the film but would certainly attract original fans).[46] Notions of community, friendship and shared experience are important themes in most Transformer fan output: from Jamieson's booklet sign-off "'til all are one!" which comes from the 1986 movie, to his own web-blog on the www.TheTransformers.Net website. Nostalgia clearly plays a key role in Jamieson's personal blogs; on his page he starts by confessing his first experiences as a kid collecting the toys: "My first Transformer was Inferno.... I thought he was so cool, he led to my being driven away from the road that was *Star Wars* and down the Transformers path." Then he moves on to describe key moments in his childhood when he remembers the toys giving him joy and pleasure: "One of my favourite transformer moments was playing with Jetfire on the coach on the way to swimming in school."[47] As well as the emotional attachment he had with the toys, Jamieson expands upon the other important part of being a modern collector by describing valuable and rare toys in a collection:

> The rarest tf [transformer] I ever had was probably the find of all time, for £4 in a pokey news agents. It was the unbranded Shockwave released in the UK. The same mould as the original shockers, and the same quality but without the tf brand or stickers, and for some reason a dark grey. Very nice though.[48]

In this blog extract we can see how collecting rare examples from childhood, even better if you had them when they were first released, is important to fans and their position within the online community — previous studies have highlighted how degrees of cult fandom and subcultural capital can be gauged through levels of consumption, knowledge and esteem within a particular fan community⁴⁹—however, it is also clear that personal experience shared with the group is also integral to the memorialization of *The Transformers* as adult/child television. This form of collecting, in which fans get just as much enjoyment as financial gain from things they collect, corresponds to the type of consumption known as "curatorial consumption." Each piece in a person's collection conveyed a sense of personal and social history and it was curatorial "in that possession, preservation, and orderly succession of ownership superseded the immediate use dictated by industrial production."⁵⁰ The memories attached to the toy and its collection distinguish the fan experience as a form of nostalgia rather than a process of consumer capitalism. Furthermore, since "the collection may provide its owner with an omnipotent sense of mastery,"⁵¹ we can also see how Jamieson's knowledge and ownership of the rare toy set his revelation in the contexts of subcultural hierarchies that "operate to establish the ownership" and exclusivity of cult texts within a specific fan group.⁵²

Daz Jamieson's blog calls attention to these characteristics in that he also includes pictures of his children and says, "I popped into Toys R Us to buy my 2½-year-old son a reissue Optimus Prime for Christmas. I already have one of course, otherwise I could never let him play with one in front of me." Such sharing of experience, and protectionism of perceived valued property from 2½-year-old children, alludes to the "masculinity of cult" as defined by Joanne Hollows as the ways in which "many of the key consumption practices that constitute cult fandom" (collecting, viewing, reading fanzines, etc.) are naturalized as masculine in opposition to the gendered femininity of the cultural mainstream (popular film and television).⁵³ In distancing themselves from the "feminine shopper" and adopting more "assertively masculine" attitudes to consumption, male fans like Jamieson are participating in the collecting ritual that has historically been "imagined as masculine" in comparison to the idea that women merely bought objects as part of routine and domesticated consumerism.⁵⁴ Of course, there could be arguments put forward that Transformers were marketed as "boys' toys" and therefore would continue that pattern into adult collection, and Hollows makes the case that "the collector is [not] an 'essentially' masculine figure," but it is interesting to see how Jamieson denotes playing with Transformers as a boyish pursuit (as long as there are duplicates) and therefore their collection as an adult male pasttime.⁵⁵

Simon Plumbe and Sven Harvey, co-organizers of the annual "Auto Assembly" Transformers convention in the UK, have initiated a communal blog on their website where fans can leave and share their childhood memories of the series and toys. "Transformers Memories: 20 Years of Robots in

Disguise" was conceived as "an extensive archive of fan memories of Transformers," including thoughts on episodes, characters, first memories, and favorite toys.[56] Plumbe's first entry likewise covers these main themes in that he says, "I was what you call a late starter to Transformers. Sven had been trying to convert me for years ... since then, I've got a small corner of my room taken over with a toy display, comics and DVDs everywhere and I've even converted my fiancée into being a fan. Sven would be proud." Not only does this show fans as adult collectors of child toys but it also challenges the common stereotype of them being socially maladjusted bachelors; Plumbe has friends, family and a fiancée — a situation recently replicated and subverted in *The 40 Year Old Virgin* (2005).[57] The lifelong fascination for Transformer memories, to be retold and recounted in a communal web-blog, can be related to the notion of timeless film reception Annette Kuhn calls "enduring fandom": Defined as "loyalty to a star which continues throughout the fan's life, and even beyond the star's death."[58] In the case of enduring Transformer fans, they remain loyal to the product long after Generation One stopped being made — collecting toys on eBay, at conventions, through fan clubs — but also continue to share in their memorialization of the mythos surrounding the product by rewatching the cartoons and following similar patterns of induction into the collecting community.

Conclusion

As we have seen in this last section, through the various self-confessed experiences and fan memories, *The Transformers* can now be characterized by the necessary function of Matt Hills' idea of "affective play" and fans' imagined subjectivity rather than through the tropes of the children's animated television genre and the real play experienced in childhood — affective play "deals with the emotional attachment of the fan" and "suggests that play is not always caught up in a pre-established 'boundedness' or set of cultural boundaries, but may instead imaginatively create its own set of boundaries and its own auto-'context.'"[59] The fans' relationship with the fictional text, that which is created and sustained in the repackaged DVDs, rereleased merchandise, the associated childhood experiences and pseudo-memorialization of the cartoon series, is more important than the actual text itself. The interrelated, constantly expanding universe of *The Transformers* has become a new ground for proving and testing personal identity and remembering past childhood events. The toys and series are reread within the contexts of modern life and fans are able to use new technologies such as the Internet to reach out to the community in order to share their thoughts on how their lives have turned out. This constant act of reflection points to what Anthony Giddens terms "the trajectory of the self," in which people are constantly trying to define themselves and their self-identity through reflexive examination of their "lifecycle."[60] Being part of a fan community, in an age of fractured society and social hierarchies, "can be viewed as a positive strategy" balancing alienation at work with camaraderie through group membership.[61] Sharing memories of a once mainstream children's TV show and popular toy range provides "the real satisfaction to individuals" who have unwittingly challenged the notion of genre specificity.

As new toys are produced, old ones repackaged, and episodes remembered, those fans that collect them do so because nostalgia and intertextuality are key components of their postmodern identities and important tools in the continued understanding of contemporary society. Sharing thoughts and memories of an intertextual childhood phenomenon such as *The Transformers* is but one way of interacting with and within this modern age of uncertainty.

TV and Filmography

The Care Bears. Syndicated. Di C Enterprises/Neluma Ltd., 1985–1988.
Child's Play. 75 episodes. LWT, 1984–1988.
"Child's Play," *The Transformers.* Written by Beth Bornstein. Directed by Terry Lennon. 30 mins, 1985.
Child's Play. Written by Don Mancini. Directed by Tom Holland. MGM/United Artists, 1988.
"Chinpoko-Mon," *South Park.* Written by Trey Parker. Directed by Eric Stough and Trey Parker. 30 mins, 1999.
Dungeons and Dragons. 27 episodes. CBS/Syndicated, 1983.
Fifi and the Flowertots. 21+ episodes. Channel Five/Nick Jr. Chapman Entertainment/Cosgrove Hall Films. 10 mins, 2005–Present.
"Forever Is a Longtime Coming," *The Transformers.* Written by Gerry Conway and Carla Conway. Directed by Ray Lee and Andy Kim. 30 mins, 1986.
GI Joe. 95 episodes + movie. Syndicated. Hasbro Inc./Marvel Productions/Sunbow, 1983–1987.
He-Man and the Masters of the Universe. 330 episodes. Syndicated. Filmation Associates/Mattel Inc., 1983–1985.
M.A.S.K. 75 episodes. Syndicated. Kenner/Ashi Pro, 1985–1986.
The Real Ghostbusters. 140 episodes. ABC/Syndicated. 1986–1991.
She Ra: Princess of Power. 93 episodes. Syndicated. Filmation Associates/Mattel Inc., 1985.
South Park. 139+ episodes, 1 movie, 6 specials. Syndicated/Comedy Central, 1997–Present.
Teenage Mutant Ninja Turtles. 193 episodes. CBS/Syndicated, 1987–1996.
Teenage Mutant Ninja Turtles. 103+ episodes. FOX/Syndicated, 2003–Present.
The Forty Year Old Virgin. Written by Judd Apatow and Steve Carell. Directed by Judd Apatow. Universal Pictures, 2005.
The Transformers. 98 episodes. Syndicated. Hasbro Inc./Marvel Productions/Sunbow/Akom, 1984–1987.
The Transformers: The Movie. Written by Ron Friedman. Directed by Nelson Shin. Marvel Productions/Sunbow Productions/Rank Film Distributors, 1986.
The Transformers. Written by Alex Kurtzman and Robert Orci. Directed by Michael Bay. Dream Works SKG/Paramount/TriStar Pictures/Hasbro Inc., 2007.

Acknowledgments

I would like to thank the British Academy and the Centre for European and International Studies Research at the University of Portsmouth for awarding me funds to attend the 2006 Popular Culture Association/American Culture Association Conference in Atlanta, Georgia where I presented a shorter version of this chapter.

Notes

1. The series was inspired by the original toyline of transforming robots produced by the Japanese Takara Corp., which was sold in the U.S. and Britain by Hasbro.
2. David Butcher, "Marketing Mania." *Radio Times* May 14–20 (2005): 61.
3. Justin Wyatt, *High Concept: Movies and Marketing in Hollywood* (Austin: University of Texas Press, 1994), 20.
4. Ibid., 22.
5. Ibid., 153.
6. For an analysis of the term *affective play*, a topic to which I will be returning later in this chapter with regard to adult fans of *The Transformers*, see Matt Hills, *Fan Cultures* (London: Routledge, 2002), 90–113.
7. Wendy Hilton-Marrow and David T. McMahan, "*The Flintstones* to *Futurama*: Networks and Prime Time Animation." In *Prime Time Animation: Television Animation and American Culture*. Ed. Carol. A Stabile and Mark Harrison (London and New York: Routledge, 2003), 78.
8. Paul Wells, *Animation and America* (Edinburgh: Edinburgh University Press, 2002), 81.
9. Stephen Kline, *Out of the Garden: Toys and Children's Culture in the Age of TV Marketing* (London: Verso, 1993), 221.
10. Timothy Burke and Kevin Burke, *Saturday Morning Fever: Growing Up with Cartoon Culture* (New York: St. Martin's Griffin, 1999), 57–58.
11. David Hubka, "Globalization of Cultural Production: The Transformation of Children's Animated Television, 1980 to 1995." In *Global Culture: Media, Art, Policy, and Globalization*. Ed. Diane Crane, Nobuko Kawashima, and Ken'ichi Kawasaki (New York: Routledge, 2002), 242.
12. Ibid., 251.
13. Stephen Kline, "The Empire of Play: Emergent Genres of Product-based Animations." In *In Front of the Children: Screen Entertainment and Young Audiences*. Ed. Cary Bazalgette and David Buckingham (London: BFI, 1995), 151.
14. Ibid., 154.
15. David Buckingham and Julian Sefton-Green, "Gotta Catch 'em All: Structure, Agency and Pedagogy in Children's Media Culture." *Media, Culture, Society* 25.3 (2003): 384.
16. Bob Dixon, *Playing Them False: A Study of Children's Toys, Games and Puzzles* (Stoke-on-Trent, UK: Trentham Book, 1990), 265.
17. Parental concern over the commercialized nature of children's toys has even been the basis for the *South Park* (1997–present) episode "Chinpoko-Mon" (1999), in which contemporary fears of a widespread degradation of American culture due to Japanese imports are lampooned. In this episode the children of South Park are brainwashed into buying Chinpokomon toys (with the catchphrase being "Buy them all"), and the video game emphasizes the message that in order to be the master you must buy every one so that you have the power to defeat evil. Unbeknownst to the children, the toys are actually miniature antennae that help Japan launch an invasion of Pearl Harbor and the evil force that the children must defeat is America.
18. Kline, "The Empire of Play: Emergent Genres of Product-Based Animations," 162.
19. Ibid., 163–164.
20. Stefan Kanfer, *Serious Business: The Art and Commerce of Animation in America from Betty Boop to "Toy Story"* (New York: Da Capo Press, 1997), 96.
21. Hubka, "Globalization of Cultural Production: The Transformation of Children's Animated Television, 1980 to 1995," 252. Similar work has been done with the *Pokémon* phenomenon, looking not only at the globalization of popular culture and mass-produced children's toys but also at the local reception of a peculiar Japanese product around the world — see Joseph Tobin (ed.), *Pikachu's Global Adventure: The Rise and Fall of Pokémon* (Durham: Duke University Press, 2004).
22. The double meaning of the episode's title "Child's Play" is brought to preeminence when we

consider two contemporary texts with the same name: *Child's Play* (1984–1988) was the name of the popular LWT Saturday night celebrity panel game hosted by Michael Aspel, in which children provided (often hilarious) descriptions of various words and the celebrities had to guess them to win money for contestants — the innocence of child play proving to be a big hit; the horror film *Child's Play* (1988), in which the possessed toy doll Chucky terrorizes both children and adults alike, implicates the darker side of children with the uncertainties of their imaginary world — the subversion of child's play thus proves popular.

23. Dan Fleming, *Powerplay: Toys as Popular Culture* (Manchester: Manchester University Press, 1996), 102.
24. D. W. Winnicott, *Playing and Reality* (London: Tavistock Publications, 1971), 2.
25. Fleming, *Powerplay*, 201–202.
26. Buckingham and Sefton-Green, "Gotta Catch 'em All: Structure, Agency and Pedagogy in Children's Media Culture," 386.
27. Ibid., 387. See also Henry Jenkins, "'Complete Freedom of Movement': Video Games as Gendered Play Spaces." In *From Barbie to Mortal Kombat: Gender and Computer Games*. Ed. Justine Cassell and Henry Jenkins (Cambridge, MA: MIT Press, 1998), 262–297.
28. Buckingham and Sefton-Green, 394.
29. John Hartley, *The Uses of Television* (London: Routledge, 1999), 218–219.
30. Tom Engelhardt, *The End of Victory Culture: Cold War America and the Disillusioning of a Generation* (Amherst: University of Massachusetts Press, 1998), 268.
31. Ibid., 284.
32. I examine the political and cultural contexts of *Star Wars* toy action figures in greater detail in Lincoln Geraghty, "Aging Toys and Players: Fan Identity and Cultural Capital." In *Finding the Force in the Star Wars Franchise: Fans, Merchandise and Critics*. Ed. Matthew Wilhelm Kapell and John Shelton Lawrence (New York: Peter Lang, 2006), 209–223.
33. Furthermore, I would argue that *The Transformers: The Movie* (1986) can be seen as a modern-day American Jeremiad as its narrative emphasizes living and working with Transformers can bring about physical and spiritual empowerment only if people are willing to change and learn from their mistakes. Due to space this theory cannot be developed further than an endnote, but it does help to demonstrate the cultural climate of America during the conservative presidency of Reagan in the 1980s.
34. Bernadette Casey, Neil Casey, Ben Calvert, Liam French and Justin Lewis, "Genre." In *Television Studies: The Key Concepts* (London: Routledge, 2002), 110.
35. Ibid., 109.
36. Rick Altman, *Film/Genre* (London: BFI Publishing, 1999), 188.
37. Ibid.
38. Ibid., 189.
39. Ibid., 189–190.
40. Ibid., 191.
41. P. David Marshall, "The New Intertextual Commodity." In *The New Media Book*. Ed. Dan Harries (London: BFI, 2002), 69.
42. Kendall L. Walton, *Mimesis as Make-Believe: On the Foundations of the Representational Arts* (Cambridge, MA: Harvard University Press, 1990), 12.
43. Quoted in Janet Staiger, "Cabinets of Transgression: Collecting and Arranging Hollywood Images." *Particip@tions* 1.3 (2005). Available at URL: <http://www.participations.org/volume%20I/issue%203/1_03_staiger_article.htm>. Accessed 02/17/06.
44. *The Transformers* DVD box sets are just one example of the renewed interest in children's television series; once popular but short-lived series such as *Dungeons and Dragons* (1983), *GI Joe* (1983–1987) and *The Real Ghostbusters* (1986–1991) are keenly sought on DVD so that fans can rewatch the episodes and relive childhood memories.
45. Daz Jamieson, "Episode Guide." *The Transformers* Season Two Part One DVD Box Set, Metrodome/Hasbro Inc./TV-Loonland Company, 2003.
46. "Transformers (2007 film)." Wikipedia, the free encyclopedia. Available at URL: <http://en.wikipedia.org/wiki/Transformers_(2007_film)>. Accessed 02/24/06.
47. "Member: Daz Jamieson (Starscream)." Available at URL: <http://www.thetransformers.net/member.asp?/MID=10&Skin=1>. Accessed 02/24/06.
48. Ibid.
49. See Mark Jancovich, "Cult Fictions: Cult Movies, Subcultural Capital and the Production of Cultural Distinctions." *Cultural Studies* 16.2 (2002): 306–22; Mark Jancovich and Nathan Hunt, "The Mainstream, Distinction, and Cult TV." In *Cult Television*. Ed. Sara Gwenllian-Jones and Roberta E. Pearson (Minneapolis: University of Minnesota Press, 2004), 27–44.

50. The work of G. McCracken as interpreted by Jonathan David Tankel and Keith Murphy, "Collecting Comic Books: A Study of the Fan and Curatorial Consumption." In *Theorizing Fandom: Fans, Subculture and Identity*. Ed. Cheryl Harris and Alison Alexander (Cresskill, NJ: Hampton Press, 1998), 59.

51. Russell W. Belk, *Collecting in a Consumer Society* (London: Routledge, 2001), 70.

52. Nathan Hunt, "The Importance of Trivia: Ownership, Exclusion and Authority in Science Fiction Fandom." In *Defining Cult Movies: The Cultural Politics of Oppositional Taste*. Ed. Mark Jancovich, Antonio Lázaro Reboll, Julian Stringer, and Andy Willis (Manchester: Manchester University Press, 2003), 186.

53. Joanne Hollows, "The Masculinity of Cult." In *Defining Cult Movies: The Cultural Politics of Oppositional Taste*. Ed. Mark Jancovich, Antonio Lázaro Reboll, Julian Stringer, and Andy Willis (Manchester: Manchester University Press, 2003), 37.

54. Ibid., 46.

55. Ibid., 47.

56. "Transformers Memories: 20 Years of Robots in Disguise." Available at URL: <http://www.autoassembly.org.uk/>. Accessed 02/24/06.

57. Bachelor Andy Stizer lives alone surrounded by his vintage and pristine boxed toys and action figures; before meeting Trish he epitomizes the geeky fan/collector stereotype. After revealing his passion for toys to Trish he uses her expertise in online trading to sell his toys and make a profit, and his enduring passion for the figures turns out to be beneficial when approached from a more orthodox (culturally acceptable) position.

58. Annette Kuhn, "'That day *did* last me all my life': Cinema Memory and Enduring Fandom." In *Identifying Hollywood's Audiences: Cultural Identity and the Movies*. Ed. Melvyn Stokes and Richard Maltby (London: BFI, 1999), 135.

59. Hills, *Fan Cultures*, 112.

60. Anthony Giddens, *Modernity and Self-Identity: Self and Society in the Late Modern Age* (Cambridge: Polity Press, 1991), 14.

61. Karen Ross and Virginia Nightingale, *Media Audiences: New Perspectives* (Basingstoke: Open University Press, 2003), 126.

11

Subcultural Tastes, Genre Boundaries and Fan Canons

BRIGID CHERRY

Any genre definition is a contested site and yet generic classification remains important within both popular discourse and academic analysis. For genre audiences in a wider sense and for fan communities in particular, the conception of genre is a foundation of taste and viewing preferences, and thereby of identity. The material presented here explores how fan tastes and demographic profiles contribute to the establishment of genre definitions and a fan canon. It is based on the findings from a longitudinal study of horror fans and followers drawn from a selection of face-to-face and online communities and from the wider audience of teens and viewers in their early twenties. Firstly, the chapter determines how fans engage with cinematic horror and argues that modes of emotional affect not only define the boundaries of the genre for the fans, but how these are correlated with demographic and identity groups. Secondly, it argues that cultural competencies are a factor in the formation of fan communities and this correlates with the development of fan canons. Finally, the significant films within the canon are considered and it is suggested that gendered, national and other identity groupings are a crucial factor in the placement of films within the canon. These findings highlight the diversity of horror cinema with the canon reflecting a cultural economy of fandom encompassing difference in terms of gendered aesthetics, historical moments and national cinemas. This has implications for our understanding of audiences, the dichotomy between different sections of the fan communities (including the general teen audience) and how we conceptualize the horror genre.

Defining Horror

In order to evaluate the main findings of this study it is important to begin by exploring approaches to the genre itself and how the genre audience is stratified. Horror cinema is an indefinite term, and the genre itself is extremely flexible, not least in that it is composed of a large number of heterogeneous film styles and narrative structures taking in atmospheric chillers, psychological thrillers, various kinds of occult or supernatural cinema and special effects–driven splatter and gore films, as well as the classic Gothic horrors and monster movies. Undoubtedly, what is conceived of as "the horror genre" has changed over time and is subject to retrospective reclassification (as with the acceptance of certain examples of art cinema into the canon of horror[1]). Examples of both popular and academic discourses surrounding horror cinema suggest that definitions of horror can fluctuate widely and that the accepted boundaries of the genre can be both extremely fluid and a site of contention.[2] Within the long history of the genre, different styles and cycles have dominated at particular cultural moments and these have appealed to different identity groups at different times. The intended audience has shifted according to shifts and changes in the genre.[3] In recent years — not only with the slasher and neo-slasher film cycles, but with successes such as *The Blair Witch Project* (1999) and the *Ring* films, the horror genre has been aimed principally at the younger teen market (many horror films gaining a 15 certificate in the UK) and the 18–24 year olds who constitute Hollywood's key audience segment. In addition, horror sub-genres have been the marketed and distributed with particular niche markets in mind — slasher films to the teen audience, splatter films to the specialist (male) fans (gorehounds), or even sold under the banner of an associated genre to a mainstream audience (as with the marketing of *The Silence of the Lambs* [1991] as a thriller, for example).

Despite the difficulties with genre classification, however, the horror film is one of the few generic types widely regarded, by audiences, the industry and the popular media, as a distinctive film genre. The horror genre is seen by Robin Wood (and others) in a unique light and is expected to have a discrete and strongly loyal audience, the vast majority of film viewers either showing a strong liking for the genre or a total dislike, with little feeling in between these extremes.[4] The generic diversity, however, taken together with the separation and marginalization of the loyal (or fan) audience that marks a liking for horror out as a subcultural taste, means that individual responses and sensibilities, which play a large part in the viewer's personal preferences, can lead to heterogeneity of tastes both between the fan and intended audiences and within the fan community. Although the more recent forms of horror may be most important in considering the tastes of the contemporary audience, the constant recycling of older films (including repeat screenings on television, archive releases on video and DVD, major retrospectives such as that at the National Film Theatre in November 2004, and the annual horror film festivals in Edinburgh, London and Manchester) means that all forms and eras of horror cinema have continuing relevance to the fan audience. As fan critics such as Kim Newman and Mark Kermode[5] also recognize, the fan audience (for Kermode in particular this audience consists of male aficionados of gore and other "hardcore" horror) tends to have a high level of generic competence. Accordingly, a fan canon of horror cinema might be expected to have much in common with historical or academic accounts of the genre, but would not be solely focused on dominant or contemporary trends in horror cinema. This is borne out by fan discourses circulating around the essential ingredients of "horror" or lists of recommended, favorite or greatest (the scariest, for example) horror films. These are not necessarily agreed upon by fans, however, and it would be a mistake to assume a unified subculture. Nevertheless, such discourses, together with the privileging of particular kinds of horror or particular films or filmmakers, might ultimately lead to fan canons of horror cinema or dominant definitions of horror within the fan community, but these might well be fragmented depending upon the demographics of the particular fan group and the identity group membership or degree of "fanishness" of its individual members. As Mark Jancovich has demonstrated,[6] horror is constructed by different social groups according to their relationship with the term.

In particular, popular assumptions about the horror film audience — for example, as evidenced by the aiming of horror films at a youth and frequently male demographic — raise important questions not just about the widely accepted classification of horror as a teen and/or masculine genre but how the genre is conceived by different groups at different times and how individual films are received and classified. It is the knowledge of this diversity within the genre, not only historically but across the range of national horror cinemas, that marks out the fan from the more casual (though frequent) viewer of horror (particularly the intended youth audience of contemporary horror cinema). Within the horror fan communities these cultural competencies are a vital currency.[7] Thus, fan communities, in addition to writers of academic or popular histories and media critics, can contribute to (or indeed create) a canon of horror cinema. And, as with the development of any other canon, dominant fan discourses can lead to the circulation and acceptance of particular canonical models of the genre or particular films being held in high regard. Though differences of opinion may arise frequently, certain views, which may divide along lines of either taste or identity group, can be marginalized by more dominant patterns of opinion (this is particularly evident among the female fan community[8]). More importantly, various segments of the fan community may hold quite different views from the wider audience about what constitutes both a "horror genre" and an ideal or "archetypal" horror film.

Researching Taste

Since differences between identity groups and also between fans and the intended audience might both be expected to produce differences in conceptions of the genre and the adoption of canonical texts, the research was designed around collecting responses from as diverse a sample of fan and general audiences as possible. The project seeks to address whether it is possible to construct a model of the genre based on empirical research of the horror fan subculture (or, indeed, the intended audience), and what such a model might tell us about either a fan canon of horror cinema or the fans themselves. In order to address these questions, a small-scale study taking in a representative sample of active horror fans (those taking part in organized face-to-face or online fan groups) was carried out. Participant observation of six fan groups was undertaken and a sample of 45 fans provided data via questionnaire and/or interview. The observed groups include the Horror in Film and Fiction e-mail list, the Yahoo! group Wheels of Terror, the newsgroups alt.horror and rec.arts.horror, members of the London Vampyre Society and the associated Vampire Exchange and Information Network, and the fans who stayed in contact after attending a course on horror cinema at the National Film Theatre. A control group of eight regular horror film viewers aged between 15 and 20 was also recruited from colleges in West London in order to identify the differences that might arise between the intended (youth) and the subcultural (fan) audience.

The concern here is not with the composition of the horror film audience (though this undoubtedly affects popular ideas about horror — particularly it being a masculine genre) but rather with possible core definitions of the genre that fan audiences make, what elements they regard as essential, their notions about the boundaries (if any) of the genre and the classifications or labels that they place on films. Obviously, responses and classifications (the latter is undoubtedly correlated with the former — what is "scary" for example will depend to a large extent upon personality, personal tastes and experiences) will be varied. A key concern here is therefore whether identity group membership affects the fans' conceptions of the genre, and if it does, in what ways. The study was designed and participants recruited in order to identify possible areas of difference. Equal numbers of male and female fans were selected, with an equal split between those aged 25–34 and those aged 35 or older (the oldest recruit was 48). Fans representing a range of sexualities, disabilities and ethnic groups were sought (though it did not prove possible in this small-scale study to produce representative samples of each). One-quarter of the participants declared themselves to be something other than heterosexual, just under one-eighth had a disability, and all but two were Caucasian.[9] Three of the control group are male and five female; two — both female — are of mixed-ethnic backgrounds; one declared herself to be bisexual, another as "label-less," and one male professed not to know his sexuality.

Emotional Affect

The first key finding of this study confirms that definitions of the genre horror are to a large extent correlated with what fans define as scary, disturbing or frightening. However, this is qualified by frequent suggestions that long-term fans do not (or no longer) find the examples they cite or that they accept as key horror films personally scary. Fans in particular (as opposed to the teen audience) are aware that age and desensitization means they are not always affected in ways intended by filmmakers. Nonetheless, modes of emotional affect are always important and sometimes problematical — especially revulsion and the shiver sensation, and these are linked to cinematic horror in its widest sense and not restricted only to accepted forms of horror cinema. This produces an extremely fluid genre definition, one that may be extremely personal and serves to reinforce the fan's identity as someone who enjoys frightening films of various forms (not necessarily formulaic horror films).

Among the fans in general there is broad consensus on a core definition of the genre, and this remains relatively stable across gender, age and other demographic or identity group categories. Commonly expressed definitions of horror include combinations of conventions from supernatural themes, unnatural monsters and elements intended to scare. A 36-year-old male fan who works as a software developer typically defines the genre as "movies where the primary goal is to cause sympathetic fright or dread to the viewer, often with a supernatural element." Of these essential elements, the most significant is, unsurprisingly, that films should usually be scary or terrifying in some way. The definition of horror as scary films highlights a problematical area for fans and this exposes the first of several contradictions in the fans' attempts to negotiate their cultural competencies and personal tastes. Since the majority of fans' attraction to the genre dates from childhood or early adolescence — a time in their lives when they first learned that they enjoyed being scared by horror films, they have a very specific idea of scariness as an emotional response. For example, a 25-year-old female fan says that "when I was younger *Cujo* [1983] bothered me because I had a thing with dogs, rabies, and realistic horror." Such comments do indicate that individual fans may respond more to films that contain horrific events or themes that they relate to on a very personal level and that have echoes of formative experiences.

A small number of fans (approximately one-third) also find it hard to name many or any horror films they consider to be good examples of scary films. For example, a female fan says that it is "hard to think of any." She goes on to say, "I rarely get scared by horror films, even as a kid I didn't get bothered." This is fairly typical of horror fans, a significant number claiming not to be scared by horror films, even as children. Although there is consensus that horror consists of scary films, as adults, many fans do not find horror particularly scary, frightening or horrific in general, and this is not the key reason why they like the genre. These fans accept a core definition of horror as scary films — one female fan qualifies her definition by stating that there should be an intent to scare on the part of the filmmaker, but they emphasize that the intent does not always work on them personally. Some do, however, continue to seek out films with the potential to scare them. These fans attempt to recreate the emotional responses of childhood by looking on the fringes of or outside the genre for suitable horrific and scary material. Films mentioned in this respect include *Eraserhead* (1978) and *The Vanishing* (1988). This undoubtedly affects the fans' definitions of the genre. For example, a 44-year-old female fan defines horror as an emotion and says that she would "describe as horror cinema any film that attempts to provoke that emotion." For her, Lars von Trier's *Dancer in the Dark* (2000) evokes that emotion and is, therefore, a horror film. There is strong evidence here of a tendency for fans to regard the ability to scare as a more important factor than supernatural, monstrous or even gory elements in categorizing the genre. One male librarian aged 41 states that films do not have to be promoted as horror to belong in the genre; the key criteria for this fan is where "scaring the audience is clearly one of the goals of the filmmaker" and he gives *Deliverance* (1972) as an example. Another fan, a 37-year-old female librarian, states that "horror cinema can include parts of films or whole films that would generally be seen as 'belonging to' a genre other than horror." The definitions of horror thus arising among these fans frequently tend toward definitions of cinematic horror (as opposed to horror cinema). This distinction is one that has been applied by Steven Schneider in his discussion of horror aesthetics,[10] though here there is clearly a personal element in what the individual fans find scary. In terms of canonical definitions, then, an intent to scare is considered essential, but on an individual level, the scary elements can vary immensely and be present in non-horror films.

The inherent contradiction here, namely that horror is (or should be) by definition scary, yet few horror films are scary on a personal response level, leads to some interesting conceptions of the genre and this further leads to some fans regarding the boundaries of the genre as extremely flexible. Typically, many of the fans offer qualifications to their core definitions, though this is more often to accommodate films widely classified as horror already (but which they might not enjoy or find horrific). However, this can also occur in order to be inclusive of the enjoyable responses some fans seek from cinematic horror (within or without the genre) and these are often modes of emotional affect other than scariness.

Demographic Factors

Clearly, then, modes of affect, and emotional and physical responses to films determine the boundaries of the genre for the fans, but these are often correlated with identity and demographic group, particularly with respect to gendered identities. In addition, fans are aware that they have to negotiate — not unproblematically in some cases — different aesthetic and sub- or quasi-generic sets of conventions of horror. Again, fans, unlike the teen audience, are aware of the different historical and national forms of horror and fans in particular seek out cinematic horror other than that on current release in cinemas — in this respect conditions of viewing can also be extremely important. These are key factors that fans take into account when discussing significant examples of the genre and thus influencing the development of fan canons.

The most mentioned secondary affect is suspense, and this is deemed important for slightly more of the fans than fear or terror. Both suspense and fear or terror are given importance across categories of both age and gender. Other affects, however, are correlated with demographic factors. Anxiety for characters is far more likely to be given importance by female and older fans, and slightly less likely by non-heterosexual or disabled fans. It is not entirely clear why this should be, though several fans express empathy with the monster and this may impede the process of identifying with the victim/protagonist. Certainly in this respect, Tanya Kryzwinska, Sue-Ellen Case and others have theorized lesbian identification with the female vampire and female fans who were marginalized as children or adolescents (for example, being bookish or geeky) express identification with some kinds of monsters.[11] Frights, jumps or shocks are more likely to be given importance by the younger fans — and this correlates with the importance of more recent forms of horror cinema (slasher films as well as science fiction horror hybrids such as *Alien* [1979]) for these fans. The shiver sensation or goosebumps are weighted more heavily by female fans who, in general (and this is borne out by the earlier study of the female horror film audience), prefer more imaginative, atmospheric and uncanny forms of horror that might elicit this mode of affect rather more than splatter films, which they generally reject due to the high levels of gore and lack of atmosphere. Male fans were slightly more likely to mention revulsion or nausea as key affects of the genre than female fans, though overall this was deemed to be the least important affect (and only of significance to those fans with a specific interest in splatter or gore films). This suggests that fans are approximately divided according to whether they have a personal preference for uncanny or graphic horror[12] — and certainly the evidence from this and other studies suggests that fan communities exist around both types and some fans actively select or prefer one over the other. This is not to suggest, though, that many fans do not enjoy both forms or that a preference for one leads to outright rejection of all films in the other category. For example, female fans who generally dislike gore and splatter enjoy films such as *Hellraiser* (1987), which is deemed atmospheric in spite of the gore.[13] Noel Carroll's suggestion[14] that the audience can be divided into average and specialized viewers is not, then, unproblematical and gender may be only one factor to influence definitions and categorization among a range of fan profiles and identities (female fans resemble Carroll's average viewers much more closely than the specialized category, and yet they also exhibit typical fan behaviors and responses and desire the "negative" emotions that horror arouses, albeit in different areas of the genre to male fans). Certainly, it appears to be important to consider gendered tastes and feminine or similar aesthetics of horror cinema (Harry M. Benshoff analyses a queer aesthetic, for example[15]). In this respect, it should be noted that while the differences in preferred modes of affect between able-bodied and disabled fans or between heterosexual fans and those of other sexualities (gay, bisexual, other) are of low statistical significance, the fact that they do exist within this small-scale study indicates that textual accounts of the genre need to consider the full range of the audience.

Formative Experiences

When asked to list the films they considered the scariest examples of horror, there was a significant correlation between films the fans found scary as younger viewers and their definitions of essential features of horror. For fans, these formative experiences influence their tastes and preferences and thereby their perceptions of the genre. Since generic competence is a feature of the subcultural taste, the contradictions this creates are recognized by the fans. A number make exceptions to their definitions either to accommodate non-horror films they find horrific or to include types of horror that they are aware are widely considered to be part of the genre but that they do not respond to as horror. Some of the fans find horror-comedies funnier than they find them scary, but they knowingly stretch their definition of horror in order to include such films. (*Tremors* [1990] and *Shaun of the Dead* [2004] are examples mentioned here.) Those fans who emphasize the supernatural as a key element often acknowledge the difficult position this causes with respect to more realistic horror categories. One female fan defines the genre as "movies with supernatural themes, witches, monsters not of this natural world." She specifically excludes films such as "mad tigers rampaging and attacking people [which] would be more thriller or suspense rather than horror," although other fans disagree and might classify such films as belonging to the horror subgenre of aberrant nature. (*The Birds* [1963] is mentioned by one male fan.)

More often, however, although supernatural elements are widely mentioned in the core definitions, exceptions are frequently made by the fans in order to accommodate films with horrific or frightening killers that have no supernatural themes or elements. (*The Silence of the Lambs* and *The Texas Chain Saw Massacre* [1974] are cited in this respect.) In the same way, one female fan, a 48-year-old secretary, (almost unwillingly) expands her core definition of horror to include "gorefests" such as *Cannibal Holocaust* (1980). Although this fan does not find these kinds of films scary (stating that "I think there should be some effort to frighten the viewer at some level, not just make them want to heave"), she considers them to be examples of horror and includes them because "I know people think gore equals scare." When questioned as to how she knows this she states that it is through observations of fellow fans: "My sexist theory about it is that it's mostly guys who think this way, and it's because they're so typically spooky about blood." Such examples of "extreme cinema" and "video nasties" have long been associated with horror, but for a significant number of fans (especially women) these appear not to meet the key criteria of being able to elicit fear or terror and they, therefore, have to make exceptions for these films in their definitions. Certainly, the fans seem to knowingly divide the genre along lines of gore or suspense and atmosphere. One male fan, a 27-year-old journalist, defines horror as films that set out to scare, instill fear or make the viewer feel uncomfortable, but he divides these into two types: "Some films do this primarily through images, giving gore drenched, tortuous scenes that linger — and others (and my inclination) serve up images that burn themselves into the mind with clever writing and haunting themes." Primarily, fans are aware of the negotiations they are required to make in order to accommodate their own and their fellow fans' definitions of horror, and they frequently accept that "breaking the rules" is necessary.

Not all fans, however, are able to clearly articulate a definition of horror based on generic or other cinematic codes or modes of emotional affect. While one or two express circular or ambiguous definitions (one states that the horror genre is simply a collection of horror films), others specify external factors. The intent of the filmmaker is sometimes acknowledged: one female fan defines horror films as those "made by people who consider them horror movies." Other fans are specific about viewing conditions; a 29-year-old male incorporates the experience of viewing in an audience into his core definition: horror has to be viewed in a cinema. More commonly, fans make reference to viewing in a darkened room as a key aspect of the genre. (This is obviously a major factor in creating an atmosphere that amplifies the modes of emotional affect, particularly being scared.) This reveals an interesting approach to genre, in which experiences of viewing conditions are given some importance, and this raises questions about generic models in the era of The Horror Channel, the DVD and home cinema. For example, a 28-year-old male reports that viewing alone or in company can change one's responses to a film; he cites *The Texas Chain Saw Massacre* as an example of this, stating that it is only scary "if watching it alone, if with a group it is very funny." Previous research has also suggested that female fans view horror films at home more frequently than at the cinema (because they feel marginalized for their aberrant taste or they have no one to attend screenings with),[16] suggesting that models of the genre and of the spectators based on cinema attendance might be ignoring key segments of the audience.

Cultural Competencies

Regardless of viewing conditions, however, fan definitions of the genre are often centered around what for them are key films that elicit the desired affects. Within the fan audience, in particular, cultural competencies are a key factor in the formation of fan communities. (There is some suggestion this also occurs within the teen audience, though this is restricted to recent horror films with a high marketing profile or genre "classics.") The value of certain competencies and generic knowledge within the cultural economy of horror fandom varies across identity groups, most notably with respect to gender. Personal tastes are crucial here, with fans seeking out others with similar tastes — within these groupings fans rely on each other for examples of "great" horror films and recommended titles. The sharing of knowledge and ideas is a key factor in the development of discourses within the group and thereby the fan canon. The formation of fan canons is thus correlated with identity and subgroups within the wider fan community. This can also be at odds with the film industry's classification of films as horror, and with the media's marketing and reviewing of films, and by implication the wider (and teen) conceptions of the genre.

As is the nature of any subcultural taste, the fans are very knowledgeable about the genre, although the various fan communities may place very different values on different aspects of generic competence and fan behavior. Female fans, for example, are much less likely than male fans to deem collecting ephemera or factual knowledge about the genre important or to read the specialist horror magazines, whereas they might privilege certain feminine aesthetics and characterizations and to specify a romantic or erotic element as important.[17]

However, regardless of the value placed on certain cultural competencies, all the fans are cosmopolitan in their tastes and like many different kinds of horror. Comments such as "I watch it all" or "I will give anything a try" are common. Within fan communities, recommendations from fellow fans and opinions imparted during discussion of particular films are important. (Indeed, this is a primary activity observed within both face-to-face and online communities.)[18] A 28-year-old male fan states that he is especially likely to watch a film "if someone else recommends it to me," thus suggesting that within particular groups, fans rely on each other's opinions. In general, the fans are very open-minded and accepting of new or different examples of horror. Even when a fan generally dislikes one type of horror subgenre, this does not necessarily mean they choose never to view them. As a 36-year-old male software developer states, "I dislike slasher [films], but I'll watch one occasionally."

However, even though the fans generally like a wide range of different types of horror films, contradictions again arise over what constitutes the genre. Some fans reject films that veer too far away from their core conception of horror or overlap too much with other genres. A 29-year-old female teacher says: "I can't stand that when I think I am watching a horror movie, and then it turns into more of an action movie than a horror movie. That drives me nuts." Marketing is a key issue here; fans may feel exploited at being sold a film as horror when it does not match their core concept of the genre. In addition, while some generic hybrids are popular with many of the fans (sf-horror and serial-killer films), others tend to divide them. Horror-comedy, for example, is a contested area: one female fan states: "I hate the ones that are supposed to be funny — like *Shaun of the Dead*, I like my horror to be scary." There are obviously some further contradictions emerging here. It is clear that the genre remains a contested site within and between fan communities, the point here primarily being that the personal often overrides other considerations. Observations suggest that fans orient themselves with others of a like-mind or (mostly good-naturedly) agree to disagree. Fandom also tends to divide along lines of personal taste and background. For example, the Horror in Film and Fiction group consists mainly of fans who tend to be slightly older, are often educated to university or post-graduate degree level, and who desire to discuss or analyze the full range of horror film and fiction in depth. The newsgroups, by contrast, appear to attract younger and predominantly male fans and discussion is centered on the latest releases and older accepted classics (the Romero zombie films, for example). Other groups — the VEIN and NFT horror groups — have very specific links with face-to-face communities and are used to prolong or arrange face-to-face interactions (including film viewings and social gatherings) as well as discussing relevant topics. The film discussions that form the center of fan discourses circulating in each group do differ, but this is not to suggest that fans are influenced to any large extent by other members. Rather, fans gravitate towards those groups that contain like-minded fans and those containing fans who disseminate opinions they respect. This might mean, however, that smaller groups of fans with oppositional or different views on the genre are isolated from the larger community and their definitions of the genre may not be so widely heard. We might, though, expect analysis of the fan canon of horror cinema to reflect these minority views.

Canonical Texts

The final key area then is to explore the formation of a fan canon of horror cinema and its relationship to other formations of canonical texts. The acceptance of films into a canon is often dependent on how well a film measures up to an idealized set of aesthetics or modes of affect. Again, chosen films correlate with identity and demographic groupings. Overall, however, the fan canon parallels accepted canons of horror cinema in many respects; this is not unexpected, since fan input into populist debate is well established, while fans can also be dependent on the general availability and accessibility of films. There are clear differences, though, in certain key respects from general and widespread populist conceptions of the genre that are reflected in the fan canon. This is the main area of difference between fans and teen audiences. The fan audience includes a stronger and wider awareness of historical and national horror cinemas, and is accepting of a wider tradition of horror with a greater variety of aesthetics and affects.

In order to determine the shape of a fan canon of horror cinema, the fans were asked to give examples of significant (and favorite or scariest) horror films. The most mentioned films are *Alien, The Exorcist* (1973), *Halloween* (1978), *The Thing* (1982), *Dawn of the Dead* (1978), *The Evil Dead* (1983), *Evil Dead 2* (1987), *Hellraiser, The Haunting* (1963), *The Shining* (1980), and *Suspiria* (1977). These films (including the two sf-horror hybrids) are widely acknowledged classics of the genre and are also some of the most well-known and popular examples. These choices reflect key moments in the recent history of horror cinema, and parallel canonical histories and academic accounts. Though none of the above films dates from before the 1960s, a significant minority of early horror films were put forward by fans. Twenty-three percent of all the films cited were from the '30s, '40s and '50s; these include *Freaks* (1932), *King Kong* (1933), *The Bride of Frankenstein* (1935), *The Fly* (1958), *The Invisible Man* (1933), and *Cat People* (1942). The stronger emphasis on more recent examples is exaggerated further in the control group. Among the control group the films listed are predominantly recent examples of horror cinema; that is, films released within the last few years (or readily available on DVD) and no films earlier than the '70s were listed. This, as might be expected, is a clear difference between the intended horror film audience and the fan subculture that possesses greater knowledge of the history of the genre. However, it is the older and more educated fans that recognize the full history of the genre and this is just one of the minority viewpoints represented.

There is also some suggestion that the fans are divided along lines of gender in their selections. Half of the films listed above are liked equally by male and female fans, though others reveal significant differences along gender lines. *Hellraiser* is deemed to be a significant film almost exclusively by female fans, while *The Thing* is named almost entirely by male fans. Significantly more male fans named *Dawn of the Dead, Halloween* and *Suspiria*, females *The Haunting*. This is confirmed by the favorite films of the female audience, which again suggests a feminine aesthetic of horror.[19] And while the fan canon (in comparison with the general audience) demonstrates knowledge of genre history and variety, it should also be noted that this (condensed) fan canon also hides a significant number of films from the wider sphere of horror cinema that the various fan "minorities" acknowledge; examples of other films mentioned include Hammer films (largely named by British fans) and vampire films (predominantly cited by female fans and those who identify as Goth), as well as classics of German Expressionist, Italian and Japanese cinema. The fan canon, as might be expected in comparison with other canons, tends in the main to reflect a dominant American and masculine position, but also reflects the diversity of many decades of international horror and its variety of audiences.

Genre Boundaries

These findings, the contradictions raised by the fan definitions of horror as well as the shape of the canon, confirm that the notion of the genre being distinct or easily definable is a misconception. As the control group's conceptions of the genre reveal, dominant contemporary forms of horror with large-scale marketing and visibility can mask the range and variety of horror cinema that has emerged throughout its history both within and outside Hollywood. Fan audience responses also raise the question of horror aesthetics and how these might lead to quite different models of genre that appeal to different identity groups within the audience. Certainly, genre definitions and canons seem incomplete without taking the (often hidden) female audience into account. In addition to fans holding a much more historical account of genre than the intended audience, it is clear that a feminine aesthetic of atmospheric and emotional horror exists alongside the typically masculine aesthetic of gore and violence, though elements of both graphic and uncanny horror may be present in both forms. A fragmented and fluid definition of horror is therefore important since different patterns of fan taste are clear and fan conceptions of the genre have widened the boundaries in order to include cinematic horror (which is often related to personal preferences as well as identity factors such as nationality, gender and age). While these examples may reflect the horror fan's nomadic interests as much as their classifications of the genre, they illustrate the difficulties with keeping horror confined within distinct genre boundaries especially where gendered aesthetics and modes of emotional affect are concerned.

Notes

1. S. S. Prawyer, *Caligari's Children: The Film as Tale of Terror* (New York: Da Capo Press, 1980), 8–47.

2. See for example Mark Jancovich, "Genre and the Audience: Genre Classifications and Cultural Distinctions in the Mediation of *The Silence of the Lambs*." In *Hollywood Spectatorship: Changing Perceptions of Cinema Audiences*. Ed. Melvyn Stokes and Richard Maltby (London: BFI Publishing, 2001), 33–45.

3. See Rhona Berenstein, *Attack of the Leading Ladies: Gender, Sexuality, and Spectatorship in Classic Horror Cinema* (New York: Columbia University Press, 1996), 60–77, on classic horror film marketing or Peter Hutchings, *Hammer and Beyond: The British Horror Film* (Manchester: Manchester University Press, 1993), 4–11, on the press coverage of Hammer films.

4. Robin Wood, "An Introduction to the American Horror Film." In *Planks of Reason*. Ed. Barry Keith Grant (Metuchen, NJ: Scarecrow Press, 1980), 173.

5. See Kim Newman, "The Pleasures of Horror." *Sight and Sound London Film Festival Supplement* October (1992): 16–18 and Mark Kermode, "I Was a Teenage Horror Fan: Or, 'How I Learned to Stop Worrying and Love Linda Blair.'" In *Ill Effects: The Media/Violence Debate*. Ed. Martin Barker and Julian Petley (London: Routledge, 1997), 57–66.

6. Jancovich, "Genre and the Audience."

7. Bourdieu's model of the cultural economy underlies this, though it is not without difficulties—see Matt Hills, *Fan Cultures* (London: Routledge, 2002), 50–58.

8. See Brigid Cherry, "Refusing to Refuse to Look: Female Viewers of the Horror Film." In *Identifying Hollywood Audiences*. Ed. Richard Maltby and Melvin Stokes (London: BFI Publishing, 1999), 187–203, for a fuller discussion of the female horror film audience.

9. Since this was primarily a self-selecting group, it did not prove possible to recruit fans from other ethnic backgrounds on this occasion, though this should not be taken as strong evidence that horror fandom is predominantly white. Since the Wheels of Terror group is an online community for disabled fans and their friends, it proved somewhat easier to recruit from this identity group. In general, the Internet has given many fans with disabilities wider access to the fan community outside fan conventions.

10. Steven Jay Schneider, "Toward an Aesthetics of Cinematic Horror." In *The Horror Film*. Ed. Stephen Prince (Piscataway, NJ: Rutgers University Press, 2004), 146.

11. See Sue-Ellen Case, "Tracking the Vampire." *Differences: A Journal of Feminist Cultural Studies* 3.2 Summer (1991): 1–20; Tanya Krzywinska, "La Belle Dame Sans Merci?" In *A Queer Romance—Lesbians, Gay Men and Popular Culture*. Ed. Paul Burston and Colin Richardson (London: Routledge, 1995), 99–110; Cherry, "Refusing to Refuse to Look."

12. See Cynthia Freeland, *The Naked and the Undead: Evil and the Appeal of Horror* (Oxford: Westview Press, 2000), 215–271 for a wider discussion of these categories.

13. Brigid Cherry, "Broken Homes, Tortured Flesh: *Hellraiser* and the Feminine Aesthetic of Horror Cinema." *Film International* May 17 (2005): 11–12.

14. Noel Carroll, *The Philosophy of Horror or Paradoxes of the Heart* (London: Routledge, 1990), 191–195.

15. Harry M. Benshoff, *Monsters in the Closet: Homosexuality and the Horror Film* (Manchester: Manchester University Press, 1997), 233–235.

16. Cherry, "Refusing to Refuse to Look," 189.

17. Ibid., 199.

18. Brigid Cherry, "Stalking the Web: Horror Film Marketing, Celebration and Chat on the Internet." In *Horror Zone*. Ed. Ian Conrich and Julian Petley (Verso, forthcoming).

19. Cherry, "Broken Homes, Tortured Flesh," 11.

12

Monster Legacies

Memory, Technology and Horror History

PETER HUTCHINGS

When it comes to the history of film genres, the dictum "The more you know, the less you know" seems particularly apt. During the 1970s and 1980s, critical writing about genre relied on the apparently reasonable assumption that there were distinctive groupings of films out there that could be known and classified with some precision. After all, commercial cinema organized itself largely through genres, and part of the impulse behind film studies' turn to genre was to get closer to the ways in which cinema actually operated as a medium (as opposed to the more "elitist" authorship-based approaches of the late 1950s and 1960s[1]). But as our knowledge of genre history has developed, this reasonable assumption has become increasingly difficult to sustain.

In part, this has to do with an acknowledgement that film genres might be considerably more heterogeneous and dispersed than earlier accounts had supposed. Historicist work, for example, has broken up overly cohesive generic "identities" through rescuing particular subgenres and cycles from the critical margins (for example, Peter Stanfield on the singing cowboy film[2]) or through recovering discarded genres such as, for example, the travel and jungle movies of the 1920s and 1930s that, when classified at all nowadays, usually end up in the horror or action genres.[3] An increased critical interest in non–American national cinemas also has implications for genre histories that have in the past been based largely on Hollywood production. Generic groupings such as, to name but a few non–American generic variants, European westerns and thrillers, East Asian horror films and Indian melodramas all raise significant questions about the overall shape and coherence of the film genres to which they in some way seem to belong. Given this, it is perhaps not surprising that discussions of film genres now frequently focus on generic cycles, tightly defined groups of films operating within specific historical and/or national sites and contexts, rather than struggling to identify what qualities bind together all the films perceived as belonging to any particular genre. For recent examples of this localizing tendency, see Tim Bergfelder on German generic variants of the 1960s, Antonio Lázaro Reboll and Andrew Willis on genres in Spanish cinema, and Steve Neale on contemporary American generic developments.[4]

It is not just our understanding of the historical and national configurations of genres that has become more complex, however. The process by which generic identity itself is assigned to particular groups of films has also been thrown into question. Instead of finding that identity solely within the films themselves, in their shared themes or iconography, genre critics will now often seek out those extratextual elements that help to produce a sense of generic intertextuality, that bind the films together in ways that are not immediately apparent from the films themselves. For example, Neale has written of the need to engage with "the role of industrial and journalistic discourses in establishing a generic corpus,"[5] while Rick Altman has argued that "genres are not inert categories shared by all (although at some moments they seem to be), but discursive categories made by real speakers for particular purposes in specific situations."[6] Altman identifies producers, exhibitors, critics and spectators as genre users (and genre definers), with the discursive activities of these various groups not necessarily cohering into a common agreement about the identity or history of any particular film genre. There are possibilities here for contested genres, with one group of users disagreeing with another group's definition of a particular genre, and also for "critical" genres, generic identities circulated by critics that do not necessarily match the original production categories of the films in question — with film noir perhaps the most notable example of a critical term applied retrospectively to a group of films.[7]

The realization that film genres need to be seen in terms of the discursive activities of "genre users" as well as in terms of the films themselves has proved very productive so far as the generation of theoretical and historical work is concerned. However, its implications for an understanding of how genres actually function for specific audiences have not been fully explored. Most notably, our sense of the particular sites — institutional, technological and national — where genres operate as discursively bound entities remains relatively undeveloped and lacking in nuance.

This chapter seeks to address this via a focus on the horror genre and through invoking particular memories of watching horror films. Memory and genre history — one subjective and private, the other existing in the public sphere — are not usually connected, but making such a connection can cast a new and interesting light on the genre in question. In essence, the chapter offers the story of a personal encounter with a film genre, albeit a story that is not especially interested in the personal significance of the encounter but instead wants to identify those sites where the encounter occurred and in relation to which memories of a particular genre were subsequently formed and sustained. Although the chapter is intended as a contribution to genre history, it proceeds in an unashamedly unchronological way. In fact, its theme might be said to be how we as spectators can often end up watching genre films in a manner that is out of synchronization with conventional notions of genre definition and genre history.

Memories of Horror

So there I am, in the DVD store, looking at this big box set of horror DVDs. It's the Universal Monster Legacy Collection, an assemblage of classic Universal horror films of the 1930s and 1940s, and it's so large that it does not fit onto the regular racks but instead perches imposingly on the top shelf. I'm thinking about buying it. Why? Because I want it, of course. But why do I want it? That's a more difficult question to answer, and the more I think about it, the more I find myself conjuring up memories of viewing Universal horror films in very different circumstances back in the 1970s. For horror enthusiasts living in Britain during the 1970s, the advent of autumn usually meant Saturday late-night double bills of horror films on BBC2. My memory of them was that a Universal horror film of the 1930s or 1940s was followed by a Hammer horror film of the 1950s or 1960s. I can recall screenings of individual films, both of first encounters with horrors seen many times since, such as Universal's *Dracula* (1931) and *Frankenstein* (1931) and Hammer's *Dracula — Prince of Darkness* (1966) and *The Reptile* (1966), and of films that did not seem to fit neatly into the established double-bill format — some of Val Lewton's 1940s horror work, for example, or an oddity like *Superbeast* (1972). However, these memories, although apparently more specific, actually feel fragile and tentative; it is possible that my first viewing of, say, *The Reptile* occurred elsewhere, on another channel, at another time. By contrast, the memory of the double-bill is more diffuse — I find it hard to date it with any precision — but also much stronger. Perhaps this is because it is the memory of a pattern that is repeated over time, a pattern involving a relatively old horror film followed by a relatively new horror film. But arguably it also has something to do with the way in which this memory is bound up with what it meant to watch television in Britain during the 1970s. In other words, it is not just a memory of horror films but also a memory of a particular institutionally defined experience of watching horror films, an experience that has now been lost.

There were only three television channels in Britain in the 1970s — BBC1, BBC2 and ITV — and no cable, satellite TV or domestic video playback technology. From the perspective of today, it seems a situation in which the act of viewing was defined very authoritatively by the institution of television, with minimal choice and with times of viewing entirely shaped by the television schedules. If you wanted to watch these horror films, you had to stay up late rather than just set the video recorder. In an era of single television households, you might also have had to contend with alternative attractions showing at the same time on another channel, and indeed my memory of watching the double bills is intertwined with a recollection of obstacles to viewing that were not always overcome (e.g., missing the opening scenes of the first film in the double bill because my father insisted on watching the football highlights on the other side).

If for no other reason, this memory of the horror double bill is useful because it reminds us of something that is both obvious and significant, namely, that films can continue to circulate and be seen long after their initial release. We are constantly surrounded by films from different periods, in the cinema, on television, video and DVD. However, this apparently banal fact rarely impacts much upon film genre histories, which tend instead to focus overwhelmingly on the moment of production. A history of 1940s horror cinema, for example, is likely to deal mainly, if not exclusively, with films produced during that decade. If horror films from the previous decade are mentioned at all, it will be in the interests of establishing how the 1940s version differed from what had gone before. The re-release of 1930s horror films during the 1940s — and the distinct possibility that sections of the 1940s audience might have been seeing these older films for the first time alongside the newer versions — is hard to incorporate within a developmental model of genre history in which one cycle of production is seen as inevitably superseded and made redundant by another cycle. In a related way, my experience of horror in the 1970s stands at odds with the conventional genre-historical accounts of that decade, with these usually focusing on the new traumatic horror offered by the likes of *The Exorcist* (1973) and *The Texas Chainsaw Massacre* (1974). For me, and I assume for many others too, horror in the 1970s meant instead not just the Universal/Hammer double bills but also horror on television rather than in the cinema.

This leads to a second significant point, namely, that experiences of film genres are mediated by institutions and technologies that have their own historical specificity. I have already suggested that the experience of the horror double bill was also an experience of a particular moment in television history. Clearly, these horror films were being positioned and framed institutionally in order to render them appropriate for domestic viewing. This involved scheduling them at the very end of the day's schedule on BBC2, a minority interest channel. It also involved some humor in their presentation, with the offscreen continuity announcers cracking jokes about how nervous they were to be alone in the TV studio late at night (and in so doing acting as mild-mannered versions of the wisecracking horror hosts who ushered horror films onto U.S. television during the 1950s).

Seeing a genre in terms of the sites of its reception and the formats of its delivery to its audiences is probably an even more pressing issue now than it was back in the 1970s. First video and then DVD (with the possibility soon of new streaming technologies that will eventually supersede DVD) have driven further the dispersal of movie watching away from cinemas, to the extent that today most people watch their films at home rather than in public auditoria. While there is a lot of critical interest in the ways in which viewers deploy audio-visual and digital technologies, this usually involves an exploration of formations of taste, especially in the context of fan cultures and fan communities, rather than thinking about the history or identity of film genres. The partial exception to this relates to "critical genres," constructions or modifications of generic identities emanating from audiences and/or critics rather than from the film industry. Even here, however, the function of video and DVD tends to be seen as primarily archival, offering a view of the way things were that can be used to generate new exciting perspectives on the films in question. For example, Christine Gledhill has noted, "'Old' films circulate amongst us still, enabling film and critical production to hook back into the past and dust off apparently worn-out formulae for present uses and possible renaming."[8] What such a comment fails to acknowledge is not just that the methods for the circulation of old films are themselves of historical significance but also that the ways in which certain films get marked as "old" is far from straightforward (e.g., old as in "classic," or — and this relates especially to recent horror DVD releases — old as in a film from the past that you now have the opportunity to see uncut for the very first time). Indeed, it seems that distinctions between past and present are not nearly as clear as might be imagined within current generic configurations.

This section began with a memory of watching horror on television three decades ago. But memory is not just a trace of the past; it is also a formation of the present, of standing in that DVD store and contemplating a box set of old movies, with the relationship to a remembered past characterized by a sense of loss. What has been lost here, however, is not the films in question but rather a particular institutional framing and presentation of those films. This chapter has been arguing that in order to bring nuance to genre history and generic identities, there needs to be some engagement with changing patterns in the circulation of genre films. It has also been suggested that, so far as the viewing of films is concerned at least, things are very different now from how they were back in the 1970s. People still go to the cinema, of course (although the cinemas themselves might look somewhat different), but they are also viewing films in other ways and in other places, and the presentation of genres has been adapted to suit this. In order to grasp what this entails in practice, we can at last turn to an object that offers itself both as absolutely up-to-date and as a testament to the origins of a particular film genre — the Universal Monster Legacy DVD Collection.

It's a Universal Picture!

The Universal Monster Legacy Collection is designed to impress. Fifteen DVDs contain seventeen Universal horror films along with nine documentaries (including the feature-length *Universal Monsters*), trailers, production photographs and stills. Eight of the horror films have voice-overs by horror historians, and there is the option of watching the 1931 Bela Lugosi *Dracula* with a new score by Philip Glass. As a cross-section of Universal horror, the Collection offers a judicious mix of the well-known — for example, *Dracula*, *Frankenstein*, *The Mummy* (1932), *Bride of Frankenstein* (1935) and *The Wolf Man* (1941) — and the relatively obscure, notably the Spanish-language version of *Dracula* that was filmed on the sets used for the Lugosi version and the 1946 B-movie *She-Wolf of London*. As an added attraction, small busts of Lugosi as Dracula, Boris Karloff as Frankenstein's monster and Lon Chaney Jr. as the Wolf Man are also included in the package.

There is no doubt that Universal was a major player in 1930s and 1940s U.S. horror but, unsurprisingly, the historical-contextualizing material contained on the DVDs rarely acknowledges the range of other companies contributing to the formation of horror during this period. Instead, the Legacy Collection clearly seeks to establish a proprietorial claim to the past of the horror genre, although at the same time it is articulating this in relation both to new products and to new markets and technological platforms. In effect, what one finds here is Universal's strategic promotion of its own economically valuable "legacy" in a way that blurs past and present and that interlinks cinema and DVD release.

The first wave of DVD releases under the Legacy banner — three collections of, respectively, Universal's *Dracula*, *Frankenstein* and *Wolf Man* films — occurred in the United States in April 2004, just one month before the cinema release of the Universal blockbuster movie *Van Helsing*, a special-effects laden extravaganza packed full of references to old Universal horror films and featuring in its cast Dracula, Frankenstein and werewolves. A second clutch of DVD sets — collections of *The Mummy*, *The Invisible Man* and *The Creature from the Black Lagoon* cycles — in October 2004 coincided with the DVD release of *Van Helsing*. The release of this material in Britain does not appear to have been tied in as tightly to *Van Helsing*, and, surprisingly, the British version of the Legacy Collection box set — which was released in October 2004 — contains more films than the American version. At the time of writing, the U.S. *Mummy*, *Invisible Man* and *Black Lagoon* sets are not available as Region 2 DVD releases (which might explain why the British Legacy Collection includes *The Mummy*, *The Invisible Man* and *The Creature from the Black Lagoon*). The close association of *Van Helsing* with the Legacy Collection clearly helped to root the blockbuster firmly in a cinematic past but it also provided a context in which Universal's back catalogue of horror films could be renewed and updated.[9]

This kind of commercial activity bears out Rick Altman's claim that studios prefer generic cycles to genres as a whole because they can own and exploit the cycles.[10] The fact that the Legacy DVD collections in all their manifestations offer recyclings of previously released material — not just released in the cinema but on video and in some cases on earlier DVDs as well — underlines this yet further. What we see here is an example of a now common marketing practice for DVD whereby "special editions" of older films are produced that add new material — new scenes and/or new features — or offer new combinations of films in box sets in an attempt to update the product and, presumably, get consumers who have bought the earlier versions to buy the more up-to-date ones too.

Horror fans, and indeed historians of horror (who are probably also horror fans), might well buy the Legacy Collection in order to get hold of the best quality versions of "classic" Universal horror films currently available in the market. But they, and especially the historians, could also profitably consider how the Collection does not just contain old films and new extras but also offers, perhaps inadvertently, fascinating glimpses into the ways in which horror has been and continues to be constructed discursively. The Legacy package presents itself as coherent and cohesive but actually it is unstable and fragmented, and the signs of that instability and fragmentation are everywhere.

It is apparent, for example, in the choice of the films to be included in the Collection. Some of these seem uncontentious. It would be hard to find many today who would not classify *Dracula, Frankenstein, Bride of Frankenstein* and *The Wolf Man* as horror (although some might want to classify the *Frankenstein* films as science fiction as well). However, it is worth pointing out that *Dracula* in particular was not initially marketed as a horror film but rather as a macabre thriller. The term "horror" barely featured in the original 1931 press book for the film and it was only later that it was reclassified as horror. The press book is included in the published version of the Dracula screenplay.[11] Indeed, one can see this process at work within the Collection itself. The *Dracula* trailer included as an extra on the *Dracula* DVD is not the original 1931 trailer; instead it advertises the re-release of the film by RealArt Pictures in the early 1950s. The trailer's insistent branding of the film as horror — "In all the annals of horror, one name stands out as the epitome of evil.... Back from the grave ... Bela Lugosi, the Master of Horror" it screams — can be seen in this respect as part of a broader discursive refiguring of the horror genre, one that involves a retrospective designation of films as "horror" that were not originally thought of in that way. This process started early, as is evidenced in a short comedy film from 1932 included in the Collection that is entitled simply *Boo!* In this, scenes of a man nervously reading horror stories are intercut with scenes from the Universal productions *Frankenstein* and *The Cat and the Canary* (1927) as well as excerpts from F. W. Murnau's *Nosferatu* (1922) (although, unexpectedly, none from the Lugosi version of *Dracula*). *Boo!* makes connections between films that on their initial release were classified differently from each other, it associates them all with a particular and singular scary affect (as is shown via the responses of the fictional spectator to them), and via a voice-over that explicitly labels this type of experience a "horror story." In this respect, *Boo!* might be a better candidate for "first horror film" than any other candidate from the early 1930s, simply because it so self-consciously constructs itself as a horror film (although the search for generic origins is itself as much a discursive maneuver as it is a historical enterprise).

In other places too, the Legacy Collection exhibits a certain vagueness in the constitution of the horror genre. One wonders whether it is anything other than the association of the director James Whale with horror that gets *The Invisible Man* (1933) included. Similarly, *Phantom of the Opera* (1943) appears to be more of a romantic melodrama than a horror, and, given the emphasis in the Collection on the 1930s and 1940s, *The Creature from the Black*

Lagoon (1954) seems to have wandered in from the wrong decade. Of course, one can make cases for and against these films as horror (and Whale's fantasy-themed post–Frankenstein films for Universal were initially marketed in relation to the horror genre). In terms of the Collection itself, their inclusion seems to be about offering both variety and added value. All three films are separated out from the Dracula, Frankenstein and Werewolf films and, along with *The Mummy*, placed in a separate "Classic Monsters" section within the box set, as if the manufacturers of the Collection were unsure what else to do with them. In the United States, having separate sets for the Mummy, Invisible Man and Black Lagoon cycles solved this problem.

But even the classic monster cycles or franchises turn out to be not as cohesive as they might at first appear. The Dracula and Frankenstein sections hold together reasonably well in contrast to those 1940s films that feature multiple monsters when cyclical classifications become confused, with the placing of *House of Dracula* (1945) in the Dracula section and *House of Frankenstein* (1944) in the Frankenstein section looking fairly arbitrary (especially given that the Wolf Man appears in both films). The Wolf Man section is yet more fragmented; the Lon Chaney Jr. version of *The Wolf Man* is not a sequel to Universal's first werewolf film *Werewolf of London* (1935), and one of the films in this section, *She Wolf of London*, is not a sequel and not a werewolf film either but instead a psychological thriller that owes more to the 1940s films of Val Lewton than it does to Universal horror of either the 1930s or 1940s.

From this perspective, the important thing demonstrated by the Legacy Collection is that even within the confines of one particular studio there is both a heterogeneity of genre production and a pragmatic generic relabeling of product as and when market circumstances dictate, and that the Collection is just the most recent example of this, with traces of earlier relabelings exhibited within the Collection itself.

How users of the Legacy Collection respond to this is another matter entirely, of course, and not something with which this article is occupied (although a quick survey of Internet discussions of the Collection does reveal some debate about whether certain films belong there). What interests me more is the way in which all this information — the films, the contextualizing material — is delivered to its audiences. All along I have been stressing how old films can be rendered "new," and the newness of the old Universal horror films in the Collection is very much bound up with the fact that they come in up-to-date DVD format. The capacity of DVD to offer in compressed form easily accessible streams of images, sounds and information bestows a visual and auditory richness on the package of films, but at the same time it also inadvertently reveals fissures and contradictions in the discursive construction of a particular generic identity. It follows that new DVD markets are far from being neutral repositories of the generic past but are instead re-presenting that past in various ways. It also seems that the past that is being invoked and reworked is not just a production-based past but can also, intentionally or otherwise, involve previous methods for circulating and exhibiting the films in question.

Previously Banned

So there I am, still in the DVD store, contemplating the purchase of the Legacy Collection, partly, I think, out of nostalgia, a yearning for a past "telephile" moment that can never be recaptured. Although the Collection does not directly refer to this particular moment of exhibition, presenting its films as "classic," as already-seen (even if you have not seen them before), lends itself very effectively to this memorial form of attraction.

But then my gaze moves along the shelves and — with a mental grinding of gears — I see several DVDs with the words "Previously Banned" featuring prominently on their covers, and then another box set entitled "The Box of the Banned." A different set of historical associations and memories are instantly invoked, relating this time not to television in the 1970s but instead to the 1980s video boom. As is now well known, the release on video in Britain during the early 1980s of extremely violent and gory horror films led to a moral panic about "video nasties" — five of which are collected together in The Box of the Banned — and the subsequent imposition of a draconian video censorship under the auspices of the 1984 Video Recordings Act. Far from staunching the flow of video horror, however, this censorship seems to have contributed to the formation of a fan culture built largely around the illicit circulation of video copies of banned horror films. Something similar occurred in the United States, where state-sponsored censorship was not really an issue but where video technology facilitated the circulation of controversial or forgotten horror and exploitation films and in so doing helped to develop underground or marginal video subcultures. The ensuing videos were often — usually, so far as I can recall — poor quality, third-, fourth- or fifth-generation copies, occasionally with Japanese or Dutch subtitles. But the grunginess of the video product, far from being an imperfection, functioned in the 1980s and 1990s as a badge of honor, a marker of an integrity that had anti-commercial, anti-official culture and anti-state resonances within the formation of self-consciously oppositional or countercultural identities.[12]

Returning to the DVD store, one can argue that The Box of the Banned and its ilk deliberately invoke a memory of that particular set of viewing formations while also mourning its loss, a loss that, ironically, has been brought about in part by the ascendancy of the DVD format over video technology. Other factors involved in this repositioning of video nasties include a relaxation of British video censorship and an increased commercial interest in alternative or cult products, with several distribution companies set up specifically to exploit this kind of material. Within such a context, the "Previously Banned" label is as much a commercial renewal of a product as the re-presenting of old films in the Legacy Collection. While there is not the direct proprietorial connection with contemporary releases that one finds with the Legacy Collection, the contemporary release of hard-edged and nasty horror films such as *Saw* (2004), *The Devil's Rejects* (2005) and *Wolf Creek* (2005) suggests a commercial context in which old video nasties might prosper. However, the emphasis in the DVD re-releases is on quality — quality of image and sound, quality of packaging (including extras) — within the market place, and the undeniable commercial value of this previously underground material seriously undermines its erstwhile status as a totemic object around which oppositional fan cultures might be constructed. Having said this, the affective pull of this particular reconfiguration of a moment in horror history is less strong for me as I stand in the DVD store than that exerted by Universal horror (and Hammer horror as well), mainly because I was only tangentially involved in this kind of video fan culture during the 1980s and 1990s. But that's just me, and again, a rudimentary search on the Internet quickly finds horror fans waxing nostalgic about the 1980s video nasties, with this often provoked by the release of ex-video nasties on DVD.

As noted above, some of the implications of looking at horror in terms of patterns of re-release are straightforward. Old films continue to circulate and, now more than ever, old films outnumber new films in the market place. It follows that an inclusive approach to horror, or any genre, needs to engage with the ways in which these films, old and new, are configured in relation to each other at particular moments in genre history. In the case of my DVD store, this would entail thinking not just about the relationship between the DVDs and current cinema releases but also about the propinquity of The Legacy Collection and The Box of the Banned on the store's shelves. Such an enterprise necessarily involves an engagement with technological shifts in the delivery of films to audiences, shifts that in themselves go beyond the confines of any genre but that can impact on genres in an uneven, non-uniform and sometimes idiosyncratic manner (e.g., the special status of video technology within horror history).

But this still leaves unexplored the role of memory in all this. So far I've just used my own memories to open up areas for investigation and have not reflected much on the status of the memories themselves. But perhaps these memories, as subjective and personal as they might be, also form part of a particular historical configuration. Perhaps they are especially encouraged and indeed shaped by the DVD market itself. After all, the sort of material I have been discussing—the Legacy Collection, The Box of the Banned—is eminently collectable, arguably more so than video, and the desire to collect seems very much bound up with acts of memory. As Walter Benjamin noted in his 1931 essay on book collecting, "Every passion borders on the chaotic, but the collector's passion borders on the chaos of memories."[13] Owning the Legacy Collection (or The Box of the Banned if that's more your thing) becomes a means of organizing and getting close to one's memories, with nostalgia built into the process of consumption. And for those who have not seen these films before, who will be seeing them for the first time on DVD (just as I was seeing them for the first time in those horror double-bills back in the 1970s), perhaps they too are setting the terms for future acts of memory, for those moments in an unknown, post–DVD cyberfuture when they will become nostalgic for the good old days of DVD collectability.

Benjamin goes on to suggest that, for the collector at least, "ownership is the most intimate relationship that one can have to objects. Not that they come alive in him; it is he who lives in them."[14] If this is the case, then the DVD, in its technical superiority over video, in its compactness and sleekness and in its sheer collectability, is the most intimate audio-visual format to date. The ways in which it articulates genre histories and invokes memories of genre films can help to form an intimate bond with the consumer, a bond through which the consumer can engage with and reflect upon his or her own historical experiences of the genre in question. But just as Benjamin's desire for books was issued in the context of the disruption of the "aura" of objects by emergent mass cultures, so the desire for DVD takes place in the context of its possible marginalization as new streaming technologies come online. Horror films will probably continue to be made—they have been in constant production since the 1930s—but the terrains upon which we engage and bond with these, and the genre in general, are likely to change again. Simply looking at the films in themselves does not really help us to understand a process that in a most profound way is constitutive of the horror genre. As is always the case with film genres, the story of production, which has been so prominent in critical writings about genre, turns out to be just one small element in a much larger and ever-changing picture.

Notes

1. Peter Hutchings, "Genre Theory and Criticism." In *Approaches to Popular Film*. Ed. Joanne Hollows and Mark Jancovich (Manchester: Manchester University Press, 1995), 59–78.
2. Peter Stanfield, *Horse Opera: The Strange History of the 1930s Singing Cowboy* (Urbana: University of Illinois Press, 2002).
3. Cynthia Erb, *Tracking King Kong: A Hollywood Icon in World Culture* (Detroit, MI: Wayne State University Press, 1998).
4. Tim Bergfelder, *International Adventures: German Popular Cinema and European Co-Productions in the 1960s* (New York and Oxford: Berghahn, 2005); Antonio Lázaro Reboll and Andrew Willis (eds.), *Spanish Popular Cinema* (Manchester: Manchester University Press, 2004); Steve Neale (ed.), *Genre and Contemporary Hollywood* (London: BFI Publishing, 2002).
5. Steve Neale, "Questions of Genre." In *Film Genre Reader II*. Ed. Barry Keith Grant (Austin: University of Texas Press, 1995), 163.
6. Rick Altman, *Film/Genre* (London: BFI Publishing), 101.
7. James Naremore, *More than Night: Film Noir in Its Contexts* (Berkeley: University of California Press, 1998).
8. Christine Gledhill, "Rethinking Genre." In *Reinventing Film Studies*. Ed. Christine Gledhill and Linda Williams (London: Edward Arnold, 2000), 227.
9. For details of the various versions of the Legacy Collection, see Kim Newman, "Monster, Inc." *Sight and Sound* 15.1 (2005): 79.
10. Altman, *Film/Genre*, 115–121.
11. Dracula — Universal Film Scripts Series, Classic Horror Films, Volume 13 (Absecon, NJ: Magic-Image Filmbooks, 1990).
12. See Jeffrey Sconce, "Trashing the Academy: Taste, Excess and an Emerging Politics of Cinematic Style." *Screen* 36.4 (1995): 371–393 and Joan Hawkins, *Cutting Edge: Art-Horror and the Horrific Avant-Garde* (Minneapolis: University of Minnesota Press, 2000) for discussions of the American forms of this, and Peter Hutchings, "The Argento Effect." In *Defining Cult Movies: The Cultural Politics of Oppositional Taste*. Ed. Mark Jancovich, Antonio Lázaro Reboll, Julian Stringer, and Andrew Willis (Manchester: Manchester University Press, 2003), 127–141 on the British version.
13. Walter Benjamin, "Unpacking My Library." In *Illuminations* (London: Pimlico, 1999), 61–62.
14. Ibid., 69.

13

"Just Men in Tights"

Rewriting Silver Age Comics in an Era of Multiplicity

HENRY JENKINS

"A creation is actually a re-creation, a rearrangement of existing materials in a new, different, original, novel way."

— Steve Ditko[1]

In late 2004, Warren Ellis (*Transmetropolitan, Global Frequency, Planetary*) launched an intriguing project — a series of one-shot comics, each representing the first issue of imaginary comics series. Each was set in a different genre — *Stomp Future* (Science Fiction), *Simon Spector* (supernatural), *Quit City* (aviator), and *Frank Ironwine* (detective). In the back of each book, Ellis explains: "Years ago I sat down and thought about what adventure comics might've looked like today if superhero comics hadn't have happened. If, in fact, the pulp tradition of Weird Thrillers had jumped straight into comics form without mutating into the superhero subgenre we know today. If you took away preconceptions about design and the dominant single form.... If you blanked out the last sixty years."[2]

Ellis's fantasy, of a world without superhero comics, is scarcely unique. Several decades earlier, Alan Moore's *Watchmen* (1986-87) constructed a much more elaborate alternative history of comic genres.[3] In a world where superheroes are real, comic fans would seek out alternative genres for escapist entertainment. Moore details the authors, the storylines, and the rise and fall of specific publishers, as he explains how the pirates' genre came to dominate comics production. Passages from the imagined DC comic series, *Tales of the*

Black Freighter, run throughout *Watchmen*, drawn in a style that closely mimics E.C. comics of the early 1950s.

Would a filmmaker conjure up an imagined history of Hollywood in which the western or the musical never appeared? Would a television creator imagine a world without the sitcom? Why would they need to? In both cases, these genres played very important roles in the development of American popular entertainment but they never totally dominated their medium to the degree that superheroes have overwhelmed American comic book production. In fact, as Gerard Jones and Will Jacobs note in *The Comic Book Heroes*, there was no point from the 1940s to the 1970s when superheroes represented more than 20 percent of the total product of the American comics industry,[4] but they have dominated sales charts in recent decades and are now so central to our understanding of the medium that we read their dominance retrospectively across comics history.

In *Understanding Comics*, Scott McCloud demonstrates what we would take for granted in any other entertainment sector — that a medium is more than a genre: "When I was little I knew EXACTLY what comics were. Comics were those bright, colorful magazines filled with bad art, stupid stories, and guys in tights.... If people failed to understand comics, it was because they defined what comics could be too narrowly.... The world of comics is a huge and varied one. Our definition must encompass all these types."[5]

I fully support McCloud's efforts to broaden and diversify the content of contemporary comics. I fear that what I am about to say might well set back that cause a bit. But what interests me in this chapter is the degree to which comics do indeed represent a medium that has been dominated by a single genre. After all, nobody really believes us anyway when we say that comics are "more than just men in tights." So, what if we accepted this as a starting premise — "you got me!" — and examined the implications of the superhero's dominance over American comics.

Understanding how the superhero genre operates requires us to turn genre theory on its head. Genre emerges from the interaction between standardization and differentiation as competing forces shaping the production, distribution, marketing, and consumption of popular entertainment. A classic genre critic discussing most other media provides a more precise description of the borders and boundaries between categories that are already intuitively understood by media producers, critics, and consumers. Genre criticism takes for granted that most works fall within one and only one genre, with genre mixing the exception rather than the norm. The genre theorist works to locate "classic" examples of the genre — primarily works that fall at the very center of the space being defined — and uses them to map recurring traits or identify a narrative formula.

Comics are not immune to industrial pressures towards standardization and differentiation, yet these forces operate differently in a context in which a single genre dominates a medium and all other production has to define itself against, outside, in opposition to, and alongside that prevailing genre. Here, difference is felt much more powerfully *within* a genre than *between* competing genres and genre mixing is the norm. The Superhero genre seems capable of absorbing and reworking all other genres. So, *The Pulse* (2003–present) is about reporters trying to cover the world of the Marvel superheroes, *1602* (2003) is a historical fiction depicting earlier versions of the superheroes, *Spiderman Loves Mary Jane* (2004–present) is a romance comic focused on a superhero's girlfriend, *Common Grounds* (2003-2004) is a sitcom set in a coffee house where everyone knows your name — if not your secret identity, *Ex Machina* (2004–present) deals with the Mayor of New York who happens to be a superhero, and so forth. In each case, the superhero genre absorbs, reworks, and accommodates elements of other genres; or perhaps we might frame this the other way around: writers interested in telling stories set in these other genres must operate within the all-mighty Superhero genre in order to gain access to the marketplace. And alternative comics are defined not simply as alternative to the commercial mainstream but also as alternative to the superhero genre. As Brian Michael Bendis explains, "In comics, if it don't have a cape or claws or, like, really giant, perfect spherical, chronic back-pain-inducing breasts involved, it's alternative."[6] Yet, to be alternative to the superhero genre is still to be defined by — or at least in relation to — that genre.

From Continuity to Multiplicity

Writing about *Chinatown* in 1979, John Cawelti described a crisis within the Hollywood genre system. Classic genres were being deconstructed and reconstructed, critiqued and parodied, and mixed and matched in films as diverse as *Chinatown* (1974), *Blazing Saddles* (1974), *McCabe and Mrs. Miller* (1971), and *The Godfather* (1972). These films, Cawelti argues, "do in different ways what Polanski does in *Chinatown*: set the elements of a conventional popular genre in an altered context, thereby making us perceive these traditional forms and images in a new way."[7]

What happened to film genres in the 1970s closely parallels what happened to superhero comics starting in the early 1980s. Geoff Klock's *How to Read Superhero Comics and Why*, for example, identifies what he calls the "Revisionary Superhero Narrative" as a "third moment" (after the Golden and

Silver Ages) that runs from *Dark Knight Returns* and *Watchmen* (both 1986) through more recent works such as *Marvels* (1994), *Astro City* (1995), *Kingdom Come* (1996) and *League of Extraordinary Gentlemen* (1999), among a range of other examples.[8] Starting with Miller and Moore, he argues, comic books reexamined their core myths, questioning the virtue and value of their protagonists, blurring the lines between good guys and bad guys, revisiting and recontextualizing past events, and forcing the reader to confront the implications of their long-standing constructions of violence and sexuality. Cawelti's description of what *Chinatown* brought to the detective genre might easily be describing what *Dark Knight Returns* brought to superhero comics: "*Chinatown* places the hard-boiled detective story within a view of the world that is deeper and more catastrophic, more enigmatic in its evil, more sudden and inexplicable in its outbreaks of violent chance."[9]

Underlying Klock's argument is something like the theory of genre evolution that Cawelti outlines:

> One can almost make out a life cycle characteristic of genres as they move from an initial period of articulation and discovery, through a phase of conscious self-awareness on the part of both creators and audiences, to a time when the generic patterns have become so well-known that people become tired of their predictability. It is at this point that parodic and satiric treatments proliferate and new genres gradually arise.[10]

We might see the Golden Age as a period of "articulation and discovery," the Silver Age as one of classicism when formulas were understood by producers and consumers, and Klock's "third age" as one in which generic exhaustion gives way to a baroque self-consciousness. Yet, subsequent genre critics have argued for a much less linear understanding of how diversity works within genres. For example, Tag Gallagher notes that the earliest phases of a genre's development are often charged with a high degree of self-consciousness as media makers and consumers work through how any given genre diverges from other and more established traditions.[11] Cawelti himself acknowledges that the forces of nostalgia hold in check any tendency to radically deconstruct existing formulas.

Rather than thinking about a genre's predetermined life cycle, we might describe a perpetual push and pull exerted on any genre; genre formulas are continually repositioned in relation to social, cultural, and economic contexts of production and reception. Genres are altogether more elastic than our textbook definitions suggest; they maintain remarkable abilities to absorb outside influences as well as to withstand pressures toward change, and the best authors working in a genre at any point in time are highly aware of their materials and the traditions from which they came.

That said, there are shifting institutional pressures placed on genres that promote or retard experimentation. David Bordwell has described those pressures as the "bounds of difference," noting that even moments in production history that encourage a high degree of standardization (understood in terms of adherence to formulas and quality standards) also are shaped by countervailing pressures towards novelty, experimentation, and differentiation.[12] Bordwell notes, for example, that the Hollywood system always allowed what he calls "innovative workers" greater latitude for experimentation as long as their films enjoyed either profitability or critical acclaim and preferably both. The so-called revisionist superhero narratives reflected a growing consumer awareness of authorship within the medium. Historically, comics publishers imposed limits on that experimentation in order to preserve the distinctive identities of their most valuable characters in a system in which multiple writers work on the same franchise and there was constant and rapid turnover of employment. Here, the mainstream publishers loosened those constraints for at least some creative workers. Rather than looking for a period of revisionism, we might better be looking for how far creators can diverge from genre formulas at different historical junctures.

Painting with broad strokes, we might identify three phases, each with their own opportunities for innovation:

1. As the comic book franchises take shape, across the Golden and Silver Ages, their production is dominated by relatively self-contained issues; readers turn over on a regular basis as they grow older. Franchises are organized around recurring characters, whose stories, as Umberto Eco has noted with regard to Superman, get defined in terms of an iterative logic in which each issue must end more or less where it began.[13] Under this system, creators may originate new characters or totally recast existing characters (as occurred at the start of the Silver Age), but they have much less flexibility once a comic franchise starts.

2. Somewhere in the early 1970s, this focus on self-contained stories shifts towards more and more serialization as the distribution of comics becomes more reliable. Readers have, by this point, grown somewhat older and continue to read comics over a longer span of their lives; these readers place a high value on consistency and continuity, appraising both themselves and the authors on their mastery of past events and the web of character relationships within any given franchise. Indeed, this principle of continuity operates not just within any individual book but also across all the books by a particular pub-

lisher so that people talk about the DC and Marvel universes. The culmination of the continuity era might well have been Marv Wolfstein's *Crisis of Infinite Earths* (1985), a 12-issue "event" designed to mobilize all the characters in the DC universe and then cleanse away competing and contradictory continuities that had built up through the years. Instead, as Geoff Klock notes, the "Crisis" led to more and more "events" that further splintered and fragmented the DC universe but also accustomed comic readers to the idea that they could hold multiple versions of the same universe in their minds at the same time.[14]

3. Today, comics have entered a period in which principles of multiplicity are felt at least as powerfully as those of continuity. Under this new system, readers may consume multiple versions of the same franchise, each with different conceptions of the character, different understandings of their relationships with the secondary figures, different moral perspectives, exploring different moments in their lives, and so forth. So that in some story lines, Aunt May knows Spider-Man's secret identity while in others she doesn't; in some Peter Parker is still a teen and in others, he is an adult science teacher; in some, he is married to Mary Jane and in others, they have broken up, and so forth. These different versions may be organized around their respective authors or demarked through other designations — Marvel's Ultimate or DC's All Star lines, which represented attempts to reboot the continuity to allow points of entry for new readers, for example. In some cases, even more radical alterations of the core franchises are permissible on a short-term and provisional basis — say, the election of Lex Luther as president or the destruction of Gotham City. Beyond the two major companies, smaller comics companies — Image, Dark Horse, Top Cow, ABC, etc.— further expand upon the superhero mythos, often creating books designed to directly comment on the DC and Marvel universes by using characters modeled on comic book icons. And beyond these direct reworkings of the DC and Marvel superheroes, there are, as noted earlier, any number of appropriations of the superhero by alternative comics creators.

In each case, the new system for organizing production layers over earlier practices — so that we do not lose interest in having compelling stories within individual issues as we move into the continuity era nor do comics readers and producers lose interest in continuity as we enter into a period of multiplicity. Even at the present moment, DC remains more conservative in its efforts to produce a coherent and singular continuity across all the books it publishes, and Marvel is more open to multiple versions of the same character functioning simultaneously within different publications.

Writing in 1991, Roberta Pearson and William Uricchio use the Batman comic as an example of the kinds of pressures being exerted on the superhero genre at a moment when older texts were continuing to circulate (and in fact, were recirculated in response to renewed interests in the characters), newer versions operated according to very different ideological and narratalogical principles, a range of auteur creators were being allowed to experiment with the character, and the character was assuming new shapes and forms to reflect the demands of different entertainment sectors and their consumers. They write,

> Whereas broad shifts in emphasis had occurred since 1939, these changes had been, for the most part, consecutive and consensual. Now, newly created Batmen, existing simultaneously with the older Batmen of the television series and comic reprints and back issues, all struggled for recognition and a share of the market. But the contradictions amongst them may threaten both the integrity of the commodity form and the coherence of the fans' lived experience of the character necessary to the Batman's continued success.[15]

The superhero comic, they suggest, may not be able to withstand "the tension between, on the one hand, the essential maintenance of a recognizable set of key character components and, on the other hand, the increasingly necessary centrifugal dispersion of those components."[16] Retrospectively, we can see Pearson and Uricchio as describing a moment of transition from continuity to multiplicity.

Do Superheroes Get Exhausted?

In his *Chinatown* essay, Cawelti identifies three core factors leading to the genre experimentation in 1970s cinema: "I would point to the tendency of genres to exhaust themselves, to our growing historical awareness of modern popular culture, and finally to the decline of the underlying mythology on which traditional genres have been based since the late nineteenth century."[17] Each of these pressures can be seen as working on the superhero genre during the period that Uricchio and Pearson were describing. Individually and collectively, these forces led to the current era of multiplicity.

For example, comics writer Ed Brubaker falls back on a theory of "generic exhaustion" to explain *Gotham Central* (2003–present), his series depicting the everyday beat cops who operate literally and figuratively under the shadow of the Dark Knight. Brubaker argues that by shifting the focus off the superhero and onto these everyday men and women, he can up the emotional stakes:

> Batman is never going to get killed by these guys, and he's not going to allow them to kill the ballroom of people they're holding hostage. Because Batman, by the rulebook you're given when you're writing it, has to be infallible. He can't get frozen solid and broken into pieces and have Robin become the next Batman. But you can have a Gotham city cop frozen and broken into pieces in front of his partner, and suddenly Mr. Freeze is scary again.[18]

Kurt Busiek, on the other hand, has stressed the elasticity of the superhero genre, arguing that superheroes can take on new values and associations as old meanings cease to hold the interest of their readers:

> If a superhero can be such a powerful and effective metaphor for male adolescence, then what else can you do with them? Could you build a superhero story around a metaphor for female adolescence? Around midlife crisis? Around the changes adults go through when they become parents? Sure, why not? And if a superhero can exemplify America's self image at the dawn of World War II, could a superhero exemplify America's self image during the less-confident 1970s? How about the emerging national identity of a newly-independent African nation? Or a nontraditional culture, like the drug culture, or the "greed is good" business culture of the go-go Eighties. Of course. If it can do one, it can do the others.[19]

We can see this process of renewing the core meanings attached to the superhero figure in such recent books as the Luna Brothers's *Ultra* (2004-2005), which depicts superheroes as celebrities whose relationships become the material of tabloid gossip magazines (with its central plotline clearly modeled after the Ben Affleck/Jennifer Lopez romance), or *Dr. Blink, Superhero Shrink* (2003–), in which superheroes are neurotics who need help working through their relationship issues and suicidal tendencies (including a suicidal superhero doomed to disappointment since he is invincible and flies whenever he tries to throw himself off tall buildings). In both cases, we see the genre's building blocks being attached to a new set of metaphors.

Second, Cawelti argues that Hollywood's generic transformations were sparked by a heightened audience awareness of the history of American cinema through university film classes, retro-house screenings, television reruns, and serious film criticism. More educated consumers began to demand an acknowledgment of genre history within the newer movies they consumed. Similarly, Matthew J. Pustz contends that the fans' interest in comic continuity reflected a moment when older comics became more readily accessible through back issues and reissues.[20] A focus on continuity rewarded fans for their interest in the full run of a favorite franchise, though it might also act as a barrier to entry for new readers who often found continuity-heavy books difficult to follow. The contemporary focus on multiplicity may similarly reward the mastery of longtime fans but around a different axis of consumption.

More and more, fans and authors play with genre mixing as a way of complicating and expanding the genre's potential meanings. Writing about television genres, Jason Mittell has challenged the claims made by postmodernist critics that such genre mixing or hybridity leads to the dissolution of genre; instead, he suggests that these moments in which two or more genres are combined heighten our awareness of genre conventions: "the practice of generic mixture has the potential to foreground and activate generic categories in vital ways that 'pure' generic texts rarely do."[21] Mittell's prime example is the merging of horror and teen romance genres within *Buffy the Vampire Slayer*, but he could just as easily be talking about DC's Elseworlds series, which exists to transform the superhero genre through contact with a range of other genre traditions. For example, *The Kents* (2000) is almost a pure western linked to the Superman franchise through a frame story in which Pa Kent sends a box of family heirlooms to Clark so that he will understand the history of his adopted family.[22] *Red Son* (2004) deals with what might happen if the rocket from Krypton had landed in Russia rather than the United States and thus works through how Superman would have impacted several decades in Russian history.[23] *Superman's Metropolis* (1997) mixes and matches elements from Fritz Lang's German expressionist classic with the Superman origin story.[24] As the series is described on the back of each issue, "In Elseworlds, heroes are taken from their usual settings and put into strange times and places — some that have existed, or might have existed and others that can't, couldn't, and shouldn't exist. The result is stories that make characters who are as familiar as yesterday seem as fresh as tomorrow."[25] The Elseworld books read the superheroes as archetypes that would assert themselves in many different historical and generic contexts; they invite a search for the core or essence of the character even as they encourage us to take pleasure in their many permutations. If we can tinker with his costume, his origins, his cultural context, even his core values, what is it that makes Superman Superman and not, say, Captain Marvel or Captain America? *Speeding Bullets* (1993) pushes this to its logical extreme: fusing the origins stories of Batman and Superman to create one figure — which is bent on using its super powers to exert revenge for his parent's deaths.[26]

Third, Cawelti reads the genre transformations of the 1970s cinema in relation to a declining faith in the core values and assumptions that defined those genre traditions half a century earlier. Alan Moore made a similar argument for the cultural importance of the revisionist superhero comics: "As anyone involved in fiction and its crafting over the past fifteen or so years would be delighted to tell you, heroes are starting to become rather a problem. They aren't what they used to be ... or rather they are, and therein lies the heart of the difficulty. We demand new themes, new insights, new dramatic situations. We demand new heroes."[27]

This search for "new heroes" is perhaps most spectacularly visible if we examine how the comics industry has responded to the growing multiculturalism of American society and the pressures of globalization on its markets. So, Marvel has created the "mangaverse" series focused on how their established characters would have looked if they had emerged within the Japanese comics industry: the Hulk transforms into a giant lizard and Peter Parker trains as a ninja. Similarly, Marvel released a series of *Spider-Man: India* (2004) comics, timed to correspond with the release of *Spider-Man 2* (2004) in India and localized to South Asian tastes. Peter Parker becomes Pavitr Prabhakar and Green Goblin becomes Rakshasa, a traditional mythological demon. Marvel calls it "transcreation," one step beyond translation. Such books appeal as much to "pop cosmopolitans" in the United States (fans who are seeking cultural difference through their engagement with popular culture from other countries) as they do to the Asian market — indeed, *Spider-Man: India* appeared in the United States more or less simultaneously with its publication in South Asia.[28]

At the same time, the mainstream comics industry has begun to experiment with giving alternative comics artists a license to play around with their characters. For example, David Mack, a collage artist, has ended up not only doing covers for Brian Bendis's *Alias* (2001–2004) series but also doing his own run on *Daredevil* (2003). Peter Bagge, whose *Hate* (1990–1998) comics epitomized the grunge influence on alternative comics, was hired to do *The Monomaniacal Spiderman* (2002) in which Peter Parker reads Ayn Rand and gets fed up with the idea that he has any kind of "great responsibility" to look after less powerful people. DC comics, on the other hand, has published a series of *Bizarro* (2001, 2005) collections in which alternative artists tell their own distinctive versions of the company's pantheon of superheroes with the framing device that these are what comics look like in the Bizarro world where everything is the exact opposite of Earth. In no other medium is the line between experimental and commercial work this permeable.

Reverse Engineering Superman

This mixing, matching, and mutating of genre categories has a much longer history within popular culture. As Rick Altman notes, "Genre mixing, it now appears, is not just a postmodern fad. Quite to the contrary, the practice of genre mixing is necessary to the very process whereby genres are created."[29] Our current tendency to describe works retrospectively based on the contemporary genre they most closely resemble has the effect of repressing the more complex process by which new genres emerge from existing categories of production. Altman concludes, "The early history of film genres is characterized ... not by purposeful borrowing from a single pre-existing non-film parent genre, but by apparently incidental borrowing from several unrelated genres.... Even when a genre already exists in other media, the film genre of the same name cannot simply be borrowed from non-film sources, it must be recreated."[30] The superhero comic, in fact, undergoes this process of recreation not once but multiple times: first, in the early Golden Age, when the superhero genre takes shape from elements borrowed from pulp magazines and second, in the early Silver age, when superhero comics reemerge from the generic soup that characterized comic production in the post-war era.

The most common accounts for the emergence of the superhero genre stress the fledgling comics industry's response to the commercial success of Superman. In *The Amazing Adventures of Cavalier & Klay* (2001), Michael Chabon vividly depicts the process by which comics creators sought to reverse engineer Superman to generate new characters:

> If he's like a cat or a spider or a fucking wolverine, if he's huge, if he's tiny, if he can shoot flames or ice or death rays of Vat 69, if he turns into fire or water or stone or India Rubber. He can be a Martian, he could be a ghost, he could be a god or a demon or a wizard or a monster. Okay? It doesn't matter because right now, see, at this very moment, we have a bandwagon rolling.[31]

Yet, a somewhat different picture emerges within Gerard Jones's account of early superhero comics. Jones uncovered a handwritten note from Joe Simon and Joel Schuster, the teenage boys who created Superman, suggesting they were rehearsing possible publicity slogans: "The greatest super-hero strip of all time!... Speed-Action-Laughs-Thrills-Surprises. The most unusual humor-adventure strip ever created!... You'll Chuckle! You'll Gasp! It must be seen to be believed!"[32] Superman is already being read against a larger genre tradition ("the greatest super-hero strip of all time!") and at the same time, the comic is being promoted through a diverse range of emotional appeals ("Speed-action-laughs-thrills-surprises," etc.).

Siegel and Schuster correctly describe their creation ("the most unusual humor-adventure strip ever created!") as, in effect, bounding over the walls separating various genres. Thomas Andrea has, for example, noted that the superhero figure emerged from a range of different science fiction and horror texts.[33] Gerard Jones cites even more influences — including Popeye in the comic strips, the pulp novels of Edgar Rice Burroughs, and *The Scarlet Pimpernel*.[34] We might note the ways that masked heroes from the pulp magazines, including The Shadow, the Phantom, The Spider, and Zorro, modeled the capes and masks iconography and the secret identity thematic of the subsequent superhero comics. The pulp magazines have been described as developing and categorizing many 20th-century genres, yet the economics of pulp magazine production also meant that the same writers worked within multiple genre traditions and in many cases, the same story was revised slightly in order to be sold to several different publications.[35] In early comics, a writer — say, Jack Kirby — might produce work across the full range of pulp genres in the course of their career and thus would be able to draw on multiple genre models in their superhero work. The intensity of comics production — new stories about the same characters every month and in some cases, every week — encouraged writers to search far and wide for new plots or compelling new elements while the openness of comics, where you draw whatever you need, made it cheap and simple to expand the genre repertoire.

The titles of the publications that gave birth to the earliest superheroes have become dead metaphors for later generations of readers who have taken for granted that *Detective Comics* (1937) is where Batman stories are found, *Action Comics* (1938) plays host to Superman, and *Marvel Mystery* (1939–1949) is where the Human Torch first emerged. Yet, each of those titles defines a somewhat different genre tradition. As a result, Superman, Batman, and the Human Torch, while all read as superheroes today, were originally understood in somewhat different contexts.

The Silver Age restored the relations between the superhero genre and other closely related traditions. The superheroes had been so over-used for patriotic purposes during the Second World War that they seemed dated by the post-war era. At the same time, GIs had found comics a lightweight and portable means of popular entertainment and were continuing to read them as they returned home, creating a strong pull towards adult content.[36] By the late 1940s and early 1950s, superhero books competed with horror, romance, science fiction, western, true crime, jungle adventures, swordplay, and so forth. This push towards more mature content provoked backlash and moral panic (best embodied by Frederick Wertham's *Seduction of the Innocent* [1954]) as reformers struggled to make sense of the presence of adult themes in a medium previously targeted to children. The Comics Code cleared away many of those emerging genres, paving the way for a reemergence of the superhero by the end of the 1950s at DC and in the early 1960s at Marvel. Or so the story is most often told.

Yet, again, this story simplifies the ways that the superhero comics of the

Silver Age emerged from a more diverse set of genre traditions. As Gerard Jones and Will Jacobs note, for example, the 1950s saw the rise of a range of books like *Challengers of the Unknown* (1958–1971), *Mystery in Space* (1951–1966), *The Sea Devils* (1961–1967), and *Black Hawk* (1957–1968); their teams of scientists, soldiers, and adventurers were prototypes for the later superhero teams such as the Justice League, The Avengers, The Defenders, or the Fantastic Four.[37] It is no accident, given DC editor Julius Schwartz's history as a science fiction fan and as an agent for important writers in that genre, that the first significant superhero to emerge in almost ten years was the Martian Manhunter.[38] When Schwartz began to retool and relaunch such established DC characters as The Flash, Green Lantern, Hawkman, and the Atom, he first tested the popularity of these characters through anthologies that cut across multiple genres: The Flash first appeared in *Showcase* (1956–1970) while the Justice League emerges in *The Brave and The Bold* (1955–1983).

Similarly, Marvel had a distribution contract with DC that limited how many books could be issued each month and somewhat restricted their use of superhero content.[39] The earliest issues of the successful Marvel franchises situate these protagonists in relationship to other genre traditions with the heroes dwarfed on the original *Fantastic Four* (1961–present) cover by a giant green monster, with the *Incredible Hulk* (1961-1962) depicted as a "super-Frankenstein" character,[40] with *Iron Man* built around the iconography of robots and cyborgs, and *Spider-man* first appearing in the pages of *Amazing Fantasy* (1962). While these characters today are viewed as archetypical superheroes, they had previously been read — at least in part — in relation to these other genres.

These various franchises carry traces of those other genres even as they are reread within a now more firmly established superhero tradition. Jonathan Lethem, for example, writes: "Kirby always wanted to drag the Four into the Negative Zone — deeper into psychedelic science fiction and existential alienation — while Lee, in his scripting, resolutely pulled them back into the morass of human lives, hormonal alienation, teenage dating problems and pregnancy and unfulfilled longings to be human and normal and loved and not to have the Baxter Building repossessed by the City of New York."[41] By the same token, as Jason Bainbridge has noted, the two companies that dominated superhero production, then and now, have chosen to pull towards different genre conventions with DC embracing action-adventure stories with their focus on plot and Marvel embracing melodrama with its focus on character.[42] What I am describing here as the era of multiplicity exaggerates and extends the generic instability that has been part of the superhero comic from the start.

I hope the above discussion has moved us beyond thinking of revisionism as simply a phase in the development of the superhero genre. We have seen that from the beginning, the superhero comic emerged from a range of different genre traditions; that it has maintained the capacity to build upon that varied history by pulling towards one or another genre tradition at various points in its development; that it has maintained its dominance over the comics medium by constantly absorbing and appropriating new generic materials; and that its best creators have remained acutely aware of this generic instability, shifting its core meanings and interpretations to allow for new symbolic clusters. Through all of that, I have shown that comics are indeed more than "just men in tights."

Notes

1. Arlen Schumer, *The Silver Age of Comic Book Art* (Portland, Oregon: Collectors Press, 2003), 59.
2. Warren Ellis, *Warren Ellis's Apparat,* Volume One (Rantoul, IL: Avatar Press, 2005).
3. Alan Moore, *Watchmen* (New York: DC Comics, 1986).
4. Gerard Jones and Will Jacobs, *The Comic Book Heroes: The First History of Modern Comic Books—From the Silver Age to the Present* (New York: Prima, 1996).
5. Scott McCloud, *Understanding Comics* (New York: HarperCollins, 1994), 2–4.
6. Brian Michael Bendis, *Fortune and Glory: A True Hollywood Comic Book Story* (Portland, OR: Oni Press, 2000).
7. John Cawelti, "*Chinatown* and Generic Transformation in Recent American Films." In *Film Genre Reader*. Ed. Barry Keith Grant (Austin: University of Texas Press, 1986), 191.
8. Geoff Klock, *How to Read Superhero Comics and Why* (New York: Continuum, 2002). There are a number of problems with this formulation. For starters, the notion of a "revisionary superhero narrative" assumes some classic definition of the superhero comic that is being revised by a more self-reflexive generation of comics creators and fans; yet, as I will show shortly, it is hard to know at what point the superhero genre could be described in such static or generically pure terms. The superhero genre seems to have always been in a state of revision or re-invention.
9. Cawelti, "*Chinatown* and Generic Transformation in Recent American Films," 189.
10. Ibid., 200.
11. Tag Gallagher, "Shoot-Out at the Genre Corral: Problems in the 'Evolution' of the Western." In *Film Genre Reader*. Ed. Barry Keith Grant (Austin: University of Texas Press, 1986), 202–216.
12. David Bordwell, "The Bounds of Difference." In *Classical Hollywood Cinema*. Ed. David Bordwell, Janet Staiger, and Kristin Thompson (Madison: University of Wisconsin Press, 1985), 110.
13. Umberto Eco, "The Myth of Superman." In *Arguing Comics: Literary Masters on a Popular Medium*. Ed. Jeet Heer and Kent Worcester (Jackson: University of Mississippi Press, 2004), 146–164.
14. Klock, *How to Read Superhero Comics and Why*, 21.
15. William Uricchio and Roberta E. Pearson, "'I'm Not Fooled by That Cheap Disguise.'" In *The Many Lives of the Batman: Critical Approaches to a Superhero and His Media*. Ed. Roberta E. Pearson and William Uricchio (New York: Routledge, 1991), 184.
16. Ibid., 190.
17. Cawelti, "*Chinatown* and Generic Transformation in Recent American Films," 200.
18. Tom Spurgeon, "Interview with Ed Brubaker." *Comics Journal* 263 (2002): 91.
19. Kurt Busiek, "Introduction." In *Astro City: Life in the Big City* (New York: Image, 1999), 7–8.
20. Matthew J. Pustz, *Comic Book Culture: Fan Boys and True Believers* (Jackson: University of Mississippi Press, 1999).
21. Jason Mittell, *Genre and Television: From Cop Shows to Cartoons in American Culture* (New York: Routledge, 2004), 155.
22. John Ostrander, Timothy Truman, and Tom Mandrake, *Superman: The Kents* (New York: DC, 2000).
23. Mark Millar, *Superman: Red Son* (New York: DC, 2004).

24. Randy L'Officier, Ray Thomas and Ted McKeever, *Superman's Metropolis* (New York: DC, 1997).
25. Text quoted on the back cover of every Elseworld's book.
26. J. M. Dematteis, *Superman: Speeding Bullets* (New York: DC, 1993).
27. Alan Moore as quoted in Jeffrey A. Brown, "Introduction." In *Batman: Dark Knight Returns*. Frank Miller (New York: DC, 1986), 1.
28. Henry Jenkins, "Pop Cosmopolitanism: Mapping Cultural Flows in an Age of Media Convergence." In *Fans, Bloggers, and Gamers: Exploring Participatory Culture* (New York: New York University Press, 2006), 152–172.
29. Rick Altman, *Film/Genre* (Berkeley: University of California Press, 1999), 143.
30. Ibid., 34.
31. Michael Chabon, *The Amazing Adventures of Kavalier & Clay* (New York: Picador, 2001), 94.
32. Gerard Jones, *Men of Tomorrow: Geeks, Gangsters and the Birth of the Comic Book* (New York: Basic, 2004), 115.
33. Thomas Andrea, "From Menace to Messiah: The History and Historicity of Superman." In *American Media and Mass Culture: Left Perspectives*. Ed. Donald Lazere (Berkeley: University of California Press, 1987), 124–138.
34. Jones, *Men of Tomorrow*, 115–116.
35. Paul Allen Carter, *The Creation of Tomorrow: Fifty Years of Magazine Science Fiction* (New York: Columbia University Press, 1977).
36. For a useful history of this era, see Bradford W. Wright, *Comic Book Nation: The Transformation of Youth Culture in America* (Baltimore: Johns Hopkins University Press, 2001).
37. Jones and Jacobs, *The Comic Book Heroes*, 19–32.
38. Julius Schwartz, *Man of Two Worlds: My Life in Science Fiction and Comics* (New York: HarperCollins, 2000).
39. See, for example, Jordan Raphael and Tom Spugeon, *Stan Lee and the Rise and Fall of the American Comic Book* (Chicago: Chicago Review Press, 2003).
40. Schumer, *The Silver Age of Comic Book Art*, 82.
41. Jonathan Lethem, "The Return of the King, or, Identifying with Your Parents." *Give Our Regards to the Atomsmashers!: Writers on Comics*. Ed. Sean Howe (New York: Pantheon, 2004), 3–22.
42. Jason Bainbridge, "Worlds within Worlds: The Role of Superheroes in the Marvel and DC Universes." Men in Capes conference, University of Melbourne, Melbourne, Australia, June (2005).

Notes on Contributors

Harry M. Benshoff is associate professor of radio, television, and film at the University of North Texas. His research interests include topics in film genres, film history, film theory, and multiculturalism. He has published essays on *Dark Shadows* fan cultures, blaxploitation horror films, Hollywood LSD films, and *The Talented Mr. Ripley* (1999). He is the author of *Monsters in the Closet: Homosexuality and the Horror Film* (Manchester University Press, 1997), and co-author of *America on Film: Representing Race, Class, Gender and Sexuality at the Movies* (Blackwell Publishers, 2004), *Queer Cinema: The Film Reader* (Routledge, 2004), and *Queer Images: A History of Gay and Lesbian Film in America* (Rowman & Littlefield, 2006).

Andrew Caine is the author of *Interpreting Rock Movies: The Pop Film and Its Critics in Britain* (Manchester University Press, 2004). His work has also appeared in *Scope*, *The Velvet Light Trap* and the *Journal of Popular British Cinema*.

Brigid Cherry is a lecturer in media arts/film and television at St. Mary's University College, Twickenham, where she teaches courses on the horror genre, cult film and television, and music in popular culture. She has researched horror film fandom, particularly the female audience, and other cult and fan audiences. Her recently published work in this area has focused on the feminine aesthetic of horror. She has also published work exploring identity in science fiction fandoms, both online and face-to-face, and in particular has looked at the impact of nationality and geography on British fans in local and multi-national fan communities. She is currently researching responses to images of the Gothic and death in alternative music videos.

Lincoln Geraghty is principal lecturer in film studies and subject leader for media studies in the School of Creative Arts, Film and Media at the University of Portsmouth. He serves as editorial advisor for *The Journal of Popular Culture*, *Reconstruction*, and *Atlantis* with interests in science fiction film and television, fandom, and collecting in popular culture. He is author of *Living with Star Trek: American Culture and the Star Trek Universe* (IB Tauris, 2007) and *American Science Fiction Film and Television* (Berg, forthcoming) and the editor of *The Influence of* Star

Trek on Television, Film and Culture (McFarland, 2008) and *Future Visions: Examining the Look of Science Fiction and Fantesy Television* (Scarecrow, forthcoming).

Su Holmes is reader in television at the University of East Anglia. She is the author of *British Television and Film Culture in the 1950s: Coming to a TV Near You!* (Intellect Books, 2005), and *Entertaining Television: The BBC and Popular Programme Culture in the 1950s* (forthcoming), and the co-editor of *Understanding Reality Television* (Routledge, 2004), *Framing Celebrity: New Directions in Celebrity Culture* (Routledge, 2006) and *A Reader in Stardom and Celebrity* (Sage, 2007). She has published widely on the subjects of British television history, reality TV, quiz shows and celebrity, and she is currently writing a book on quiz/game shows for Edinburgh University Press.

Peter Hutchings is reader in film studies at Northumbria University. He is the author of *Hammer and Beyond: The British Horror Film* (1993), *Terence Fisher* (Manchester University Press, 2002), *Dracula* (IB Tauris, 2003) and *The Horror Film* (Longman, 2004), and he also co-edited *The Film Studies Reader* (Hodder Arnold, 2000) with Joanne Hollows and Mark Jancovich. He has written numerous articles and chapters on British cinema, horror and science fiction cinema, and genre theory and criticism.

Mark Jancovich is professor of film and television studies at the University of East Anglia, UK. He is the author of several books: *Horror* (Batsford, 1992), *The Cultural Politics of the New Criticism* (Cambridge University Press, 1993), *Rational Fears: American Horror in the 1950s* (Manchester University Press, 1996), and *The Place of the Audience: Cultural Geographies of Film Consumption* (with Lucy Faire and Sarah Stubbings, BFI, 2003). He is also the editor of several collections: *Approaches to Popular Film* (with Joanne Hollows, Manchester University Press, 1995), *The Film Studies Reader* (with Joanne Hollows and Peter Hutchings, Arnold/Oxford University Press, 2000), *Horror, The Film Reader* (Routledge, 2001), *Quality Popular Television: Cult TV, the Industry and Fans* (with James Lyons, BFI, 2003), *Defining Cult Movies: The Cultural Politics of Oppositional Taste* (with Antonio Lazaro-Reboll, Julian Stringer and Andrew Willis, Manchester University Press, 2003), and *Film Histories: An Introduction and Reader* (with Paul Grainge and Sharon Monteith, EUP, 2006). He was also the founder of *Scope: An Online Journal of Film Studies*; and is currently series editor (with Eric Schaefer) of the Manchester University Press book series *Inside Popular Film*. He is currently writing a history of horror in the 1940s.

Henry Jenkins is the DeFlorz Professor of Humanities and the co-director of the Comparative Media Studies Program at MIT. He is the author or editor of 11 books on various aspects of media and popular culture, including *Textual Poachers: Television Fans and Participatory Culture* (Routledge, 1992), *From Barbie to Mortal Kombat: Gender and Computer Games* (MIT, 2000), and *Hop on Pop: The Politics and Pleasures of Popular Culture* (Duke, 2003). His most recent works are

Convergence Culture: Where Old and New Media Collide (New York, 2006), *Fans, Gamers and Bloggers: Exploring Participatory Culture* (New York, 2006), and *The Wow Climax: Tracing the Emotional Impact of Popular Culture* (New York, 2006). He spends much of his endowed chair on purchasing comics at the Million Year Picnic at Harvard Square.

James Russell is lecturer in film studies at De Montfort University. His research deals with the impact of commercial imperatives and creative agendas on Hollywood film production trends since the 1940s. His published work includes journal articles and book chapters on the animated films of DreamWorks SKG and the history of the Hollywood studios. He is author of *The Historical Epic and Contemporary Hollywood* (Continuum, 2007).

Jason Scott is lecturer in media and film at Trinity and All Saints College, Leeds. His primary research interests encompass the historical reception of film, and film cultures, particularly in relation to European, American and British films. His Ph.D. thesis, "Discourses Recognizing Aesthetic Innovation in Cinema — Bonnie and Clyde, a Case Study," adopted a historical reception approach, applying discourse analysis to critical and wider receptions of the film. He is currently working on a book on film reception, as well as developing his research on critical receptions, the role played by critics and other discourses in characterizing films.

Janet Staiger is William P. Hobby Centennial Professor in Communication and professor of women's and gender studies at the University of Texas at Austin. She teaches critical and cultural studies of film, television, and other media. Her most recent publications include *Media Reception Studies* (New York, 2005), *Authorship and Film* (co-edited with David Gerstner, Routledge, 2002), *Perverse Spectators* (New York, 2000), and *Blockbuster TV* (New York, 2000).

Liza Treviño holds a Ph.D. in cinema-television critical studies from the University of Southern California in Los Angeles. She has always been fascinated by the "industry" of the entertainment industry. Her research interests focus on points in popular culture where tensions between art and commerce erupt and expose the different ways identity, taste, and class circulate across American media. Dr. Treviño currently holds the director of research position at the NBC and CW television affiliates in Austin, Texas.

Andrew Willis is senior lecturer in media and performance at the University of Salford. He is the co-author (with Peter Buse and Nuria Triana Toribio) of *The Cinema of Alex de la Iglesia* (Manchester University Press, 2007), the editor of *Film Stars: Hollywood and Beyond* (Manchester University Press, 2004), and co-editor of *Spanish Popular Cinema* (with Antonio Lazaro Reboll, Manchester University Press, 2004) and *Defining Cult Movies: The Cultural Politics of Oppositional Taste* (with Mark Jancovich, Antonio Lazaro Reboll and Julian Stringer, Manchester University Press, 2003).

Index

Abbott and Costello 21, 22
Abbott and Costello Meet Frankenstein 21
ABC 145, 234
aberrant nature 209
Accident 58, 61
Ackerman, Forrest J 8
Action Comics 240
action genre 3, 74, 211, 216, 241
Adelaide 62
Adler, Renate 96
adult film 4, 53, 65, 66
adventure films 2, 3, 73
The Advocate 97, 100
Affleck, Ben 41, 236
Airline 161, 167
Alfie 54, 57, 65
Alfred Hitchcock Presents 6, 112, 113, 114, 118
Alias 238
Alien 5, 208, 213
alien invasion genre 3
All in the Family 130
Allied Artists 95
Alphaville 60
alt. horror 204
Altman, Rick 3, 27, 37, 125, 127, 130, 133, 143, 152–153, 162, 191–192, 217, 222, 238–239
Amadeus 147
The Amazing Adventures of Cavalier & Klay 239
Amazing Fantasy 241
Amazing Stories 1
AMC Theatre 106
American Film 38
The American Film Musical 127
American International Pictures (AIP) 126
American Sunbow Productions 184
Anderson, Christopher 43
Andrea, Thomas 239
Andrew, Lynn 150
Andrews, Dana 90
animal comedy 132

animal (wild) pictures 3
animated television 187, 189, 191
The Apprentice 161
The April Fools 57
April Love 134
Argento, Dario 6, 112–116, 118
art cinema 40, 41, 53, 99
Arthur, Paul 89
El Asfalto 119–120
Aspel, Michael 199
Astaire, Fred 127, 128, 136
Astor, Mary 79
Astro City 232
At Home at the End of the World 42
At the Angelika 41–43, 47
Attenborough, Richard 80
Avakian, Aram 95
avant-garde 35, 36
aviator genre 229
Axelrod, George 58
Aznavour, Charles 95

Babington, Bruce 144
Bacall, Lauren 71
Bach 138
The Bachelor 161
backstage musical 135, 136
Bacon, Kevin 40
Bad Lad's Army 177
Bagge, Peter 238
Bailes, Alison 42, 47
Bainbridge, Jason 241
Balagueró, Jaume 121
Balcon, Michael 56
Il Bambola (The Devil) 114
Bancroft, Anne 108
The Band Wagon 136, 138, 139
Barker, Clive 7
Barnes & Noble 44
Barnfield, Graham 161
Barthes, John 95
Batman 151

Bava, Mario 112
Bazalgette, Peter 162
BBC (British Broadcasting Corporation) 6, 167–171, 218–220
The Beach 167
Beach Boys 134
beach movies 134
The Beatles 56
Bedazzled 57, 59, 62, 63
Belushi, John 130, 131
Ben-Hur 144, 146
Bendis, Brian Michael 231, 238
Benjamin, Walter 227
Bennett, Joan 81
Benshoff, Harry M. 9, 208
Bergfelder, Tim 217
Bergman, Ingmar 88
Bergman, Ingrid 79
Berlin, Irving 128
Bernadotte, Siro 118
Berry, Chuck 141
Best in Show 139, 140
Beyond the Valley of the Dolls 93, 95–97, 99, 100–104, 106–107
BFI Film Classics 97
Les Biches 61
Big Brother 159, 161, 162, 167–170, 172, 174, 175
The Big Picture 40
Bignell, Jonathan 175
biographies 3
The Bird with the Crystal Plumage see *La Uccello dalle Piume di Cristale*
The Birds 209
Bizarro 238
black comedy 99
Black Hawk 241
Black Robe 155
Black Sabbath 129
The Blair Witch Project 202
Blake, Michael 146, 152
Blazing Saddles 231
blood melodrama 75
Blow Up 54, 59, 65
The Blue Dahlia 90
Blue Hawaii 134
Blues and Twos 161
Bogart, Humphrey 2, 79, 80, 82
Bonner, Frances 162, 174
Boo! 223
Boom! 93, 94, 97, 98, 102, 103, 107
Boone, Pat 129, 134
Borde, Raymond 80
Bordwell, David 53, 83, 88, 233
Boston After Dark 100, 101, 103
Bourdieu, Pierre 94, 98, 99, 106, 215
The Box of the Banned 225–227
Boys in the Band 98
Bradbury, Ray 117
Brando, Marlon 95

The Brave and the Bold 241
Braveheart 10, 155
Bravo 37, 38, 40, 46
Breaking Up America 38
Bride of Frankenstein 21, 213, 221, 223
Brighton Rock 80, 81, 83, 90
Britton, Pamela 90
Broadcast 166
Brogan, Hugh 152
Brooks, Mel 22
Brooks, Peter 71, 90
Brosnan, John 20, 25
Brown, James 134
Brown, Phil 85
Brubaker, Ed 235
Buchanan, Jack 138
Buckingham, David 186
buddy film 125
Buffy the Vampire Slayer 6, 125, 126, 237
Buiza, Carlos 119
Bull Durham 147
Burke, Kevin 183
Burke, Timothy 183
Burroughs, Edgar Rice 240
Burton, Richard 94, 95, 102
Busiek, Kurt 236
Butcher, David 182
Butler, Ivan 22
Butler, Judith 106
Bye Bye Braverman 56, 57, 59, 61
Byron, Lord 138

The Cabinet of Dr. Caligari 84
Cablevision Systems Corporation 37
Caine, Andrew 10
Camille, Michael 192
Cammell, Donald 96, 100
La Campana del Infierno (The Bell of Hell) 120
Candide 95
Candy 63, 93, 95, 97, 100–102, 104, 107
Cannes Film Festival 42, 56
Cannibal Holocaust 209
Captive Wild Woman film series 31
The Care Bares 183
Carreras, Enrique 117
Carroll, Noel 208
Casablanca 79, 90
Case, Sue-Ellen 207
Cassavetes, John 36
Castaway 2000 167–170
Castillo, Edward D. 149
Cat and the Canary 223
Cat Ballou 57, 58, 59
Cat People 213
Catch Us If You Can 126
Caughie, John 161
Cavalier 101
Cawelti, John 144, 231–232, 235–237
celebrity challenge series 161

The Celestine Prophecies: An Adventure 150
Celluloid Mavericks 35
C'era una Volta il West (Once Upon a Time in the West) 113
Chabon, Michael 239
Chadwick, June 124
Challengers of the Unknown 241
Champlin, Charles 38, 96, 97, 101, 104
Chaney, Lon 1, 18
Chaney, Lon, Jr. 18, 20–21, 24–26, 221
Channel Five 182
Channel Four 125, 167, 169, 172, 174
Channing, Carol 108
Chaplin, Geraldine 62
Charisse, Cyd 138
Chase, Chevy 130
chat shows 162
Chaumeton, Étienne 80
Cherry, Brigid 11
child star pictures 3
children's television 182, 184, 185, 190, 196
Child's Play (film) 199
Child's Play (television series) 199
"Child's Play" (*The Transformers* episode) 185, 187–189, 198
chillers 202
Chinatown 231, 232, 235
Christian Science Monitor 153
The Christine Jorgensen Story 98
Cimino, Michael 142, 145
Citizen Kane 86
The Clampers 167
Clarens, Carlos 19, 21, 22
Clemens, Brian 6
The Climax 18
Coates, Craig 159, 174
Cohan, Steven 126
Collins, Jim 151
Comden, Berry 136
comedy 3, 10, 53–58, 124–126, 139, 140, 190
comedy drama 55
comedy prizefight film 55
The Comic Book Heroes 230
comic or parodic Western 144
Common Grounds 231
concert film 134
Cook, David A. 144
Cook, Harold 95
Cooper, Gary 146
Cooper, James Fenimore 155
Corbett, Kevin 46
Corman, Roger 7
Corner, John 160, 171, 173
Coronation Street 159
Corrigan, Timothy 41
Costner, Kevin 10, 142, 144–148, 150, 151, 152, 153, 154, 155, 156
costume picture 54, 55
Cotten, Joseph 83
Couldry, Nick 164

counter-cinema 35
Coward, Noel 94, 102
Cozzi, Luigi 115, 116
Cream 128
The Creature from the Black Lagoon 222–224
criminal-adventure thriller 75
Crisis of Infinite Earths 234
Criss Cross 80, 82, 90, 91
Cronenberg, David 7
Crossfire 80, 82, 86
crossover genre 53
The Cruise 167
El Cuervo 119
Cujo 206
Cul-de-Sac 62
Cullen, Peter 193, 194
Cunningham, Michael 42
Curtis, Jamie Lee 7

Daily Mail 171
The Damned 99
Dancer in the Dark 206
Dances with Wolves 10, 142–148, 150–156
Dances with Wolves: The Illustrated Story of the Epic Film 153
Danko, Rick 135
Daredevil 238
dark comedy 59
The Dark Corner 82
Dark Horse 234
The Dark Knight Returns 232
Dark Waters 30
Dawn of the Dead 213
Day of the Dead 8
The Day of the Triffids 54
DC Comics 229, 234, 237–238, 240, 241
Dead Reckoning 80, 81, 82, 83, 90
deCarlo, Yvonne 80
de Certeau, Michel 47, 49
Deep Purple 129
de la Iglesia, Alex 121
Deliverance 206
Deloria, Philip J. 150
DeMille, Cecil B. 144
DePalma, Brian 146
Destination D-Day 169
Detective Comics 240
detective fiction/film 112, 229, 232
Detour 81, 82, 83, 90
The Devil's Rejects 226
Dillard, R.H.W. 25, 26
Disney (corporation) 185
Disney, Walt 43
Disneyland 43
Ditko, Steve 229
Divorce American Style 57, 58
Dixon, Bob 184
D.O.A. 90
Doane, Mary Ann 81, 86
Dr. Blink, Superhero Shrink 236

Doctor Faustus 60, 62, 65
Dr. Jekyll and Mr. Hyde (character) 22
Dr. Jekyll and Mr. Hyde (film) 4, 5, 26
Dr. Strangelove 63
documentary 160, 169–173, 190
docusoap 161
Dogville 42
Doherty, Thomas 133
Don't Look Back 134
Dos Passos, John 76
Double Indemnity 75, 77, 78, 85
Dowling, Doris 90
Dracula (character) 17, 20, 22, 23, 25, 26, 28, 29
Dracula (film) 1, 15, 23, 25, 120, 218, 221, 222, 223
Dracula — Prince of Darkness 218
Dracula's Daughter 26
drama 10, 54, 58, 124, 125, 140
Drescher, Fran 131
Driving School 161
drug film 99
Dungeons & Dragons 199
Dyer, Richard 75, 125
Dylan, Bob 134

Ealing Studios 56
EastEnders 159, 160
Eastwood, Clint 154
Ebert, Roger 95, 100, 153
Eberts, Jake 147
EC Comics 230
Eco, Umberto 233
ecological drama 142
The Ed Sullivan Show 136
The Edwardian Country House 169, 170
8 Mile 125
Ellis, Warren 229
Eminem 125, 126
Empire 7
Encyclopedia of American Independent Filmmaking 35
End of the Road 93, 95, 97–101, 105, 107
Endemol UK 162
Engelhardt, Tom 189
epic 10, 142–145, 152–153, 155–156
episodic reality soap 161, 168
Eraserhead 206
Evans, Peter William 144
Everson, William K. 25
The Evil Dead 213
The Evil Dead 2 213
Ex Machina 231
The Exorcist 213, 219
experimental film 35, 36
exploitation cinema/film 9, 37

The Facts in the Case of M. Valdemar 119
Faking It 174
Fame Academy 161, 171

family life comedies 3
Famous Monsters of Filmland 8
Fan Cultures 198
Fandango 146
Fangoria 8
Fantasia 101
fantasies 3, 182
Fantastic Four 241
Far and Away 155
Farber, Manny 77
farce-murder-mystery 53
Farrell, Colin 42
Farrow, Mia 95
Fast Times at Ridgemont High 131, 132
Faulkner, William 76
Fellini Satyricon 101
La Femme Mariée 60
Ferncase, Richard 36, 37
Feuer, Jane 127, 136, 137, 162
Field of Dreams 147, 152
Fifi and the Flowertots 182
Fifty Key Television Programmes 165
Film/Genre 37, 125
film noir 2, 4, 6, 9, 28, 74–76, 79, 81, 83–87, 89, 217
Film TV Daily 105
Filmax 121
Films and Filming 103
Fine Madness 57, 62
Fiske, John 167
Fitzgerald, F. Scott 76
500 Nations 155
Flaming Star 127
Fleming, Dan 186
Flinn, Carol 89
Florey, Robert 26
The Fly 213
fly-on-the-wall documentaries 167, 173
Ford, Glenn 81
Ford, John 8
"Forever Is a Long Time Coming" (*The Transformers* episode) 188
formatted documentary 161, 168
The 40 Year Old Virgin 196
Foucault, Michel 50
4 Mosche di Velluto Grigio (4 Flies on Grey Velvet) 114
Fox, James 96
Frank, Alan 17, 19, 21, 24, 25
Frank Ironwine 229
Frankenstein (character) 17, 22–23, 25–26, 29–30
Frankenstein (film) 1, 15, 21, 26, 28, 218, 221, 222, 223
Frankenstein Meets the Wolf Man 18, 20, 26
Freaks 213
Freddie and the Dreamers 137
Freund, Karl 23
Friday the 13th 7
Friedman, James 164

Fright Night 7
The Frontier House 169
Fulci, Lucio 8

Gallafent, Edward 111
Gallagher, Tag 232
Gallent, Chris 114
game show 159, 160, 162, 166–167, 169, 174
gamedoc 161, 167, 171
gangster and G-man pictures 3, 99
Gardner, Ava 85
Garfield, John 91
Garland, Alex 167
Gaslight 6, 30
Il Gatto a Nove Code (The Cat o' Nine Tails) 114
Genre and Hollywood 34
Genre and Television 162, 178
Georgy Girl 54, 57, 65
Geraghty, Christine 165
Geraghty, Lincoln 10–11, 199
Gernsback, Hugo 1
Geronimo: An American Legend 155
Gerry and the Pacemakers 137
Gettysburg 155
The Ghost of Frankenstein 18, 19, 21, 25, 26
G.I. Joe 199
gialli 112–113, 115–116
Gibson, Mel 155
Giddens, Anthony 197
Gifford, Denis 7, 18–20, 24
Gilda 81, 82, 85
Gimme Shelter 125, 134, 135
The Girl Can't Help It 133
Gladiator 155
Glass, Philip 221
Gledhill, Christine 71–73, 75, 89, 220
Global Frequency 229
Godard, Jean-Luc 56, 60, 61, 65
The Godfather 231
Gold, Ronald 62, 65, 66
Goldstein 57, 62
gore films 202, 208
Gosford Park 170, 172
The Gospel According to Matthew 59
Gotham Central 235
Gothic horror 202
Grahame, Gloria 82
Grau, Jorge 120
The Great Gatsby 78
The Great TNT 141
Green, Adolph 136
Greene, Graham (actor) 149
Greene, Graham (writer) 75
Greer, Jane 84
Grossman, Albert 135
Guest, Christopher 124, 130, 139
Gundle, Stephen 113
Guns n' Roses 129
Gunsmoke 111

Hagan, Jean 139
Hairspray 40
Haley, Bill 133
Hall, Sheldon 144
Hallelujah the Hills 63
Halloween 7, 213
Hamer, Robert 56
Hammer 7, 214, 218, 219, 226
Handel, Leo 3
Hanks, Tom 41
The Happening 57–59, 63
A Hard Day's Night 53, 55, 56, 63, 126, 127
Hardy, Phil 21
Hartley, John 187
Harvey, Sven 195–196
Hasbro 183, 198
Hate 238
The Haunting 213
Hayworth, Rita 81, 84
He-Man and the Masters of the Universe 183
The Heat Is On 168
Heaven's Gate 142, 145, 147
Heggessey, Lorraine 168
Hellraiser 208, 213
Hell's Kitchen 171–173
Help! 57, 59, 126, 127
Hemingway, Ernest 76
Hendra, Tony 124, 130
Hendrix, Jimi 129
Henry, Buck 95
Here We Go Round the Mulberry Bush 58
Hill, Claudio Guerin 120
Hills, Matt 119, 196, 198
Hillyer, Lambert 26
Historias para no dormir (Stories to Keep You Awake) 6, 117–122
historical epic 10, 152
historical reality documentary series 161, 169
historicals 3, 143, 231
History Channel 170
history documentary 169
Hitchcock, Alfred 113
Hoffenberg, Mason 95
Holiday Showdown 174
Hollinger, Karen 85
Hollows, Joanne 195
Hollyoaks 167
Hollywood Citizen News 97, 102
Hollywood Genres 7
Hollywood Herald Examiner 97
Hollywood Production Code 72, 79, 93
Hollywood Reporter 97, 100
Hollywood TV 43
Hollywood vs. America 150
Holmes, Sherlock 29, 31
Holmes, Su 10
The Honey Pot 57, 58, 62
Hopewell, John 121
horror 1–7, 9, 11, 15–21, 25, 27, 29, 30, 52,

54, 73, 99, 110–113, 115, 117, 119–122, 201–214, 216–220, 222–227, 237, 239, 240
The Horror Channel 210
horror-comedy 99, 209, 212
The Horror Film 22
Horror in Film and Fiction 204
Horror in Film and Literature 212
horror-suspense 118
House 7
House of Dracula 25, 224
House of Frankenstein 25, 224
How the West Was Won 144, 145, 146, 152
How to Read Superhero Comics and Why 231
Howard, Ron 155
Howard, Trevor 91
Hubka, David 184, 185
Hudson, Rock 62
Hull, Henry 25
Humphries, Reynold 22
Hunchback of Notre Dame 1
Huston, John 95
Hutchings, Peter 11, 16
Huyssen, Andreas 75

I Walked with a Zombie 20
Idle, Eric 132
IFC Center 48, 49
IFC Rant 33, 41, 43, 44
Image 234
In a Lonely Place 82, 83
In the Cool of the Day 54
Incredible Hulk 241
independent film 33–36, 38–40, 42–45, 47
Independent Film Channel (IFC) 33–35, 37–48, 50
Independent Spirit Awards 42, 150
Inner Sanctum (film series) 31
Intermission 42
Interview 96
The Invisible Man (character) 31
The Invisible Man (film) 213, 222, 223
The Invisible Man Returns 19
The Invisible Ray 19
Iron Maiden 129
Iron Man 241
ITV 168, 169, 171, 172, 177, 219

Jacobs, Jason 6
Jacobs, Lea 72
Jacobs, W.W. 119
Jacobs, Will 230, 241
Jagger, Mick 96, 129, 135
Jailhouse Rock 126
James, Henry 119
Jamieson, Daz 193–195
Jancovich, Mark 6, 8, 49, 110, 203
Jane Eyre 6
Jaws 106
Jenkins, Henry 11, 88, 186
JFK 155

The Jimi Hendrix Experience 128
Joe Millionaire 161
Johnson, Candy 126
Johnson, Van 58
Johnston, Claire 89
A Jolly Bad Fellow 56
Jones, Gerard 230, 239, 241
Jones, James Earl 95
Joyce, James 76
Joyrich, Lynn 111
jungle stories 216, 240

Kael, Pauline 93
Kahn 77
Kanfer, Stefan 185
Karloff, Boris 6, 18, 19, 21, 221
Kasdan, Lawrence 145, 146
Kasdan, Margo 144, 145
Kaufman, Anthony 44
Kawin, Bruce 23
Keach, Stacy 95
Kelly, Gene 130, 138
Kenner 183
Kentis, Chris 43
The Kents 237
Kermode, Mark 203
Kerr, Paul 84, 88
Kilborn, Richard 169, 173
The Killers 81, 82, 85, 86, 90
King, Stephen 7
King Creole 127, 133
King Kong (character) 22
King Kong (film) 213
Kingdom Come 232
Kirby, Jack 240, 241
Kiss Me Deadly 82, 84, 90
Klimovsky, Leon 116
Kline, Stephen 184, 185
Klinger, Barbara 4, 9, 16, 53, 65
Klock, Geoff 231, 232, 234
The Knack 56, 62, 63
Knight, Arthur 96
Kozloff, Sarah 76
Kramer vs. Kramer 88
Krassner, Paul 101
Kressing, Harry 95
Krutnik, Frank 74, 75, 88, 89, 90
Kryzwinska, Tanya 207
Kuhn, Annette 196

Ladd, Alan 80, 90
Ladette to Lady 174
The Lady from Shanghai 80, 82, 84, 85
Lake, Ricki 40
Lake, Veronica 80
Lancaster, Burt 80, 81
Lang, Fritz 237
Lansbury, Angela 95
Lardner, John 77
Lasia o raddoppia? (*Double or Quit?*) 113

The Last Emperor 144
The Last of the Mohicans 155
The Last Waltz 125, 134, 135
Laura 6, 30, 90, 91
Laurel and Hardy 99
Lawrence of Arabia 153
The League of Extraordinary Gentlemen 232
Led Zeppelin 129
Lee, Spike 155
Lee, Stan 241
Lennon, John 139
Leone, Sergio 113
Leroux, Gaston 117
LeRoy, Mervyn 144
Lester, Richard 53, 63
Lethal Weapon 2 151
Lethem, Jonathan 241
Leutrat, J.L. 64
Lewton, Val 15, 20, 22, 218, 224
Life 96, 105
lifestyle television 162
Little Big Man 144, 145
loathsome film 9, 92–107
LoBrutto, Vincent 36
London Vampyre Society 204
Lonesome Dove 145
Lopez, Jennifer 236
Lord Love a Duck 57, 58, 60
Los Angeles Herald Examiner 99
Los Angeles Times 96, 153
Losey, Joseph 54, 94, 95
Lost Weekend 2, 4, 28
Love Me Tender 127, 133
love stories 3
The Loved One 57, 58
Lugosi, Bela 19, 21, 221, 223
Lumet, Sidney 54, 57
Luna Brothers 236
Lyndon, Neil 172

MacDonald, Edmund 81
Mack, David 238
MacMurray, Fred 77
Macready, George 81
makeover programs 161
Malcolm X 155
Mallet, Timmy 193
Maltby, Richard 53, 54, 143
The Maltese Falcon 77, 79
Mamoulian, Rouben 26
Man Made Monster 19
Mann, Michael 155
La Marca de Hombre Lobo (*The Mark of the Werewolf*) 116
Marquand, Christian 95
Marsh, Carol 81
Marshall, P. David 192
Martin, Eugenio 120
Marvel Comics 231, 234, 235, 238, 240, 241
Marvel Mystery 240

Marvel Productions 184
Marvels 232
Marx, Karl 36
Marx Brothers 57
La Maschera del Demonio (*Mask of the Demon*) 112
Masculin, Feminin 60
M.A.S.K. 183
Mattel 183
Maxwell, Ronald F. 155
McCabe and Mrs. Miller 231
McCall, Davina 159
McCloud, Scott 230
McDonnel, Mary 149
McGaa, Ed 150
McKean, Michael 124, 130
Medavoy, Mike 147
Medical Aspects of Human Sexuality 96
Medved, Michael 150, 151
Meeker, Ralph 84
Méliès, Georges 1
meller 52, 54
Melo Talk 73
melodrama 2, 4, 9, 52, 71–76, 81, 84–90, 111, 216, 241
Menta, Narcisco Ibáñez 117, 120
Mercer, John 88
Mercury Theater 76
Merritt, Greg 35
Meyer, Moe 102, 103
Meyer, Russ 95
MGM 4, 5, 126, 133, 136
Mickey One 63
A Mighty Wind 140
Mildred Pierce 90
The Milk Train Doesn't Stop Here Anymore 94
Miller, Frank 232
Mills, Jeremy 169
Minority Report 42
The Miracle of Morgan's Creek 77
Miramax 41
Mis Terrores Favoritos 120
Mister Buddwing 62, 63
Mitchum, Robert 82, 86
Mittell, Jason 161–164, 166, 170–171, 175, 178, 237
mock documentary 125, 132
Modernist or Anti-Western 144
Mon Oncle 38
Monash, Paul 104
Mondadori 112
The Monkey's Paw 119
Monogram 27
The Monomaniacal Spiderman 238
monster movies 202
Monty Python's Flying Circus 132
Moore, Alan 229, 232, 237
Moreau, Jeanne 108
Morgan! 57, 59
Morrissey, Paul 36

Motion Picture Exhibitor 104, 106
Motion Picture Herald 105
Movie Star, American Style, or, LSD, I Hate You! 61
Movieline 44
Mozart 138
MPAA (Motion Picture Association of America) 93, 104
Mullen, Megan 39, 41
The Mummy (character) 17, 23, 25–27, 29
The Mummy (film) 19, 21, 23, 120, 221, 222, 224
The Mummy's Curse 18, 24
The Mummy's Ghost 19
The Mummy's Hand 18, 19, 20, 23
The Mummy's Tomb 18, 19, 23
El Muñeco 119
Murders in the Rue Morgue 26
Muriel 97
Murnau, F.W. 223
Murphy, Keith 200
Murray, Susan 168, 170
musical 3, 54, 99, 124–128, 130, 133–134, 139–140, 230
musical comedies 3
musicals (serious) 3
Musicals and Beyond 126
Myra Breckenridge 93, 95–99, 101–105, 107–108
mysteries 3, 112
Mystery in Space 241

Naremore, James 2, 28, 75, 76, 79, 88
Nasty Nick 159
National Cowboy Hall of Fame 153
National Film Theatre 203, 204, 212
National Lampoon 130, 132
National Lampoon's Animal House 130, 131, 132, 139
Neal, Tom 81
Neale, Steve 2, 34, 53–55, 64, 73, 75, 77, 88–89, 130, 143, 145, 152, 154, 162–163, 217
neo-slasher 202
New Line 155
New Republic 77
New Statesman 172
New York magazine 153
New York Post 153
New York Times 29, 93, 96, 100, 153
New York Times Magazine 41
New Yorker 77
Newman, Kim 7, 8, 203
news 190
Newsweek 96, 97, 99, 101, 105, 130, 153
Nichols, Bill 173
Nick Carter et le trefle rouge 60
Night of the Living Dead 7, 8
Nightmare Movies 7
Nightmare on Elm Street 5, 7

The 1940s House 169
The 1900 House 169
Nixon 155
No Profanar el Sueño de los Mertos (*The Living Dead at the Manchester Morgue*) 120
La Noche de Walpurgis (*The Werewolf's Shadow*) 116
Nosferatu 223
Notes on Camp 101

oater 52, 54
oater comedy 54
Obras Maestras del Terror (*Masterpieces of Horror*) 117
O'Brien, Edmond 85, 90
The Observer 172
occult cinema 202
off-beat film 9, 52–66
"Once More with Feeling" 125
Once Upon a Time in the West see *C'era una Volta il West*
The 100 Greatest Musicals 125
1001 Movies to See Before You Die 124
One Way Pendulum 57, 59
Open Range 146, 154
Open Water 43
Operation Bikini 54
Ordinary People 88
Ordinary Television 162
Orion Pictures 10, 147, 152, 156
Osbourne, Ozzy 128
Ouellette, Laurie 168, 170
Out of Africa 170
Out of the Past 82, 84, 90
Outsider Features 36

El Pacto 119
Pánico en el Transiberiano (*Horror Express*) 120
Paramount Pictures 77, 79
paranoid woman's film 6, 28
Parker, Edwin 18
Paul, William 130
Pearson, Roberta 235
Peckinpah, Sam 8
Peñafiel, Luis 117
Penn, Arthur 63, 144, 145
Peppermint Frappe 62
Performance 92–97, 99–101, 104–107
Peterson, Lowell 84
Petulia 97
Phantom Lady 6, 30
Phantom of the Opera 1, 2, 18, 19, 223
Pierce, Jack 18
The Pioneer House 169
Pitfall 80, 82
Place, Janey 84
Planetary 229
Platinga, Carl 128
Platoon 147
The Player 170

Plaza, Paco 121
Pleasence, Donald 7
Plumbe, Simon 195, 196
Poe, Edgar Allan 117, 119, 121
Pokémon 184–186, 198
Polan, Dana 29
Polanski, Roman 231
Police, Camera, Action 161
The Politics and Poetics of Camp 102
Poor Little Rich Girls 173, 174
Pop Idol 161, 171
Popstars 167, 171
Porfirio, Robert G. 83, 88
Porky's 130, 131
pornography 9
La Porta sul Buio 6, 113–116, 118, 122
Porter, Cole 128
The Postman Always Rings Twice 90
Powell, Dick 80
Premiere 44
Presley, Elvis 126, 127, 129, 133, 134
The Pretty Things 129
Pretty Woman 170
Prince, Harold 95
Prince, Stephen 145
Prince, William 82
Producer's Releasing Corporation 27
Production Code 82, 88, 90
Production Code Administration (PCA) 4, 53
Profile 38
Psycho 120
psychological drama 75
psychological melodrama 75
psychological thriller 75, 202, 224
The Pulse 231
Pustz, Matthew J. 236

Queen 137
Quién Puede Matar a un Niño? (*Who Can Kill a Child?*) 116
Quit City 229
quiz shows 162, 190
Quo Vadis 144

Rachel, Rachel 62
Radio Times 182
Radiotelevisione Italiana (RAI) 113–116
Rainbow Tribe: Ordinary People Journeying the Red Road 150
Rains, Claude 80
Ramsay, Gordon 171
Ramsay's Kitchen Nightmares 172, 173
Rand, Ayn 238
Rashomon 86
Rat Pfink a Boo Boo 61, 63
Rawhide 111
Ray, Nicholas 2
Ready, Steady, Go 136
Reagan, Ronald 189, 199
real crime 161, 163

The Real Ghostbusters 199
real-life documentary series 173
RealArt Pictures 223
reality-game shows 161
reality TV 10, 159–168, 170–175
Reality TV: Remaking Television Culture 168
Re-Animator 7
Rebecca 6
Reboll, Antonio Lázaro 117, 118, 217
rec.arts.horror 204
Red Son 237
Redfield, James 150
Redford, Robert 39
Redgrave, Vanessa 108
Reed, Rex 95
Rees, Laurence 169, 170, 177
Reiner, Rob 124, 125, 130, 132
The Reptile 218
Resfest 45
La Residencia (*The Finishing School*) 116, 118, 120
Return of the Living Dead 8
Revenge 151
Reynolds, Debbie 58
Reynolds, Kevin 146
Richard, Cliff 126
Richards, Keith 129
The Ring 202
The Rise of Cable Programming 39
RKO 15, 22
Robards, Jason 58
The Robe 144
Robertson, Cliff 58
Robertson, Robbie 135
Robinson, Edward G. 77, 80
Robinson, James 172
Robocop 147
Rock Around the Clock 133, 134
rock movie 124, 125, 128, 133, 134, 137, 140
Rock, Rock, Rock 133, 134
rockumentary/rock documentary 10, 126, 134, 140
Rocky 106
The Rocky Horror Picture Show 48
Rodgers and Hammerstein 128
Roeg, Nicholas 96, 100
Rogers, Ginger 127
The Rolling Stones 128, 129, 134
romance 133, 231, 237, 240
romantic meller 54
romantic melodrama 72, 223
romantic pictures 3, 4
romanticomedy 52
Romero, George A. 7, 212
Romney, Jonathan 135
Rosza, Miklos 85
Rubin, Martin 126
Run, Lola, Run 47
Running with the Devil 141
Russell, James 10

The Rutles: All You Need Is Cash 132
Ryan, Robert 80

Samson and Delilah 144
San Sebastian Horror Film Festival 117
Sarne, Michael 92, 95, 103, 105
Saturday morning children's television 190
Saturday Night Live 130, 132
Saturday Review 96, 97
Savage, Ann 81
Saving Private Ryan 155
Saw 226
The Scarlet Pimpernel 240
Schafter, Steven 130
Schatz, Thomas 7
Schickel, Richard 96
Schindler's List 155
Schjeldahl, Peter 100
Schneider, Steven 207
Schrader, Paul 85
Schuster, Joel 239
Schwartz, Julius 241
sci fi meller 54
science fiction 1, 5, 73, 117, 182, 190, 208, 223, 229, 239–241
science fiction-horror 208, 212, 213
Scorsese, Martin 40, 135
Scott, Jason 9
Scott, Lizabeth 80
Scream 3
The Sea Devils 241
Seconds 60, 62, 65
Secret Ceremony 93, 95, 96, 97, 99, 105, 107
Seduction of the Innocent 240
Sefton-Green, Julian 186
Seitz, George B. 155
El Ser 121
serial killer films 212
Serious Business 185
serious dramas 3
Serling, Rod 6
Serrador, Narciso Ibañez 6, 116–121
sex comedy 99
sex film 100
sex, lies & videotape 36, 39
Shaun of the Dead 209, 212
She-Wolf of London 221, 224
Shearer, Harry 124, 130
Shelley, Percy Bysshe 138
She-Ra, Princess of Power 183
Shingler, Martin 88
The Shining 213
The Ship 169
Shipwrecked 167
Shock Xpress 7, 8
Showcase 241
Siedelman, Susan 40
Sight and Sound 133
The Silence of the Lambs 147, 202, 209
Silent Night with Jose Carreras 38

Silverado 145, 146, 152
Simmons, Jean 58
Simon, Joe 239
Simon, John 92, 93, 94, 96, 100, 102, 103, 104, 105, 106
Simon Spector 229
The Simpsons 139
Singin' in the Rain 136, 138, 139
singing cowboy film 216
Siodmak, Curt 24
Sirk, Douglas 4, 71
situation comedy 57, 163, 230, 231
6 Peliculas Para no Dormir (6 Films That Won't Let You Sleep) 121
1602 231
The $64,000 Question 113
slapstick comedies 3
slasher movies 8, 100, 202, 208, 211
Smashing Time 57
soap opera 102, 111, 160, 163, 166, 167, 190
socially significant pictures 3
La Socrate (The Socratic One) 61, 63
Soderbergh, Steven 40
Something for Everyone 93, 95, 97, 99, 100, 103, 104
Son of Dracula 18, 20, 21, 25, 26
Son of Frankenstein 18, 21, 22, 25
Sontag, Susan 101
sophisticated comedies 3
The Sound of Music 99
South Park 198
Southern, Terry 95
specialty film 37
Speeding Bullets 237
Spellbound 6, 30
Spider-Man: India 238
Spiderman Loves Mary Jane 231
Spider-Man 2 238
Spielberg, Steven 155
splatter films 202, 208
Squanto: A Warrior's Tale 155
Stack, Robert 71
Stacy's Knights 146
Staiger, Janet 9, 88
Stanfield, Peter 216
Stanwyck, Barbara 77
Star Trek 5, 182
Star Wars 106, 182, 183, 194, 199
Starr, Ringo 95
Stevenson, Robert Louis 117
Stoker, Bram 24
Stomp Future 229
Stone, Oliver 155
Streisand, Barbra 108
Studlar, Gaylyn 90
Summer Holiday 126, 134
The Sun Also Rises 78
Sundance Channel 39, 46
Sundance Film Festival 36, 39, 41, 42
Sunday Calendar 104

Sunset Boulevard 91
Superbeast 218
superhero genre 11, 74, 229, 230, 231, 233, 239, 240, 241, 242
Superman's Metropolis 237
supernatural 202, 229
The Supremes 134
Survivor 161, 167, 169, 170
suspense 117
Suspiria 213
The Swimmer 62, 64
swinging film 57, 65
swordplay genre 240

Takara Corporation 198
Talbot, Lawrence 24, 26
Tales of the Black Freighter 229, 230
talk show 160
The TAMI Show 134, 141
Tankel, Jonathan David 200
Tarantino, Quentin 40
Tavernetti, Susan 144, 145
Taylor, Elizabeth 94, 95, 102, 103
Tea and Sympathy 100
teen television 6
Teenage Command Performance 141
Teenage Mutant Ninja Turtles 183
teenpic 133, 140
Television 166
The Television Genre Book 6, 162, 165
Televisual 166
Tell Me in the Sunlight 62
Testimone Oculare (Eyewitness) 114
The Texas Chainsaw Massacre 7, 209, 210, 219
That Was Rock 141
That'll Teach 'Em 177
Therapy TV 161
The Thing 213
The Third Man 83, 84, 90, 91
This Gun for Hire 80, 83
This Is Spinal Tap 10, 124–128, 130–140
Thompson, Kristin 53, 88
Thomson, David 145
Thriller (Clemens) 6
thriller (genre) 2, 6, 25, 60, 73, 75, 87, 202, 216, 223
Thriller (Karloff) 6
Thunderheart 154
Tierney, Gene 90
Tig Productions 147
Time 77, 96, 99, 102
The Time Out Film Guide 124
Titanic 10, 155
TNT 155
Tolson, Andrew 174
Tombstone 10, 154
El Tonel 119
Top Cow 234
Torres, Sara 117
Total Recall 151

tough-thriller 75
Toulouse-Lautrec 38
Tourneur, Jacques 22
Toys"R"Us 195
traditional western 144; *see also* western
tragedy 71
Il Tram (The Tram) 114, 116, 118
The Transformers 10, 181–199
The Transformers: The Movie 199
Transmetropolitan 229
El Trapero 119, 121
trash film 35
travel film 216
Tremors 209
The Trench 169
Treviño, Liza 8
Trip to the Moon (Le Voyage Dans la Lune) 1, 2
Tristan, Dorothy 95, 105
Troma 7
Troy 10
true crime 240
Tudor, Andrew 19, 20, 22
Turner, Graeme 34, 162
Turner, Ted 155
Turow, Joseph 38, 42, 46
TVE 117, 118, 120, 121
Twentieth Century Fox 95, 96, 100, 102, 104
The Twilight Zone 6, 112, 118
Twitchell, James B. 18, 20, 22, 24
Two or Three Things I Know About Her (Deux ou trois choses que je sais d'elle) 60, 61
2001: A Space Odyssey 101
Tyler, Parker 89
Tyler, Tom 18, 19

La Uccello dalle Piume di Cristallo (The Bird with the Crystal Plumage) 112, 113, 115
Ultra 236
underground film 35
Understanding Comics 230
Unforgiven 10
United Artists 142, 145, 147
Universal Monster Legacy Collection (DVDs) 11, 218, 221, 223–227
Universal Monsters 221
Universal Studios 3, 16–25, 27, 29, 31, 95, 155, 218–219, 221–223, 226
unscripted drama 161
The Untouchables 146, 152
Urbizu, Enrique 121
Uricchio, William 235
US Magazine 130

Valenti, Jack 104
Valley of the Dolls 94, 95, 101
Vampire Exchange and Information Network 204, 212
Van Dyke, Dick 58
Van Helsing 222
The Vanishing 206

Van Zoonen, Lisbet 166
Variety 9, 52–55, 59–61, 64–66, 77, 96, 101, 121, 151
Veronica Guerin 42
Il Vicino di Casa (*The Neighbour*) 114, 115
Vidal, Gore 95
Vietnam Western 144
Village Voice 146
Virgin 44
Virgin Encyclopedia of Stage and Screen Musicals 125
Voltaire 95
von Trier, Lars 42, 206

Wagon Train 111
Wakey Wakey Campers! 177
Walking in the City 47
Wall Street Journal 97
Waller, Gregory 6
Walser, Robert 141
Walton, Kendall 192
war films 2, 3, 73
war meller 54
Warhol, Andy 36, 96
Warner Brothers 96
Watchmen 229, 230, 232
Waterhole No. 3 54
Waters, John 40
Watson, Dr. 29, 74
Wayne, John 130
way-out films 58, 59, 65
Webb, Clifton 91
Le Weekend 60, 61
weird thrillers 229
Welch, Racquel 95
Welker, Frank 193, 194
Welles, Orson 76, 80, 83
Werewolf of London 24, 25, 224
Wertham, Frederick 240
West, Mae 95
western 3–4, 8, 10, 52–54, 64, 99, 111, 122, 130, 133, 142–144, 146, 152–154, 156, 216, 230, 237, 240
Whale, James 22, 223, 224
What's New Pussycat? 57, 58, 59
Wheatley, Helen 119
Wheels of Terror 204, 215

Whitesnake 129
The Who 128, 129
whodunit 112
Who's Crazy? 62, 63
Wife Swap 172, 173, 174
Wild in the Country 127
Wilder, Billy 75, 79
Williams, Linda 75, 88, 89
Williams, Tennessee 94, 98
Williams, Tony 90
Willis, Andrew 6, 9, 217
Wilson, Jim 146, 147
Winnicott, Donald 186
Wiseman, Frederick 36
The Wizard of Oz 127
Wolf, Leonard 25
Wolf Creek 226
The Wolf Man (character) 17, 20, 22–27, 29–30, 221, 224
The Wolf Man (film) 24–26, 221–224
Wolfstein, Marv 234
Woman in the Window 6, 30, 80, 81
woman's picture 4
Wonderwall 62
Wood, Mary P. 112
Wood, Robin 202
Woodfall studio 56
Woodstock 134
Woolf, Virginia 76
Woolworth's 185
Work Is a Four Letter Word 56, 57, 59, 66
Worland, Mark 15
Wright, Will 144
Written on the Wind 71, 72, 90
The Wrong Box 56, 57, 60, 61, 63
Wyatt Earp 10, 146, 154

The Yardbirds 128
Yellow Submarine 101
York, Michael 95
Young Frankenstein 22

Zanuck, Darryl 96
Zanuck, Richard 96
La Zarpa 119
zombie films 212

www.ingramcontent.com/pod-product-compliance
Lightning Source LLC
Chambersburg PA
CBHW051215300426
44116CB00006B/578